Individual Health Insurance Planning
Thomas P. O'Hare and Burton T. Beam, Jr.

Financial Planning: Process and Environment
Craig W. Lemoine

Fundamentals of Insurance Planning
Burton T. Beam, Jr., and Eric A. Wiening

Fundamentals of Financial Planning
David M. Cordell (ed.)

Fundamentals of Income Taxation
James F. Ivers III and Thomas M. Brinker, Jr. (eds.)

McGill's Life Insurance
Edward E. Graves (ed.)

McGill's Legal Aspects of Life Insurance
Edward E. Graves and Burke A. Christensen (eds.)

Group Benefits: Basic Concepts and Alternatives
Burton T. Beam, Jr.

Planning for Retirement Needs
David A. Littell, Kenn Beam Tacchino, and Paul J. Schneider

Fundamentals of Investments for Financial Planning
Walt J. Woerheide

Fundamentals of Estate Planning
Constance J. Fontaine

Estate Planning Applications
Ted Kurlowicz

Planning for Business Owners and Professionals
Ted Kurlowicz, James F. Ivers III, and John J. McFadden

Financial Planning Applications
Craig W. Lemoine

Advanced Topics in Group Benefits
Burton T. Beam, Jr., and Thomas P. O'Hare (eds.)

Executive Compensation
Paul J. Schneider

Health and Long-Term Care Financing for Seniors
Burton T. Beam, Jr., Nancy P. Morith, and Thomas P. O'Hare

Financial Decisions for Retirement
David A. Littell (ed.)

D1303772

The American College® is an independent, nonprofit, accredited institution founded in 1927 that offers professional certification and graduate-degree distance education to men and women seeking career growth in financial services.

The Center for Financial Advisor Education at The American College offers both the LUTCF and the Financial Services Specialist (FSS) professional designations to introduce students in a classroom environment to the technical side of financial services, while at the same time providing them with the requisite sales-training skills.

The Solomon S. Huebner School® of The American College administers the Chartered Life Underwriter (CLU®); the Chartered Financial Consultant (ChFC®); the Chartered Advisor for Senior Living (CASL®); the Registered Health Underwriter (RHU®); the Registered Employee Benefits Consultant (REBC®); and the Chartered Leadership Fellow® (CLF®) professional designation programs. In addition, the Huebner School also administers The College's CFP Board—registered education program for those individuals interested in pursuing CFP® certification, the CFP® Certification Curriculum.

The Richard D. Irwin Graduate School® of The American College offers the master of science in financial services (MSFS) degree, the Graduate Financial Planning Track (another CFP Board-registered education program), and several graduate-level certificates that concentrate on specific subject areas. It also offers the Chartered Advisor in Philanthropy (CAP®) and the master of science in management (MSM), a one-year program with an emphasis in leadership. The National Association of Estate Planners & Councils has named The College as the provider of the education required to earn its prestigious AEP designation.

The American College is accredited by **The Middle States Commission on Higher Education**, 3624 Market Street, Philadelphia, PA 19104 at telephone number 267.284.5000.

The Middle States Commission on Higher Education is a regional accrediting agency recognized by the U.S. Secretary of Education and the Commission on Recognition of Postsecondary Accreditation. Middle States accreditation is an expression of confidence in an institution's mission and goals, performance, and resources. It attests that in the judgment of the Commission on Higher Education, based on the results of an internal institutional self-study and an evaluation by a team of outside peer observers assigned by the Commission, an institution is guided by well-defined and appropriate goals; that it has established conditions and procedures under which its goals can be realized; that it is accomplishing them substantially; that it is so organized, staffed, and supported that it can be expected to continue to do so; and that it meets the standards of the Middle States Association. The American College has been accredited since 1978.

The American College does not discriminate on the basis of race, religion, sex, handicap, or national and ethnic origin in its admissions policies, educational programs and activities, or employment policies.

The American College is located at 270 S. Bryn Mawr Avenue, Bryn Mawr, PA 19010. The toll-free number of the Office of Professional Education is (888) AMERCOL (263-7265); the fax number is (610) 526-1465; and the home page address is theamericancollege.edu.

Huebner School Series

EXECUTIVE COMPENSATION
Twelfth Edition

Paul J. Schneider

THE
AMERICAN
COLLEGE PRESS

HS342-12

This publication is designed to provide accurate and authoritative information about the subject covered. While every precaution has been taken in the preparation of this material, the authors, and The American College assume no liability for damages resulting from the use of the information contained in this publication. The American College is not engaged in rendering legal, accounting, or other professional advice. If legal or other expert advice is required, the services of an appropriate professional should be sought.

© 2011 The American College Press
270 S. Bryn Mawr Avenue
Bryn Mawr, PA 19010
(888) AMERCOL (263–7265)
theamericancollege.edu
All rights reserved
ISBN-10: 1-58293-036-8
ISBN-13: 978-1-58293-036-7
ISSN: 1541-3977
Printed in the United States of America

CONTENTS

ACKNOWLEDGMENTS

I would like to express my appreciation to Monica Haley for her support and insight in helping to produce the revisions to this text.

Paul J. Schneider, JD, LLM

Adjunct Professor of Pensions
Guardian/Deppe Chair in Pensions
and Retirement Planning

Learning Objectives

An understanding of the material in this chapter should enable the student to

1. Describe the tests used under the federal tax law to determine deductibility of compensation.

2. Describe the problems associated with, and the procedures for determining, reasonable salary levels.

3. Determine when the company can claim a deduction for a salary payment and when the employee must report the income.

4. Explain the procedures to follow when instituting a bonus plan and other considerations in connection with the design of a bonus plan.

5. List advantages and disadvantages of the use of reimbursement arrangements where a portion of compensation is held to be unreasonable.

6. Determine a "best salary" plan from an income tax standpoint for the sole stockholder of a corporation and list problems associated with such a plan.

7. Explain the tax considerations for the company and the stockholder-executive of a buyout of the executive's stock and employment contract.

8. Advise an S corporation and other pass-through entities on compensation planning for stockholder-executives.

REASONABLE COMPENSATION AND OTHER TAX-LAW ISSUES

The broadest impact of the tax law on compensation planning comes from Sec. 162(a)(1), which provides that an employer can deduct "a reasonable allowance for salaries or other compensation for personal services actually rendered." This provision has been part of the income tax law since its inception.

The regulations, Reg. Sec. 1.162-7(a), broaden this rule into a two-part test:

- whether the payment was purely for services (the intent test)—that is, was it a disguised gift or dividend
- whether the amount paid was reasonable

The consequence of failing to meet these tests is that the employer's deduction for compensation will be disallowed in part or even entirely. The part that is disallowed will be treated as some other kind of payment (such as a gift or dividend) depending on the facts.

As a practical matter, the Sec. 162(a)(1) issue is primarily raised in the context of compensation arrangements for closely held businesses. In a closely held business, the executives are often the same people as the members of the corporate board, or they are closely related or allied, so there is a question of whether the amount of compensation was actually agreed on between the executive and the board in an arm's-length negotiation.

Assuming that an employee who is also a shareholder is planning to take a given amount out of the company in a given year, it is generally in the corporation's economic interest (and therefore in the shareholder's interest) to maximize the portion of this amount that is compensation and therefore deductible. When dividends were taxed at the same rate as compensation income (prior to 2003), the employee who was also a shareholder had the same interest as the corporation and therefore also wanted to maximize the compensation portion of his or her corporate withdrawal and minimize the dividend amount. For this reason the IRS traditionally has assumed that the negotiation was not arm's length and has closely scrutinized compensation amounts in closely held corporate audits.

Under recent tax law (JGTRRA 2003) dividends are taxed together with capital gains under a complex scheme that probably would have been unthinkable in the days before computerized tax preparation. The result is that dividends are taxed at the same rates as net capital gain.[1] Since the capital-gain rates are also reduced by JGTRRA, the upshot is that dividends

---

1.   This dividend treatment applies to "qualified dividend income" as defined under Code Sec. 1(h)(11)(A). Generally all dividends as defined under Code Sec. 316 from domestic corporations as well as certain foreign corporations are included. Interest from money market funds or life insurance dividend payments are not included.

factors vary from case to case and from one court to another. Due to the variability in how and when particular factors are applied, other courts prefer to be guided by an approach that is referred to as the hypothetical independent investor test. Both of these approaches are discussed below.

Factor Tests

The most often applied approach involves lists of factors that are taken into account in determining whether compensation is reasonable. In almost all cases no one factor is considered determinative so that previous decisions have little precedential value. Thus, each new case is treated on its own merits. As a consequence, there is a significant potential for courts to allow their analysis to become overly subjective. Some of the factors considered in court cases (and often specifically listed by the courts in the various cases) include[4]

- the employee's qualifications and training
- the nature, extent, and scope of the employee's duties
- the prevailing rates paid to comparable employees in a comparable business
- the ratio of compensation to gross income and to net profits (before salaries and federal income tax)
- whether compensation is set by corporate directors
- the correlation between the employee's compensation and stockholdings
- the corporation's dividend history
- prevailing economic conditions
- whether the payments were a necessary inducement for the employee to remain with the employer
- the financial condition of the company after payment of the compensation
- the scarcity of qualified employees
- whether a discretionary bonus was paid at the end of the year

The IRS has its own list of favorable and unfavorable factors in the *Internal Revenue Manual*[5] and other sources:[6]

---

4. The lists here are based on those in the Martin and Harris article cited above.
5. IRM, Part IV, Examination.
6. See note 4 above.

Favorable factors:

- long hours
- uniqueness of the employee's contribution
- success in turning the company around
- the company's above-average growth or profitability
- experience level of the employee
- high productivity and effectiveness of the employee
- bonus arrangements entered into prior to becoming a stockholder
- whether the employee was offered a higher salary by outsiders
- inability of the employee to control compensation levels or dividends
- salary compared favorably with that of employees of other similar companies
- employee was undercompensated in previous years
- high return on equity

Unfavorable factors:

- compensation rate exceeded that of comparable companies
- lack of dividend payments
- inappropriate compensation formulas
- lack of unique employee skills
- employee spent little time on the job or worked less than in previous years
- board of directors was not independent
- salary increased without increase in duties
- bonus formulas changed because of high profits

These factors are not applied mechanically (or at least they're not supposed to be) but are guides for an analysis of the true factual situation. Most of them are self-explanatory, but some of the important ones deserve additional comment.

Several of the factors involve the company's dividend history. In determining whether a payment is a disguised dividend, the courts consider the following facts, among others:[7]

---

7. See Raby and Raby, *Accountants' Advice and Reasonable Compensation*, 16 Pension and Benefits Update No. 2, Tax Analysts, Oct. 26, 1999.

- whether a high percentage of the corporation's net income (before salaries and taxes) is paid to shareholder-employees
- whether the corporation paid dividends
- whether incentive compensation plans benefit only shareholders and are calculated to some degree based on stock ownership

If no dividends have been paid in prior years, this is generally a red flag for unreasonableness of compensation. However, if the corporation can convincingly show a business reason for not paying dividends it may successfully fend off the IRS or win in court on this issue.[8] Likewise, compensation not being paid in the same ratio as stockholdings is evidence that it's not a dividend, but this evidence is not necessarily conclusive.[9]

Another important factor in closely held companies is low compensation in prior years as justification for higher compensation later. The IRS recognizes that in the start-up phase, many small business owner-employees put most of their money back into the business rather than taking it out in compensation. Later catch-up additions are reasonable; however, the total compensation over the entire period must be reasonable.[10]

Also the compensation that must meet the reasonableness test includes all elements of compensation—salary, bonus, retirement plans, benefits, long- and short-term incentives, and so forth. Compensation includes both current and deferred compensation. However, since nonqualified deferred compensation, though earned currently, is not deductible by the corporation until it is received in future years, it often does not figure directly in an IRS challenge of the amount deducted in a given year.

Hypothetical Independent Investor Test

Recent court cases in this area have often invoked the hypothetical independent investor test. The test works like this: The corporation's rate of return on equity is compared to what an independent investor would expect. If the corporation's rate of return is less than this, it suggests that profits are

---

8. Rev. Rul. 79-8, 1979-1 CB 92.

9. Reg. Sec. 1.162-7(b)(1).

10. *Alpha Medical, Inc. v. Commissioner*, 172 F.3d 942 (6th Cir. 1999, *rev'g on other grounds* 74 T.C.M. 893 (1997) and *Devine Brothers, Inc. v. Commissioner*, T.C. Memo 2003-15.

being drained off in the form of excess compensation.[11] There currently is no single accepted method for determining the rate of return, but it is clear that the return on investment includes amounts reinvested in the business as well as dividends paid out. An increase in the market value of the shares is also apparently a factor in return. Some courts add a "factors" test to the independent investor analysis.[12] For example, the Tax Court balances the multi-factor and independent investor tests and explains that it applies the multi-factor test "through the lens of an independent investor."[13]

In 2009 the Seventh Circuit Court of Appeals gave the taxpayer a significant victory while confirming that the independent investor test should be applied in lieu of the multi-factor test. In *Menard, Inc. v. Commissioner*, 560 F. 3d 620 (7th Cir. 2009), rev'g TCM 2004-207, the Court of Appeals reversed the Tax Court's decision that found a large portion of a multimillion dollar bonus paid to a closely-held corporation's founder/majority shareholder/CEO to be a nondeductible dividend. The appellate court struck down the "flimsy" analysis of the Tax Court and concluded that company patriarch John Menard's bonus compensation was reasonable.

In *Menard,* the facts involved a classic reasonable compensation scenario. The taxpayer was Menard, Inc., a Wisconsin corporation that under the name "Menards" sold hardware, building supplies and related products through retail stores spread throughout the Midwest. It had 138 stores in 1998, the tax year at issue, and was the third largest retail home improvement chain in the United States, behind only Home Depot and Lowe's. The corporation was founded in 1962 by John Menard and through 1998 he was the company's chief executive. The uncontradicted evidence demonstrated that Menard was a workaholic. He worked 12 to 16 hours a day, 6 or 7 days a week, involving himself in every aspect of his firm's operations and determining everyone's compensation. The facts supported a conclusion that Menard did work that in a publicly traded company would have been the responsibility of several additional employees. Thus, Menard was a very successful businessman. Under his guidance, Menards revenues grew from $788 million in 1991 to

---

11. This test is generally associated with the case of *Elliots, Inc.*, 716 F.2d 1241 (9th Cir. 1983). The company in that case was paying an annual bonus equal to about 50 percent of the net profits but had returns on equity of 21 percent and 19 percent in the years in question.

12. However, at least one court has abandoned the "factor" test in order to rely solely on the independent investor analysis. See *Dexsil Corp. v. Commissioner*, 147 F. 3d 96 (2d Cir. 1998), *rev'g and rem'g* 69 T.C.M. 2267 (1995).

13. See *Miller & Sons Drywall, Inc. v. Commissioner*, T.C. Memo 2005-114.

$3.4 billion in 1998 and the corporation's taxable income grew from $59 million to $314 million during that same period. The corporation's rate of return on shareholders' equity in 1998 was 18.8 percent, higher than that of either Home Depot (16.1 percent) or Lowe's (13.7 percent).

Menard owned all of the corporation's voting shares and 56 percent of the corporation's nonvoting shares, the balance being owned by family members, two of whom were senior executives of the corporation. Like the corporation's other executives, Menard was paid a modest base salary, and also participated with them in a profit sharing plan. In 1998 his base salary was $157,500 and he received a profit sharing bonus of $3,017,100. However, the bulk of Menard's compensation was paid in the form of a "5 percent bonus" program that yielded him a bonus payment equal to 5 percent of the corporation's net income before income taxes. In 1998 the 5 percent bonus amounted to $17,467,800, which gave Menard total compensation for that year in excess of $20 million.

The 5 percent bonus program was adopted in 1973 by the corporation's board of directors at the suggestion of the corporation's accountant who advised the board that Menard should have his own bonus plan because of his commanding role in the management of the corporation. The board in 1973 included a shareholder who was not a member of Menard's family and who voted for the adoption of the bonus program. The 5 percent bonus had remained in effect since 1973 and there was no indication the 5 percent bonus had been called into question by the board since its adoption. The unrelated shareholder left the board in 1998 which thereafter consisted of Menard, a younger brother who worked for the corporation and the corporation's treasurer.

There was no indication that the shareholders were unhappy with their 18.8 percent rate of return or that the corporation's success was due to any windfall factors in 1998 or in any prior year. Finally, the 5 percent bonus was subject to a reimbursement agreement. Pursuant to this agreement Menard became obligated to reimburse the corporation should the deduction of any portion of Menard's compensation be disallowed by the Internal Revenue Service (IRS). Menard never paid dividends to its shareholders.

Looking at this factual context, the Tax Court did not question the reasonableness of Menard's base salary or the profit sharing bonus, but did focus on the amount of the 5 percent bonus. The Tax Court found that a portion of the 5 percent bonus was both excessive and intended to be a dividend. The court was able to address this latter issue by determining that in addition to satisfying the independent investor test, compensation must qualify as a "bona fide expense" in order to be deductible. The IRS had introduced evidence suggesting that the compensation was a disguised dividend which required the court to inquire into whether, as a matter of fact, the taxpayer had a compensatory purpose for the payment, even if the payment was otherwise reasonable in amount. The Tax Court concluded primarily for two reasons that a portion of the 5 percent bonus was a disguised dividend. The first reason was based on the facts that the taxpayer had never paid a dividend and that the 5 percent bonus appeared, for all practical purposes, to be no different from a dividend, that is, a profit based, year-end amount paid to the majority shareholder. The court reasoned that when large shareholders base their compensation on a percentage of profits, the arrangement may suggest an attempt to distribute profits without declaring a dividend. The court's second reason relied on the fact that the 5 percent bonus was subject to a reimbursement agreement if the IRS disallowed it as a corporate deduction. The court found that such reimbursement provisions suggest that the taxpayer had preexisting knowledge that the compensation was intended, in part, as a disguised dividend.

In analyzing the reasonableness of Menard's compensation, including the 5 percent bonus, the Tax Court acknowledged that an appeal of its decision would go to the Seventh Circuit Court of Appeals and thus, it had to apply the independent investor test of *Exacto Spring Corp. v. Comm.*, 196 F. 3d 833 (7th Cir. 1999). As previously described, this test, as adopted by the Seventh Circuit, provides that if a hypothetical independent investor would consider the rate of return on her investment in the taxpayer corporation a higher rate of return than she had any reason to expect, then, notwithstanding the CEO's exorbitant salary (as it might appear to a judge or other modestly paid official), the compensation paid to the corporation's CEO is presumptively reasonable. However, this presumption of reasonableness may be rebutted if an extraordinary event was responsible for the corporation's profitability or if the executive's position was merely titular and his job was actually performed by someone else.

The Tax Court did not dispute the proposition that Menard's compensation satisfied the independent investor test, but the court found that the inquiry did not end there. Despite the limited circumstances which the Seventh Circuit believed that the presumption of reasonableness could be rebutted under the independent investor test, the Tax Court nevertheless felt compelled by the regulations under Sec. 162(a) to consider evidence of compensation paid to CEOs in comparable companies in determining whether the presumption of reasonableness under the independent investor test is rebutted by the fact that the CEO is paid substantially more than the CEOs of comparable companies. Accordingly, the Tax Court was willing to expand the basis on which the presumption of reasonableness can be rebutted and to find that the presumption of reasonableness could be rebutted by evidence demonstrating that the CEOs of the corporations in the taxpayer's same business, such as Home Depot and Lowe's, were paid substantially less than the taxpayer paid its CEO. In 1998 the CEO of Home Depot received compensation of $2.8 million and Lowe's CEO received compensation of $6 million. The Tax Court found this evidence to be sufficient to rebut the presumption of reasonableness established by the taxpayer's rate of return on investment.

In determining what portion of Menard's compensation was reasonable, the Tax Court used a formula that determined what Menard's compensation would have been had he been the CEO of Home Depot and if Home Depot had achieved a rate of return equal to that of the taxpayer. This formula assumed that the corporation's rate of return drives CEO compensation. The result of the Tax Court's calculation was about $7 million and the Tax Court ruled that all compensation paid to Menard in 1998 in excess of that amount was unreasonable. Consequently, the Tax Court held that the portion of Menard's compensation in excess of $7 million was not deductible and was also a disguised dividend.

The taxpayer appealed the Tax Court's decision to the Seventh Circuit Court of Appeals. In a decision written by Judge Posner, the appellate court strongly disagreed with the Tax Court's analysis and conclusion. It found that the Tax Court's holding was based on a "flimsy" analysis of the taxpayer's bonus program and a "wrongheaded" comparison between Menard's compensation and the compensation paid to the CEOs of the taxpayer's competitors.

By way of background, the Court of Appeals began its opinion by pointing out that by making a payment to a shareholder/employee in the form of a salary payment, rather than as a dividend, a closely-held corporation is able to obtain a deduction for the payment while the recipient receives taxable income in either event. Accordingly, by treating a dividend as salary, the corporation will reduce its income tax liability without (in 1998) affecting the income tax liability of the recipient. In 1998 the highest marginal income tax rate of 35 percent was applicable to both salary and dividends. In addition, the Court of Appeals noted that the shareholders of a publicly owned corporation rein in the ability of corporate officers to take salary rather than paying dividends, but if, in a closely held corporation, the corporate officers/owners are paid more salary than they otherwise might be entitled to in order to avoid paying a dividend and to beat the corporate income tax, there is no one to complain, other than the IRS.

The circuit court recognized that it is difficult to analyze a case, like Menards, where the corporation pays a high salary to its CEO who works full time, but is also the sole or controlling owner of the corporation. It noted that the standard of reasonableness set forth in the Treasury regulations, which provides that to be reasonable the amount of salary must be the same as "would ordinarily be paid for like services by like enterprises under like circumstances," is not an operational standard. It requires a comparison in situations where no two corporations and no two CEOs are the same and thus, the standard is difficult to apply. Moreover, if a comparison is going to be made, the total compensation packages of the CEOs should be taken into account, including deferred compensation, severance pay, and employee perks as well as the amount of risk in the executives' compensation.

The court further noted that other courts have attempted to operationalize the reasonableness standard by considering multiple factors that relate to optimal compensation. But the Seventh Circuit had rejected that approach as being too vague and too difficult to apply on an objective basis to be of much utility. This is particularly the case where no comparative weight is assigned to any of the factors. Consequently, the Seventh Circuit, in an attempt to bring a degree of objectivity to the analysis, established the independent investor test which creates the presumption that "when the investors in his company are obtaining a far higher return than they had any reason to expect, [the owner/employee's] salary is presumptively reasonable." However, the court recognized that this presumption could be rebutted by evidence that the company's success was a consequence of extraneous factors, such as a windfall profit which was unrelated to anything done by the owner/employee, or that the company intended to pay the owner/employee a disguised dividend rather than salary. Finally, the court said that a comparison with the compensation of executives of other companies can be helpful "if—but it is a big if—the comparison takes into account the details of the compensation package of each of the compared executives, and not just the bottom line salary."

Looking at the facts in the *Menard* case, the Court of Appeals confirmed that none of the taxpayer's shareholders were disappointed with the 18.8 percent rate of return and that the company's success in 1998 or any prior year was not due to any windfall factors. Addressing the Tax Court's holding that the 5 percent bonus was intended as a dividend, as evidenced by the reimbursement agreement between Menard and the taxpayer and because the 5 percent bonus looked more like a dividend than like salary, the court found that it was prudent and not necessarily in Menard's personal financial interest for the taxpayer to require Menard to reimburse the taxpayer in the event that the IRS should disallow a compensation deduction. With respect to the 5 percent bonus looking like a dividend, the court argued that dividends are generally specified dollar amounts per share rather than a percentage of profits. Moreover, by tying Menard's compensation to the taxpayer's pretax profits, the taxpayer increased Menard's incentive to work hard and to increase profits, which has no application to a non-employee shareholder. Finally, the fact that the 5 percent bonus was paid at the end of the year did not impress the Court of Appeals which found the timing of the payment to be the most practical approach to paying the bonus since that is when annual earnings are known, as opposed to the payment of a dividend which usually occurs on a quarterly basis.

The Court of Appeals then focused on the Tax Court's main argument which was that the portion of Menard's compensation that exceeded the compensation paid to comparable CEOs should be treated functionally as a dividend and not a bonus. Addressing this argument, the Court of Appeals made the following points:

- Salary was just the beginning of a meaningful comparison, because it is only one component of a compensation package. All of the various components have to be compared, not just salary.

- Risk is an important factor in an executive's compensation structure. A risky compensation structure implies that the executive's compensation is likely to vary substantially from year to year. The Tax Court ignored the fact that Menard's compensation would have been substantially less than $20 million if the taxpayer experienced a bad year.

- The IRS seemed to be cherry picking, given that the 5 percent bonus had been in effect for 25 years before the IRS decided to challenge it.

- The Tax Court's formula for calculating Menard's reasonable compensation was an arbitrary approach which disregarded (i) differences in the total compensation packages payable to the CEOs of the companies being compared, (ii) differences in whatever business challenges faced the companies in 1998 and (iii) differences in the responsibilities and performances of the other CEOs.

- The Tax Court failed to consider the possibility which the evidence supported that since the taxpayer's three other corporate officers were modestly compensated, Menard really did the job of multiple employees.

- The Seventh Circuit confirmed its disagreement with the proposition that a bonus contract executed by a non-controlling shareholder may be viewed as reasonable while the same contract executed by a controlling shareholder may be viewed as unreasonable simply because the latter executive does not need an incentive bonus to call forth his best effort. As a controlling shareholder he will receive the economic benefit of the profits of the business in any event. The court argued that holding that a controlling shareholder/executive can never receive an incentive bonus would not make any sense since bonuses are not intended to reward motivation, but rather they reward performance.

For all these reasons, the Court of Appeals found that the Tax Court's decision that Menard's compensation for 1998 was unreasonable constituted clear error and had to be reversed. This appellate decision clearly gives corporate taxpayers reason to be optimistic about how reasonable compensation claims will be reviewed in the future.

Approximately one year after *Menard* was decided by the Seventh Circuit, the Tax Court had another opportunity to address the issue of reasonable compensation. In *Multi-Pak Corporation*, TCM 2010-139 (2010), the Tax Court reviewed the taxpayer's deduction for compensation paid to its sole owner/CEO/COO and upheld the compensation deduction for the entire $2.02 million paid in 2002, but reduced the compensation deduction in 2003 by approximately 37 percent to $1.28 million, which was still significantly more than the $660,000 compensation amount that the IRS determined was reasonable. The key factors that the Tax Court cited to support its determination of the allowable deductions included the following: (i) the owner performed varied jobs; (ii) the owner made all important operational decisions; (iii) the owner was the driving force behind the taxpayer's success; (iv) the rise in revenues and sales in 2002 could almost all be attributed to the owner; and (v) an independent investor would accept the taxpayer's return on equity for 2002, but due to a drop in revenues and sales in 2003, the negative return on equity in 2003 would not have been acceptable to an independent investor. Thus, in 2003 reasonable compensation had to be less than the amount paid to the owner. Unlike its opinion in *Menard*, the Tax Court in *Multi-Pak* dismissed as a relevant factor the compensation paid to CEOs of comparable companies, because the comparable companies selected by the compensation experts were not enough like the taxpayer to make the comparison meaningful. Instead the Tax Court focused more on the independent investor test in making its decision than it had in *Menard*. Thus, it appears that the independent investor test is gaining greater traction in the Tax Court.[14]

Although it is too soon to make any definitive determinations, corporate taxpayers can be hopeful that the *Menard* and *Multi-Pak* decisions will change the standards and the methodology by which the IRS and the Tax Court will resolve reasonable compensation cases in the future. Nevertheless, financial professionals, even those in the Seventh Circuit, should continue to exercise caution when advising clients on compensation planning matters. Until the Tax Court and the other Circuit Courts clearly adopt the independent investor test, as applied by the Seventh Circuit, corporate taxpayers should take into account the multi-factor test when determining compensation. In particular, planners should pay particular attention to the executive's contributions to the company in terms of hours worked, specialized expertise and performance of multiple roles. Compensation information for comparable positions in similar companies is also important. Furthermore, a prudent planner should consider the following suggestions:

- A methodology for determining each executive's compensation level should be developed as soon as possible by the corporation and that methodology should be followed consistently in years with both profits and losses. In certain circumstances the implementation of this suggestion may require the corporation to engage the services of a consultant who specializes in compensation planning.
- Corporate minutes should document the reasons why a given amount of compensation was decided upon.
- Where there is more than one shareholder-employee, compensation should not be paid in proportion to stockholdings.
- If the corporation is profitable, some dividends should be paid, unless there is a valid business reason for retaining earnings. Any

---

14. The Tax Court's opinion in *Multi-Pak* is appealable to the Ninth Circuit which is a multi-factor test jurisdiction, even though the Ninth Circuit will consider whether a hypothetical independent investor would be willing to compensate an executive as he was actually compensated. However, given the taxpayer's success with respect to 2002, an appeal by the taxpayer is not likely. The IRS may also be willing to accept a partial victory and thus, may decide not to appeal as well.

such business reason should be documented in the corporate minutes.

- The payment of compensation should take place at various times during the year, rather than waiting until year end. Incentive compensation, based on year-end results, can be paid after the end of the year, but some compensation should nevertheless be paid on a regular basis throughout the year.

- The corporation should monitor its shareholders' return on equity as well as the return on equity of any competitors who are publicly traded. This comparison should be taken into account by the corporation in setting the compensation levels for its executives.[15]

PUBLICLY HELD CORPORATIONS AND THE $1 MILLION LIMIT—SEC. 162(M)

The "reasonable compensation" analysis discussed above is never used to challenge compensation paid to executives in publicly held corporations. The various state and federal laws relating to disclosure of information, shareholder rights, the election of boards of directors, and other factors tend to make most of the issues in the reasonable compensation case law as applied to closely-held corporations, irrelevant in the case of publicly held corporations. However, especially in recent years, the size of compensation packages for the CEOs and other officers of publicly held corporations has come into question, and various approaches to limiting the high levels of their remuneration have been discussed.

One pertinent provision in the Code is Sec. 162(m), which specifies that an employer's deduction exceeding $1 million for "employee remuneration" is not allowable. However, this provision has limited application as indicated by the following:

- It applies only to publicly held corporations. A *publicly held corporation* is any corporation with equity securities that must be registered under the Securities Exchange Act of 1934—generally a company with securities traded on a securities exchange.

- It applies only to compensation paid to the chief executive officer and to the four highest compensated officers, as defined under federal securities law.

---

15. See Friske and Smith, "The Status of the 'Independent Investor' Test in Reasonable Compensation Determinations," 31 *The Tax Advisor* 406 (June 2000).

- It does not apply to compensation paid on a commission basis or to certain other performance-based compensation.

Because of the limited applicability of Sec. 162(m), it generally is not a factor in planning for the types of executive compensation paid by the closely held businesses that are the focus of this course. Also, even for the publicly held corporation, a substantial part of the very large compensation packages paid to CEOs and to other corporate officers that have attracted criticism are structured to qualify as performance-based and therefore are not subject to the deduction limitations set forth in Sec. 162(m).

DETERMINING EXECUTIVE COMPENSATION LEVELS

In a closely held company, executive pay will be determined by the owners' needs or wishes as to how much money should be taken out of the business in the form of compensation, subject to tax-law limitations on reasonable compensation. For publicly held companies, however, the determination of executive compensation is a matter of fiduciary responsibility to the shareholders. Fundamentally, the person or group of persons ("compensation committee") responsible for determining executive pay has the responsibility of paying compensation at a level sufficient to attract and keep the kind of executives needed to maintain the company's profitability and share values. Critics of compensation practices of large corporations, such as John Bogle of the Vanguard mutual fund organization, have suggested that in today's environment this process has become corrupted. They argue that managerial interests rather than shareholder interests dominate the process because decisions are made by a closed circle of self-interested people. As a result, executives are given incentives to operate the company in the interests of short-term investment profits that increase their equity-based compensation packages rather than building long-term share values. However, even though this issue is beyond the scope of this chapter, it should be noted that the Dodd-Frank Wall Street Reform and Consumer Protection Act contains provisions that are intended to make compensation committees more independent and to make executive compensation subject to greater disclosure and subject to greater shareholder review. Thus, for our purposes we will assume that compensation committees operate, as they should, in the interests of shareholders in general, and therefore in the overall long-term interests of the company.

There are two broad ways to determine the compensation of any employee:

- Determine the market value of the position.
- Evaluate the position itself for its intrinsic value to the company.

For top executives, the market value approach tends to dominate. After all, the company's need is to attract the right person from a relatively small pool of suitable executives, and the market will primarily determine the compensation level. For lower level positions with a much larger pool of potential hires, it is more difficult to determine the market level of compensation and a position-evaluation system may be more appropriate. In particular, the goal of compensation policy for lower level employees is usually to help provide a sense of fairness or equity within the company, and position-evaluation techniques are helpful for this purpose; but internal fairness is generally not (at least in today's environment) considered relevant to high-level executive compensation.

Determining the market rate of compensation usually involves surveys, formal or informal, of comparable positions in comparable companies. No two high-level positions are exactly alike, so surveys provide only a range of compensation levels. It is then up to the company compensation managers to determine how much to offer for the job in order to attract the right kind of person. The people that the company wishes to target will generally be keenly concerned that they are being paid at a competitive level.

Relating the compensation offered and paid over the executive's career to market levels not only helps attract and keep the right people, but it also helps to justify the level to company stakeholders—directors, shareholders, customers or clients, employees, and the IRS and other government regulators.

In evaluating compensation levels, it is important to take into account all forms of compensation, both current and deferred, and including all fringe benefits and perquisites. This involves a process of evaluation that sometimes is problematic, especially where compensation is based on future stock values. In addition, since competitiveness of compensation levels is the criterion for determining these levels, it is important that both the company and the targeted employees generally value the proposed benefits according to the same general considerations.

PREPARING FOR IRS CHALLENGE

From IRS audit guidelines, it appears that on audit the IRS looks at factors like the following in determining that compensation is unreasonable:

- salary for the current year that is substantially more than the executive was paid in the preceding year
- bonuses paid close to the end of the company's taxable year
- the fact that no dividends, or only a small amount of dividends, were paid in recent years
- salary that is paid in proportion to stockholdings

There are no procedural steps that can insulate a compensation arrangement against challenge by the IRS or other corporate stakeholders. However, a prudent course of action would include the following:

- The specific dollar amount of salary should be set forth and documented at the beginning of the year. For formula-type arrangements, the formula should be set forth.
- The company should set forth a complete explanation of how the amount of salary was reached. This includes a statement of the executive's qualifications and value to the company, a history of undercompensation in prior years (if this is a factor), studies of comparable executives, and special duties or expenditures required of the executive such as entertaining, etc.
- The company should make and preserve a written record of the decision as part of either the minutes of the directors' meeting or the employment contract specifying which conditions indicating reasonableness of salary were satisfied.

Some areas in documentation may require particular attention since they are often challenged.

- If surveys of executive pay indicate that the executive in question is receiving more than the normal pay in his or her field, the company should document the reasons for this. Exceptional qualifications or achievements should be presented to the board and put in a written report.
- The argument that high current compensation levels reflect underpayment of the executive in prior years has been accepted by the courts in tax cases and is theoretically accepted by the IRS. However, such an assertion must be clearly documented. Also, it is possible that corporate stakeholders might be more resistant to this argument than the IRS, so the case must be made that

this executive must be kept and compensated for earlier services, rather than hiring someone else at a lower rate of pay.

YEAR OF DEDUCTION

Generally as an individual taxpayer, an executive will report income using the cash method of accounting. A cash-method taxpayer reports income when it is actually paid or the money is irrevocably available to him or her under the constructive-receipt doctrine. If an executive has a drawing account, but must repay amounts not earned through the performance of services, the executive is taxable on the amount when it is earned.

The company, whether it uses a cash or accrual method of accounting, can deduct only the compensation paid for services that were actually rendered by the end of the taxable year for which the deduction is claimed. Amounts paid before services are rendered are deductible pro rata over the period in which they will be rendered.

EXAMPLE
Employee Fern has a contract for supervising the repair of hurricane damage providing a payment of $240,000 for 24 months of services. Because of Fern's unique talents, the parties negotiate an agreement for payment in two installments at the end of 2010 and 2011. In 2010 Fern rendered 2 months of services and the company paid Fern $120,000 on December 31, 2010. Fern must report $120,000 of compensation income for 2010. The company can deduct $20,000 of this for 2010 (2/12 of $120,000).

The 2½-Month "Safe Haven" Rule. As a general rule, an accrual-method company deducts accrued business expenses, for the year the expense is accrued, while it may not be paid until a later year. However, compensation expenses are subject to a stricter rule. Accrued compensation for a given year of the employer can't be deducted for that year unless the payment is made to the employee or independent contractor within 2½ months after the end of the employer's year. (Reg. Sec. 1.404(b)-IT, Q and A-2).

This rule provides some inherent tax leverage because the employee, as a cash-method taxpayer, reports income in the year received. So for example, if an employee receives compensation income for 2008 services on March 14, 2009, from an accrual-method employer that uses a calendar year, the employer deducts the amount for 2008 but the employee pays tax on the amount in 2009. The employer has the use of the tax money for the compensation deduction for an additional year, and it can share this benefit with the employee in the form of greater effective compensation levels.

There is a limitation on this leverage, however. If the employee is a 50 percent or more shareholder of the company making the payment, the corporation cannot take a deduction until the year the amount is included in the executive's income; there is no 2½-month "safe haven." See Code Sec. 267(a).

The use of the 2½-month safe haven is most appropriate in the case of a bonus amount that is based on annual results and often cannot be computed before the end of the year. If the bonus is paid within 2½ months after the end of the year, the safe haven preserves the company's deduction of the bonus amount for the year in which the bonus was earned.

CASH BONUS PLANNING ISSUES

Bonus arrangements sometimes run into reasonable compensation problems because they may look to the IRS like an ad hoc, last-minute method of distributing excess corporate profits (hence dividend treatment or compensation for services other than the current year's services). In general, however, the IRS will recognize a bonus arrangement as resulting in reasonable compensation if it was (a) a fair bargain, (b) arrived at in arm's-length negotiation, and (c) agreed to before the services were performed. These criteria are the guidelines for planning a successful bonus arrangement.

A company planning to institute a bonus plan should arrange to tailor the incentive to the performance of the particular executive, decide on the bonus before it is earned, and reduce the arrangement to writing in either an employment contract or board of directors' resolution.

It is important that the decision to pay a bonus be made early in the tax year and a formula for doing so worked out to avoid a charge by the IRS that such payment is not a bona fide payment for current services. If it is considered a dividend, the payment would not be deductible by the corporation. If it is considered additional compensation for past services, such additional payment could raise the question of whether the total compensation for that past time was reasonable. The company should adopt a written bonus plan that includes provisions for defining profits if the bonus depends on profits, a time limit for the agreement to be in force, a periodic review of the plan, and arbitration of disputes.

Although bonuses usually depend on profits, they also could be based on such things as the price of the company stock during a certain period or at year-end, dividends, sales, costs, or some basis connected with the particular job to be accomplished by that executive.

Although cash bonuses must meet the requirement of reasonableness, the fact that there is some risk attached as to whether or not the executive actually receives that amount can enlarge the limits of reasonableness. The test of reasonableness is governed by the circumstances existing at the time the contract is entered into rather than those existing when the company is audited by the IRS.

EXAMPLE

For the current year, Aldo receives cash compensation of $400,000 plus a bonus of $300,000 based on excellent current-year operating results, for a total of $700,000. The formula that provides the $300,000 bonus was negotiated at the beginning of the current year. The criteria for computing the bonus are realistic for the business—that is, there is a reasonable likelihood that no bonus could result. According to guidelines that all parties accept, a reasonable cash compensation level for Aldo would be $600,000 annually. The IRS will not necessarily disallow the additional $100,000 that Aldo receives, because it was based on a formula under which Aldo had a reasonable risk of not receiving it as of the time when the compensation arrangement was negotiated.

Some other design points can be noted:

- If more than one executive is to be paid a bonus based on profits, there must be a prior determination of whether profits are to be computed before or after the other bonuses are paid.
- In the case of a large company with various subsidiaries or divisions, a decision must be made as to whether the bonus is to depend on results of the whole company or a particular part of the company.
- Corporate philosophy will determine whether the regular salary should be at a fairly high competitive level and the bonus minimal (unless the executive's performance is outstanding), or whether the salary should be minimal and the bonus directly reflective of the company's position that year.

- The plan can be structured as a "target" arrangement, under which there is no bonus unless profits (or other measuring element) reach a certain level. Above that level, the bonus is a percentage of profits up to a higher level, with a higher percentage-of-profits bonus above that level, and so on. Any realistic formula of this type can be used.

- An incentive bonus plan can be designed for a group of executives by creating a bonus "fund" equal to a percentage of profits; executives covered under the plan then receive a portion of the bonus fund, usually proportional to their cash compensation.

Defining Profits

An important part of drafting an incentive agreement is the definition of "profits" for purposes of the agreement. The definition of profits is necessary, of course, in order to determine the amount of incentive compensation based on profits. There are no tax or other rules that constrain this definition. The method of determining profits must be specified in the agreement. Profit could be the amount shown as profit in the financial statement, taxable income for federal income tax purposes, or it could be determined in some other specified way. If the company has affiliates, their profits can be factored into the bonus plan, or the plan can be based on just the entity that employs the executive.

If profits are based on the current accounting system, however, a change in the accounting method might require the company to keep a special set of books for the bonus plan. If profit is based on taxable income, the profit picture, and therefore the bonus, would vary with the tax laws; the agreement can be drafted to minimize or eliminate this variation by basing tax-related provisions on the tax law at the time of the adoption of the agreement. But such refinements correspondingly increase the burden of administering the agreement.

Ongoing Administration of Bonus Plans

A compensation plan or agreement is subject to changes in the business, tax, or other environments. Tax rates or rules applicable to compensation or benefits change often. And business conditions for a given company can change, often virtually overnight by a competitor's introduction of a better product, the company's acquisition of a large new client or customer, and so on. The level of compensation determined originally, or the original formula, may produce a compensation for later years that is inappropriate for business conditions or possibly unreasonable under the tax law's reasonable compensation requirement.

Compensation agreements therefore should generally have limited terms, especially for cash compensation and incentive bonus arrangements. Deferred-compensation or pension arrangements have longer terms as to the ultimate payout of amounts already earned. These arrangements, however, should, like those for current compensation, provide for periodic changes in the amount of benefit accrued currently.

Incentive bonus plans in particular are inherently short-term arrangements, since future profits and other measures of business success are hard to predict. These plans are typically subject to periodic renegotiation.

STOCKHOLDER-EXECUTIVE ISSUES

Reimbursement Agreements

Where employees are also owners of the company, and especially where the company is small or closely held, it is difficult to make a distinction between the stockholder-employees' economic interests and those of the company. This issue is highlighted when deduction of allegedly excessive compensation amounts is disallowed by the IRS. If the disallowance stands, the executive must still pay taxes on the full amount received. (Typically, the excess amount would be treated as a dividend, and generally subjected to a lower rate of tax than the ordinary income.) But the corporation would lose its tax deduction and its taxes would increase. The aggregation of the company and its owners would therefore lose money to Uncle Sam in the amount of the tax increase resulting from the disallowance, less the reduction in income taxes, if any, resulting from dividend treatment to the employee-shareholder.

It appears that this situation could be "fixed" if the compensation payment could be reversed in part:

EXAMPLE
Addvul Co. requires stockholder-employee Kramer, as part of her employment contract, to repay any compensation amount for which Addvul can't take a compensation deduction. If Kramer has a binding legal obligation to repay, the tax law allows a business expense deduction for the repayment. Suppose that for the year 2010, Kramer receives compensation of $400,000. In 2012, the IRS audits Addvul's returns for 2010 and disallows $100,000 of Kramer's compensation as excessive. Kramer repays the excess $100,000 to Addvul in 2012. For 2010, Kramer would be taxable on $400,000. Addvul's taxable income for 2010 would be increased by $100,000, reflecting the disallowed deduction. For 2012, Kramer could deduct the $100,000 repayment she makes to Addvul. The repayment is not taxable to Addvul since its 2010 income was already increased to reflect this amount.

The repayment agreement technically provides a remedy for disallowance, but it has disadvantages:

- Generally, only a very large shareholder, one whose financial interests are essentially identical with those of the corporation, would have a financial interest in agreeing to a repayment agreement. For most employees, their interest is to "take the money and run." Nonshareholders and minority owners should not enter into repayment agreements.

- Even a large shareholder-employee may be reluctant to enter into a repayment agreement since the agreement may require the employee to come up with a large cash payment resulting from a circumstance beyond his or her control—an IRS audit.

- Some shareholders may be suspicious that the existence of a repayment agreement will provide a disincentive for corporate management to vigorously contest IRS audits of compensation arrangements. The problem here is that if compensation deductions are disallowed and executives make a repayment to the company, the company's financial position is improved. So it is seemingly in the company's interest to acquiesce in the IRS disallowance where a repayment agreement exists.

- Probably worst of all, it is generally considered among tax practitioners that repayment agreements are a "red flag" for the IRS—an indication that compensation amounts are likely excessive. IRS agents generally will learn of the existence of repayment agreements because typical IRS practice in corporate audits is to ask to examine existing employment agreements.

Nevertheless, a repayment agreement serves a valid legal and economic purpose where a determination of a tax liability contradictory to that anticipated by the parties would be disadvantageous to at least one of the parties. Rather than giving up on the transaction or spending time and money obtaining IRS rulings or legal opinions, the parties may agree to indemnify against such an adverse tax result, thus mitigating the risk and allowing the transaction to go forward. While a determination may be made that a particular compensation arrangement is earned and reasonable, it is not beyond doubt that the IRS may be successful in challenging some of the compensation as being nondeductible. Thus, the parties are only being prudent in providing that if the expected tax consequences do not materialize, then one party will protect the other party against the unintended adverse tax consequences. For courts to automatically determine that compensation is unreasonable due to the existence of a repayment agreement is bad tax policy.

CLAUSE COVERING REPAYMENT OF EXCESSIVE COMPENSATION

Any payment made to _____ [the executive] as salary, commission, bonus, or other compensation for personal services, which shall be disallowed in whole or in part as a deductible expense by the Internal Revenue Service, shall be reimbursed by _____ [the executive] to _____ [the company] to the full extent of such disallowance, not later than _____ days after demand for reimbursement is made by _____ [the company]. In lieu of such reimbursement by _____ [the executive] the Board of Directors of _____ [the company] may at its discretion direct that amounts be withheld and deducted from _____'s compensation until the amount owed to _____ [the company] shall be recovered.

"Best Salary" Considerations

Corporate and individual tax rates differ. The idea behind the best salary concept is that there is an optimum salary rate for shareholder-executives that, taking into account the different rates of corporate and individual tax, provides the minimum tax cost to the entire business entity (corporation plus shareholders). The best way to understand the concept is to look at examples such as those in the Review Questions at the end of this chapter.

EXAMPLE

Here's a very simple example to illustrate the concept. Suppose Zilch Co. has $50,000 of income remaining after paying all expenses except compensation for Veeble, the sole owner-CEO of Zilch. It's assumed that the applicable corporate tax on $50,000 is $7,500. If $50,000 is paid as salary to Veeble, Veeble's tax would be $6,785. Therefore, the full $50,000 should be paid as salary to Veeble since it would save the corporate enterprise taxwise.

The usefulness of the best salary concept is weakening as individual tax rates have in recent years begun to dip below corporate rates, thereby usually making it advantageous to maximize salary payments rather than accumulating income and taxing it at corporate rates. Other factors also have relegated the best salary concept to a largely theoretical idea:

- It makes sense only for a sole owner, or for a group of similarly situated executives who are owners of the corporation, because a nonowner does not have an inherent direct economic interest in helping the company save on its tax bill.

- The practice of not paying corporate profits out as dividends or compensation can run into problems with the "accumulated earnings tax" of Code Sec. 512. This tax was designed to encourage payment of corporate income as dividends to shareholders rather than to shelter it as investment income within the corporation. Under the accumulated earnings tax, a corporation can accumulate only a total of $250,000 ($150,000 for a personal-service corporation) without showing a business need for the accumulation.

Buying Out a Retiring Stockholder-Executive's Interest

Corporate buyout packages of shareholders cover a lot of ground that is not relevant to this book. However, there are compensation-planning issues that can be involved when a shareholder-executive retires or otherwise terminates employment, and the parties wish to design a buyout package for the retiree. Typically, the retiree will receive a combination of payment for the shares he or she sells back to the company and a deferred-compensation/severance package of current or deferred cash.

From a tax perspective, this type of planning is interesting because the two parties—the executive and the company—tend to have opposing interests. On the one hand, the company would like to maximize the extent to which the package constitutes current or deferred compensation. This is because the company can deduct the amount of any payment that represents compensation. On the other hand, the departing employee would prefer to receive as much of the total payout as possible as a current or deferred payment for his or her stock, because that payment would be treated as capital gain: Only the amount that exceeds the departing employee's basis would be taxable and would be subject to the favorable capital-gain tax rates. But a payment for the departing employee's stock is not deductible by the company.

In planning these buyout packages, it should be noted that there is no way to guarantee that the IRS will accept the parties' allocation of the amount between capital gain and compensation. On audit of the company or the executive, the IRS may, and often does, question the allocation and may choose to recharacterize the payments.

In trying to avoid an IRS challenge, probably the best way to support the compensation element of the payout is to adopt a deferred-compensation agreement early in the executive's career that spells out the amount of deferred compensation to be paid at retirement or termination of employment, making it clear that this amount is truly paid on account of the employee's services over his or her career.

However, even if the compensation element is part of a late, ad hoc severance agreement, the parties fortunately have an ace in the hole in this argument with the IRS. Because the corporation and the employee have different interests with regard to the characterization of the amount, there can be a good argument that the allocation results from an arm's-length negotiation between adverse parties. In general, the IRS tends to defer to an arm's-length allocation where it can be demonstrated by the taxpayer.

S Corporation Stockholder-Executives

An S corporation is a corporation that is eligible to make, and has made, an election under the tax law to be taxed as a pass-through entity somewhat like a partnership. (Taxation of an actual partnership, however, has many unique features not shared by S corporations.) For nontax state corporate law purposes, an S corporation is treated as a bona fide corporation. The S corporation election has become very popular and is often recommended by accountants for smaller corporations, since it tends to save taxes by eliminating income tax at the corporate level. It can also avoid taxation of shareholders or corporations upon the ultimate liquidation of the corporation, a problem with regular or "C" corporations.

Since all income of an S corporation is passed through to its owners (shareholders) in proportion to their ownership, shareholder-employees are often under the impression that compensation planning is irrelevant. However, a determination of what portion of the amount taxable to a shareholder-employee constitutes "compensation" as opposed to a dividend-type payment is important taxwise for a number of reasons:

- Social Security and Medicare taxes are based on compensation, not on the total amount taxable to the shareholder-employee. Attempts to report artificially low salaries for this purpose have been aggressively thwarted by the IRS, but they are still sometimes suggested (unwisely) as a way to save taxes.

- Qualified plan and other fringe benefit plan contributions or benefits are often based on compensation. For example, if a qualified pension plan formula provides for an employer contribution of 20 percent of compensation, then a reduction in "compensation" will result in a disallowance of part of the pension plan contribution as well as a reduction in the employee's pension.

- The amount of compensation paid to executives has a significant effect on important accounting aspects of the S corporation.

With regard to the third item, there are at least two significant issues that should be noted illustrating the importance of compensation.

First of all, compensation paid by an S corporation is a deduction to the S corporation subject to the same "reasonable compensation" limit applicable to regular corporations. Consequently, as with a regular corporation, denial of a deduction can increase the corporation's taxable income. However, since there is no corporate level tax, the amount of the disallowed deduction becomes taxable to the S corporation's shareholder or shareholders as distributable net income.

EXAMPLE
Freeh Co., an S corporation, pays Glitch, its sole shareholder and CEO, a $450,000 salary, makes a contribution of $40,000 to Glitch's account in a qualified plan, and has $60,000 left as undistributed earnings. Glitch pays taxes on the $450,000 salary and on the $60,000 of undistributed earnings, for a total of $510,000. However, if $25,000 of the compensation deduction is disallowed, the company's earnings increase by $25,000, but Glitch still pays taxes on a total of $510,000—that is, $425,000 of salary, $25,000 of distributed net income, and $60,000 of undistributed net income.

In addition, denial of a compensation deduction can create additional income for nonemployee stockholders. For example, suppose in the above example Glitch was a 50 percent stockholder; with the balance of the stock owned by Zlota, Glitch's mother. If Glitch's compensation is deductible in full, he is taxed on $480,000, Glitch's salary plus half the earnings. Zlota is taxed on the other half of the earnings, or $30,000. If $25,000 of Glitch's compensation is disallowed, then both shareholders have additional income of $12,500 each. Note that Zlota has this additional taxable income even though the corporation has parted with the funds on which she is taxed, having paid them to Glitch.

This result possibly could be avoided by having Glitch enter into a repayment agreement, with the disadvantages discussed earlier, or the shareholders might enter into a side agreement dealing with this contingency.

It is interesting to note that in an S corporation, the IRS can be concerned that compensation is unreasonably low as well as unreasonably high. Stock from an S corporation may be transferred to children or other family members as a useful income-splitting device if it is a bona fide transfer and if the children or family members are in low tax brackets. In diverting income to children in this way, salaries of those stockholders actually working for the company should be kept at a level of compensation that reasonably reflects the value of their services to the company. If the IRS considers the compensation to be unreasonably low, it will act to tax the amount of salary that it determines to be reasonable by reallocating a portion of the corporate income distributed to a nonemployee-shareholder. Factors affecting what this amount is include the factors previously discussed under reasonable compensation, and, in this situation, especially what was considered a reasonable salary prior to the transfer of the stock. Furthermore, this discussion is equally applicable to other pass-through entities, such as limited liability partnerships and limited liability companies, which elect to be taxed as partnerships.

ADDITIONAL RESOURCE

Sample Incentive Compensation Agreement

AGREEMENT made this _____ day of _____ between _____ hereinafter, "the company") and_____ (hereinafter, "the employee").

WITNESSETH

1.   [Employee's duties, term of contract, etc.]

2. As compensation of the employee's services hereunder, the company agrees to pay the employee: (a) a salary of $_____ per annum, payable semimonthly, and (b) an additional amount (hereinafter, "incentive compensation") equal to _____ percent of the amount of consolidated net earnings of the company and its subsidiaries, except that in no event shall incentive compensation exceed _____ percent of salary.

   Consolidated net earnings of the company shall be such earnings as are determined by the independent accounting firm employed by the company as its auditors, and shall reflect deduction for federal income taxes, compensation of all kinds paid to the employee, and all other proper charges. The determination of consolidated net earnings made by such accounting firm shall be final and binding on company and employee, and no adjustments in incentive compensation shall subsequently be made because of adjustments in federal income taxes or other items. The consolidated net earnings for purposes of this incentive computation shall be computed not later than 60 days after the end of the company's fiscal year and distribution on any incentive compensation shall be made not later than 75 days after the end of that fiscal year.

3. et seq. [Clauses unrelated to incentive compensation.]

IN WITNESS WHEREOF the company and the employee have executed this agreement as of the day and year first written above.

[company]

by _____   _____

[title]   [employee]

Alternative Clauses Based on Profits. Below are alternative clauses that may be substituted in the Sample Incentive Compensation Agreement above.

A._____ percent of the first _____ of profits [consolidated net earnings or other definition]. _____ percent of the next _____ of profits _____ percent of the next _____ of profits. And so on.

In some agreements the percentage of profits to be paid drops as profits rise; in others, the percentage rises-for example, 2 percent of the first $500,000, 3 percent of the next $1 million, and so on.

B. _____ percent of the profits in excess of _____ percent of the sum of the company's average amount of capital employed during the year.

This bases the award on profits that exceed some predetermined rate of return on invested capital.

C. _____ percent of profits in excess of $ _____.

This is somewhat similar to the preceding clause, basing the award on profits that exceed a predetermined dollar amount.

CASE PROBLEM

Roberts Steel and Supply Co., Inc., is a steel fabrication business owned by three stockholder-officers and one spouse. Roberts started the business as a sole proprietorship. In 1992, Roberts and DeMarco incorporated the company. DeMarco is a civil engineer and had prior experience in this field. At that time, the company had two trucks and some machinery. Taft began to work for the company in 1992, first as a truck driver and then as a salesperson. At first, the company was only in the business of fabrication and installation of reinforcing steel. Later a structural steel division supplying structural steel components was added. Now the company occupies two large adjacent buildings and employs 300 people, some of whom are seasonal employees.

Roberts, as president, is in charge of the company's operations. DeMarco is general manager of the reinforcing steel division, and Taft is general manager of the structural steel division. All three officers devote their full time and attention to the company's affairs. They regularly work between 55 and 70 hours in a 6-day week. They are the only executive officers and the only ones that have supervisory responsibility.

Since 1996 Roberts, DeMarco, and Taft have been the only officers and directors of the company. Roberts's compensation from 1996 to last year ranged from a low of $80,000 to $200,000. Last year he was a 34 percent shareholder.

Over the last 5 years, DeMarco's compensation has increased from $80,000 to $120,000. He was a 22 percent shareholder last year. Taft became an officer in 1997, and his compensation has since increased from $65,000 to $110,000. He owned 13 percent of the stock last year.

Roberts's wife holds the balance of the stock. The highest paid employee other than these officers is a salesperson who earned $42,000 last year.

Prior to 1999, the officers received irregular bonuses. In 1999, the officers agreed to set aside 40 percent of the net profits before income taxes as a management bonus to be distributed between the three officers. (Roberts usually received 46 percent of this amount; DeMarco and Taft received 27 percent of the bonus.) There was no bonus plan for any other employees. Forty percent was chosen in order to leave an adequate amount of working capital available for the business.

Last year the three officers were compensated as follows:

	Salary	Bonus	Pension Plan	Total
Roberts	$50,000	$130,000	$20,000	$200,000
DeMarco	50,000	60,000	8,000	120,000
Taft	45,000	59,000	6,000	110,000

The above totals represent an increase of $50,000 for Roberts over the preceding year; $40,000 for DeMarco; and $34,000 for Taft.

The company's tax returns for 2001 were audited by the IRS, and there was no objection to the bonus formula at that time.

The company never paid dividends. As of last year, the company had an earned surplus of $600,000.

The IRS has disallowed $80,000 of the compensation paid to these three executives under the bonus arrangement last year as a deduction for the company. (They disallowed $40,000 for Roberts, $20,000 for DeMarco, and $20,000 for Taft.)

To support its position against this IRS challenge as to the deductibility of the salaries, the company submitted the following table comparing the company's income with the industry-wide average and with income of other companies of comparable size.

Comparison of Selected Data with Industry Sample for Last Year		
(American Institute of Steel Construction—AISC)		

I. Income before Federal Income Taxes as a Percentage of Sales

	Roberts AISC Company	Group	$2.5MM—$5MM Companies
Last year	7.43%	3.51%	3.70%

II. Income after Federal Income Taxes as a Percent of Net Worth

	Roberts AISC Company	Group	$2.5MM—$5MM Companies
Last year	14.45%	5.32%	6.28%

III. Income after Federal Income Taxes as a Percentage of Total Assets

	Roberts AISC Company	Group	$2.5MM—$5MM Companies
Last year	8.28%	3.28%	3.80%

There was no comparison of compensation paid by the various companies.

1. What factors support the IRS position that the compensation paid to the three executives exceeds reasonable compensation?

2. What arguments can be made on the company's behalf in favor of deductibility?

CHAPTER REVIEW

Review Questions

1. What is the two-part test for deducting compensation payments? [1]

2. What is included in "compensation" for purposes of the tests in objective 1, question 1? [1]

3. Aldo, a skilled engineer, started a consulting business some years ago. He and his two partners incorporated the business shortly thereafter. In its early years the owners put most of the company's earnings back into the business. After 10 years the business is doing well; Aldo's salary for this year is $650,000. Aldo's wife, Beth, also has begun working for the business as a marketing consultant 2 days per week at a salary of $50,000. An IRS auditing agent has challenged the company's compensation deductions for Aldo and Beth. What arguments can be made against the IRS position? Assume all corporate documents and employment agreements are in good order. [1]

4. Surgical Suppliers, Inc., has four shareholders, three of whom are principal employees of the business. The three principal employees are founders of the business and have grown it into a company with gross receipts in the millions. The stock is currently valued at $20 million and has grown at a rate of 10 percent for the past 8 years. Each year the owners have reinvested over $1 million of earnings in business equipment and real estate. The three principals are each currently receiving $700,000 in annual salary. This is more than twice the average salary of the highest paid employees at their closest competitor, a branch of a large corporate chain operation located across town. How would you defend the salary amounts in the event of an IRS audit? Assume that an independent consultant will testify that an investor in this business would expect a 10 percent return based on the risks involved. [1]

5. Bache Company, a listed corporation, wants to employ Jefferson Barnes as its general manager. What problems may the company face if the amount of salary agreed on is excessively high? [2]

6. What important steps should a company take when establishing salaries for executives in order to preserve the deduction as reasonable compensation? [2]

7. Clyde Davis is controller of the Moore Chemical Company that has annual sales of $150 million. His salary is $70,000. An industry study shows that salaries of controllers range from $25,000 to $65,000 in companies with comparable sales. Davis has been with this company for 5 years. Prior to that, he worked for another chemical company in a junior financial capacity. He is in charge of all planning and day-to-day operations for this company. Moore's income has been increasing during the past 3 years, and this is due in large part to Davis's ability to foresee trends. Stockholders have received an average return of 10 percent on their money over the past 3 years and the market price of the stock has increased from $26 to $48 during this time. Company prospects continue to be good. [2]

    a. What factors included above prove that Davis's compensation is reasonable?

    b. What further information would be useful in determining whether the salary was reasonable?

8.   a.   In the following situations, what facts act as a justification for a salary that is larger than normal? [2]

   i. After 10 years as marketing director of a competing company, Peter Emerson has agreed to join Rand Company in the same capacity. He is the recognized expert on marketing of Rand's product and, in fact, it appears that his suggestions will result in 80 percent increased earnings for Rand Company by the end of 2 years.

   ii. Although Robert Swenson is president of the Able Baker Company, he also performs the function of general counsel representing the company in all union negotiations and before all regulatory agencies.
   b. In the following situations, what facts justify the executive's salary increase as being reasonable?

   i. George Romberg received an $80,000 salary 2 years ago when the company he worked for was still operating in the red. This year, the company showed a profit, thanks primarily to the fact that Romberg reorganized his department saving the company $800,000. Romberg's salary for this year was increased to $160,000.

   ii. Irving Harrison was hired as a manager at a salary of $40,000 when Russell Glass Company was formed 6 years ago. After several unprofitable years, while Harrison continued to earn $40,000, Russell is finally making a profit. Harrison's salary was increased to $180,000 this year.

9.   Sam Evans is the vice president and a major stockholder of Evans Company, a closely held corporation. In November of this year when it became clear that Evans Company, a calendar-year taxpayer, was going to have an extremely profitable year, the company agreed to pay Sam a bonus of $500,000 in addition to his salary of $250,000. (Last year Sam's salary and bonus had totaled $300,000.) The bonuses paid to Sam and the two other stockholder-employees were proportional to their stockholdings. No amounts labeled as dividends were paid to any stockholders.

   What factors might lead the IRS to consider the $500,000 bonus as a dividend rather than salary? [2]

10. In the following situations, when will the company deduct the salary payment, and when will the executive be taxed on it? [3]

   a. Excello Corporation, a corporation using the accrual method, has an employment contract with Paul McCarthy. Under the terms of this contract, McCarthy agrees to work for the company for 2 years, from November to November, for a total of $60,000. For mutually advantageous reasons, the company agrees to pay him the entire amount next year. Both the company and McCarthy are calendar-year taxpayers.

   b. Under the terms of Dale Golden's employment contract as a salesperson for Superior Bargain Company (a cash-basis corporation), he is paid on a commission basis and any advance in excess of the commission he earns must be returned. Golden has been paid $40,000 under his drawing account for this year. By the end of the year, however, he had earned $35,000 and the difference is charged to his account for next year. (The difference is considered as a draw against commissions to be earned next year.) Next year, he earns $50,000 and draws an additional $45,000. Both the company and Golden are calendar-year taxpayers.

11. In the following situations, when will an accrual-method calendar-year company deduct the bonus payment, and when will the executive report it as income? [3]

   a. Hayden Company, Inc., is obligated to pay Edmond Frazier (who is not a shareholder) a bonus for this year in the amount of one percent of company profits in excess of $1 million. It will not be determined until February of next year that company profits for this year are $2 million, and the payment ($10,000) will be made at that time.

   b. Crystal Corporation adopted a bonus plan this year under which it is committed to annually allocate a certain amount to a bonus fund though not to any particular individual. Next year on March 1 it will apportion this fund between a specified group of nonshareholder-executives.

12. David West, president and a 60 percent stockholder of Pitman Company, is owed $70,000 for the current year by the company under his employment contract. Assume it has not been paid by the end of the year. Both West and the company are calendar-year taxpayers. However, the company is an accrual-basis taxpayer, and West is a cash-basis taxpayer. In the following situations: (i) when does West report the income, and (ii) when, if ever, can the corporation take a deduction? [3]

    a. Pitman Company pays West in April of next year and withholds the tax on this amount at that time.

    b. Pitman Company pays West the $70,000 in February of next year. It has withheld the tax due on this amount in the current year.

13. Christie Corporation is to pay vice president Marple $80,000 under a bonus agreement entered into with him this year. The IRS determines that $65,000 of this amount is reasonable compensation. How much must Christie pay Marple under the bonus agreement, and how much is deductible by the company for tax purposes? [3]

14. Fetter Corporation is planning to institute a bonus plan. [4]

    a. What preliminary steps would you recommend they take?

    b. What provisions should Fetter Corporation include in writing (either the employment contract or the resolution of the board of directors) establishing the bonus plan?

15. Mark Cohen receives a salary of $12,000. Senior Corporation plans to pay him a bonus of $50,000 if profits increase by 5 percent over the preceding year. Executives in other companies who do similar work receive a total pay of $25,000. Explain whether this presents any tax problems for either Cohen or Senior Corporation. [4]

16. Blue Bell Corporation is going to institute a bonus plan based on profits. What advice and suggestions could you give them specifically related to the issue of profits? [4]

17. If several managerial employees, as defined in the plan, are going to be entitled to a bonus based on profits, what additional factor enters into the computing of profits? [4]

18. General Service Company has several subsidiary companies. What special considerations are there with respect to such a company regarding a bonus plan dependent on company profits? [4]

19. Albert Harris, Jr., son of the president of Sample Manufacturing Company, has been working as a junior executive at an annual salary of $15,000 since January of this year. In November of this year, Harris's father arranges to award him a bonus of $25,000 in spite of the fact that the company made a profit only because another executive was able to salvage some of the bad deals Harris had entered into. State what factors indicate whether the IRS would recognize this bonus as reasonable compensation. [4]

20. Exxoff Company pays Joe V. Reif, a vice president, a salary of $95,000. Reif has minimal stockholdings in Exxoff. There has been a final determination by the IRS that $15,000 of this salary is not reasonable. Exxoff had been considering entering into a reimbursement arrangement with Reif calling for him to pay back to Exxoff any future salary held to be unreasonable by the IRS. List some of the considerations against the use of such a reimbursement arrangement. [5]

21. James Bowen is president and sole stockholder of Merten Company. For this year the net corporate income (before deducting Bowen's salary) will be $300,000. Assuming he is married with two exemptions, what would the best salary be from an income tax standpoint for Bowen? [6]

22. Frank Slick, P.C., is a sole-practice lawyer operating in corporate form. His professional corporation earns $140,000 this year. What is the "best salary" for Frank? [6]

23. List the main drawbacks in connection with such a best salary plan. [6]

24. Roman Tile Company wants to buy out the 10 percent interest of Angelo Gallo who is vice president of the company. Gallo paid $200,000 for his stock 3 years ago. He also was given an employment contract for $140,000 per year. That contract has 3 years yet to run. Both the company and Gallo have agreed on a total buyout price of $700,000. In the following situations, how much is capital gain to Gallo, how much is ordinary income, and what amount can the company deduct? [7]

    a. The buyout agreement allocates $300,000 as the price of the stock and $400,000 to buy the employment contract.

    b. The agreement allocates $400,000 to the stock and $300,000 to buy out the contract.

25. How is income of an S corporation taxed? [8]

26. Edward Sellers is president and a 50 percent stockholder of Allied Shoe Company, an S corporation. Corporate income this year was $500,000. Since dividends are taxable to Sellers whether or not they are distributed to him, explain whether it makes a difference to (a) the company and (b) Sellers how payments to him are apportioned between salary and dividends. [8]

27. David McMullin, sole stockholder and president of an S corporation, had received a salary of $200,000 last year. There was no undistributed taxable income after the salary. This year McMullin plans to make a bona fide transfer of 40 percent of his stock to his son, Pat, who is now in college and who will come into the business upon his graduation from college. The father also plans to take a salary of $100,000 for this year. The remaining earnings of the corporation, $100,000, will be taxable dividend income divided between the two stockholders ($60,000 to David and $40,000 to his son, Pat). Pat will have no other income this year besides the dividends from this stock.

What is the likely tax treatment for the father and the son? [8]

Answers to Review Questions

1. Generally under the regulations, in order to be deductible under Sec. 162, a payment must (1) be intended as compensation and (2) be reasonable in amount. [1]

2. Compensation includes not only cash compensation but also the value of employee benefits including deferred compensation, such as retirement plans. [1]

3. There is never any single answer to tax issues based essentially on the facts of a situation, such as whether compensation is reasonable. However, Aldo's compensation can be defended based on the various "factors" used by the courts and the IRS. For example, Aldo's compensation was low in the initial years of the business; his current high compensation level can be considered a valid "catch-up." Also, Aldo has specific skills as an engineer that command a premium salary. Although dividends were not mentioned in the question, if it's true that no dividends were paid by the company, this can be explained by the fact that earnings were put back into the growing business. Beth's compensation is more difficult to justify under the factors analysis. Facts would have to be developed showing that her $50,000 compensation is reasonable for the work that she does. [1]

4. The compensation for Surgical Suppliers's owner-employees may be difficult to justify under a purely factors analysis, since it is not stated that they have any special skills. Their compensation is arguably higher than that of a comparable employer such as their

big-company competitor. However, the "hypothetical independent investor" test would help their case greatly, since the facts indicate that the rate of return on investment in Surgical Suppliers is higher than expected. Therefore, the shareholders are not being deprived of return on investment by the payment of excessive salaries.

Tax considerations play an important role in cash compensation planning. Payments made to an employee as compensation for services are deductible company expenses if they are reasonable. The cash outlay to the company for reasonable salary payments is 65 percent of the amount paid when the top marginal corporate federal income tax rate is about 35 percent (and the outlay is even less where state income tax must also be paid). [1]

5. The company can deduct only "reasonable" compensation. If it is determined that a particular salary is excessive, the company may not deduct the excess amount over what is considered reasonable. This makes the cash outlay to the company 100 percent of the amount considered excessive.

Stockholder discontent and generally adverse publicity also are negatives connected with payment of excessive salaries. [2]

6. Important steps that a company should take when setting executive salaries include the following: [2]

   - The specific dollar amount of salary should be set at the beginning of the year.
   - The company should set forth a complete explanation of how the amount of salary was reached.
   - The company should make and preserve a written record of the decision as part of either the minutes of the directors' meeting or the employment contract specifying which conditions indicating reasonableness of salary were satisfied.

7. There are no clear, indisputable answers to these situations, but what is most appropriate for each one follows. [2]

   a. Comparing the facts in the question with the list of "factors" on pages 1.5–1.7 shows favorable results.

   b. Additional information on the rate of return an investor should receive in this situation would be helpful to compare with the 10 percent actual rate for purposes of the independent investor test.

8. A larger salary than is usually paid for a comparable position in a comparable company can be justified by such circumstances as superior qualifications and outstanding performance, the need to hire away from a competing firm, greater responsibility than counterparts in other companies, individual achievement resulting in company achievement, or that the executive was, in fact, underpaid during the start-up period of the company. [2]

9. Factors that alert the IRS to the fact that payments made to the stockholder-employee are dividends rather than salary include [2]

   - The bonus was decided upon close to the end of the company's tax year.

   - The company has paid only a small dividend, if any, in recent years.

   - Salary or bonus is proportionate to stockholdings.

10. The cash-basis executive reports income when it is actually paid or the money is irrevocably available to him or her. If an executive has a drawing account but must repay amounts not earned through performance of services, the executive is taxable on it when it is earned.

    The company, whether it uses a cash or accrual method, can deduct only the compensation paid for services that were actually rendered by the end of the taxable year for which the deduction is claimed. Amounts paid before services are rendered are deductible pro rata over the period in which they are rendered. [3]

    a. McCarthy reports the entire amount as income next year. The company deducts the following amounts each year:

       $5,000 this year (2/24 of $60,000)

       $30,000 next year (12/24 of $60,000)

       $25,000 in 2 years (10/24 of $60,000)

    b. Superior Bargain Company deducts $35,000 for this year and $50,000 for next year. Golden reports $35,000 for this year and $50,000 for next year.

11. As a general rule, an accrual-method company deducts bonus payments, like other business expenses, for the year the bonus is earned even though it may not be either paid or computed until the following year. However, unlike noncompensation expenses, the payment must be made within 2½ months after the end of the

employer's tax year. The executive reports the bonus as income for the year it is received. If the employee is a 50 percent or more shareholder, however, the corporation cannot take a deduction until the year the amount is included in the executive's income; there is no 2½-month "safe harbor." [3]

    a. Hayden Company, Inc., takes the deduction for this year; Frazier reports it next year.

    b. Crystal Corporation takes deduction for this year; individuals report it next year.

12.   [3]

    a.

        (1) next year

        (2) when it is entered into West's income

    b.

        (1) next year

        (2) next year

13. A company must pay a bonus it has contracted to pay even if the IRS denies a deduction to the company. Christie Corporation must pay $80,000 but can only deduct $65,000. [3]

14. A company planning to institute a bonus plan should arrange to tailor the incentive to the performance of the particular executive, decide on the bonus before it is earned, and reduce the arrangement to writing in either an employment contract or resolution of the board of directors.

It is important that the decision to pay a bonus be made early in the tax year and a formula for doing so worked out to avoid a charge by the IRS that such payment is, in fact, either additional compensation for past services or, in the case of a major stockholder, dividends. If it is considered additional compensation for past services, such additional payment could raise the question of whether the total compensation for that past time was reasonable. The company should adopt a written bonus plan that includes provisions for defining profits if the bonus depends on profits, a time limit for the agreement to be in force, a periodic review of the plan, and arbitration of disputes.

Although bonuses usually depend on profits, they also could be based on such things as the price of the company stock during a certain period or at year-end, dividends, sales, costs, or some basis connected with the particular job to be accomplished by that executive. [4]

15. Although cash bonuses must meet the requirement of reasonableness, the fact that there is some risk attached as to whether or not the executive actually receives that amount can enlarge the limits of reasonableness. The test of reasonableness is governed by the circumstances existing at the time the contract is entered into rather than those existing when the company is audited by the IRS. [4]

16. If a bonus is to be based on profits, the method of determining profits must be specified in the agreement. Profit could be the amount shown as profit in the financial statement, taxable income for federal income tax purposes, or it could be determined in some other specified way.

    If profits are based on the current accounting system, however, a change in the accounting method might require the company to keep a special set of books for the bonus plan. If profit is based on taxable income, the profit picture, and therefore the bonus, would vary with the tax laws. [4]

17. If several people are to be paid bonuses based on profits, there must be a prior determination of whether profits are to be computed before or after the other bonuses are paid. [4]

18. In the case of a large company with either subsidiaries or various divisions, a decision must be made as to whether the bonus is to depend on results of the whole company or a particular part of the company. Corporate philosophy will determine whether the regular salary should be at a fairly high competitive level and the bonus minimal (unless the executive's performance is outstanding), or whether the salary should be minimal and the bonus directly reflect the position of the company for that year. [4]

19. The IRS will recognize a bonus arrangement as resulting in reasonable compensation if it was (a) a fair bargain, (b) arrived at in arm's-length negotiation, and (c) if it was agreed to before the services were performed. [4]

20. In some situations, a company will enter into a reimbursement arrangement with an executive to provide for reimbursement if the IRS disallows a salary deduction because the amount is excessive. Such agreements in themselves can sometimes lead to an inference by the IRS of excessive compensation and deter the

company from defending against an IRS challenge. Although the employee is taxed on any unreasonable amount as a dividend, the maximum tax rate will be the same. Consequently, the employee is still better off financially by retaining it and paying the tax rather than repaying the whole amount, even though the repayment would be deductible. However, the corporation will lose its deduction. [5]

21. The purpose of a "best salary" plan is to minimize the total tax paid by the company and the stockholder-executive. A best salary plan is most advantageous in the case of an individual entrepreneur.

    Depending on Bowen's actual taxable income after deductions, a salary between $200,000 and $250,000 produces the lowest total taxes. Corporate taxes rise steeply above $100,000 of corporate income. [6]

22. For a personal-service corporation, income can never be taxed at a lower rate at the corporate level unless the taxpayer's effective tax rate is more than 35 percent. Thus, here it is advantageous to pay all income out as salary (or as deductible employee benefits). [6]

23. Because use of a best salary plan can result in salary fluctuations, is geared to corporate income, and can best be determined late in the year, a portion of such salary may not be deductible by the corporation. By retaining income for purposes of minimizing total tax, the corporation might subject itself to the accumulated-earnings tax. This tax can apply to accumulated earnings in excess of $250,000 ($150,000 in the case of professional corporations). [6]

24. In those cases in which an executive-stockholder's interest in company stock and employment contract are both bought out, the executive and the company may have different interests in how the total sum is allocated for income tax purposes. The company benefits more from the amount allocated to salary payments since it is deductible by the corporation (but taxable as ordinary income to the employee). The employee benefits more from an amount allocated to stock purchase since that would be taxed as capital gain (but that amount is not deductible by the corporation). The allocation should be spelled out in the final buyout agreement. [7]

a.	capital gain	$100,000
	ordinary income	$400,000
	corporation deducts	$400,000
b.	capital gain	$200,000
	ordinary income	$300,000
	corporation deducts	$300,000

25. S corporations are exempt from federal corporate income tax in most cases, and stockholders are taxable on their share of corporate income whether or not it is actually distributed as dividends. [8]

26. Although the maximum tax rate on personal-service income and dividends is the same, only salary will be taken into account when determining retirement, death, and disability benefits. It does not make a difference to the company, but it does make a difference to Sellers. [8]

27. S corporation salaries to stockholder-executives cannot be set at an unreasonably low level as a way of having family members save on taxes.

    An S corporation income shift is not successful if it is accompanied by a decrease in the salary of family members actually working for the company to a point where the salary does not reflect the value of services to the company. In such a case, the IRS will increase the amount taxed as salary to an amount considered reasonable. [8]

Learning Objectives

An understanding of the material in this chapter should enable the student to

1. Explain the advantages of deferring tax on compensation income.
2. Relate client situations to nonqualified deferred-compensation benefit formulas.
3. Explain the appropriate use and design of withdrawal provisions.
4. Describe nonqualified plan provisions relating to vesting, financing, and deferring nonemployee income.
5. Explain the constructive-receipt and economic-benefit doctrines and their applications, if any, to informally financed nonqualified deferred-compensation plans.
6. Explain why and how ERISA must generally be avoided in a nonqualified deferred-compensation plan.
7. Explain how nonqualified deferred-compensation plan agreements and benefits are treated for Social Security (FICA) purposes.
8. Describe income and estate tax treatment of death benefits payable under a deferred-compensation agreement in the event the employee dies prior to receipt of all benefits.
9. Describe the special factors that determine the income tax treatment of deferred-compensation (salary continuation) arrangements for stockholder-employees of a closely held corporation and the tax treatment of the corporation.
10. Compare the attributes and drawbacks of qualified retirement plans and unfunded nonqualified deferred-compensation plans.
11. Explain how nonqualified deferred-compensation benefits figure in the definition of compensation for fringe-benefit-plan purposes.
12. Describe benefits under a salary continuation plan that can provide an incentive to improve work performance for a given employee or group.
13. Describe methods of paying benefits in case of early termination.

Both this chapter and the next discuss the general subject of nonqualified deferred-compensation plans that have not been formally "funded." The absence of formal funding implies that the employee must rely on the unsecured promise of the employer to pay the benefits under this plan. As will be demonstrated, however, the fact that no assets may be set aside beyond the employer's reach as security for the payment of these benefits does not prevent the employer from establishing an asset reserve (a financing mechanism) in which general assets of the employer are earmarked for the payment of plan benefits. In fact, the employer should not create a liability without a financing mechanism to meet the future obligation.

The fact that the plans discussed here are nonqualified is of considerable importance in their utilization in an employer's total employee benefit plan strategy. Because these plans do not seek to be treated as qualified under the Treasury regulations, the employer is free to discriminate as to who will be covered and the benefit levels that will be provided. This is particularly true if the plan is limited to a select group of management or highly paid employees.

The primary purpose of deferring compensation is to defer the taxation of that compensation with the goal of ultimately maximizing the after-tax dollars that will be available to the employee. Arrangements that effectively defer taxation and benefit provisions of a deferred-compensation plan that maximize the tax leverage are the central focus of these chapters.

Nonqualified deferred-compensation plans play a critical role in the compensation of key employees and executives. These plans provide retirement savings and tax-deferred income beyond the restrictions imposed on qualified retirement plans. Nonqualified deferred-compensation plans are very flexible and can be designed to help meet specific goals of the employer and employee.

Broadly speaking, a nonqualified deferred-compensation plan is a plan that provides tax-deferred compensation to an employee and does not meet the requirements of the Internal Revenue Code and ERISA for a "qualified plan." In practice, nonqualified deferred-compensation plans have the following characteristics, among others:

- The plan is unfunded (for reasons discussed here) and is based on the employer's unsecured contractual promise to pay benefits. Various arrangements discussed here can provide some degree of certainty of payment for the executive, but no irrevocable fund for the exclusive benefit of the employee can be set aside as in a qualified plan.
- Benefits are generally provided only to a selected group of executives or highly compensated employees—or even to a single executive only.

- The primary object of the plan is to provide compensation income that is not taxed currently but is taxed when benefits are payable.
- These plans usually focus on providing retirement benefits, but deferral for specified periods of years is also common.
- Disability, death, and in-service withdrawal provisions are often included.
- The employer's tax deduction is not available when the compensation is earned, but is tied to the year in which the employee includes the amount in income.

Since the last edition of this book, Code Sec. 409A has become fully effective; final regulations have been issued; and all transition rules have become obsolete. The requirements of Sec. 409A have changed the entire landscape of the design and taxation of nonqualified deferred compensation plans. The enhanced role played by Sec. 409A will be reflected in the discussion of nonqualified deferred compensation in this chapter.

TAX ADVANTAGES OF DEFERRAL

An initial question in assessing the benefits of a nonqualified deferred-compensation plan is whether the plan's tax deferral is actually a significant benefit. Of course, it is always better to pay taxes later rather than sooner, because during the deferral period the employee has the use of the potential tax money that otherwise would go to the government. The issue is the magnitude of the benefit and the risks of losing that benefit.

One issue is the effect of future tax increases. Executives might wonder whether it is wise to defer compensation if tax rates are expected to increase. After all, they reason, wouldn't it be more advantageous to use an executive bonus plan or a secular trust or some other form of current compensation and pay taxes at current rates rather than defer taxes but pay them at increased future rates?

The second question deals with the impact on the employer of reducing corporate tax rates. Financial services professionals are discovering that corporate costs for nonqualified plans have actually gone down along with corporate tax rates. Many are wondering if there's ever been a better time to recommend a nonqualified plan.

The third question deals with how cost-effective nonqualified plans are to the employer. The recent attention given to the shift in tax rates has once again raised the question of whether the deferral of a corporate deduction under a nonqualified plan can be as cost-effective to the employer as paying out compensation currently on a deductible basis or making deductible contributions to a qualified plan.

A final question that came to the fore with the bull market of the 1990s is whether tax deferral through investment in assets that receive capital-gain treatment is better than deferred compensation. As an alternative to a deferred-compensation plan, an executive might opt to take income currently and invest it in (hopefully) appreciating capital assets. Is the result better than deferred compensation since the capital gains are not taxed currently unless the assets are sold, and, when ultimately sold, the gains are taxed at the maximum 15 percent capital-gain rate rather than as ordinary income taxable at up to 35 percent?

Benefits of Deferral

The first question raised was whether executives would be better served by paying taxes currently under an executive bonus plan or secular trust as opposed to participating in a nonqualified deferred-compensation plan. The answer varies depending on the following:

- the tax rate when funds are distributed
- the length of the deferral
- the interest rate that deferred funds earn

These factors come into play because the central issue is whether the deferral of current taxation (that is, the present value of the use of dollars that otherwise would be payable in current income tax) will offset the probable increase in tax rates. In other words, if an executive uses a nonqualified deferred-compensation agreement today, he or she is able to invest one dollar for every dollar put aside. If, on the other hand, the money were paid out currently under an executive bonus plan or secular trust, the executive would only have 65 cents out of every dollar to invest, since 35 cents would be paid in taxes. The 35 cents on a dollar (or the amount of the tax rate) that does *not* have to be paid currently if a nonqualified plan is established can be likened to an interest-free loan from the government. The question then becomes, at what point will the interest earned on a certain interest-free loan be enough to offset the increase in taxes paid out due to the *probable* increased tax rate? The following table sets forth the amount of time it will take to reach breakeven, taking into account various future tax rates and projected after-tax interest rates.

Table 2-1 Years until Breakeven for Deferred Compensation Assuming Tax Rates Will Increase and Current Rate Is 35 Percent			
Current Tax Rate	35%		
Future Tax Rate	37%	40%	50%
Rate of Return	Years to breakeven		
3%	2.916434	6.884728	17.8895
5%	1.791861	4.219672	10.89656
7%	1.310896	3.079327	7.901623
10%	0.951554	2.226584	5.658209

These figures can be displayed on an Excel or Quattro Pro worksheet where

$$N(\text{number of years to break even}) = \frac{\ln(1 - t_f) - \ln(1 - t_c)}{\ln\left[1 + i(1 - t_f)\right] - \ln(1 + i)}$$

$$i = \text{rate of return}$$
$$t_c = \text{current tax rate}$$
$$t_f = \text{future tax rate}$$

For a comprehensive look at deferral break-even analysis, see Doyle, "Creative Wealth Planning Techniques," in the *Financial Services Professional's Guide to the State of the Art.* Fourth Edition, © 1997, The American College.

EXAMPLE

Employee Charles Able has a current tax rate of 35 percent and has the option of deferring $10,000 under his company's nonqualified top-hat plan or having the money paid out under a currently taxable executive bonus agreement. If Able projects that a 50 percent individual tax rate will apply when his distribution occurs and that he can earn a before-tax interest rate of 7 percent on deferred funds, Able would be better off under the nonqualified plan if the deferral period is longer than 7.9 years. If, however, the deferral period is less than 7.9 years, then Able would be better off from a tax standpoint under an executive bonus plan.

In addition to the monetary concern, executives must also factor a *security concern* into their decision to defer under a nonqualified plan. One conclusion is that if the executive's employer becomes insolvent, the executive will probably end up losing his or her promised benefit. Therefore, the decision to defer under a nonqualified plan is not an economic decision alone; other factors must also be considered.

Pass-Through Entities

Not all employers are subject to tax at the entity level. Employers who are not treated as a taxpayer with respect to their earnings and losses are generally referred to as "pass-through" entities. As this name implies, the pass-through entity's earnings and losses, instead of being taxed initially at the entity level, are passed through and are taxed to the owners of the entity in proportion to their ownership interests. The forms of pass-through entities include sole proprietorships, general, limited and limited liability partnerships, S corporations and limited liability companies. The latter become pass-through entities if they elect for tax purposes to be taxed as a partnership. More and more, these pass-through entities are being used by small businesses due to their flexibility and the favorable tax treatment.

When a pass-through entity considers adopting a nonqualified plan, it must evaluate the impact on its owners of the tax rule that contributions to nonqualified plans are not deductible by the employer until the deferred compensation is taxable to participants and the tax rule that earnings on deferred compensation are taxed to the employer as they accrue.

EXAMPLE 1

Sunset Vacations, Inc. (Sunset) is a C corporation. Sunset's effective combined federal and state corporate tax rate is 20 percent. Sunset has revenues of $1 million in 2010 and spends $950,000 on currently deductible ordinary and necessary business expenses. Sunset also establishes a nonqualified plan for its CEO and deposits the remaining $50,000 of its 2010 revenues into a rabbi trust. The $50,000 deposit to the rabbi trust earns $5,000 of taxable interest. Sunset will pay corporate tax on $55,000, the $50,000 of revenues that is not offset by any tax deduction and the $5,000 of interest earned in the rabbi trust. Thus, given its 20 percent tax bracket, Sunset will pay $11,000 in taxes for 2010.

EXAMPLE 2

The same facts as Example 1, except that Sunset is a limited liability company that has elected to be taxed as a partnership. Thus, Sunset is not a tax-paying entity. Instead, its owner, Bill, reports Sunset's earnings and losses on his personal income tax. Bill has an effective combined federal and state personal income tax rate of 40 percent. For 2010, Bill will pay tax on Sunset's $50,000 of revenues and on the $5,000 of interest income earned in the rabbi trust. Thus, given Bill's 40 percent tax rate, Bill will have to pay $22,000 in additional income taxes for 2010. In effect, Bill has paid the income taxes for Sunset's CEO. Now, eventually, Bill will obtain a tax benefit from the deduction that is generated when the total deferred compensation is paid to Sunset's CEO. However, in the meantime, Bill has lost the use of the $22,000 that he paid in income taxes in 2010 and the additional income taxes that will be paid in subsequent years until the deferred compensation is paid to the CEO.

As the above examples illustrate, there is a different financial analysis that has to be performed in connection with the adoption of a nonqualified plan by a pass-through entity. Not only must the nonqualified plan be beneficial for the covered employee, it must also not result in a financial detriment to the owners of the pass-through entity or if there is financial detriment to the owners, it should be a detriment that represents an acceptable cost of doing business.

Impact of Reduced Corporate Rates

The reduction of top corporate tax rates some years ago from 46 percent to 35 percent reduced the up-front cost to high-income corporations of providing a nonqualified plan and tended to encourage the growth of such plans. It costs about $1.85 to provide each benefit dollar in a nonqualified plan at the 46 percent tax rate, and it costs about 35 cents less ($1.50) to provide each benefit dollar at the 35 percent tax rate. The reason it costs the corporation more than one dollar to provide one dollar's worth of benefit under both circumstances is because the corporation is deferring its deduction by using a nonqualified plan. (You can ascertain the per-dollar current cost by dividing [1 − current corporate tax rate] into $1.) The net effect of the reduction in corporate tax rates has been to mitigate the up-front cost of the plan, that is, to lower the cost of deferring the eventual deduction, because the deduction that cannot be taken currently is smaller under the new tax structure. (When benefits are paid out and the corporation can take its deduction, the deduction will not be based on what was set aside but rather on the original investment plus earnings. Furthermore, if those predicting tax increases are correct, the "down-the-road" deduction might be *more* valuable than it would be if it could be taken currently.)

This type of analysis can illustrate to the employer the net cost to the corporation of providing a nonqualified plan. This in turn motivates the employer to consider whether a qualified plan, executive bonus plan, or a cash-payment alternative would be more effective.

The Cost Effectiveness of the Nonqualified Plan

A nonqualified deferred-compensation plan should be strongly considered for two important reasons. First, unlike a qualified plan, a nonqualified plan allows the employer to discriminate with regard to who will be covered and how much each covered employee will receive. Second, unlike an executive bonus plan (at least as currently used) or a cash-payment alternative, the nonqualified plan can place restrictions on an executive receiving payment (forfeiture provisions) and thus either achieve business goals or recoup forfeited funds so the plan either accomplishes what it was intended to accomplish (retain key employees) or the firm gets its money back.

EXAMPLE

Jamestown Manufacturing is excited about providing a qualified plan for its employees, but it has a problem. In order to provide a 15 percent contribution for its executives, Jamestown has to provide a comparable contribution for its non-highly compensated employees (NHCEs). The payroll for its highly-compensated employees (HCEs) is $1,000,000 (10 HCEs with an average salary of $100,000). The payroll for the NHCEs is $3,000,000 (120 employees with an average salary of $25,000). The qualified plan would therefore cost Jamestown $600,000 per year (15 percent x $4,000,000 aggregate salaries).

Jamestown can cut its costs in half, exceed its goal for HCEs, and still come close to achieving its goal for NHCEs by providing a 5 percent 401(k) plan with a dollar-for-dollar match and a 10 percent supplemental executive retirement plan (SERP). Both HCEs and NHCEs would have a 10-percent-of-salary qualified retirement savings account (5 percent reduced salary and 5 percent employer contribution). HCEs will have a total of 20 percent of pay going toward retirement (the 10 percent qualified and 10 percent from the SERP). The cost to the employer, however, would only be $300,000 per year.

5% contribution for all employees ($4,000,000 payroll)	$200,000
10% for HCEs only ($1,000,000 payroll)	$100,000
	$300,000

Jamestown may still believe that the nonqualified plan is not tax efficient ($1.51 to provide a $1 benefit), but it must admit that it is cost efficient (a $300,000 annual savings).

EXAMPLE

Instead of providing a retirement plan for its employees, Jamestown is considering paying out salary under a current compensation program because of the high cost of nonqualified benefits. Jamestown should consider that the cost of nonqualified benefits will be offset either partially or totally by forfeitures under the nonqualified plan. In other words, if only two of the 10 HCEs forfeit their benefits under the nonqualified plan's golden handcuffs provision, the plan will recapture $20,000 in contributions (10 percent contributions x $100,000 salary x 2 employees) for each year contributions were made, thus mitigating the loss of a current tax deduction.

Deferred Compensation versus Capital Gains

While the idea of investing after-tax dollars in capital-gain assets as an alternative to deferred compensation may appear attractive because of the lower tax rates on capital gains, it appears that the nonqualified deferred-compensation plan generally gives better results. In an article investigating these alternatives (Russell, "When Does Income Deferral Make Sense?" *RIA Pension and Benefits Week*, May 8, 2000) the author summarizes the results as follows:

> No matter [how] long the investment period before retirement, or the type of investments made, executives will receive higher total distributions (net of federal income taxes and capital-gains taxes) from the deferral plans than from outside investments.

A principal reason why this is the case is that any kind of outside investment plan loses some of its value annually to taxes, since it is not realistic to assume the investment consists of the same unchanged portfolio throughout the deferral period. But even if an unrealistic situation of no loss of taxes (no realized capital gains until retirement) is assumed, for a given rate of return the nonqualified deferred-compensation plan does better for the executive since the initial investment is unreduced by taxes (to the executive) at the outset, while the outside investments must be made from after-tax dollars. The tax rate difference at payout (35 maximum rate versus 15 percent) can't overcome this initial advantage given the benefits of deferral.

The tax rate of 15 percent for dividends (since 2003) further reduces, but does not eliminate, the advantage of deferral. However, unless Congress changes the law, the lower tax rate on dividends will no longer apply after 2010.

BENEFIT FORMULAS

The benefit formula is the basic starting point in designing or explaining a nonqualified deferred-compensation plan. Executives covered under the plan want to know first what benefits the plan provides rather than methods of financing those benefits, such as corporate-owned life insurance arrangements. Benefit formula design is very flexible for nonqualified deferred-compensation plans; formulas can be designed for the specific needs of specific employees. Some common benefit formula approaches are summarized below.

Salary Continuation Formula

The salary continuation formula generally refers to a type of nonelective nonqualified deferred-compensation plan that provides a specified deferred amount payable in the future. A salary continuation plan provides benefits in addition to other benefits provided under other plans and requires no reduction in the covered employee's salary. As a simple example, the contract might provide: "At retirement, disability, or death, the XYZ Corporation will pay you or your designated beneficiary $50,000 a year for 10 years starting at age 65."

Plan designers will develop a benefit formula for the plan that reflects the objectives of both the employer and employee and will carry out the design decisions that have been made. Some typical examples of benefit formulas are listed below.

Salary Continuation—Fixed Amount

Under this benefit formula, the retirement benefit is not tied to future compensation levels but uses a formula that allows for easier advance financing. For example, the benefit might be "$1,000 multiplied by the number of months of employment subsequent to this agreement, in monthly installments equal to 1/120 of the total amount, payable for 10 years."

Salary Continuation—Percentage of Final-Average Compensation

This benefit formula provides a benefit based on the employee's compensation at retirement, which is usually averaged over several years (generally at least 3). This type of formula is similar to those used in qualified defined-benefit plans.

Salary Continuation—Excess Benefit

This type of formula is tied into the employer's qualified plans and is designed to provide benefits in excess of the limits for qualified plans (see below for further discussion). The formula might provide a monthly benefit at retirement equal to some percentage of the employee's compensation (say, 60 percent of final-average compensation) *less* the amount provided by specific qualified plans maintained by the employer.

As these examples indicate, a salary continuation formula generally uses a defined-benefit type of formula to calculate the benefit amount. However, the formula is not subject to the limitations applicable to qualified defined-benefit plans such as limitations on benefits or the amount of salary used in the formula. A nonqualified salary continuation plan for a selected group of executives with similar formulas for the entire group is sometimes referred to as a "SERP" (supplemental executive retirement plan).

Salary Reduction Formula

A salary reduction formula involves an elective deferral of a specified amount of the compensation the employee could have taken but chose not to take. The employer contribution under this type of plan can be in the form of a "bonus" without actual reduction of salary. The plan is somewhat similar to a defined-contribution type of qualified plan, although qualified plan restrictions do not apply.

The amount deferred each year under a salary reduction formula is generally credited to the employee's "account" under the plan. When benefits are due, the amount accumulated in this account determines the amount of payments. Payment is generally in the form of a lump sum, but the account balance can also be paid in an equivalent stream of periodic payments. The amount ultimately payable can be determined in any manner the parties wish. Some typical approaches are introduced below.

Salary Reduction—Investment Account—Employer Investment Discretion

Salary reduction amounts are deposited to a reserve account invested at the employer's discretion in mutual funds, stocks, bonds, securities, life insurance, or other assets. At retirement, the employee's benefit is equal to the resulting account balance payable in a lump sum, annuity, or installments.

Salary Reduction-Employer-Guaranteed Return

Salary reduction amounts are either invested in an actual account or merely credited to a book account. Any amounts actually set aside are invested at the employer's discretion. At retirement, the employee's benefit is equal to the amounts set aside, plus interest credited annually at a stated rate or at a rate tied to some fixed standard such as Moody's Corporate Bond Average, the federal rate or other indexed rate, the rate on specified assets, or some other standard specified in the deferred-compensation agreement. This benefit can be paid out in a lump sum, annuity, or installments.

Note

In a salary reduction arrangement (or any other nonqualified deferred-compensation plan), the employer has no obligation to actually set assets aside. The participant's account can be purely an accounting concept existing only on paper. In that case, when payment becomes due, the employer pays it out of its current assets. This points out the fact that all nonqualified deferred-compensation plans are essentially based only on the employer's contractual obligation to pay benefits. However, employees may seek greater security.

Excess-Benefit Plan

Under ERISA Sec. 4(b)(5), an excess benefit plan that is unfunded is not subject to Title I of ERISA (which contains the reporting and disclosure, participation, vesting, funding, and fiduciary responsibility provisions).

Excess-benefit plans are those designed to provide benefits only for executives whose annual projected qualified plan benefits are limited under the dollar limits of Code Sec. 415 ($195,000 in 2010). An excess-benefit plan makes up the difference between the percentages of pay top executives are allowed under Sec. 415 and what rank-and-file employees are allowed. In other words, highly compensated employees receive the difference between the amount payable under their firm's qualified plan and the amount they would have received if there were no benefit limitations under Code Sec. 415.

However, note that an excess-benefit plan cannot restore benefits lost under the $245,000 (2010 indexed figure) compensation limitation rather than Sec. 415. This severely limits the usefulness of these otherwise very flexible, ERISA-free plans. Sec. 409A also will have an impact on the usefulness of these plans. Under Sec. 409A certain qualified plan elections are allowed to affect nonqualified deferred compensation only if certain special rules are met and the effect is limited in the manner outlined in the regulations. Thus, as a general rule, an excess benefit plan should stand on its own, rather than relying on elections or features that are part of its related qualified plan.

EXAMPLE
Suppose a company's qualified plan provides a general benefit of 50 percent of salary. For an executive retiring with average compensation of $300,000, the plan formula would dictate a retirement benefit of $150,000 annually. However, the formula can be applied only to the first $245,000 (2010) of the executive's compensation, so the executive's benefit is actually 50 percent of $245,000, or $122,500. The "lost" $27,500 of benefits cannot be restored under an excess benefit plan since the benefit was not reduced by Sec. 415 (but rather by the compensation limit of Sec. 401(a)(17)).

Although the excess-benefit formula as strictly defined under ERISA may not be available, many nonqualified plan benefit formulas are related to qualified plan formulas and are designed to "make the executive whole"—that is, to provide an amount that makes up the difference between the benefit the executive would get under the company's qualified plan without the limitations of either Sec. 415 or Sec. 401(a)(17), and the amount actually available under the qualified plan.

401(k) Mirror Plan

With this type of plan, the nonqualified plan salary reduction is tied to the company's qualified 401(k) plan; the employee's nonqualified contribution is a fraction or multiple of the amount contributed to the 401(k) plan. Sec. 409A affects these plans in the same manner as discussed above with respect to excess benefit plans.

Stock Appreciation Rights (SARs) and Phantom-Stock Formulas

The benefit formula in the plan can be determined on the basis of the value of a specified number of shares of employer stock, or contributions to a salary reduction formula can be stated in terms of shares of employer stock rather than cash. Generally, no actual shares are set aside, nor are shares of stock necessarily actually distributed. The value of the employer stock simply is the measuring rod by which the benefits are valued. Obviously, this type of formula provides a substantial incentive for the executive and, from the employer viewpoint, matches the size of benefits with company success.

Note

No firm distinction between SARs and phantom-stock formulas has been established among benefit practitioners. However, a phantom-stock benefit generally refers to a plan formula that sets aside actual shares of stock for an employee when the plan is adopted. It includes a provision that the employee receive the actual shares or equivalent cash at the date of payment. An SAR formula provides that the employee's future benefit is to be determined based on the appreciation in value of the company's stock over the period between adoption of the plan and the exercise of the SAR. In most cases the payment due upon the exercise of the SAR is made in cash, but in some cases it may be made in actual shares of stock.

401(k) Pour-over Plan

Under this type of arrangement an executive's excess deferrals in a 401(k) plan (amounts in excess of those allowed under the ADP tests applicable to 401(k) plans) are poured over into a nonqualified deferred-compensation plan. The IRS originally did not allow this on the grounds that it was a "subsequent election" violating the constructive-receipt principle (see discussion below). A later ruling, PLR 9524007 permits this type of plan. With reforms in 401(k) administration rules under recent law, excess contributions are less likely to occur, so this type of plan has become less significant. Sec. 409A could have an effect on these plans, as was discussed above with respect to 401(k) mirror plans.

SEC. 409A REQUIREMENTS

The reason for the Sec. 409A provisions is a view in Congress and the Treasury Department that prior restrictions for nonqualified plans were not stringent enough to justify the deferral of taxes on the amounts in question. However, by its terms, Sec. 409A does not affect the tax rules or other legal requirements applicable to nonqualified deferred compensation under prior law. Thus, nonqualified deferred compensation plans must still satisfy the two judicially sanctioned doctrines of constructive receipt and economic benefit and must still avoid the ambit of Code Sec. 83. Nevertheless, Sec. 409A does address three specific aspects of nonqualified deferred compensation, i.e., deferral elections, the holding of assets and the timing and form of benefit distributions. In dealing with these three areas, Sec. 409A eliminates specific abuses identified over the past several years, codifies certain of the government's preexisting administrative positions and replaces amorphous judicial doctrines with relatively bright line rules designed to bring a greater degree of uniformity and certainty to the various forms of nonqualified deferred compensation that were being made available under pre-Enron executive compensation practices.

By way of summary, the principal requirements of Sec. 409A include the following:

- There is a broad definition of NQDC plans that includes any plan, agreement, or arrangement that provides for the deferral of compensation, other than a tax-qualified employer plan or any bona fide vacation leave, sick leave, compensatory time, disability pay or death benefit plan.[16]

- An initial election to defer compensation must be made prior to the beginning of the taxable year in which the services are to be performed. There are two exceptions to this requirement which apply to (i) deferral elections by newly eligible participants who are given a 30-day grace period and (ii) performance-based compensation where the performance period is 12 months or more. In the latter case the deferral election can be made up to 6 months prior to the end of the performance period.[17]

- Nonqualified deferred compensation may only be distributed upon the occurrence of any of the following six specified events: a separation from service, the participant's death or disability,

---

16. Treas. Reg. Sec. 1.409A-1(a).
17. Treas. Reg. Sec. 1.409A-2.

a specified time (or fixed schedule) provided under the plan or elected by the participant at the date of deferral, a change in ownership or effective control of the corporation or in the ownership of a substantial portion of the assets of the corporation, or the occurrence of an unforeseen emergency (generally a severe financial hardship as defined in Code Sec. 457).[18] Distributions of nonqualified deferred compensation may no longer be made based on a haircut provision under which a small penalty (such as 6%) was imposed on the amount withdrawn or a trigger determined by the corporation's failing financial health. Unfortunately, under prior law, a haircut provision was an important safeguard. If the employee felt that financial or other conditions within the company might threaten the employee's deferral compensation benefit, the employee could withdraw his money under the plan's haircut provisions. It was a form of safety valve that no longer exists.

- Specified employees (as determined under Sec. 416) of a publicly traded corporation may not receive a distribution of nonqualified deferred compensation for at least 6 months following a separation from service.[19]

- A taxable event will occur if the corporation transfers assets to an offshore trust (even if the trust is otherwise subject to the claims of the corporation's creditors) used for the purpose of paying nonqualified deferred compensation.[20]

Sec. 409A generally applies to amounts deferred on or after January 1, 2005, but grandfather rules do apply. Amounts deferred before January 1, 2005 are generally not subject to Sec. 409A as long as the deferred compensation arrangement is not materially modified after October 3, 2004. Amounts are considered deferred before January 1, 2005, if an employee had a legally binding right to the deferred amount and the right to the deferrals was earned and vested as of December 31, 2004.

A nonqualified deferred compensation plan is not limited to an arrangement between an employer and an employee, but includes arrangements between any person who is the recipient of services and the person providing the services. Thus, arrangements covering corporate directors, independent contractors, agents, consultants, and partners can be a nonqualified deferred compensation plan subject to Sec. 409A. Likewise, the service providers

---

18. Treas. Reg. Sec. 1.409A-3.
19. Sec. 409A (a)(2)(18)(i); and Treas. Reg. Sec. 1.409A-1(i).
20. Sec. 409A(b)(1).

who may be subject to Sec. 409A can include individuals, personal service corporations or similar non-corporate entities. (Similar to the nomenclature used in the Sec. 409A regulations, the individual who is providing the services covered by the nonqualified deferred compensation plan will be hereafter referred to as a "service provider" and the individual receiving those services will hereafter be referred to as a "service recipient.")

Definitions of Nonqualified Deferred Compensation and Nonqualified Deferred-Compensation Plan

Sec. 409A regulates compensation deferred under arrangements that are part of a nonqualified deferred-compensation plan. The term nonqualified deferred-compensation plan is defined simply as any plan that provides for the deferral of compensation. In deciding whether a plan provides for the deferral of compensation, the Sec. 409A regulations require that determination to be made at the time the service provider has a legally binding right to the compensation under the plan. In effect, this means that once a deferral of income occurs, it cannot be retroactively changed to recharacterize it as something else.

A nonqualified deferred-compensation plan need not be a plan, as defined under ERISA. Instead, it can be an agreement, method, or arrangement that applies to a single person or to a group. Moreover, the plan can be unilaterally adopted by the service recipient or can be negotiated by both parties. But there are a number of statutory and regulatory exceptions to the definition of nonqualified deferred-compensation plan. Generally, Sec. 409A excepts qualified employer plans (Sec. 401(a) qualified plans, 457(b) plans, 403(a) and (b) annuity plans, SEPs, SIMPLEs and government excess benefit arrangements under Sec. 415(m)) and any vacation leave, sick leave, compensatory time, disability pay, or death benefit plan. In addition, the Sec. 409A regulations except Archer medical savings accounts, health savings accounts, any medical reimbursement arrangement that satisfies the requirements of Code Secs. 105 and 106 and certain foreign arrangements from the definition of a nonqualified deferred-compensation plan.

A plan provides nonqualified deferred compensation if, under the terms of the plan and the relevant facts and circumstances, a service provider has a legally binding right during a taxable year to compensation that pursuant to the terms of the plan is or may be payable in a later year. A legally binding right to compensation exists if a service provider is entitled to such compensation under contract, statute, or any other enforceable law, even if contingencies must occur in order for the deferred amount to become payable. Therefore, rights to severance pay upon a future involuntary termination of employment or bonuses that vest upon the satisfaction of certain service requirements are considered legally binding rights at the time the employment agreement, reflecting the severance rights or bonuses, first becomes effective despite such contingencies. However, if the contingencies constitute substantial risks of forfeiture, they will cause the compensation not to be subject to Sec. 409A until they lapse.

A legally binding right to compensation is not affected when the right is subject to a substantial risk of forfeiture. For example, suppose an agreement entered into in 2008 provides that deferred compensation attributable to services performed in 2008 will vest in 2010. This is a legally binding right created in 2008 that will not be paid until a later year; thus, the agreement provides for a deferral of compensation under Sec. 409A. Although a substantial risk of forfeiture will not affect the legally binding nature of nonqualified deferred compensation, the substantial risk of forfeiture does prevent nonqualified deferred compensation from being taxable. A substantial risk of forfeiture exists if entitlement to money or other property is conditioned on the performance of substantial future services by any person.

A substantial risk of forfeiture also exists if entitlement is tied to the occurrence of a condition related to the purpose of the compensation, such as the service provider's performance or the service recipient's business activities—for example, the attainment of a prescribed level of earnings or an initial public offering. However, merely refraining from the performance of services, such as required by a noncompete provision, is not sufficient to constitute a substantial risk of forfeiture for this purpose.

Accordingly, unless the requirements of some specific exemption or exception are satisfied, the following types of compensation plans are now considered nonqualified deferred-compensation plans subject to Sec. 409A: employment and buy-sell agreements with deferred payments, voluntary deferred-compensation plans, supplemental executive retirement plans (SERPs), incentive compensation and bonus plans, separation pay plans, phantom stock plans, change of control retention plans, and discounted stock options and stock appreciation rights (SARs).

Short-Term Deferrals and Other Exceptions

The Sec. 409A regulations describe several circumstances in which nonqualified deferred compensation is not considered to have occurred for purposes of Sec. 409A. Chief among these are short-term deferrals. Short-term deferrals will not be considered nonqualified deferred compensation for purposes of Sec. 409A if, absent an election to defer the payment until a later date, the terms of the plan at all times require payment (and the payment is actually or constructively received by the service provider) by the later of: (a) the date that is two and one-half months from the end of the service provider's first taxable year in which the payment is no longer subject to a substantial risk of forfeiture, or (b) the date that is two and one-half months from the end of the service recipient's year in which the payment is no longer subject to a substantial risk of forfeiture. For example, the short-term deferral exception would apply to a contractual obligation to pay severance benefits in a lump sum to an executive immediately after an involuntary termination of employment, that condition being considered a substantial risk of forfeiture.

On the other hand, the short-term deferral exception will not apply if the plan provides that payment will be made on or after any date or upon the occurrence of any event that will or may occur later than the applicable two and one-half month period, even if payment is actually made before the end of the short-term deferral period. Thus, if an employment agreement provides for a lump-sum severance payment following any termination of employment, the payment will not qualify as a short-term deferral. In that case there is no substantial risk of forfeiture, and payment can be made following the end of the allowable short-term deferral period. As illustrated by this example, an amount that is never subject to a substantial risk of forfeiture is considered to be no longer subject to such risk of forfeiture on the date the service provider has a legally binding right to the amount.

Another situation in which the Sec. 409A regulations provide for an exception from the statutory requirements are separation payments made in connection with an involuntary termination of employment or a window program, that is, typically an arrangement providing an incentive from the employer to encourage early retirement or termination of employment by its employees during a limited period of time. This exception applies if the entire amount of payments to the service provider does not exceed two times the service provider's annual compensation or, if less, two times the limit on annual compensation that may be taken into account for qualified plan purposes under Sec. 401(1)(17) ($245,000 in 2010). In addition, the amount must be paid no later than the end of the second calendar year after the termination of employment. If certain conditions are satisfied, the Sec. 409A regulations also treat payments made due to a voluntary termination for good reason as an exception to the Sec. 409A requirements.

Timing of Deferral Elections

For a deferral election to be considered properly made under Sec. 409A, it must be irrevocable and must specify (i) the amount of compensation being deferred; (ii) the timing of when the deferred compensation will ultimately be paid out; and (iii) the form in which the deferred compensation will ultimately be paid out. For bonuses that relate to services provided over one or more years, the deferral election with respect to such bonuses must be made before any services are performed during the bonus period. Accordingly, a 2008 election must be made with respect to a 2009 through 2010 bonus period, even if payment of the bonus will not be made until 2011. "Evergreen" elections are also permitted, that is, an initial or subsequent deferral election for one year remains in effect for the following year unless terminated or changed before the last day of the year preceding the year in which the election is to be effective. For example, an evergreen election for 2008 remains in effect for 2009 if it is not terminated or changed by December 31, 2008.

There is a special deferral election rule applicable to newly eligible service providers. Under this rule if a service provider becomes newly eligible, he or she can make a deferral election within 30 days after he or she becomes eligible, but only with respect to compensation payable for services performed after the election.

In addition, a special deferral election rule applies to performance-based compensation. A deferral election with respect to performance-based compensation may be made no later than 6 months before the end of the period over which the performance is measured and prior to when the amount is readily ascertainable. Performance-based compensation is defined as "compensation where the amount of, or entitlement to, the compensation is contingent on the satisfaction of preestablished organizational or individual performance criteria relating to a performance period of at least 12 consecutive months in which the service provider performs services." However, compensation will not be considered performance-based if the required level of performance is substantially certain of being attained at the time the criteria is established. In other words, it must not be known at the outset that the performance criteria will be satisfied. In order for any performance criteria to be considered preestablished, they must be put in writing at least 90 days after commencement of the performance period.

Another requirement of Sec. 409A relating to deferral elections is that as long as certain timing requirements are satisfied, an election can be made to delay the timing, or change the form, of a previously elected distribution. The Sec. 409A regulations elaborate on this provision by authorizing a subsequent election to delay a payment or to change the form of a payment if:

- The plan requires that any such subsequent election relating to a payment that is to be made at a fixed time or pursuant to a fixed schedule may not be made less than 12 months prior to the date the first amount was scheduled to be paid. In other words, an election to postpone must be made at least 12 months before any payment is scheduled to be made;

- The plan requires that the subsequent election may not take effect until at least 12 months after the date on which the subsequent election is made. In other words, if a distribution event occurs within 12 months of having chosen a new distribution date or a new form of distribution, the distribution must be made in accordance with the original distribution method; and

- The plan requires that the redeferral payment must be deferred for a period of not less than 5 years from the date such payment would have otherwise been made. During that 5-year period distributions may be made on account of death, disability, or unforeseeable emergency, but not on account of separation from service or change of control.

For purposes of applying these subsequent election rules, the term "payment" refers to each separately and objectively identified amount to which a service provider is entitled under a plan at a particular date. Under this definition a life annuity is treated as a single payment with the first date that a payment could be made being considered the payment date. However, changing from one type of life annuity to another type of life annuity, before any annuity payment has been made, is not considered a change in the time or form of payment, as long as the old and new annuities are actuarially equivalent, using reasonable actuarial assumptions.

Similarly, a series of installment payments is treated as a single payment, unless the plan provides that at all times the right to the series of installment payments is to be treated as a right to a series of payments for purposes of Sec. 409A. The difference between a single payment and a series of separate payments may be significant. For example, if a 5-year installment payment is treated as a single payment and is scheduled to commence on January 1, 2009, then consistent with the 5-year delay rule, a service provider could change the time and form of payment to a lump sum payable on January 1, 2014, provided the other conditions for making a subsequent election are met. On the other hand, if a 5-year installment payment is designated as five separate payments for the years 2009 through 2014, then the service provider could not change the time and form of payment to a lump-sum payment to be made on January 1, 2014, because the annual payments for 2010 through 2014 would not have been deferred for at least 5 years.

Finally, there are three circumstances in which a plan may be amended in order to provide for a delay of a deferred-compensation payment to a date following the designated payment date without having the delay treated as an impermissible payment date or a subsequent election. However, once such an amendment applies to an amount of nonqualified deferred compensation, it may not thereafter be disregarded and payment must be delayed if the condition exists. Any failure to apply the amended provision will be treated as a prohibited acceleration of benefits.

The three circumstances are: (i) the service recipient reasonably determines that the service recipient's tax deduction with respect to such payment would be limited or eliminated by application of Sec. 162(m); provided that the payment is made as soon as possible when the deduction will not be limited or eliminated by Sec. 162(m) or in the calendar year in which the service provider separates from service; (ii) the service recipient reasonably anticipates that the making of the payment will violate a term of a loan agreement or other similar contract to which the service recipient is a party and such violation would cause material harm to the service recipient; and (iii) the service recipient reasonably anticipates that the making of the payment will violate Federal securities laws.

Distribution of Benefits

Sec. 409A(a)(2)(A) significantly limits the circumstances under which nonqualified deferred compensation can be paid. A nonqualified deferred-compensation plan will fail to satisfy the distribution restrictions of Sec. 409A(a)(2)(A) unless distributions cannot be made earlier than (i) a separation from service, (ii) the date a service provider becomes disabled, (iii) the date of a service provider's death, (iv) a specified time or pursuant to a fixed schedule specified in the plan, or (v) the occurrence of an unforeseeable emergency (hereafter together referred to as the "enumerated events"). A distribution may also be made on account of a change of control event involving any of the following: (i) the service provider's employer, (ii) the service recipient or other corporation liable for the nonqualified deferred-compensation payment, or (iii) the parent corporation of the employer or service recipient. For a public company's "specified employees," as defined for purposes of the "top-heavy plan" rules found in Code Sec. 416(i), there is an additional 6-month waiting period, commencing with the date of separation, before any distribution of deferred compensation can be made on account of a separation from service. Finally, the acceleration of distributions is prohibited, except as provided in the Sec. 409A regulations.

Because it may not always be administratively feasible to make payment on the exact date stated in the plan, a payment will generally be treated as made on the specified payment date, if the payment is made on the specified payment date or any later date within the same calendar year that the payment is due, or if later, by the 15th day of the third month after the date the payment is due or no earlier than 30 days before the designated payment date. Furthermore, where nonqualified deferred compensation is payable upon a specified event, it is permissible for distributions to be made upon an objectively determinable date or year following the specified event, for example, July 1 following the service provider's separation from service, as long as the plan so provides.

The Sec. 409A regulations elaborate on these distribution requirements in several respects. It is permissible for a plan to provide for a distribution of nonqualified deferred compensation on the "earliest of" or "latest of" more than one of the enumerated events. Furthermore, a different form of distribution can be used for payments occurring before or after a particular date. For example, a plan can provide a lump-sum payment if separation from service occurs before age 65, and installment payments if the separation occurs on or after age 65. This rule also allows for different forms of distribution to be associated with different payment events. Thus, the nonqualified deferred-compensation payments triggered by a change of control can be made in the form of a lump sum, while all other nonqualified deferred compensation payments are made in five installments.

With respect to the 6-month delay of payments to specified employees, the plan must set forth the manner in which it will implement the 6-month delay. A plan, for example, could provide that payments during the 6-month period are accumulated and paid upon another date, for example, the day after the end of the 6-month period, or the plan can treat the end of the 6-month period as the payment commencement date. These provisions can be amended at any time, but such amendment cannot become effective for 12 months, except in the case of an initial public offering when the amendment can be effective immediately.

The occurrence of an "unforeseeable emergency" is determined in a similar manner to a hardship withdrawal under a Sec. 401(k) plan, but without the safe harbors. In other words, payments to satisfy an unforeseeable emergency are allowable only upon severe financial hardship of the service provider or a beneficiary resulting from illness or accident or other similar extraordinary and unforeseeable circumstances from events beyond the control of the service provider or beneficiary. Only the amount necessary to satisfy the need can be withdrawn. Moreover, an emergency will not qualify to the extent that the emergency can be relieved by insurance, liquidation of other assets, or cessation of any deferrals under the plan. Clearly, plan administrators must take care in making the determination of the need and the service provider's other available assets and may want to borrow procedures and representations from the hardship withdrawal regulations for Sec. 401(k) plans.

Tax Consequences

A nonqualified deferred-compensation plan that satisfies the rules of Sec. 409A will be taxed under the same rules as applied under prior law. Assuming the requirements of prior law have been satisfied, the executive includes the nonqualified deferred compensation in gross income when the executive receives it; the employer deducts the nonqualified deferred compensation from gross income when the executive includes it in income; and the investment income, if any, attributable to the nonqualified deferred compensation between the time of the initial deferral and the time of distribution is taxed to the employer.

On the other hand, a nonqualified deferred-compensation plan that fails to satisfy the new requirements of Sec. 409A will result in accrual-based taxation for the affected executive. This means that in each year the executive will include in gross income the total amount of vested nonqualified deferred compensation, including actual or notional investment returns, if any, less any amounts included in income in all prior years. Sec. 409A also imposes a flat 20 percent surtax on the nonqualified deferred compensation taxable to the executive. If (i) a nonqualified deferred-compensation plan initially meets the requirements of Sec. 409A, but subsequently fails them, or if (ii) the nonqualified deferred compensation plan is noncompliant from its inception, but such noncompliance is not discovered until after vesting has occurred, the executive must pay an interest charge, that is, the IRS underpayment rate plus one percentage point, from the time of the initial vesting of the nonqualified deferred compensation. The interest charge is applicable to the hypothetical underpayment of tax arising from the failure to include the nonqualified deferred compensation in income when initially vested. For example, assume that a participant enters into a nonqualified deferred-compensation plan that complies with Sec. 409A in 2008 and that the nonqualified deferred compensation is vested in 2009. The plan is amended in 2010 so that it no longer complies with Sec. 409A, but the noncompliance is not discovered until 2012. In 2012 the participant will be required to pay interest at the higher rate on the imputed underpayment of tax, arising from her failure to include her nonqualified deferred-compensation in income in 2010 and 2011.

Correction Programs

As is readily apparent from the above discussion of the Sec. 409A requirements, Sec. 409A is a far-reaching and very complex statutory provision that imposes severe adverse tax consequences on the plan participants in the event of noncompliance. The IRS has recognized this and has provided two programs to taxpayers which are intended to allow plan sponsors to correct certain violations of Sec. 409A, without requiring participants to pay the full amount of the otherwise applicable penalties.

The first correction program was issued in IRS Notice 2008-113[21] which provided relief for certain operational failures, including the following four categories of unintentional operational errors:

- Errors arising from failures to defer, early payments, excess deferrals and below-market stock rights that are corrected in the same taxable year as the errors occurred.
- Errors arising from failures to defer, early payments, excess deferrals and below-market stock rights that are corrected in the taxable year immediately following the taxable year in which the errors occurred.

---

21. 2008-51 I.R.B. 1305. Although IRS Notice 2008-113 makes obsolete the guidance under IRS Notice 2007-100, taxpayers may continue to rely on the relief provided in IRS Notice 2007-100 for operational failures that occurred in taxable years beginning before 2009, or may choose to follow the relief provided in IRS Notice 2008-113 for those pre-2009 operational failures.

- Errors arising from failures to defer, early payments, and excess deferrals that do not exceed a threshold amount ($16,500 in 2010) and that are corrected by the end of the second taxable year immediately following the taxable year in which the failure occurred.
- Errors arising from failures to defer, early payments, and excess deferrals, regardless of the amount and the status of the service provider as long as the correction is made by no later than the end of the second taxable year immediately following the taxable year in which the failure occurred.

In order to obtain the benefit of any of the available corrections, the company has the burden of establishing that the operational error was inadvertent and unintentional, that the error satisfies the eligibility requirements for the available relief and that the company has otherwise satisfied the requirements of Notice 2008-113. The following are several of the general requirements that are prerequisites to being eligible for the relief provided by the notice:

- The company must implement "commercially reasonable" steps to avoid a recurrence of the error.
- The service provider must not already be under examination by the IRS.
- Relief is not available if before or in the year of the correction, the company experiences a substantial financial downturn or other economic issue indicating that a deferred payment would not be paid when due in the future.
- If the service provider must repay the company any erroneously paid amount, he or she must repay the gross amount determined without regard to the payment of any withholding and employment taxes.
- The notice's information and reporting requirements must be satisfied. Generally, the company is required to provide a disclosure statement to both the IRS and the service provider regarding the failure.

The extent of the relief available under Notice 2008-113 depends on when the correction is made. Thus, it is important to uncover an operational failure as soon as possible. For any failure that involves an early or delayed payment, including an improper deferral, such failure may be corrected by repaying the amount to the employer or service provider, respectively, in the same taxable year. If that occurs, there is no inclusion in income and no Sec. 409A penalty is imposed. If a failure by a non-insider is corrected in the year following the year in which the failure occurred, and the failure involves an early payment, a failure to defer, a delayed payment or an excess deferral, there are income tax adjustments and possibly the payment of interest, but the relief for this category of failure is still the avoidance of any Sec. 409A penalty.

Finally, the relief provided in connection with the correction of a failure that falls within either category 3 or category 4, described above, is generally to make the amount involved in the failure subject to income tax and subject to the 20 percent penalty tax under Sec. 409A, but not to the additional interest associated with a tax underpayment.

The second correction program was issued in IRS Notice 2010-6 and offers employers an opportunity to correct plan documents that are not compliant with Sec. 409A. This document correction program is intended to encourage taxpayers to review their nonqualified deferred compensation plans to identify plan provisions that fail to comply with the requirements of Sec. 409A and to correct those provisions promptly. Early correction is important not only because the relief is generally not available once the taxpayer is under audit, but also because some of the relief is time sensitive. For example, assume that a plan provides for payment upon a change in control which is defined in a manner that is not consistent with the Sec. 409A definition. If the change in control has not yet occurred, the employer can amend the definition of "change in control" to be Sec. 409A-compliant, with the amendment effective immediately. However, if a change in control, as defined before the amendment, occurs within one year after the correction, 25 percent of the deferred compensation that would have been paid under the pre-amendment definition must be included in income — even though the payment isn't made because the corrected definition applies. Similar rules apply for many of the other corrections, often with 50 percent of the deferred compensation having to be included in income.

Under a special transition rule, taxpayers can avoid the Sec. 409A income inclusion otherwise required for the correction relief, such as the type described above due to the impermissible event occurring within one year after the correction, as long as the document failure is corrected by December 31, 2010. However, if an improper payment was made (or should have been made, if the amended definition applied) by December 31, 2010, there is also an operational failure that must be corrected under Notice 2008-113. The correction of the operational failure may independently require income inclusion.

Only certain types of document failures are eligible for relief under Notice 2010-6. Some of the plan provisions that may be Sec. 409A violations, but are nevertheless eligible for correction, include:

- An otherwise permissible payment event such as "termination of employment," "disability," "separation from service," "change in control," or "acquisition" that is not defined in the plan document, or is improperly defined.

- A payment period that is more than 90 days following a permissible payment event, or a payment period that is dependent upon the participant executing a noncompetition or nonsolicitation agreement or a release of claims that may extend the payment period beyond the allowable 90 days.

- An impermissible payment event, such as an initial public offering (that does not otherwise constitute a change in control as defined in the Sec. 409A regulations) or enrollment of a child in college.

- Impermissible alternative payment schedules that apply depending on which payment trigger occurs, for example, a lump sum if the participant has an involuntary separation from service versus ten annual installments if the participant has a voluntary separation from service.

- Employer or participant discretion to change the time or form of a payment that is due, such as the discretion to pay in a lump sum or annual installments, discretion to delay payments if certain cash flow targets are not met, or discretion to make subsequent deferral elections.

- Employer discretion to accelerate payment events, such as discretion to pay before the participant separates from service even though the plan provides for payment upon separation from service.

- Impermissible reimbursements, like country club dues, after separation from service.

- Failing to include the 6-month delay for payments to "specified employees".

- Provisions that don't comply with Sec. 409A's initial deferral election timing rules, such as applying the election deadline for performance-based compensation to a bonus that does not qualify as performance-based compensation.

OTHER DESIGN ISSUES

Vesting

A deferred-vesting provision (generally referred to simply as a "vesting" provision) is designed to provide a risk to the employee that part or all of the deferred compensation will be forfeited if the employee fails to meet certain conditions. These provisions are designed primarily to meet employer interests in keeping a valuable employee. They do not serve the interests of the employee, and generally most employees covered under a nonqualified deferred-compensation plan will prefer to have immediate, full vesting of their benefits. This is particularly true for the salary reduction type of benefit formula, since it appears to the employee as if he or she has given up cash compensation that would otherwise be available.

If the employer succeeds in imposing a vesting provision, it can be as strict or as liberal as the employer wants it to be. As discussed below, in practice the ERISA vesting provisions do not apply to nonqualified plans and the plan is not limited to the 2- to 6-year graded or 3-year/100 percent vesting schedules applicable to qualified defined contribution plans and the 3- to 7-year graded or 5-year/100 percent vesting schedules applicable to qualified defined benefit plans.

The most stringent vesting provision, designed to encourage a key employee from ever leaving the employer, would be a provision that benefits are payable at retirement (or at prior death) only if the employee is still actively working for the employer at that time. An employee would lose all benefits (or, depending on the vesting schedule, most benefits) if employment is terminated prior to the target date of retirement or death.

In a plan using a salary reduction type of formula with an "account balance" for the participant, some designers provide different rates of return based on whether the employee remains in service until retirement or leaves earlier. In effect, this is a type of vesting provision. For example, the plan might provide that the participant's account balance will be credited with a compounded return of 10 percent if the participant terminates employment before retirement, but if the employee stays until retirement the rate of return will be 15 percent. In effect, the plan provides immediate vesting of the participant's deferrals and a 10 percent rate of return. The plan also provides an additional 5 percent rate of return that is not vested until retirement.

Financing Formula

Obviously, an employer should establish a financing mechanism to meet its (contingent) future promises. Although for tax reasons (see below) the employer gives the employee merely an unsecured promise that the benefits will be paid, accounting and financial procedures clearly suggest the wisdom of a method to allocate dollars to an asset or reserve fund held by the employer. This reserve fund can be a type of life insurance policy, money market account, mutual funds, stocks, certificates of deposit, or some other form of investment. This subject is discussed more extensively in the next chapter.

Deferring Other Income

Many senior executives in publicly held corporations serve on the boards of other publicly held companies. The fees for such "outside" directors may be substantial (commensurate with their responsibilities and potential liabilities). Many outside directors do not currently need that income, because they are well paid by their regular employers. An executive can defer these fees until retirement by signing an agreement with the corporation prior to the commencement of the year the money is earned. "Interest" can be added to the deferred amounts each year at a rate possibly one or two points above prime. If the arrangement is structured in accordance with the rules discussed here, the executive does not pay tax on either the deferred amounts or the interest until he or she receives payment.

TAXATION OF THE EMPLOYEE

The plans discussed here are generally intended to provide one primary objective—the deferral of income taxation to the employee until benefits from the plan are paid. Achieving this clear objective involves some complex but important technicalities of the tax law. These technicalities underlie all tax planning for executive compensation (not just nonqualified deferred compensation), so the planner must be thoroughly familiar with them. Apart from the requirements of Code Sec. 409A, there are fundamentally four requirements that will be listed first and then discussed in detail.

Tax Law Requirements

- The plan must be unfunded for tax purposes.
- There must be no actual receipt or "constructive receipt" of benefits before the employee intends the benefits to be taxable.

ERISA Requirements

- The plan must be unfunded for ERISA purposes.
- The plan must meet the "top-hat" exclusion (that is, it must cover only a "select group of management or highly compensated employees").

These four points will be explained in more detail in the material that immediately follows, but those interested in pursuing this material further should be aware that this 4-point summary is somewhat oversimplified. In designing a complex executive compensation plan the provisions of Sec. 409A and the Sec. 409A regulations must also be carefully considered by the advisers of both the employer and the employee.

Unfunded Plan Requirement—Tax Issues

In the employee benefit area, the term *funded plan* has a very specialized meaning. For tax purposes, the distinction between a funded plan and an unfunded plan involves the question of whether the employee has received *property* from the employer or simply received the employer's promise to pay in the future. For income tax purposes, the treatment of a transfer of property is very different from that of a simple promise. If the employer transfers property to the employee, the amount and timing of taxation are determined under the rules of Code Sec. 83.

Summary of Sec. 83 Rules
If an employer transfers property to an employee as compensation for services, the employee is taxed on the fair market value of that property in the first year in which there is no substantial risk of forfeiture. In other words, to defer taxation on property transferred as compensation, the employee must have a risk of forfeiture.

By contrast, to defer taxation on a simple promise, the requirements of Sec. 409A and constructive-receipt rules (discussed below) must be satisfied.

The definition of a funded plan for tax purposes, in effect, draws a line as to what will be considered a promise (governed by the constructive-receipt doctrine); anything over this line will be considered property (governed by Sec. 83).

In the tax sense, a plan is of course considered unfunded if there is no fund of any kind set aside. However, the plan is also considered unfunded even if the employer has set aside money or property to the employee's account, as long as the assets are available to the employer's unsecured creditors. The

IRS has ruled that the assets can be protected against the employer itself, but must at least be available to the employer's unsecured creditors. In other words, the view of the IRS is that in an unfunded plan, the employee's rights to any assets set aside must be no better than those of unsecured creditors.

Practical methods of informal funding or "financing" a nonqualified deferred-compensation plan are discussed in the next chapter.

Constructive Receipt and Sec. 409A Limitations

Under the constructive-receipt doctrine (Code Sec. 451), an amount is treated as received for income tax purposes (even if it is not actually received) if it is "credited to the employee's account, set aside, or otherwise made available."

Constructive receipt does not occur if the employee's control over the receipt is subject to a "substantial limitation or restriction." A requirement that payment of deferred compensation cannot be made until the passage of a specified time period is usually considered a substantial limitation or restriction. In a typical deferred-compensation plan, for example, if the plan provides that an amount is not payable for 5 years or not payable until the employee terminates employment or retires, it will not be constructively received before that time. A risk of forfeiture—a plan provision that specifically provides for a possibility of loss of the benefits—is not required in order to avoid constructive receipt.

If a nonqualified plan uses salary reductions to fund the plan, the employee's election to reduce salary must be made in accordance with the requirements of Sec. 409A (discussed earlier in this chapter). Similarly, plan distribution provisions must also be designed to comply with the requirements of Sec. 409A (as discussed earlier in this chapter).

In designing distribution provisions, the planner should be aware that Code Sec. 409A(a)(3) prohibits any "acceleration of the time or schedule of any payment under the plan."

However, apart from payments to satisfy an unforeseeable emergency, there are several other circumstances when nonqualified deferred-compensation payments may be accelerated under Sec. 409A. These circumstances include the following:

- Payment to someone other than the service provider of amounts required to be paid as the result of a domestic relations order, as defined for tax-qualified retirement plan purposes;

- Payment necessary to comply with divestitures required by conflict of interest rules;

- If taxes are due upon a vesting event under a Sec. 457 (f) plan, payment may be made in an amount necessary to pay the required taxes;

- Payment by December 31 of the calendar year in which a service provider separates from service (or alternatively, March 15 of the year following separation from service, if such separation occurs after October 15) of an entire account balance that is less than $10,000, so long as the payment results in the termination of the service provider's entire interest in the plan and the cash out is mandatory.

- Payment of employment taxes related to the plan;

- Payment of income taxes due to required income inclusion under Sec. 409A;

- Payment after termination of the plan. In two circumstances, that is, following a corporate dissolution or a corporate bankruptcy, payments can be made if the plan termination is accomplished within 12 months of the dissolution or bankruptcy.

  If the plan is terminated within 30 days before or 12 months after a change of control event, amounts may be paid from the plan as long as they are paid within 12 months from the date of the plan termination; or

  Payment after a plan termination for any other reason so long as no payment is made on account of the plan termination (other than payments that would have been payable in the absence of the plan termination) within 12 months after the termination and all payments are made within 24 months of the termination. Moreover, a similar plan that covers the same service providers may not be adopted within 5 years of the plan termination.

Finally, the Sec. 409A regulations describe two other circumstances that should not be treated as accelerations. First, an acceleration event can be specified at the time of deferral. For instance, a plan may allow payments to be made in 10 installments, but if death should occur before all of the installments have been completed, the remaining installments can be paid in a lump sum to the service provider's estate or a beneficiary. Second, if a payment is subject to a substantial risk of forfeiture and the service recipient waives the condition that gives rise to the risk of forfeiture, such waiver will not be considered an impermissible acceleration. For example, assume that a service provider is subject to a 10-year cliff vesting schedule. If the service provider terminates employment after 7 years and the service recipient waives the vesting schedule, then the service recipient would be able to make an immediate payment of nonqualified deferred compensation to the service provider without it being treated as an acceleration.

The purpose of Sec. 409A's anti-acceleration rule is to prevent executives from taking money out of a failing corporation when they see financial trouble approaching for the corporation. This is the type of practice involved in the Enron and similar corporate scandals of the last several years, and Congress decided to try to prevent such practices with new Code Sec. 409A. The new rules nevertheless sacrifice design flexibility in many situations where abusive practices are not likely.

Unfunded Plan Requirement—ERISA Issues

Funded plans are subject to the ERISA vesting and fiduciary requirements, which create design inflexibility. Under the ERISA vesting rules, the plan must have a vesting schedule that is at least as fast as the 5-year cliff or 3- to 7-year graded vesting for defined benefit plans and at least as fast as 3-year cliff, or 2- to 6-year graded vesting for individual account plans. A third alternative is 100 percent vesting with a 2-year waiting period for entry. This is the same vesting requirement that applies to qualified plans.

The use of a funded plan, containing one of these ERISA vesting schedules, is rarely acceptable in a nonqualified deferred-compensation arrangement because of the unacceptable tax consequences. Recall that a funded plan is subject to Sec. 83, which results in income taxation to the employee when the employee's benefit is no longer subject to a substantial risk of forfeiture (that is, the benefit is vested). Since the ERISA vesting rules apply, this means that income taxation can be deferred only as far as the vesting schedule extends. This amounts to a maximum of 6 years deferral (for part of the benefit if the 2- to 6-year schedule is used) and a maximum of 7 years deferral for defined benefit plans (for part of the benefit if the 3- to 7-year schedule is used).

Furthermore, a funded plan is subject to the ERISA funding requirements. This would require the plan to be funded on an actuarial basis just like a qualified plan, with periodic required minimum funding deposits, subject to the minimum funding penalties of the Code. This is generally too inflexible for most nonqualified deferred-compensation arrangements.

As a result of these unacceptable consequences, it is generally important to avoid the ERISA funding, vesting, and fiduciary requirements. The plan should therefore be unfunded. However, being unfunded is not enough to avoid ERISA; there is also a requirement that the plan be limited to the "top-hat" group.

The "Top-Hat" Group—ERISA Issues

In order to avoid ERISA, a plan must be unfunded AND must be "maintained by an employer primarily for the purpose of providing deferred compensation for a select group of management or highly compensated employees." This select group is referred to as the "top-hat" group.

Obviously, a crucial question is the definition of the top-hat group. The statutory language alone does not amount to a precise definition. Unfortunately, the Department of Labor (which is the government agency responsible for enforcing ERISA) has given few clear answers in this regard. Some rulings were established in the late 1970s; however, the DOL has given no further rulings on this issue. These early rulings tended to approve very few employees, a small percentage of the employer's total workforce, as top-hat groups. But there is no clear rule of thumb as to the percentage coverage for a top-hat group.

In a 1990 opinion letter, ERISA Op. Ltr 90-14A, May 8, 1990, the DOL provided two meaningful interpretations of the top-hat group provision. First, in the first footnote it set forth its interpretation of "primarily" as referring only to the purpose of the plan, that is, the benefits provided, and not to the participant composition of the plan. Some court cases had indicated that a few participants in a top-hat plan need not be part of the "select group" without adversely affecting the status of the plan as a top-hat plan. Thus, this footnote confirmed that as far as the DOL is concerned, if a top-hat plan extends coverage to anyone other than a member of "a select group of management or highly compensated employees," it could not qualify as a top-hat plan. In addition, in Advisory Opinion 90-14A, the DOL stated its view that the ability of an employee to negotiate the terms and conditions of a plan and to understand the significance of the risks associated with such a compensation arrangement bears on the issue of whether a plan covers a select group and thus qualifies as a top-hat plan.

Thus, Advisory Opinion 90-14A clearly took a new approach adding a test that treats only employees that do not require ERISA protection as includible in the "select group." However, that was the last official word that the DOL has had on this subject since 1990. This has left financial planners without any further guidance from the DOL as to what weight, if any, should be given to quantitative and qualitative factors in determining what constitutes a "select group" and what weight, if any, should be given to the individual employee's bargaining power in making that determination.

The courts have been available to fill the guidance vacuum created by the DOL's failure to issue meaningful interpretations of what constitutes a top-hat plan. However, over the past 25 years there have been only about 15 judicial decisions that have had to address some aspect of what constitutes a top-hat plan. Moreover, like the DOL, all of the judicial decisions that have had to focus on the meaning of "select group" generally have taken into account both quantitative and qualitative factors. This includes (1) the percentage of the total workforce invited to join the plan (quantitative), (2) the nature of their employment duties (qualitative), (3) the compensation disparity between top-hat plan members and nonmembers (qualitative), and (4) the actual language of the plan agreement (qualitative).

In terms of percentages, *Darden v. Nationwide Mutual Insurance Co.*, 717 F. Supp. 388 (EDNC 1989), a federal district court held that 18.7 percent of the workforce was too high a percentage to be a top-hat group. However, in a more recent case, *Demery v. Extebank Deferred Compensation Plan*, (216 F. 3d 283 (2d Cir. 2000), the influential Second Circuit Court of Appeals held that a plan offered to 15.34 percent of the company's employees, with about 7 to 10 percent of the workforce actually participating, was a top-hat plan. This plan was offered to a group of executives whose status was just below that of the top four highest paid executives, who had their own individually negotiated deferred-compensation plans.

Following the DOL's lead, many courts have also mentioned the requirement that the members of the select group must hold positions with their employer of such influence that through direct negotiations they are capable of designing and protecting their deferred-compensation arrangements. Until 2008, there does not appear to have been a case where the outcome turned solely on the issue of the bargaining power of the individual members of the select group. However, in 2008, the First Circuit Court of Appeals addressed the issue of the select groups' bargaining power head on. In *Alexander v. Brigham and Women's Physicians Organization, Inc. et al.*, 513 F. 3d 37 (1st Cir. 2008), the court of appeals affirmed the lower court's ruling that two deferred-compensation plans for certain surgeons whose net practice income exceeded an earnings cap imposed by Harvard University constituted top hat plans under ERISA. The court applied the traditional qualitative and quantitative analysis to determine that the deferred-compensation plans in question were maintained for a "select group."

However, the plaintiff/appellant (Alexander) who wanted the plans to be subject to ERISA requirements also argued that the district court erred in determining that Alexander's lack of individual bargaining power was irrelevant to the top-hat plan determination. Alexander's position was that every member of the select group had to possess sufficient bargaining power to influence the terms of a top-hat plan.

In addressing the argument, the appeals court first looked at the terms of the statute. It found no reference to the term "bargaining power" or any other indication that courts should take into consideration the employees' ability to bargain over the terms of their deferred-compensation plans as part of the court's determination of whether a top-hat plan exists. The court then turned its attention to DOL Advisory Opinion 90-14A as the primary authority cited by Alexander to support his "bargaining power" argument. The court, however, refused to defer to, or to even be persuaded by, the DOL opinion letter. The court viewed the letter as only speaking to Congress's purpose in including the top-hat provision in ERISA and refused to accept it as an interpretation of the provision's requirements.

The court thus found two reasons not to find any requirement for individual bargaining power in the context of a top-hat plan. First, neither the statute nor its legislative history contains any indication that Congress intended to have courts consider the employees' ability to bargain over the provisions of their deferred-compensation plans. Second, the DOL opinion letter does not constitute an interpretation of the statutory language and should not become the basis of an independent statutory test. Thus, the First Circuit is very clear in its rejection of the DOL's interpretation of the top-hat plan requirements, as found in DOL Advisory Opinion 90-14A.

In light of the *Alexander* decision and prior court decisions the following conclusions can be drawn about what constitutes a top-hat plan. First, the group of covered employees should constitute less than 10 percent of the employer's workforce, unless you are in the Second Circuit where Demery was decided. In addition, the covered employees should be identified based on their rank, position, and management characteristics. Second, the members of the top-hat group should be highly compensated in both absolute and relative terms. The current dollar limit on highly compensated employees under Code Sec. 414(q) is generally irrelevant. The employer must be able to show a substantial disparity between the compensation paid to the top-hat group and the compensation paid to all other workers. Third, employees who are not part of a select group, no matter how few in number, should not be allowed to participate. Finally, as far as individual bargaining power is concerned, in the First Circuit it is no longer a factor. In the Sixth and Ninth Circuits it is something that needs to be addressed. In other circuits it has yet to face judicial analysis and thus, it remains a possible consideration. However, the *Alexander* decision now provides a basis for persuading other courts of appeal to take the same position as the First Circuit.

ERISA Avoidance on the "No Plan" Theory

Finally, another theory should be mentioned on which ERISA coverage of a nonqualified deferred-compensation plan can be avoided. This is the theory that there is no "employee plan," but rather a simple one-time contractual arrangement. The U.S. Supreme Court in *Fort Halifax Packing Co. v. Coyne*, 482 U.S. 1 (1987) held that a one-time severance payment arrangement was not a "plan" for ERISA purposes because it "require[d] no administrative scheme whatsoever." There are also many lower court cases on this issue, which depend on their particular facts, and it is difficult to predict how a specific case will be decided.

Because this theory is primarily a defense in litigation, it is relatively useless in planning because of the wide variation in the results of the cases that have been decided. In a simple situation very close to the facts in the *Fort Halifax* case, it might be possible to advise an employer that, for example, a severance-pay plan or one-time contractual arrangement or window-type retirement arrangement is not an ERISA plan and therefore requires no ERISA compliance. For more complex deferred-compensation plans where a non-top hat group is covered, it is probably unwise to advise the employer in advance that the plan is not covered under ERISA, although of course the employer might want to take that position in court at some later time if the arrangement leads to a lawsuit by a dissatisfied employee.

Income Taxation

If the requirements of Code Sec. 409A are satisfied, employees must pay ordinary income tax on benefits from unfunded nonqualified deferred-compensation plans in the first year in which the benefit is actually or constructively received. No favorable treatment is available to payments from nonqualified plans.

Death benefits from nonqualified plans that are payable to a beneficiary are taxable as income in respect of a decedent (IRD) to the recipient. IRD is taxable income to the recipient, but the recipient is entitled to an income tax deduction for the estate tax payable on the amount of the IRD included in the estate for federal estate tax purposes.

Social Security (FICA) and Medicare Taxes

Amounts deferred under nonqualified deferred-compensation plans are not subject to Social Security and Medicare taxes until the year in which the employee no longer has any substantial risk of forfeiting the amount, provided the amounts are reasonably ascertainable. In other words, as soon as the covered executive is vested in the plan, he or she will be subject to Social Security taxes. Conceivably, this could be earlier than the year of actual receipt.

For example, if the plan provides that benefits are payable at retirement, but the benefits become vested 5 years after they are earned, then the amounts deferred will enter into the Social Security tax base 5 years after they are earned. Note that this is neither the year they are earned nor the year they are paid, a circumstance that complicates tax compliance in this situation.

Although part of the Social Security taxable wage base—the OASDI part—has an annual upper limit ($106,800 for 2010), the Medicare hospital insurance portion is unlimited. The Medicare tax rate is 1.45 percent for the employer and the employee. For higher paid executives, the inclusion of deferred compensation in the wage base during a year of active employment will not result in additional OASDI taxes if the executive's current (nondeferred) compensation is more than the OASDI wage base; however, additional Medicare taxes will be payable. This factor must be taken into account in designing nonqualified deferred-compensation plans.

Subsequent Account Earnings

If a nonqualified deferred compensation plan provides employee "account balances" and credits earnings on these accounts periodically, are there additional Social Security and Medicare taxes applicable each time the earnings are credited even after the account balance has already been included in the wage base? The regulations provide a means of avoiding this result by a "nonduplication rule." The idea of the nonduplication rule is that the Social Security and Medicare taxes should apply to compensation income only once, and thereafter any earnings on the income should no longer be subject to Social Security and Medicare taxes. The Regulations (Reg. Sec. 31.3121(v)(2)-1(d)) provide that earnings credited on a deferred-compensation account are not subject to additional Social Security and Medicare taxes—if the earnings either (a) do not exceed the rate of return on a predetermined actual investment or (b) reflect a reasonable rate of interest.

In the view of the IRS, it apparently is not difficult to meet the test for an "actual investment" contained in the Social Security regulations. A private letter ruling, Private Letter Ruling 2000 21012, explains the regulations by stating: "Plan assets do not need to be actually invested in the stated investment, nor does the investment need to be generally available to the public. For example, the investment options could be the same as those available under the employer's qualified 401(k) plan, even if one of those investment options is not generally available to the public." (Language of this ruling interprets Reg. Sec. 31.3121(v)(2)-1(d).) This ruling further notes that under the regulations "an actual investment includes an investment identified by reference to any stock index with respect to which there are positions traded on a national securities exchange . . . ." In other words, typical investments credited to the account could include the same range of stocks (including employer stock), mutual funds, etc., typically used in 401(k) plans, as well as such options as life insurance contracts. Again, remember that no actual investments need to be provided for a nonqualified deferred-compensation plan—the accounts can be merely book accounts.

Federal Estate Tax Treatment

Note: The federal estate tax was repealed for 2010. It is anticipated that the federal estate tax will be reinstated in 2011 and thereafter.

The amount of any death benefit payable to a beneficiary under a nonqualified deferred-compensation plan is generally included in the deceased employee's estate, for federal estate tax purposes, at its then present value. In other words, the present value of payments made to the employee's beneficiary will be included in the employee's gross estate. If the beneficiary is the participant's spouse, the amount will fall under the marital deduction and will produce no estate tax at the participant's death, but could be taxed at the spouse's subsequent death. For a nonspousal beneficiary, the estate tax unified credit amount is available to shelter nonqualified plan amounts up to the credit amount applicable in the year of the participant's death.

It is possible to exclude nonqualified plan benefits from the taxable estate if the plan is designed as a "death benefit only" (DBO) plan. Under a DBO plan, the employee can have no lifetime benefits available from the plan. All of the employer's nonqualified plans for the employee are aggregated in determining if there are lifetime benefits. The design of DBO plans is discussed in detail in a later chapter.

NONQUALIFIED DEFERRED COMPENSATION FOR STOCKHOLDER-EMPLOYEES

An employee-shareholder is eligible to participate in a nonqualified deferred-compensation plan. Such a plan can take the place of or enhance qualified retirement plans. A shareholder-employee can therefore enhance financial security, have income generated by the asset underlying that security taxed at low corporate rates, and obtain the benefit of a corporate tax deduction and the consequent tax leverage.

There are potential problems obtaining favorable tax treatment with respect to payouts to shareholder-employees and their families under these plans. The IRS might claim that the amounts paid are either disguised dividends or unreasonable compensation. This makes deductions more difficult than those for payments to non-shareholder-employees.

It is therefore important to document

- a contractual obligation for a corporation to make payments
- the economic benefit accruing to the corporation from the arrangement
- a nexus between the benefits and past or future services furnished to the corporation by the shareholder-employee
- a reasonable amount that is paid in relation to the past or future services provided

It is permissible to provide more extensive and valuable perquisites to a shareholder-employee than to another employee as long as it can be shown that those payments were made to reward past or present services to the corporation. Obviously the smaller amount of stock the shareholder has (and therefore the less power that individual has to divert corporate profits), the less likely it is that the IRS can successfully argue that payouts are a form of disguised dividends.

Generally the IRS will not issue rulings on the tax effect of nonqualified deferred-compensation arrangements for stockholder-employees (this is generally included in the IRS's annual list of "no-ruling" issues), so the protection of an IRS ruling is not available. Furthermore, the IRS took the position in TAM 8828004 that compensation could not be deferred for a *controlling shareholder*. However, this position was "dictum" (not a binding IRS interpretation), so the result is unclear.

M.S.D., Incorporated, 1979-2 U.S.T.C. para. 9712 (6th Cir. 1979), affg. 434 F.Supp. 113 (N.D. Ohio 1977) points out that even if salary is reasonable, the corporation's deduction may be disallowed as not being an "ordinary and necessary" expense within the meaning of Sec. 162(a). In the *M.S.D.* case two brothers (together with their respective families) each owned 50 percent of three corporations in the burglar alarm business. Under the leadership of one of the brothers, the business was built up substantially and generated exceptionally high sales and profits. During the 19-year period of business growth, the decedent-brother received only a modest ($20,000 to $30,000 per year) salary and still less in dividends. The court found that his services were clearly worth in excess of $70,000 per year, and thus no issue of reasonable compensation arose. The corporations contracted with each of the brothers to make payments to their wives after their deaths. Payment of almost $20,000 was made to the widow of a deceased brother and the corporation deducted those payments and listed them as deferred compensation. The court examined the testimony of the surviving brother concerning the reason that the corporation entered into the contract and decided that the motivation was to provide financial security for the brothers' wives and that no concern was given to obtaining a business benefit for the corporations. The M.S.D. case indicates that the business reasons for establishing a nonqualified deferred-compensation arrangement (or death-benefit-only plan) should be in writing with the appropriate corporate formalities. The agreement should be as close as possible to that which would be provided for a non-shareholder-executive whom the corporation wanted to tie into the business.

QUALIFIED RETIREMENT PLANS VERSUS UNFUNDED NONQUALIFIED DEFERRED-COMPENSATION PLANS

Comparing Nonqualified and Qualified Plans

A nonqualified deferred-compensation plan is not really an "alternative" to a qualified plan in a practical sense. The two types of plans have different uses. Nonqualified deferred-compensation plans are appropriate only for selected executives, while qualified plans cover a broad group of employees and can't discriminate in favor of highly compensated employees. Nevertheless, it is helpful to compare nonqualified plans with qualified plans to illustrate their various features.

With regard to executives, sound planning generally dictates that if the employer has a qualified plan, it should be designed to provide the best benefit possible to executives within the qualified plan rules and limitations. This planning is in order to obtain as much as possible of the qualified plan's favorable tax aspects for executives. Nonqualified plans should be used to provide additional, supplemental deferred compensation for the executives.

Advantages of a Qualified Plan

First, we'll discuss the advantages of a qualified plan to both employer and employee and how they compare with the advantages of a nonqualified deferred-compensation plan. If a retirement plan is "qualified," an employer will obtain an immediate income tax deduction for its contribution. An employer's contribution is considered an ordinary and necessary business expense.

Second, contributions made by the employer for an employee's benefit will not be taxable to the employee until benefits are actually distributed to him or her.

A third advantage of a qualified retirement plan is that earnings on the assets of the plan are typically tax exempt. In other words, unless they are considered "unrelated business income," or unless the trustee engages in certain prohibited transactions, neither the employer nor the employee is taxed on the buildup of the money or other assets set aside to meet the employer's obligation under the plan. Tax-free buildup of money is a considerable advantage.

Finally, a lump-sum distribution (in some very limited cases) is taxed under favorable 10-year income-averaging rules.

Advantages of a Nonqualified Plan

The advantages of a qualified plan can be measured against the advantages of a nonqualified deferred-compensation plan.

In a nonqualified plan, until payouts are made the employer receives no income tax deduction since nothing is set apart for the employee beyond the corporation's reach. Although accounting "reserves" may be set up, for all intents and purposes the underlying assets still belong to, and are usable by, the employer for an emergency, opportunity, or even as working capital if necessary. (In a rabbi trust, access to the assets is generally restricted to *creditors* of the corporation.) However, at the payout of the funds, the employer does receive a tax deduction for the entire amount paid out to the employee. This amount, of course, will probably have increased significantly over the amount originally invested.

From an employer's viewpoint, either a deferred-compensation or salary continuation plan serves as a tool for attracting as well as retaining key employees. It can also be used as a flexible incentive for rewarding exceptional performance.

Unlike a qualified retirement plan, a nonqualified plan allows an employer to pick and choose who will be covered, what promises will be made, and what levels of benefits will be paid. This gives the employer significant flexibility to tailor the plan to its specific needs and desires and work within a given and highly controllable budget.

Because of ERISA's vesting requirements, it is impossible to establish a strong penalty for premature voluntary termination of employment under a qualified retirement plan. This is not the case with a nonqualified plan. Such a plan is a good device for retaining key executives since it can provide that if an employee prematurely terminates employment, all or most of the benefits the employee might have received will be forfeited.

A nonqualified plan can serve as a valuable incentive offered by an employer who is not in a position to pay current compensation to a key employee, but would like to obtain that employee's services by promising to make up the present low level of income with future payments.

There are some situations in which the employer needs and desires the employee's post-employment consulting services or wants that employee to refrain from competition after employment. Where a promise to render consulting services or not to compete is important and meaningful, a provision in the contract that threatens the loss of deferred income benefits in the event such a promise is breached will motivate the employee to meet specified obligations. In the event of a breach, the employer can penalize the employee (and is compensated for any loss caused by the employee's breach) in addition to the exercise of other legal remedies.

A nonqualified deferred-compensation arrangement serves as a forced savings plan for an executive or other employee and obviously supplements other retirement income. To the extent the employee benefits from tax leverage and a low tax buildup at corporate rates, the employee is better off than may have been the case had a tax been paid and the money invested independently by the employee. In some situations an employee who forgoes the present enjoyment of compensation may receive a greater amount on a deferred basis than could have been received if paid currently.

It is instructive to compare the *disadvantages* of qualified plans and nonqualified plans.

Disadvantages of Qualified Plans

The major disadvantages of a qualified plan arise out of the complex qualification requirements. Basically, these requirements are the following:

1. The plan must be for the exclusive benefit of employees or other beneficiaries.
2. There must be a funded trust, insurance contract, or other legally binding fiduciary-type arrangement. The plan must be in writing and must be communicated to the employees.
3. Contributions made by the employer to the plan and any income earned on those contributions cannot be used by or for the benefit of the employer or recovered by the employer until or unless the plan is terminated and all liabilities to employees and their beneficiaries have been satisfied. Even then, reversions of funds to the employer are subject to a penalty tax of up to 50 percent.
4. The plan must be "permanent" and must be operated and maintained by the employer in good faith.
5. The plan cannot discriminate (in terms of contributions or benefits) in favor of highly compensated employees.

6. Although death benefits may be included in a qualified plan, they must be "incidental" and are therefore limited.

7. Stringent vesting rules must be met.

8. Qualified defined-benefit plans can't provide an annual retirement benefit of more than the lesser of 100 percent of high 3-year average compensation or $195,000 per year, as indexed for inflation (2010). Qualified defined-contribution plans must limit annual employer contributions to the lesser of 100 percent of compensation or $49,000 (2010 as indexed).

9. Only the first $245,000 as indexed (2010: $245,000) of each employee's compensation can be taken into account in the plan's benefit or contribution formula.

10. Some plans (typically smaller plans) must provide minimum "top-heavy" benefits for all participants.

These requirements (and others) make a qualified plan both inflexible and costly. Since every qualified plan must establish standards for eligibility, many employees will have to be included in the plan. (Compare this with a nonqualified plan in which an employer can choose who will benefit as long as the plan is limited to a select group of management or highly compensated employees—the very individuals the employer will probably want to benefit most.)

1. While a qualified plan cannot discriminate in favor of highly compensated employees, a nonqualified plan is typically limited to this category only. The employer can discriminate entirely in favor of key employees or executive personnel and in fact generally must cover only the top-hat group to avoid unfavorable ERISA treatment.

2. IRS approval technically is not required for either a qualified or nonqualified plan, but almost all tax practitioners consider an advance determination letter from the IRS as a near-necessity for a qualified plan. Qualification can be costly, time consuming, and uncertain. In comparison, a nonqualified plan needs no advance approval.

3. An employer will be subject to substantial retroactive tax penalties if a qualified plan or contributions to it are discontinued without a sufficient business reason. On the other hand, an employer can terminate, suspend, curtail, or omit contributions to a nonqualified plan at any time without adverse tax consequences.

4. An employer must include all eligible employees in a qualified plan as soon as certain minimum requirements are met. Increasing the number of employees who remain with the employer eventually

must increase the employer's cost. Furthermore, increasing labor costs will usually automatically increase the qualified plan cost. Conversely, the employer has complete control over the cost of a nonqualified plan and can suspend, curtail, or limit benefits at any time, as long as it has reserved the right to do so.

5. A qualified plan benefit formula is quite stringent and must be applied in the same manner to all employees who are similarly situated. Conversely, a nonqualified plan allows an employer to meet the individual needs of specific employees or recognize their differences or merits. Different benefit levels can be based on an employer's perception of merit, loyalty, need, and other factors. Different groups of key employees can be covered under different benefit formulas or different benefit plans.

Disadvantages of Nonqualified Plans

There are disadvantages to nonqualified deferred-compensation plans. Employees must wait to receive their compensation. Therefore, those who are in a position of power will doubtless bargain for greater employer promises to compensate for the length of time they must wait.

Typically, there will be no problem with an accumulated-earnings tax since the employer would not set aside such amounts without an obligation to make payments. At least one case held that the accumulation to satisfy an employer's obligation for deferred compensation is a reasonable business need. (It may be more difficult to justify a corporation's need for a large amount of funds to provide salary continuation to a controlling shareholder.)

Publicly held corporations could possibly have a different problem. A salary continuation type of plan will reduce the amount of money available as dividends to stockholders. (Obviously, this should be balanced against the increase in profits because of the retention and productivity of the covered key employee.)

The deferral aspect of a nonqualified deferred-compensation plan presents another potential problem. By definition such plans delay the reward for high performance. At the same time most plans condition payment of the continued salary on continued service. This may weaken the incentive of a competent employee and create a conservative "play it safe" attitude on the part of employees. The result could be unimaginative riskless decisions.

One additional disadvantage to the employer is the deferral of the tax deduction. A qualified retirement plan allows an immediate deduction.

This leads to certainty of tax implication. In other words, the employer can estimate the value of the deduction in the current year. However, a nonqualified deferred-compensation or salary continuation plan that will not generate a deduction for many years in the future creates tax uncertainty. The employer really can't be sure of what tax bracket it will be in, and the deduction could possibly come in a tax year in which it could be wasted.

From the employee's viewpoint there are disadvantages; the greatest is the loss of the present use and availability of money. The younger executives who have high immediate cash needs will be particularly conscious of this problem. Second, deferred income equates to the loss of earning ability during the employee's working years. An employee who forgoes a current salary increase of $5,000 could have taken the after-tax income and invested it for capital appreciation. Certainly, this factor should be a consideration in deciding whether or not income should be deferred or taken currently. It also should be considered in deciding whether to structure the plan as a defined-benefit or defined-contribution arrangement.

Perhaps the greatest disadvantage of nonqualified deferred-compensation plans is that they typically do not provide security for the employee. This means a great deal of the employee's retirement security (as well as the security of the family in the event of his or her death) must depend solely on the employer's financial ability and willingness to make the promised payments. Obviously, this problem diminishes in importance in direct proportion to the financial soundness of the company. A large publicly held corporation with a long history of business success can usually be considered financially stable (but remember Penn Central, Pan Am, etc.). Obviously, the employee's retirement security is considerably less assured in a closely held corporation.

An important factor that is often overlooked is the relationship between the qualified retirement plan in which the employee participates and the nonqualified deferred-compensation plan. To the extent compensation is deferred under a nonqualified plan, it generally cannot be considered as compensation for purposes of determining contributions or benefits under the qualified plan. If the same money was taken currently as salary, it would enhance the employee's retirement because of the formula for allocating contributions under the qualified plan.

A final disadvantage relates to the balance-sheet "visibility" of nonqualified plans. As discussed in a later chapter of this text, since such plans are unfunded, the benefit accruals increase from year to year, creating a growing company liability.

EFFECT OF DEFERRED COMPENSATION ON OTHER FRINGE BENEFITS

Under qualified corporate retirement plans, compensation of an employee for benefit or contribution purposes generally refers only to cash compensation actually paid or accrued (IRC Sec. 415(c)(3)). Deferred compensation cannot generally be included in the compensation base for a qualified plan unless it can be shown that discrimination in favor of highly compensated employees will not result. Code Secs. 414(s) and 401(a)(4).

Discrimination will occur if the proportion of compensation deferred by rank-and-file employees is less than the proportion deferred by highly compensated employees (Rev. Rul. 80-359). Therefore if a qualified plan's benefits were based on a "final 3-year" average compensation, consideration should be given to terminating contributions to the deferred-compensation plan 3 years before retirement.

A special rule applies to employees who participate in a tax-deferred annuity under Code Sec. 403(b) and under their employer's qualified plan. In Rev. Rul. 69-296 the IRS ruled that in the definition of compensation a qualified plan of an exempt employer could include amounts paid by the employer toward the purchase of nonforfeitable annuities under IRC Sec. 403(b). Similarly, the definition of compensation under the Code Sec. 415 regulations allows salary reductions in a Sec. 401(k) plan to be taken into account in defining compensation for purposes of the employer's other qualified retirement plans.

The definition of "compensation" under fringe benefit plans, such as group insurance and group long-term disability, currently depends largely on the underwriting practices of the insurer.

DEFERRED INCENTIVE COMPENSATION PLANS

Quite often an employer will want to use a salary continuation plan as a means of rewarding creative and productive employees. An incentive element can be integrated into either a fixed-benefit or a money-purchase formula. Obviously, however, it is easier to build an incentive into a money-purchase formula plan.

The easiest way to provide incentive through a salary continuation plan is to have a money-purchase formula credit to the employee's account an amount equal to a percentage of current salary. Then, as the employee receives increases in salary (which presumably reflect specified levels of performance), the credits to his account automatically increase. How can a fixed-benefit formula provide an incentive? A fixed-benefit formula, by defining the promised benefit as a percentage of the salary earned by an employee immediately (or perhaps in the 3 to 5 years) prior to retirement, will reward an employee's performance, again assuming that salary reflects performance.

What if compensation paid to an employee fluctuates in amount from year to year? For example, salespeople who are paid on commissions may receive widely varying amounts of compensation. A money-purchase formula can credit to the employee's account an amount equal to a percentage of the compensation earned on a year-by-year basis. Assuming current compensation reflects performance, deferred benefits are completely contingent upon that performance. It is possible to accomplish these same objectives through a defined-benefit formula by defining the benefit as a percentage of the average commissions earned during the salesperson's working years. The drawback to this approach is that the performance in the current year may not be reflected accurately since it is merged with performance of all other years. Perhaps a weighting approach may help solve this problem.

Some employees are responsible for corporate results that can be quantified. The benefits that a salary continuation plan provides can be designed to reflect specified goals. For instance, a money-purchase plan might provide that a salaried sales manager will be credited with a percentage of net sales. Likewise, a defined-benefit formula might define the manager's benefit as a percentage of all sales made during the manager's entire working career. Obviously this averaging does not properly weigh superior current performance, and psychologically a money-purchase approach might be more appealing.

How can an incentive formula be provided if it is impossible to measure the results of a given employee? One solution might be to establish a money-purchase plan that provides that an employee's account will be credited with a certain percentage of the corporation's current profits. In essence, this is a nonqualified profit-sharing plan. The advantage of this arrangement is that such a plan would not have to conform to the limitations and restrictions imposed on qualified profit-sharing plans.

One technique that is particularly applicable to publicly traded corporations and links the amount of the deferred benefits to the success of the employer is the use of a money-purchase plan. It assumes that all credits to the account of the employee are invested in the employer's stock. This is a form of phantom-stock arrangement.

Past-service credits can be provided to tie key long-service employees to the corporation. Either a money-purchase or defined-benefit formula can be used. Amounts determined either partially or fully by reference to the years the employee has served in the past are credited to the employee's account. Likewise, the defined benefit provided to an employee can be determined, in whole or in part, by referring to the number of years of prior service.

PROVISIONS FOR VOLUNTARY AND INVOLUNTARY EARLY TERMINATION

What happens to the benefits earned by an employee if he or she terminates employment prior to the normal retirement date specified in the deferred-compensation plan? The answer to this question depends on what the plan provides, and that in turn is determined by two elements: (a) the dominant motives of the parties to the plan, and (b) which of the two parties, the employer or the employee, is in a stronger bargaining position.

A salary continuation plan formula should include a method to determine the benefit, if any, that will be paid to an employee in the event of early termination. With a salary-reduction arrangement, the value of the early termination benefit will almost always equal at least the amount of salary the employee elected to defer prior to termination. In some cases the amounts payable will exceed the aggregate amount of salary reductions because the formula will provide for some credit for earnings on the account.

It is relatively simple to determine how much an early retirement benefit will be if the plan formula is the money-purchase type. The simplest approach is to base the benefit on the value of the employee's account as of the date of termination. If the employee is in control or in a position of power, the early termination benefit will typically be equal to whatever is in the account at that time. But if the employer was the dominant or controlling party in the creation of the plan, something less than the full value of the account may be paid to the employee in the event of early termination.

It is possible to reflect the actual number of years an employee has served prior to termination by graduating the percentage of the employee's account that is vested (nonforfeitable). For example, if an employee worked for 3 to 5 years, there would be no vesting; from 6 to 8 years, 10 percent vesting; from 9 to 11 years, 25 percent vesting; from 12 to 14 years, 50 percent vesting; from 15 to 17 years, 90 percent vesting; and 18 or more years, 100 percent vesting.

A typical revision would specify that the vesting schedule would apply if the employee terminated employment for any reason other than death or disability prior to the normal retirement date.

How is early termination reflected in a fixed-benefit formula plan? There are several ways to solve this problem. An early termination benefit can be stated as a percentage of the normal retirement benefit (for example, a person leaving within 2 years of retirement will receive 95 percent of the normal retirement benefit) or the agreement can provide a table of defined early retirement benefits. Usually these benefits will reflect the projected value of reserves the employer intends to set aside (such as a life insurance policy, mutual fund, or annuity contract) and the years of service rendered by the employee.

There is a distinction between the vesting described above and the type of vesting found in qualified plans. In a qualified plan, the employee has a legal interest that constitutes a preferred claim against a bundle of segregated assets such as the value of a life insurance policy on the employee's life or other assets held in trust for his or her benefit. But in a nonqualified plan, unless the plan is formally "funded" (which few are), "vesting" gives the employee only a general claim against the employer's total assets. The employee does not have the right to look to a specific asset for payment. And, if the plan meets the top-hat plan exemption from ERISA, the strict ERISA vesting requirements (5-year cliff or 3- to 7-year graded vesting rule applicable to defined benefit plans and the 3-year cliff or 2- to 6-year graded vesting rule applicable to individual account plans) do not apply. So the plan can have a relatively long vesting schedule or none at all.

The cause of early termination may affect the amount of benefits payable. Death, disability, and forfeiture for cause are all forms of early termination that should be considered in the drafting of a deferred-compensation plan. When a premature termination is due to death or disability, benefits are usually quite generous. Conversely, when an employee has been terminated involuntarily because of malfeasance or fraud, or leaves to work for a competitor, plans often provide that no benefits are available.

Another technique used more often in salary continuation than salary reduction plans is to suspend the payment of an early termination benefit until the normal retirement or prior death or disability of an employee. The plan must specify whether or not the value of the benefit will be increased with interest or increased or decreased to reflect investment gains or losses during the period that begins at the date of termination and ends when the benefit actually becomes payable. As in all the other provisions in a deferred-compensation plan, the liberality will depend on the employer's objectives as well as the relative bargaining powers of the parties involved.

Disability presents a number of unique problems. First, has "disability" occurred? To answer this question the plan must provide for a definition of disability. That definition inevitably leads to disputes that in turn may lead to arbitration or litigation. One solution to this problem is to shift the decision to a third party—an insurer. The plan could provide that disability exists when the insurer (under the terms of a disability policy that the corporation owns on the employee's life but not made technically a part of the plan itself) becomes obligated to pay the disability benefits specified in the policy. By referring to the disability policy as a measurement of obligation rather than as a funding vehicle, the potential for disputes diminishes significantly. It is important, however, that the plan does not obligate the employer to buy and retain disability insurance as part of the plan. Otherwise, the IRS will make a claim that the employee has received a current economic benefit in the amount that the employer was paying as premiums for the disability policy.

What happens if the disability coverage accidentally lapses or expires by its terms before the employee retires or terminates employment for some other reason? The plan can provide that in such a case the definition of disability would be the same as it was defined under the (outside) insurance policy. Although this provides a definition for disability, it does not eliminate the potential for disagreements once the policy actually is no longer in effect.

If an employee becomes disabled soon after a plan is adopted, where will the employer obtain the funds to pay a significant disability benefit (absent disability insurance coverage on the employee)? Obviously there is no tool or technique that will automatically provide sufficient cash if an employee is disabled except for some form of disability coverage owned by and payable to the employer but held and kept separate from the plan itself. How is the size of the disability benefit payable to the employee determined? One approach is to pay the employee a benefit based on the size of the assets credited at the time of the disability. The shortcoming of this approach is that the termination benefit will be small.

A second possibility for determining the size of disability benefits is for the employer to purchase disability income coverage on the life of the employee. The plan could provide that the employee be paid a given amount that is somewhat below that payable to the corporation in the event of the employee's disability.

A third approach utilizes a waiver of premium incorporated into a life insurance policy on the employee's life. Many employers will purchase life insurance on the life of a key employee to meet the obligation under either a nonqualified deferred-compensation or salary continuation plan. If the waiver-of-premium rider on the life insurance policy is used to determine the size of disability benefits, the plan provides that the employer will pay a benefit equal to the amount of premiums that are waived from a life insurance policy. (With tax leverage the payout could be twice as much as the waived premium assuming the corporation was in a 50 percent tax bracket.) For example, an employer relieved of the obligation to pay $10,000 in life insurance premiums now has $10,000 available to pay disability benefits. An employer in a 50 percent tax bracket could pay out $20,000 as salary to the disabled employee and the after-deduction cost would be $10,000. The cash value of the insurance policy continues to grow in value in the employer's hands.

CHAPTER REVIEW

Review Questions

1. Arthur Helix, aged 55, is an executive in the 35 percent marginal tax bracket. His reader and adviser has consulted her crystal ball and warned him that his marginal tax rate will reach 40 percent when Arthur retires. Assuming Arthur retires at age 65, what before-tax return on deferred-compensation amounts is required in order to make deferred compensation pay under these circumstances? [1]

2. Robert Rich, an $80,000 per year executive with Rotex, Inc., is in the process of negotiating his employment contract for next year. Instead of a salary increase, he is considering requesting $10,000 per year in deferred compensation that would be paid to him at retirement. In terms of (a) the security of his benefits and (b) the method by which the size of his benefits would be determined, what factors should Rich consider before adopting such a plan? [2]

3. Vic Valu is a key employee of Vertex, Inc. Vertex would like to tie Valu closer to the firm and is considering a plan whereby Valu's salary will be continued after he retires at age 65. What plan provisions relating to (a) Valu's security of benefits and (b) the method of determining the amount of his benefits would you recommend? [2]

4. What plan provisions would you recommend to Vertex (in question 2 above) concerning (a) the events that would prompt the payment of benefits to Valu and (b) the events that would cause the forfeiture of benefits by Valu? [2]

5. When does a service provider have a "legally binding" right to deferred compensation? [3]

6. What are the events upon which deferred-compensation may be paid without violating the provisions of Sec. 409A? [3]

7. What are the tax consequences of a deferred-compensation arrangement that does not comply with Sec. 409A? [3]

8. When is a vesting provision appropriate and what restrictions apply? [4]

9. Why is a financing formula important to an employee? [4]

10. Can nonemployee income be deferred in a nonqualified deferred-compensation plan? [4]

11. Sidney Sayles closed a large case on December 10 of last year that earned him a $25,000 commission. On December 31, because he had already earned a substantial amount during that year, Sayles asked his employer to defer payment to him of his $25,000 commission. They agreed that the commission would be paid to Sayles over the next 5 years in 5 equal installments of $5,000 each. Prior to any actual payment to Sayles, the commission dollars will remain the unencumbered asset of the employer. Explain the effect of Sec. 409A on the tax treatment of the $25,000 commission. [5]

12. To lure Ken Key to come with the firm, Kopex, Inc., has agreed to a contract that provides Key with a current salary of $75,000 per year for 3 years. In addition, 10 annual payments of $10,000 each will be paid to Key upon his termination of employment with Kopex for whatever reason. Kopex would have agreed to pay Key an annual salary of $85,000 instead of a deferred arrangement, but Key preferred to have a portion of his compensation deferred. In order to meet its future obligation, Kopex intends to purchase mutual funds that it will hold as a general asset of the corporation but which will be earmarked to meet future payments to Key. Will the constructive-receipt doctrine make the deferred payments currently taxable to Key? Explain. [5]

13. In order to provide an additional incentive to stay with the firm, Tritex Corp., has given Larry Lock, a key employee, a bonus payable 4 years from now. The bonus will be equal to one percent of the firm's net pre-tax profits measured by the firm's annual earnings 3 years from now.

     To be eligible to receive this bonus, Lock must work with the firm until December 31 of the year preceding the year in which the bonus is to be paid. If Lock terminates employment prior to that December 31, he may still be entitled to the bonus if he has both refrained from employment with a competing business and made himself available for the rendering of consulting services to the firm up through that December 31.

     Furthermore, Lock may elect on or before December 15 of the year prior to the year in which the bonus is to be paid to further defer receipt of the bonus until his retirement. However, if he elects the further deferral, then he must either continue in the service of the firm until December 31 of the year prior to the year in which a payment will be made, or, if he terminates prior to that time, he must refrain from employment with a competing business and make himself available for consulting services to the firm up to December 31 of the year preceding the year in which a payment will be made. If he does not meet either of these requirements, he will forfeit his right to the bonus. [5]

     a. If Lock does not elect to postpone receipt of the bonus until retirement, when will he have to include the bonus as taxable income? Explain.

     b. If Lock makes a timely election to defer receipt of the bonus until after retirement, when will he be taxed on the bonus?

     c. If there were no forfeiture provisions in the plan, when would Lock be taxed if

         i. he did not elect to defer receipt of the bonus until retirement age

         ii. he elected to defer receipt of the bonus until retirement age

14. What are the two requirements for avoiding the ERISA vesting, funding, and fiduciary provisions in a nonqualified deferred-compensation plan? [6]

15. Explain why a nonqualified plan may not be suitable for a relatively large group of employees, including many rank-and-file employees. [6]

16. Compare the inclusion of nonqualified plan benefits in the Social Security and Medicare tax base with their treatment for income tax purposes. [7]

17. Saul Sickle, an employee of Sintex, Inc., entered into a deferred-compensation agreement with his corporation under which he will receive $10,000 per year for 10 years following retirement. If he dies prior to retirement or after retirement but before 10 annual payments have been made, the balance of the payments due him will be paid to his named beneficiary. Assuming Sickle dies before retirement, what will be the income and estate tax treatment of the benefits paid to his beneficiary? [8]

18. All the stock of Seetex Corporation is owned equally by three individuals who are all key employees of the company. They would all like to go into semi-retirement at about age 55 and want to maintain their take-home pay thereafter at about the same level as just prior to reaching age 55.

    One alternative they are considering is to merely continue salaries at the pre-retirement level after semi-retirement.

    The other alternative they are considering is to enter into a deferred-compensation plan now that would provide a stockholder-employee with an income of approximately one-half salary after semi-retirement. In addition, under an employment agreement, the stockholder-employee would continue to receive an amount equal to one-half salary (as measured just prior to semi-retirement) in the form of salary.

    Evaluate these two alternatives with regard to the probable income tax treatment of the stockholder-employee and the corporation. [9]

19. The three stockholder-employees of Seetex Corporation have decided to enter into the following agreement: For services rendered in the past and to be rendered in the future, after a stockholder reaches age 55, the corporation will pay to the stockholder for life (or in the event of death, to the surviving spouse for 5 years following death), an annual sum equal to one-half of salary received at age 55. Such annual sum to be increased or decreased by one-half the average of any increase or decrease in the salaries of the other full-time stockholder-employees. What will be the likely income tax treatment under this arrangement for (a) the corporation, (b) a stockholder-employee, and (c) the surviving spouse? Why? [9]

20. Kent D. Sidde, president of Kentex, Inc., must decide on whether the corporation should adopt a qualified retirement plan or a nonqualified deferred-compensation plan. Help him make a decision by comparing the two with regard to each of the following: [10]

a. the timing of the corporation's income tax deduction

b. the ability to discriminate as to who will be covered

c. the extent to which benefits may be forfeitable

d. the income tax treatment of earnings on any amounts set aside to fund the plan

e. coverage for independent contractors

f. the balance-sheet impact

21. The Acme Corporation is planning to establish a qualified pension plan as well as group-term life insurance and group long-term disability plans for its full-time salaried employees. Several executives of the corporation receive discretionary annual bonuses in addition to their base compensation. These executives are also covered under an unfunded nonqualified deferred-compensation plan that provides definite retirement benefits.

What elements of compensation may or may not be included in defining "compensation" for purposes of the following fringe benefit plans? [11]

a. qualified pension plan

b. group term life plan

c. long-term disability plan

22. The Productivity Corporation is looking for an employee benefit plan that is likely to increase the performance of covered employees. Among the employees that would receive benefits from the corporation are [12]

a. Sonny Smooth, a commissioned salesperson

b. Marc Moore, salaried sales vice president

c. Spencer Lester, controller, who has been instructed by the board of directors to try to improve the company's profit picture by reducing its costs

Suggest a nonqualified deferred-compensation plan for each of these employees that will act as an incentive to improve work performance.

23. Publico, Inc., whose stock is traded on the over-the-counter market, would like to provide a deferred incentive compensation plan for its management employees that would give them an interest in the value of the company's stock. However, the corporation does not want to issue any additional shares because it does not want to dilute the value of each share of stock already outstanding. What type of plan would you recommend? Explain how such a plan works. [12]

24. How is the benefit from a nonqualified deferred-compensation plan typically determined where an employee terminates employment before retirement? [13]

25. How should a nonqualified deferred-compensation plan provide for benefits in the event of the participant's disability? [13]

Answers to Review Questions

1. From Table 2-1 (page 2.5) it appears that any before-tax return better than about 3 percent will prove advantageous on a 10-year deferral even in view of an increase in tax rate from 35 percent to 40 percent. This table illustrates the planning significance of tax deferral. [1]

2. When employees are considering a salary reduction plan—the deferral of an amount that they probably could negotiate to receive currently—they should be relatively certain that the cash that they are giving up currently will, in fact, be paid to them in the future. Consequently, the financial stability of the corporation is an important factor to employees. They will want the right to benefits to be nonforfeitable under all conditions including voluntary early termination. Furthermore, they will want to receive credit in some fashion for the earnings attributable to the accumulated salary reductions. No actual assets need to be set aside by the employer—the account can be only a book account. [2]

3. When the employer institutes a plan of salary continuation in order to tie an employee closer to the firm, the expense incurred by the employer is in addition to any amounts it is willing to pay the employee currently. To accomplish the employer's goals, plan provisions related to the security of benefits and the determination of benefits should be weighted in favor of the employer. Therefore, the employee's right to benefits often will be forfeitable upon the occurrence of certain events, particularly termination prior to normal retirement age.

   In order to provide some immediate incentive to the employee, the plan may utilize a vesting schedule whereby an increasing percentage of the employee's right to benefits will become nonforfeitable with the passage of time. Benefits are based on a formula similar to formulas used in qualified defined-contribution plans. [2]

4. When a salary continuation plan is to be established to encourage an employee to stay with the firm, benefits will generally be payable when the employee reaches retirement age or upon death prior to retirement. Depending upon the other fringe benefits offered by the employer, it may also be appropriate to provide for the payment of this benefit if the employee becomes permanently disabled prior to retirement. Before retirement, the employee may forfeit benefits if services are voluntarily terminated or if the employee is discharged for cause. After retirement, the employee may lose all or a portion of the benefits by refusing to provide reasonable consultation services to the employer or by entering into competition with the employer. [2]

5. A threshold requirement for deferred compensation to be subject to Sec. 409A is that the service provider have a "legally binding" right to such compensation. A legally binding right to compensation exists if a service provider is entitled to such compensation under contract, statute, or any other enforceable law, even if contingencies must occur in order for the compensation to actually become payable. Therefore, rights to future payments are considered legally binding rights at the time the contract or agreement providing those rights first becomes effective despite any future contingencies. However, if the contingencies constitute a substantial risk of forfeiture, they will cause the deferred compensation not to be subject to Sec. 409A until they lapse. [3]

6. There are six events upon which deferred compensation may be paid without violating Sec. 409A. They include separation from service, death, disability, certain change of control transactions, an unforeseeable emergency, and a specified date or event that is identified in advance. [3]

7. Sec. 409A generally provides that unless certain requirements are satisfied, amounts deferred under a nonqualified deferred-compensation plan for all taxable years are currently includible in gross income to the extent not subject to a substantial risk of forfeiture (and not previously included in gross income). Thus, a failure to satisfy the requirements of Sec. 409A triggers income recognition in the year in which the service provider vests in the arrangement (and in each year thereafter until the deferred compensation is fully distributed) even if he or she has not received

or directly benefited from the deferred compensation. In addition, a 20 percent penalty is imposed on the amount required to be included in income in each year. Finally, if the arrangement initially satisfied the requirements of Sec. 409A, but subsequently failed them, or if the arrangement initially failed to comply with the requirements under Sec. 409A, but such noncompliance was not discovered until a subsequent tax year, after vesting occurred, the service provider must pay an interest charge, that is, the IRS underpayment rate plus one percentage point, from the time of the initial vesting of the deferred compensation. The interest charge is applicable to the hypothetical underpayment of tax arising from the failure to include the deferred compensation in income when initially vested. [3]

8. Vesting provisions are generally in the interest of the employer rather than the employee. These provisions provide a "handcuff" that tends to keep the employee in service, at least until the vesting period has elapsed. If the plan is unfunded and covers a top-hat group, the ERISA vesting provisions do not apply, so vesting can be delayed beyond the ERISA maximums of 5-year cliff or 3- to 7-year graded vesting applicable to defined benefit plans and of 3-year cliff or 2- to 6-year graded vesting applicable to individual account plans. Almost any kind of vesting provision is permissible. [4]

9. Financing—the development of some kind of asset pool to pay the ultimate benefits—is important to the employee in order to secure the payment of benefits. Financing the plan and providing security are discussed in detail in the next chapter. [4]

10. Any kind of compensation income can be the subject of a deferred-compensation plan, such as director's fees or payments to independent contractors. The income must be an unfunded, deferred payment for services rendered in order to be deferrable under the simple constructive-receipt rules. [4]

11. The entire $25,000 would be taxed in the year it was earned. Under Sec. 409A an election to defer income must be made by the end of the year preceding the year in which the services are performed that give rise to the income. [5]

12. They are probably not currently taxable. An employee in a high income tax bracket may seek to defer a portion of income that is not yet earned to a later period of time when the employee will probably be in a lower tax bracket. As long as the deferral agreement is entered into in the year succeeding the year the income to be deferred is earned and otherwise satisfies the requirements of Sec. 409A, taxation should be deferred until the income is actually

received. The employer can establish an asset reserve to finance its future obligation by purchasing life insurance, mutual funds, or other property, provided whatever asset is used remains the unencumbered property of the employer, subject to its general creditors. These same rules apply to an arrangement between independent contractors as well as to an arrangement between employer and employee. [5]

13. [5]

    a. The bonus arrangement satisfies the requirements of Sec. 409A since it is payable on a fixed date. Accordingly, the bonus will be taxed in the year in which it is actually received.

    b. Since the redeferral election will satisfy the requirements of Sec. 409A, assuming that the date of his retirement will be more than 5 years after the originally scheduled date of payment, the bonus will be taxed in the year in which the it is actually received.

    c. (i) The removal of the forfeiture provision does not change the result in answer a., above.

    (ii) The removal of the forfeiture provision does not change the result in answer b., above.

14. In order to avoid the ERISA vesting, funding, and fiduciary provisions a nonqualified deferred compensation plan must (a) be unfunded and (b) primarily cover a select group of management or highly compensated employees (the top-hat group). [6]

15. The exact composition of the top-hat group is not entirely clear from published rulings and cases. However, it is clear that a plan covering a group that consists of a relatively large percentage of the employees—that is, more than 20 pecent—and that includes rank-and-file employees will not meet the requirements for the top-hat exclusion from ERISA. [6]

16. Income tax inclusion for the typical nonqualified deferred-compensation plan (unfunded top-hat plan) generally follows the requirements of Sec. 409A and, therefore, tax is generally not due until benefits are actually or constructively received by the employee. By contrast, deferred compensation is includible in the Social Security (FICA) taxable wage base, including Medicare, when the amounts are substantially vested. This could result in a different year of inclusion for purposes of these two taxes. A "nonduplication rule" allows earnings in

deferred-compensation accounts to avoid additional Social Security or Medicare tax treatment once the account balance has initially been subject to tax. [7]

17. *Income tax treatment.* Both deferred-compensation and salary continuation benefits will be taxed as ordinary income to the beneficiary when received. However, if the inclusion of the deferred-compensation death benefit generated a federal estate tax, the beneficiary would be entitled to an income tax deduction equal in amount to the federal estate tax paid by the estate multiplied by a fraction whose numerator is the present value of the death benefits in the employee's taxable estate and whose denominator is the gross estate.

    Estate tax treatment. For federal estate tax purposes, when a deferred-compensation agreement provides for a death benefit in addition to lifetime postemployment benefits, the present value of the beneficiary's right to receive the death benefits will be includible in the decedent-employee's gross estate. (Under a pure salary continuation agreement where no nonqualified postemployment plan benefits are payable during his or her lifetime to the employee, but a death benefit is payable to a named beneficiary, the value of such death benefit may escape inclusion in the employee's gross estate if the right to change the beneficiary was not retained. The estate tax inclusion may not generate any tax if the recipient is the employee's surviving spouse and the payment is made in a manner that qualifies for the estate tax marital deduction. [8]

18. There are some special considerations that enter into a decision to install a nonqualified deferred-compensation (salary continuation) plan for the stockholder-employees of a closely held corporation.

    Since the stockholders control the corporation, they could easily agree to simply continue their high level salaries after semi-retirement even though actual duties are curtailed. However, the question of the reasonableness of compensation is monitored fairly closely by the IRS when a stockholder-employee is involved. The reasonableness of amounts paid as current salary are generally based primarily on the current services that are being performed. Where there has been a clear curtailment of services and no reduction in salary for a stockholder-employee, the IRS is likely to find a portion of the salary to be unreasonable and treat that portion as a constructive dividend. Any amount so classified would be taxed as ordinary income to the stockholder-employee with no deduction to the corporation.

The availability of a deduction to the corporation for the payment of deferred compensation is also dependent upon the payment qualifying as a reasonable business expense during the taxable year it is paid. However, when determining whether a deferred-compensation payment is reasonable in amount so as to qualify as an ordinary and necessary business expense, it is permissible to consider the personal services actually rendered by the employee in prior years as well as services rendered in the current year. Also considered will be all compensation paid to such employee in prior years as well as in the current year. Therefore, it is possible for a deduction to be allowed even though a deferred-compensation benefit, taken together with other compensation for the current year, is in excess of reasonable compensation for services performed in the current year. This may be the case when total compensation and contributions paid to or for the benefit of the employee represent reasonable compensation for all services rendered by the employee up to the end of the current year. [9]

19. There is a possibility that such payments will be treated as dividends taxable as ordinary income to the recipient with no deduction to the corporation . The determination of the reasonableness of deferred-compensation payments is particularly difficult when the amount of the payments varies according to events that are unrelated to the services rendered by the employee. Examples would be benefits that are geared in amount to the performance of a given mutual fund or benefits that vary depending on the changes in the salary levels of other specified employees. In these instances, the benefits may turn out to be substantial in comparison to the services rendered by the employee to the corporation. In such cases, if the amounts actually paid had been stated dollar amounts in the original agreement, a portion would be disallowed as unreasonable. That is, there would be no proof that any economic benefit accrued to the corporation from the payment of such excessive amounts.

When the employee is also a stockholder of the corporation with an active voice in management, the IRS tends to scrutinize compensation arrangements closely for reasonableness and, where there is any doubt, unreasonable amounts may be treated as dividends to the stockholder-employee or the beneficiary.

However, if it could be shown that the financial risk incurred by the corporation when it agreed to pay deferred-compensation benefits based on some outside indicator was reasonable in light of the services the employee performed, it could be argued that the benefits, regardless of their ultimate size, should be considered reasonable in amount and deductible by the corporation as an ordinary and necessary business expense. (There do not appear to be any court decisions on this latter point.) [9]

20. [10]

Comparison of Various Items of Qualified Retirement Plans with Unfunded Nonqualified Deferred-Compensation Plans		
Item	Qualified Retirement Plan	Unfunded Nonqualified Deferred- Compensation Plan
a. Timing of corporation's income tax deduction	Corporation receives a deduction when contributions are made to the plan.	Corporation receives a deduction when benefits are received by employees.
b. Who must be covered by plan	70 percent of nonhighly compensated employees, or alternative test under Code Sec. 410(b).	Corporation free to discriminate as it sees fit if plan covers only independent contractors or members of management or highly compensated employees.
c. Extent to which benefits may be forfeitable	Must meet 3-year or 2- to 6-year vesting test applicable to defined contribution plans or must meet 5-year or 3- to 7-year vesting test applicable to defined benefit plans; possible faster vesting for top-heavy plans.	The qualified plan vesting rules apply if plan covers rank-and-file employees. If plan covers only independent contractors or members of management or highly compensated employees, benefits may be forfeitable in full at all times.

Comparison of Various Items of Qualified Retirement Plans with Unfunded Nonqualified Deferred-Compensation Plans		
Item	Qualified Retirement Plan	Unfunded Nonqualified Deferred- Compensation Plan
d. Tax treatment of earnings on amount set aside to fund plan	These earnings accumulate tax free but will be taxable to employee along with other plan assets when distributed to employee; no income tax deduction for employer.	These earnings will be taxed currently to the employer and will be taxable to the employee when distributed as benefits; however, employer will be entitled to an income tax deduction at that time.
e. Coverage of independent contractors, directors, and so forth	Only employees are eligible for coverage.	Independent contractors and directors may be covered in the same manner as an employee.
f. Balance-sheet impact	Not adverse if plan avoids underfunding.	Can be adverse

21.

    a. For qualified retirement plan purposes, the definition of compensation as the basis for determining benefits or employer contributions typically includes total cash compensation. The IRS permits the inclusion of nonqualified deferred-compensation credits or benefits in the definition of compensation where discrimination in favor of officers, stockholders, supervisors, and highly compensated employees does not result. Therefore, a corporation wishing to include deferred compensation will have to prove to the IRS the absence of discrimination.

    b. & c. With respect to group life insurance and group long-term disability income plans, the underwriting practice of the insurer is the key point. Some insurers will not permit deferred-compensation amounts to be included in the compensation base for purposes of group life or disability benefits. In the latter case, the replacement of current cash income necessarily precludes the inclusion of deferred-compensation benefits. [11]

22. An employer will sometimes initiate a deferred-compensation plan as a means of increasing the performance of key employees. To accomplish this, the method used to determine the benefits under the plan should contain a factor that will cause the benefits to vary directly with the measurable results of the employee's performance. The following table illustrates how this can be accomplished through a defined-benefit formula or a money-purchase formula when an employee's performance is measurable in one of three different ways: [12]

Suggested Uses of Defined-Benefit Formulas and Money-Purchase Formulas For Different Methods of Measuring Performance

Method of Measuring Performance	Defined-Benefit Formula	Money-Purchase Formula
a. Personal sales of commissioned salespeople	Benefits based on a fixed percentage of average commissions earned during working years (40 percent of average annual commissions earned). Another approach would be to accrue a benefit each year equal to a specified percentage of commissions earned during that year. (Benefits accrue at the rate of 2 percent of commissions earned each year.)	Contributions credited to employee's account each year is equal to a specified percentage of his commissions for that year (an amount equal to 10 percent of commissions earned for the year credited to employee's account).
b. Salaried employee where performance measurable by total sales of company	The same approach as (a) above can be used but with benefits based on total sales. To keep benefits reasonable, the percentage used would be smaller.	The same approach as (a) above can be used but with benefits based on total sales. To keep benefits reasonable, the percentage used would be smaller.
c. Salaried employee whose performance is measurable by employer's	The same approach as (a) above except benefits based on a percentage of average profits per year over entire working career; or each year an	Employer can contribute to employee's account an amount equal to a specified percentage of the

**Suggested Uses of Defined-Benefit Formulas and Money-Purchase Formulas
For Different Methods of Measuring Performance**

Method of Measuring Performance	Defined-Benefit Formula	Money-Purchase Formula
current profits	annual benefit is accrued based on a percentage of profits for that year.	employer's profits for the year.

23. A phantom-stock plan would be effective here. A corporation whose stock is publicly traded will sometimes provide selected employees with an interest in the stock of the corporation rather than paying direct cash compensation as an incentive to improve future work performance. Under such a plan, if the value of a corporation's stock goes up, not only will the employees covered under the plan benefit, but all stockholders will benefit. These goals can be accomplished without actually giving the covered employees stock in the corporation through a phantom-stock plan or similar plan.

    A phantom-stock plan is essentially a type of benefit formula for a nonqualifed deferred-compensation plan. An account is established for each covered employee. Although no stock is actually placed into the account, it is credited each year with a certain number of shares of stock, that is, records are kept as though the stock was placed into the account. When benefits are due in the future, their amount is measured by the dollar value of the stock that has been credited to (but never actually placed in) the employee's account. Therefore, although not an actual owner of stock, an employee has a strong incentive to improve company performance, which it is hoped will be reflected in increased value of its stock. [12]

24. The plan can provide whatever benefit for early termination that the employer and employee agree upon. Typically, the plan would pay the employee's vested benefit, if any, in a form appropriate for the benefit formula that is used. In a salary reduction formula, the payout would generally be the total of salary reductions to date, plus any earnings provided on the total account balance under the plan. In a salary-continuation formula, a reduced actuarial benefit (reduced from the retirement benefit provided under the plan) would typically be provided. [13]

25. Disability payouts present a number of problems. Typically, a nonqualified plan will pay out at least the vested benefit determined as in the preceding question. However, in the event of early disability this may be inadequate, and disability insurance should be considered in addition to the nonqualified deferred-compensation plan. [13]

Learning Objectives

An understanding of the material in this chapter should
enable the student to

1. Describe the basic features and advantages to the employer of
   establishing a financing mechanism to meet its obligations under a
   deferred-compensation or salary continuation plan and alternatives
   for meeting potential employer objectives and needs under such
   a financial arrangement.

2. Evaluate the use of a rabbi trust to hold the asset reserve in a
   financing arrangement for a nonqualified deferred-compensation
   plan.

3. Based on given employer or employee objectives, recommend or
   evaluate the propriety of given choices of investment media for
   the asset reserve established by an employer to meet its future
   obligations under a deferred-compensation agreement.

4. Explain how life insurance financing for a nonqualified
   deferred-compensation (NQDC) plan can be structured for larger
   groups.

5. Describe the secular trust and discuss when and how it is used in a
   nonqualified deferred-compensation arrangement.

6. Describe and illustrate the rules applicable to nonqualified
   deferred-compensation plans for executives of tax-exempt and
   governmental organizations.

FINANCING THE EMPLOYER'S OBLIGATION IN A DEFERRED-COMPENSATION PLAN

Since almost all nonqualified deferred-compensation (NQDC) plans are
unfunded in the formal sense, employees initiating deferred-compensation

arrangements are likely to seek ways to increase benefit security. The following approaches are commonly used:

- *Reserve account maintained by employer.* The employer maintains an actual account invested in various types of securities. There is no trust, and funds are fully accessible to the employer and its creditors. The plan is considered unfunded for tax and ERISA purposes.

- *Employer reserve account with employee investment direction.* With this variation, the employee obtains greater security by having the right to "direct" (select) investments in the account. This right must be limited to a choice of broad types of investments (equity, bonds, family of mutual funds, and so on), because the ability to choose specific investments may lead to constructive receipt by the employee.

- *Corporate-owned life insurance (COLI).* Life insurance policies on the employee's life, owned by and payable to the employer, can provide financing for the employer's obligation under nonqualified deferred-compensation plans. With life insurance financing, the plan can provide a substantial death benefit even in the early years of the plan, which is of significant value to younger employees.

- *Rabbi trust.* A rabbi trust is a trust set up to hold property used for financing a deferred-compensation plan, where the funds set aside are subject to the employer's creditors. The IRS has ruled that trusts designed in this way do not constitute formal funding in the tax sense.

- *Third-party guarantees.* In these arrangements, the employer obtains a guarantee from a third party to pay the employee if the employer defaults. The guarantor may be a shareholder, a related corporation, or a "letter of credit" from a bank. Employer involvement does raise the possibility that the guarantee will cause the plan to be deemed formally funded for tax purposes. However, it appears that if the employee acts independently of the employer to obtain a third-party guarantee, the IRS will not necessarily view the plan as formally funded.

Once an employer signs a deferred-compensation agreement, there is a potential liability that must be met at some point. There are many reasons why the employer should establish a financing mechanism to meet this liability. First, it is a sound business practice to earmark a certain amount of corporate assets each year for the eventual payment of the long-term liability inherent in a deferred-compensation or salary continuation plan. This earmarking is typically in the form of an annual increase in a special asset reserve account. As soon as the deferred liability is incurred, the increases begin and do not end until all payments are made. Second, the employee gains some assurance that the promised funds will be available at retirement. Since the fulfillment of any promise is contingent on the promisor's ability to perform, the larger the asset reserve, the more likely it is that the employer will be able to meet its promises.

Psychologically, if assets such as a life insurance contract, annuity, mutual fund, or individual stocks are set aside specifically to meet the employer's obligation under a deferred-compensation or salary continuation plan, the employer shouldn't consider them "operating assets." Although the employer could always convert the earmarked assets back into operating assets (for example, by taking out a policy loan and using the proceeds for current working capital), the employer should remember that money has a specific purpose and must be repaid.

Although it is possible to provide in the deferred-compensation agreement that the employer may not use earmarked assets for any purpose other than to pay the deferred benefits, it is unlikely that such a provision will be utilized, or even if so, it is unlikely that it will be productive. First, earmarked assets still remain within the reach of the firm's creditors even if the employer can't convert them into operating assets. An employee does not gain a position higher than an unsecured creditor through such a provision. Furthermore, the corporation's inability to reach emergency or opportunity funds may reduce the strength of the very firm that the covered employee is most concerned with enhancing.

There is a third reason to establish an asset reserve. In a salary reduction arrangement, there would be no way to measure the increases or decreases necessary in an employee's account to reflect investment gains and losses if there was no such account. In this case the investments are the determinant of the deferred benefits. The plan itself must specifically refer to the employer's investments. (Note that the employer should not be obligated to invest the amounts in the account, but that such amounts should be referred to only as a measuring device to ascertain the size of the employer's obligation.)

An asset reserve should be distinguished from the "deferred liability account" the employer creates on its books to reflect its obligation to pay the deferred benefits. An asset reserve account consists of tangible assets, while the deferred liability account is an accounting procedure in which the employer accrues its obligation to pay promised benefits in the form of periodic credits. An employer should establish a deferred liability account on its books whether or not an asset reserve is created. For accounting purposes, a mere earmarking of the assets intended to be used to provide an asset reserve is sufficient. Often an accountant will add a footnote to the balance sheet or make specific reference to both the liability and the earmarked assets in the deferred-compensation agreement.

Should the full amount promised under the plan be set aside in an asset reserve? In other words, should the reserve be fully funded or should it be "discounted"?

If an employer promises to pay a retired employee $10,000 a year for 10 years at age 65, how much of the employer's assets should be earmarked to meet that potential obligation? One factor is the length of time between the establishment of the plan for a given employee and normal retirement age. So if an employee was 45 years old and the normal retirement age was 65, there would be 20 years to fund benefits. If the employer's full liability is $100,000, the simplest approach would be to divide the $100,000 needed by the 20 years the employer has to set aside that much money. But obviously this approach does not consider the income that can be earned on the constantly growing principal. At a 10 percent assumption, a considerable amount less than $5,000 a year ($100,000 divided by 20) would be needed if the first payment was made at the beginning of each year and annual payments continued for a period of 20 years.

It is important for the employer to be realistic in assuming a rate of interest that can be earned over a long period of time. It is also necessary that only the after-tax return on assets not invested for capital be considered. (Keep in mind that where life insurance or tax-exempt bonds are used, there is no current tax on the interest increment.) To some extent taxes dilute the amount available for reinvestment. (Also consider that a portion of dividend income from stocks in a domestic corporation is excludible from taxation at the corporate level and serves to increase the amount available.)

No discounting would be appropriate in the case of a salary reduction formula since all interest and invested increments are typically credited to the employee.

Interest is not the only reason for reducing the amount set aside each year to meet the employer's obligation. Where the number of employees covered by nonqualified plans is large enough, certain actuarial concepts come into play. For instance, some of the covered employees will no longer be working for the company at normal retirement age. For example, some may work for other employers; some may die; and some may become disabled. The portion of the reserve earmarked for the benefit of employees who forfeit earmarked assets (because they've left for other employment) is available to meet the employer's obligation for participants who have remained employed. There is sometimes a release of a portion of the asset reserve where an employee terminates by death or disability. If insurance is used to provide the funds needed to pay death or disability benefits, the assets remaining in a side fund may be available to cover benefits the employer has promised to other employees.

Regardless of why termination has occurred prior to normal retirement age, actuarial anticipation is possible and can reduce the employer's periodic contributions. So in essence the employer is discounting contributions by factoring in anticipated turnover, mortality, and morbidity rates.

Tax leverage is another reason for discounting the reserve. An employer who has established a fixed-benefit plan receives a tax deduction at the time benefits are paid. This deduction is not for the amount of the original contributions to the reserve but rather for the amount actually paid out to the employee or the employee's beneficiary. So assuming benefits constitute reasonable compensation, the employer realizes a deduction in the amount of benefits paid—a much larger amount than what was set aside originally. This means that an employer in a 35 percent bracket needs to put aside only 65 percent of the promised amount because the tax deduction has been anticipated through discounting. For instance, an employer required to make $100,000 of deductible benefit payments would have a cost after its tax deductions of two-thirds that amount, $65,000. The reduction in taxes (assuming the employer's tax bracket hasn't changed) plus the money on hand in the reserve account should equal the promised benefits.

It is possible to achieve the same result in a money-purchase plan by contributing only one-half of the amount of a credit made to the employee's account. The benefit paid out to the employee is not reduced; the asset reserve anticipates the eventual tax deduction.

Should the discount in either the defined-benefit or money-purchase plan be based on an assumed or actual tax rate? Although either procedure is possible, the parties may prefer to base the discount on the actual applicable rate the employer experiences. So before an employee retires, increases in each year's reserve are based on the applicable tax rate for that year, and the size of each benefit payment is based on the applicable tax rate for the year in which the benefit is paid. Since this is often difficult or impossible to do precisely, in order to avoid complex mathematical formulas the computation of the applicable tax rate is usually based on what the employer's tax bill would be if the known taxable income of a specified prior year was taxed under current tax rates. This formula considers both changes in tax rates as well as corporate profitability trends.

RABBI TRUSTS

What Are They?

Rabbi trusts are a relatively new way to enhance security with minimal threat that the employee will be subjected to current taxation on contributions to the trust or on trust income. A rabbi trust (so called because the first one the IRS ruled on was set up to provide postretirement financial security for a rabbi) holds the assets of the plan apart from the corporation but not apart from its creditors.

The rabbi trust is a trust that holds assets that will be used to satisfy all or part of the employer's obligation. If and when the trust becomes irrevocable, the employer gives up the use of plan investments and cannot get plan assets back. Those assets are dedicated solely to the employees covered under the plan with one major exception: If the employer becomes bankrupt or insolvent, the assets become available to the general creditors of the employer, which means covered employees line up essentially like all the other creditors.

Federal Income, FICA, and FUTA Tax Treatment of the Executive and the Employer

In the original rabbi trust ruling, the IRS determined that the rabbi was not taxable on amounts irrevocably paid into a trust subject only to the claims of the congregation's creditors until the rabbi actually received a distribution of such amounts upon his death, disability, retirement, or termination of services (PLR 8113107).

Since that original ruling, a number of subsequent private letter rulings and a General Counsel's Memorandum (GCM 39230) have shaped the development and use of rabbi trusts. For example, the IRS has ruled that

- A rabbi trust is a "grantor" trust, so that all income, deductions, and credits attributable to the trust were included in computing the taxable income of the grantor-employer.
- Sec. 402(b) of the Code is inapplicable and there is no taxable income to the executive in the year in which the employer makes a contribution to the rabbi trust.
- The transfer of "property" does not occur in a rabbi trust because nothing is transferred that meets the definition of "property" as set forth in Reg. Sec. 1.83-3(3). Because Sec. 402(b) is to be applied in accordance with Sec. 83, Sec. 402(b) is not applicable to the rabbi trust situation.

When Should You Consider a Rabbi Trust?

Factors that would indicate the utility of a rabbi trust include: a fear that the management and/or ownership of the business is likely to change before all benefits will be paid; a fear that hostile new management might not honor the company's contractual obligations to its key employees; and a perceived probability that if litigation became necessary to enforce the agreement, key employees would win, if at all, only a prohibitive cost.

There are, of course, costs or risks attached to every tool or technique of estate and business planning. Three costs of rabbi trusts (aside from the legal and administrative costs of creating and maintaining them) are the following:

- Since the employer loses the use of plan assets, the assets are not available for a corporate emergency or opportunity.
- The rate of return on plan assets in the trust may be less than what could have been earned had the money been invested in the client's business.
- There is no protection against the ultimate risk of employer insolvency.

What types of assets should or should not be placed inside a rabbi trust? A deferred annuity has no particular advantage as an investment for a rabbi trust because increases in income inside the annuity are currently taxable to the employer and grantor of the rabbi trust (Code Sec. 72(u)). Tax-advantaged investments, such as municipal bonds, preferred stocks, life insurance, or a combination of these, are generally preferable.

Rabbi Trust Provisions

In previous years, rabbi trust rulings were considered by the IRS on a one-by-one basis. Currently (Rev. Proc. 92-64, Rev. Proc. 92-65) the IRS provides a "model trust" (reproduced at the end of this chapter) with provisions that meet its requirements. Rulings will be issued on a nonqualified deferred-compensation arrangement using a rabbi trust only if the IRS model rabbi trust is used. If a rabbi trust does not conform with the model, rulings will be issued only in "rare and unusual circumstances." In many cases, the use of the model trust will provide an adequate "comfort level" to the client's legal adviser, and it may not be necessary to actually apply for a ruling (with the additional expense that is involved).

The model trust generally conforms with IRS guidelines already well known from prior IRS private letter rulings. Optional paragraphs are provided to allow some degree of customization. The model contains some relatively favorable provisions. For example, it allows the use of "springing" irrevocability—that is, a provision under which if there is a change of ownership of the employer, the trust becomes irrevocable or the employer is obligated to make an irrevocable contribution of all remaining deferred compensation. Also, the model permits the rabbi trust to own employer stock. However, the model does not contain "trigger" provisions to allow acceleration of payments if the employer moves toward insolvency; the employee's rights must never be better than those of corporate creditors. The model rabbi trust also has no provision giving employees investment authority over rabbi trust assets.

Other requirements contained in the model trust, the Code, or in IRS rulings include:

- The nonqualified deferred-compensation plan must provide rules for the timing of benefit payments. Prior to Code Sec. 409A the IRS refused to rule on a plan that pays benefits merely after a term of years; the plan must pay benefits at retirement, separation, or other triggering events such as disability in order to obtain a ruling. Under Sec. 409A the employee's election as to time of receipt must be made by the employee prior to the performance of services.
- For salary reduction plans, salary reduction elections, consistent with Sec. 409A, must be made in the calendar year prior to the year in which the income is earned.
- Hardship withdrawals are permitted; however, the definition of hardship now must be consistent with the definition in the Sec. 409A regulations.

- The plan document must specifically state that it is an unfunded, unsecured promise to pay and that participants have no greater rights than unsecured creditors.
- The plan must have no "accelerated payment" or "trigger" provision that takes effect under certain adverse financial conditions or changes in ownership. The IRS has viewed these provisions as giving the employee greater rights than those of corporate creditors, and this view has been codified in Code Sec. 409A.
- Placing assets offshore as a way to limit creditor access is penalized under Code Sec. 409A.
- The plan must not have "loan to loan" offset provisions. Loan provisions can't be used as a subterfuge to avoid deferral of the right to receive benefits.
- Some flexibility on revocability may be permitted—for example, the transfer might be revocable until there is a change in control of the company.
- IRS rulings are conditional on enforceability of creditors' rights to rabbi trust assets under federal and state law.
- Apparently the IRS will not approve a rabbi trust that holds a surety bond or letter of credit to secure payment of benefits. In effect, the IRS views these arrangements as providing a secured promise to pay during insolvency, giving the executive greater rights than unsecured creditors of the corporation.

The plan designer should also consider the following employee-protection provisions that either have been approved in IRS rulings or should be approved in most cases:

- Provide that investment authority will automatically shift to the trustee of the rabbi trust in the event of an unfriendly takeover, thus preventing the "bad guys" from making investments in illiquid employer-leased real estate or an employer-related venture.
- Include some type of provision for accelerating benefit payments that enables an employer, upon an unfavorable change in tax law or an unfavorable result from an IRS audit that makes rabbi trust money taxable to participants, to immediately pay out whatever is in the trust. If neither the plan nor the trust has such a provision, the employee may incur a current tax but receive no cash to pay the tax. (Note: Any such provision would have to be consistent with Code 409A; regulations).
- Preclude the addition of new beneficiaries in the event of an unfriendly takeover, and restrict the ability of unfavorable provisions.

This prevents new management from adding plan amendments that have an adverse impact on already accrued plan benefits.

- Make it clear that liability for promised benefits is joint and several between the trust and the employer. If plan liability is shifted completely to the trust (aside from the obvious problems if trust assets are insufficient), ERISA problems may be triggered.

- Do not condition the trustee's ability to pay benefits on instructions from the employer.

- Set up a separate trust if employees of both a parent and a subsidiary corporation are to be covered by salary continuation plans. This helps to insulate trust assets and keep creditors of an insolvent corporation from reaching assets that should go to employees of a related, financially sound corporation.

Rabbi Trust Restriction for Companies with At-Risk Defined-Benefit Plans

A provision in Code Sec. 409A adds some restrictions to nonqualified deferred-compensation financing. Under this provision, if the employer is in bankruptcy or has an at-risk defined-benefit plan, any assets added to a rabbi trust or similar arrangement for funding a nonqualified deferred-compensation plan will be treated as Sec. 83 amounts; that is, vested amounts will generally be taxed immediately to the employee covered under the nonqualified deferred-compensation plan. This treatment, however, is generally limited to executives or former executives of publicly held corporations (those covered under Code Sec. 162(m) or Securities Act Sec. 16(a)).

This provision is not as broad as was originally feared, since it will not affect most closely held businesses. It is an example of what lawyers call an *in terrorem* provision. It is not expected to actually be applied very often, but is intended to discourage the behavior in question—funding executive parachutes when a company is in financial trouble.

INVESTMENT SELECTION FOR ASSET RESERVE ACCOUNT

How does an employer finance its contractual obligation under a deferred-compensation plan? There is no legal requirement to set assets aside as there is generally for qualified plans (the fiduciary requirements of ERISA). However, for prudent financial management of the company's obligation, and to provide a measure of benefit security for the employee, an asset reserve is prudent.

A number of vehicles may be used for asset reserves, and the appropriate choice or choices depend on the objectives of the business and its investment propensities. The following discussion is generally applicable to asset reserves held directly by the corporation as well as rabbi trusts, which are grantor trusts (all income, deductions, and credits, pass through to the corporation).

The discussion below will assume that whatever investment vehicle is selected, that asset will be owned solely by the corporation (or a rabbi trust), subject to rules governing corporate taxation, and will be subject to the claims of the corporation's creditors. As mentioned above, every deferred-compensation plan will reflect the attitudes, objectives, and relative bargaining positions of both the employer and employee. Where the plan is the sole source of retirement benefits, a conservative investment attitude is typically elected. Conversely, if the plan is merely a supplement to an already satisfactory qualified retirement plan, the parties may decide that a more aggressive investment policy is appropriate. Where the plan offers a significant preretirement death benefit, life insurance is the only prudent choice (at least to finance the employer's obligation under this part of the promise).

There is a clear relationship between the benefits promised and the financing method that should be selected. In other words, the accumulation vehicle must be appropriate for the amount and type of benefits.

What is the first factor that should be considered in the selection process? The employee benefit planner must first examine the agreement to see if retirement benefits will be fixed or variable in amount. If benefits are to be a fixed-dollar amount payable over a period of years or over the lifetime of the employee, the appropriate investment vehicle will probably be one that will minimize or avoid the loss of capital through adverse investment experience. The cost of this safety is the employer's loss of potential capital appreciation and the consequent lowering of plan costs.

If variable benefits have been decided on, an equity investment is appropriate. Here the participant will typically bear some or all of the risk of investment gain or loss (although most plans establish a minimum benefit amount so that if investment losses do occur, a participant will not be without some income).

If an employer is interested in using equity investments as a method of reducing costs, a compromise approach might be considered. The employee could be promised a minimum retirement benefit. In addition the employee could participate in superior investment results up to a certain amount, and the employer could receive the benefit of any excess.

Does a "pay-as-you-go" approach make sense as opposed to the purchase of one or more investment vehicles to meet deferred-compensation or salary continuation obligations? In some cases larger employers may decide that this approach makes sense, although for psychological as well as practical reasons most employers will not. Few employees will feel comfortable relying on this approach with any but the most financially sound corporations.

What are the various types of tools and techniques available for financing an employer's obligations? Where the plan promises either a fixed-dollar or guaranteed minimum-retirement benefit, certain types of investments are probably more appropriate than others. Also, the tax consequences to the corporation are an important consideration. Generally, income earned by the assets in the asset reserve or rabbi trust is taxable to the corporation or employer.

Life Insurance

The cash value life insurance policy offers guarantees that are not duplicated in other investments. An employer can know in advance the dollar amount that will be available at given stages because the contract states the policy cash value available not only at retirement but at other stages. In computing the amounts available, it is important that dividends are not considered as part of the guaranteed amounts since these are not guaranteed but merely projections.

One advantage of the cash value life insurance contract is the tax-free buildup of funds within the "wrapper" of the policy. In comparing potential returns, it is the after-tax return of a currently taxable investment that should be compared with the interest earnings on the cash value (which of course will become taxable as it is paid out).

An additional advantage of cash value life insurance is the contractual guarantee of a life annuity option. Obviously, where the plan promises a lifetime retirement benefit, such an option is extremely valuable if not indispensable.

The waiver-of-premium provision in the cash value life insurance contract provides additional protection for both the employer and employee. If the insured should become disabled prior to retirement, the corporation is relieved of the premium outlays to the insurance company, and therefore those amounts are available to be paid as a tax-deductible wage continuation benefit. (Remember that a wage continuation plan must be established prior to an employee's disability.) As mentioned in a prior objective, the corporation could now pay a disability benefit based on tax leverage. For example, if a nondeductible premium of $10,000 a year is waived for a corporation in a combined federal and state tax bracket of 50 percent, $20,000 can be paid out at no additional cost to the corporation because of the $10,000 tax savings realized by the corporation. While premiums are being waived, the policy's cash value continues to increase, which in turn assures the corporation that it will have necessary funds for payment of retirement benefits.

What are the right types of cash value life insurance policies to consider? Whole life and life paid up at 65 have been the traditional types of policies most often used. Since premiums cease at age 65, the date coinciding with typical normal retirement age and the commencement of deferred-compensation payments, life paid up at 65 has been the most popular. It is also a popular selection because of the larger cash values available at that age.

If the insured is younger or if the corporation will utilize both life insurance and another form of investment, whole life insurance is indicated. In this case the lowest premium-outlay type of policy is favored in order to maximize the amount going into the supplementary investment vehicle.

Variable and universal life products as well as interest-sensitive whole life insurance are highly useful vehicles to either supplement or take the place of traditional cash value whole life contracts.

In the case of a variable life product, the corporation obtains an asset that would produce a large sum of money in the event the employee dies; but the corporation also gains the ability to adjust the death benefit and cash value to reflect changing economic conditions. The variable life contract implies level premiums and loan and surrender values but differs in the underlying assets supporting the contract. Unlike traditional whole life, the variable life policy is supported with funds in separate accounts invested in designated instruments such as bonds, stocks, or real estate. The corporation will have a choice of two or more separate accounts in which to allocate the portion of the premium going to the cash value. While the death benefit cash value will increase or decrease based on the investment performance of the separate account, a minimum death benefit is guaranteed. The increase (or decrease) in the value of the underlying assets flows through to the corporation. This means the corporation must assume a certain portion of the risk inherent in the separate account.

Universal life is another vehicle frequently being used in deferred-compensation plans. It is a flexible-premium adjustable death benefit contract that credits current investment yield to the accumulated cash value. Insurers refer to universal life as "unbundled" life insurance because the three components—earnings, protection cost, and expenses—are separately identified.

Under universal life, the corporation pays premiums to the insurer who withdraws sufficient money to cover its expenses (loading). It then withdraws a second amount as a "mortality" charge. Any cash remaining is added to the policy's cash value, and that entire amount is then credited with an investment yield. The universal life contract is quite flexible; the amount of insurance coverage, the amount of premium, and the frequency of scheduled premium payments can all be adjusted. The corporation will be able to use the cash value as long as the contract is in force.

The third type of contract mentioned above is interest-sensitive (current-assumption) whole life. These are essentially traditional whole life products that use (a) current mortality and (b) interest earnings based on current yields rather than overall portfolio yields. In other respects the contract is identical to conventional whole life. Mutual companies generally reflect the current assumptions through the dividend formula, while stock companies make adjustments through the policy cash values and/or premiums. Premiums are basically fixed but may change based on company experience. Death benefits are guaranteed and will not fluctuate. Although the cash values are guaranteed, favorable company experience may result in increased cash value. As with traditional insurance, policy loans are available. Withdrawals can be made from dividends without impairing the base policy. With nonparticipating policies, excess accumulation values can be withdrawn subject to any surrender charges, usually without impairing the basic policy.

Is term life insurance appropriate in an NQDC plan? Typically, term life should be used only when a significant preretirement death benefit is desired, a side fund consisting of equities or other securities will provide the retirement benefit, and a disability policy will finance the employer's obligation under the disability provision. Yearly renewable term insurance provides maximum death benefit protection at minimum premium outlay. This type of contract is especially indicated where significant death benefits are to be provided for only a relatively short period of time. This is common when the employer anticipates that the investment fund will accumulate to a predetermined amount, and at that time the insurance will be terminated. An alternative is to increase corporate group insurance in lieu of individual term insurance where significant amounts can be obtained for key employees (although in many cases the purchase of individual policies on selected lives is a more economic course of action). The tax deductibility of group term premiums, combined with the income tax exclusion on the cost of the first $50,000 of coverage to the employee, and coupled with income-tax-free receipt of death proceeds by the insured's beneficiary (as well as the possible exclusion of the entire amount of death proceeds from the insured's gross estate if an absolute assignment has been used) could make group term insurance quite appealing.

If any type of life insurance is considered, it is important that plan provisions anticipate two possibilities. First, the draftsperson should consider the possibility that one or more employees covered will be uninsurable or highly rated. Second, it is essential to anticipate the possibility that if the insured dies within the contestable period of the policy (typically 2 years), the insurer will not pay death proceeds. A solution to that potential problem is to provide in the agreement between the employer and the employee that if the insurer will not pay death proceeds, there is no liability under the deferred-compensation or salary continuation plan for a death benefit to be paid (or perhaps only a minimum death benefit must be paid).

How should the insurance be arranged if it is selected as the financing mechanism? The corporation should be the policyowner, premium payer, and beneficiary. The insured participant should not be given any rights in the policy, and the deferred-compensation or salary continuation agreement should not refer to the policy. Premiums will not be tax deductible to the corporation, and proceeds should be received by the corporation income tax free. Policy cash values should be reflected as a corporate asset on the firm's balance sheet. Employees are not taxed on any current economic benefit; there are no PS 58 or equivalent taxable costs. The plan is not deemed to be formally funded for tax or ERISA purposes. Therefore, the use of the life insurance does not result in any taxable income to the employee until benefits become payable.

How much life insurance should be purchased? In most cases the plan will provide a death benefit large enough to replace the anticipated normal retirement benefit no matter when the employee dies. In a defined-benefit (salary continuation) plan, the employer can purchase life insurance equal to the present value of the promised monthly benefits as a multiple of the defined-retirement benefit (for example, 200 times the monthly benefit). If the plan is of the type with an account balance for the employee, the employer can invest a portion of the amounts credited to the employee's account in life insurance premiums. The death benefit would be equal to whatever the policy provides in death proceeds plus the vested interest of the employee in the balance of his or her account.

If the employee dies before normal retirement age, policy proceeds can be used to finance the agreed-upon death-benefit payments to the decedent's beneficiaries. When the employee retires, there are two general alternatives:

- Cost recovery is the most common alternative where the employer makes benefit payments from corporate cash flow or other corporate assets and keeps the policy intact. Then when the employee dies, policy proceeds will reimburse the employer and often add to the company's surplus. This is known as a "cost recovery" financing arrangement.
- Another alternative is for the company to pay benefits using policy cash values as well as the corporation's current cash flow. The death benefit to the corporation is therefore reduced accordingly or eliminated.

An employer that is a C corporation should purchase enough insurance to offset any corporate alternative minimum tax (AMT) on the proceeds. The amount of AMT actually due depends on the amount of the company's regular tax in the year of receipt and is difficult to predict accurately, but the AMT should be no more than about 15 percent of policy proceeds. To be safe it is suggested that the employer obtain about 17 or 18 percent more than the amount of the expected death proceeds. (Multiply the target amount by 118 percent.) Any excess can be used as key employee coverage.

The following example shows how life insurance financing operates.

EXAMPLE
Megasoft Software Corporation enters into a deferred-compensation agreement with its executive Dot Komm under which Dot agrees to defer an anticipated $10,000 annual salary increase in return for the following specified benefits:

- If Dot dies before retirement, $10,000 per year will be paid to her surviving spouse for a period equal to the number of years she was covered under the plan.

- If Dot remains employed by Mega until retirement at age 65, she will receive $20,000 per year for 10 years, in addition to other company retirement benefits.

- If Dot retires before age 65, she will receive a reduced benefit (according to a formula in the plan) beginning no earlier than age 55.

Dot's deferred $10,000 per year of compensation would have had an after-tax cost of $6,500 to the corporation if paid currently (assuming a 35 percent marginal corporate tax bracket). The corporation can use this $6,500 instead to finance Dot's benefits by purchasing a life insurance policy on Dot's life. If Dot is aged 45, about $150,000 of cash value insurance (paid up at 65) can be purchased with this $6,500 annually. The corporation would be the policyowner, the policy beneficiary, and would pay the premiums, which would be nondeductible.

If Dot died at age 50, the corporation would receive $150,000 of tax-free policy proceeds (in addition to policy dividends and perhaps interest, but reduced by any corporate AMT liability). It would have paid about $33,000 in premiums over the past 5 years. It is obligated to pay a total of $50,000 ($10,000 per year for 5 years) to Dot's surviving spouse, but since these payments are deductible to the corporation their after-tax cost is only $32,500 (65 percent of $50,000). This results in a net gain to the corporation of approximately $84,500 ($150,000 insurance proceeds less $33,000 of premiums and less $32,500 of after-tax cost of benefit payments). (This example does not take into account the time value of money, but to do so does not change the result significantly since the corporation's loss of the use of five annual premium payments is balanced by being reimbursed in advance for the 5 years of benefit payments due to Dot's surviving spouse.)

If Dot retires, policy cash values and the corporation's current cash flow could be used to finance Dot's annual benefit payments. However, under the cost-recovery approach, the corporation would keep the policy intact and use current cash flow to make benefit payments. Then, when Dot dies, policy proceeds will reimburse the corporation and often add to the corporation's surplus.

Although this example uses a traditional whole-life type of policy for illustration, other types of policies will produce similar results if they provide cash values to the employer to finance benefits as they come due.

Annuities

Fixed-dollar annuities are another means of financing an employer's obligation under the deferred-compensation or salary continuation plan. Annuity contracts can be a good fit with the employer's cash needs under the plan, and investment risks can be minimized. However, under Code Sec.

72(u), income on the contract generally is not tax deferred since the annuity is not held by or on behalf of a "natural person."

A corporation could purchase its own annual premium deferred annuity that guarantees lifetime benefits approximately equal to those promised under the plan. Obviously, if a lifetime retirement benefit or joint and survivor benefit has been promised, an annuity is particularly well suited.

A waiver-of-premium benefit could make the annuity accumulation fund self-completing so that if the annuitant became disabled prior to retirement, the employer would be relieved of premium payment obligations, and the promised benefits would still be available.

Annuities do provide some death benefits. Usually, at the death of an annuitant, payment is made equal to the greater of (a) premiums paid or (b) the annuity's cash value. Obviously, an annuity (standing alone) will not be appropriate if the plan requires substantial preretirement death benefits. But a combination of an annuity (fixed or variable) and term insurance could be a good package.

During the accumulation period the corporation, but not the covered employee, will be subject to current income taxation. At the maturity of the corporate-owned annuity, benefits will be paid to the corporation. These benefits will be tax free to the extent attributable to a return of premiums and previously taxed income. Once the corporation receives annuity payments, they can then be paid out to the retired employee as tax-deductible compensation.

Deferred annuities are often indicated when the covered employee is over age 50 if little or no preretirement death benefit has been promised.

Other Investments

What other investments may be used in an asset reserve to finance an employer's obligation under an NQDC? Some corporations will purchase corporate or U.S. government bonds, some of which produce a secure and steady payment of income. But bond prices will fluctuate, and there is always a possibility of default on corporate bonds. Interest on bonds (except for municipal bonds) is currently taxable. Therefore any comparison should take into consideration the net return.

Bond funds provide diversification and ready marketability at the cost of management fees and in some cases a sales load. There are also mutual funds consisting of short-term money funds that provide significant current yields. Tax-free municipal bonds also can be purchased through a bond fund.

Keep in mind that the investments described above provide no principal guarantees, payouts are inflexible, and interest payments typically are not automatically reinvested.

Quite often when a corporation finances its obligation through a noninsured fixed-dollar investment, it uses that money to purchase a single-premium immediate annuity from an insurer to provide the promised payout at retirement.

Variable annuities are an attempt to answer the employee's concern about the effect of inflation on a fixed-dollar payout. When a corporation buys a variable annuity, it is in essence buying accumulation units similar to the purchase of mutual fund shares. As the investment result of the insurer's separate account varies, so will the value of each unit purchased through the variable annuity. The separate account is typically invested in equities such as common stocks.

When the annuitant retires, the accumulation units can be converted into a life income option. The number of units is fixed but the value of each unit and the amount of retirement income produced will fluctuate depending on the insurer's investment results. The amount of income can change considerably although mortality and expenses are guaranteed. (If annuitants live longer than expected, the mortality guarantee is important since the insurer must continue to pay no matter how long the annuitant lives.) The expense guarantee promises that sales charges and operating costs cannot be increased once the contract is purchased.

The arrangement of a variable annuity used to finance an employer's obligation under a deferred-compensation or salary continuation contract is similar to that of a life insurance contract; the corporation names itself owner, premium payer, and beneficiary. Premiums are not deductible. When annuity payments are received by the corporation, they will be taxed much like fixed annuities, as described earlier. Once a corporation receives annuity payments, it can take that money and pay it out as tax-deductible deferred salary to the retired employee or the employee's beneficiary.

Although some variable annuity contracts allow loans, the charge for a variable annuity loan is not considered interest but rather a charge to protect the insurer against adverse financial and mortality selection. This means that no deduction is allowed for federal income tax purposes for any payment.

The corporation can surrender a variable annuity contract before the maturity date and receive the value as of that date. But there are no guaranteed cash surrender values, and some insurers impose a modest surrender charge that varies according to the contract and the length of time the contract has been in force.

A variable annuity is an appropriate device for financing deferred-compensation and salary continuation benefits as long as the employer is aware that it has all the risks and rewards of an equity-type investment. A combination of life insurance and a variable annuity can provide an excellent investment package.

Mutual funds, either alone or in combination with life insurance, should be considered in planning the asset reserve. Mutual funds provide a degree of investment diversification as well as professional money management. Typically the underlying assets of a mutual fund are primarily equities, but they can also be based on investments in bonds or money market funds.

There are fundamental distinctions between variable annuities (which also invest in common stocks) and mutual funds. All annuities, both fixed and variable, involve a sales charge, whereas mutual funds may be purchased on a "no-load" basis (although this does not mean that the investor is paying no charge whatsoever for the purchase or administration of the investment). Mutual funds, unlike variable annuities, cannot provide a guaranteed life annuity. However, many fund sponsors provide extremely flexible distribution options. Mutual funds do not guarantee either mortality or expenses. (Some funds, however, offer optional insurance in an amount sufficient to complete the contract or intended purchase amount.)

Although both mutual funds and variable annuities generally result in current income taxation to the corporation, there are distinctions. Any income or capital-gains dividends declared by the mutual fund are currently taxable to the corporation as ordinary income or as a long-term capital gain. Generally, when the corporation receives dividends from a mutual fund (as well as dividends from common or preferred stock that it holds), it can deduct 70 percent of the amount received. Code Sec. 243 (dividend deduction) for qualifying dividends means that only $30 out of every $100 received as a dividend from the stock of a domestic corporation is subject to income tax. Even if the employer corporation is in a top federal bracket of 35 percent, the effective tax rate is only 10.5 percent (35 percent times 30 percent). Capital gains are taxed to the corporation under the regular tax rules.

The corporation may use mutual funds to build up dollars, and at the employee's retirement or death it purchases a single-premium fixed or variable annuity with those dollars as an alternative to a systematic withdrawal plan, under which the value of the shares is liquidated over a given period of time. For example, if the shares are worth $100,000 at retirement, and an annual payment over 10 years is desired, one-tenth of the initial value, $100,000, will be paid the first year, one-ninth of the balance is paid in the second year, and so on.

The purchase of mutual funds is primarily an investment device, but it does not provide expense guarantees or life annuity features. The advantage of mutual funds is that there are a number of different types available and the cost or purchase is relatively low. (Remember that it is better to have a "load" fund with a good investment record than a "no-load" fund with a poor record.) Mutual funds provide neither death nor disability payments. Therefore in most cases the purchase of mutual fund shares must eventually be supplemented with life insurance and/or disability income policies.

There are devices other than life insurance policies, annuities, and mutual funds that can be used to finance an employer's obligation. A corporation may select individual common or preferred stocks. The problem here is the difficulty of creating adequate risk diversification and the cost of monitoring investment selections. Like mutual funds, individual stocks do not have any annuity guarantees, distribution options, or reinvestment facilities.

Finally, the option of investment in the employer's own stock should be mentioned. The company's own stock does not provide much additional security of payment since it generally becomes worthless or nearly so in the event of insolvency, but it may meet certain specialized needs for asset reserves. Dividends paid on company stock held by the company or a rabbi trust are not taxable to the company.

Directed Investment Provision

Can an asset reserve account or rabbi trust include a provision by which some or all of the investments are chosen by the employee? Such directed-investment provisions would be desirable from the employee's standpoint because they would give the employee some influence over the risk and return elements of the asset reserve.

The IRS position on directed investments in asset reserves has varied. Initially, the IRS appeared to take the position that employee asset direction would result in constructive receipt of the asset values to the employee. Later rulings indicated that if the employee's investment direction was only advisory (with the corporation having final discretion), then there would be no constructive-receipt problem. However, some recent rulings seem to allow mandatory investment direction by the employee. The decision to include an investment-direction provision will be dictated primarily by the interests of the employee and the employer, but if tax risks are an issue, an advisory-only provision might be preferable notwithstanding the evolving IRS view on this issue.

FINANCING NQDC FOR LARGER GROUPS—COLI/BOLI

When the group of employees to be covered by a NQDC plan is relatively large, financing the plan presents special issues, especially if life insurance financing is chosen. The threshold for a "large" plan for this purpose is typically about 25 or more employees, depending on life insurance company practices.

When the group is large, it becomes cumbersome (and possibly costly in terms of fixed policy expenses) to use individual life insurance policies for each covered employee. Perhaps more significantly, however, the "cost recovery" concept becomes more compelling with a larger group.

As discussed earlier, under the cost recovery method the employer keeps the policy in force and is ultimately reimbursed through the policy's death benefit. This approach becomes more attractive from a corporate-finance point of view as the group becomes larger and permits reasonably accurate actuarial cash-flow projections from the financing assets. In effect, the financing of the plan becomes similar to the actuarial funding of a qualified defined-benefit plan that uses life insurance as a plan asset.

There are major differences from qualified plan funding, however, which simply reflect the fact that the plan is nonqualified. The most significant are as follows:

- As with any NQDC plan, the employer does not get a tax deduction when contributing toward the financing assets, but the deduction is tied to the payment of benefits to covered employees.

- Although a rabbi trust arrangement can be used, there is no irrevocable trust for the employees' exclusive benefit as in a qualified plan; instead the assets either belong to the employer or to the rabbi trust (which is an employer grantor trust), so all earnings are taxable to the employer. (With life insurance financing, there is very little taxable ongoing income, however, unlike other potential financing assets.)
- The plan, as an NQDC plan, is designed to avoid the ERISA funding and vesting requirements.

This approach to financing larger NQDC plans is often referred to as corporate-owned life insurance (COLI) financing. The financing for bank plans is often referred to separately as "BOLI" financing, because the special state and federal regulatory rules for banks often dictate special terms in these plans, and there is in effect a separate market for life insurance arrangements.

Special Rules for Corporate-Owned Life Insurance

As a result of reported abuses involving COLI programs for large groups of rank-and-file employees, and adverse court cases in these situations, Code Sec. 101(j) was enacted in 2006 to effectively restrict COLI programs to key employees. Although pre-2006 COLI generally referred to policies covering a larger number of lives, the definition of COLI under Sec. 101(j) refers to any life insurance policy owned by an employer and as to which the employer is the sole beneficiary. Thus, Sec. 101(j) may cover an employer-owned policy on one life or an employer-owned policy on a larger group of lives. The provisions of Sec. 101(j) were developed in cooperation with the insurance industry and are intended to reflect existing *best practices*.

Under Sec. 101(j), the death benefit from a COLI policy will generally be taxable to the employer (to the extent it exceeds the premiums paid and other basis items) unless

- the insured was an employee at any time during the 12-month period before death, or
- the amount is paid to the insured's heirs, or
- the insured was a director, a highly compensated employee (as defined for qualified plan purposes under Code Sec. 414(q)), or a highly compensated individual, as defined for medical-reimbursement plan purposes under Code Sec. 105(h)(5)

      (modified to cover 35 percent, instead of 25 percent, of the highest paid employees).

- certain employee notice and consent requirements are met.

Taxation of the death benefit under a COLI arrangement would generally eliminate the favorable financial aspects of such an arrangement, so all COLI programs should be designed or amended to meet one of the exceptions to Sec. 101(j).

Generally, nonqualified deferred-compensation plans or other plans financed through COLI arrangements cover only a select group of highly compensated or management employees in order to avoid tax and ERISA complications. In most cases, the covered group will qualify for the Sec. 101(j) exceptions listed above, but all employers with these plans must review them to insure compliance.

The provision is generally effective for insurance contracts issued after the date of enactment, August 17, 2006. A contract issued under a Sec. 1035 exchange after the effective date will not be covered. Also, certain increases in death benefits after the effective date will not trigger Sec. 101(j) treatment of grandfathered contracts.

Code Sec. 101(j) also contains important notice and consent requirements. Before a policy is issued, employees must be notified in writing that their employer intends to insure their lives and the maximum face amount for which they could be insured at the time the policy is issued. Each employee must provide written consent to being insured and to allowing the coverage to continue after employment. The employee must also be informed in writing that the employer will be the beneficiary of any proceeds payable under the insurance contract.

In 2009, many of the questions prompted by the enactment of Sec. 101(j) were addressed by the IRS through the issuance of Notice 2009-48.[22] This guidance resulted from a request for information made by the American Council of Life Insurers. The notice provides significant clarification on several issues under Sec. 101(j) in question and answer format, along with an assurance that the IRS would not challenge good-faith compliance efforts based on reasonable interpretations of Sec. 101(j) before June 15, 2009, the Notice's effective date. In particular, the Notice provides guidance with respect to the notice and consent requirements. First, the Notice provides

---

22. 2009-24 I.R.B. 1085 (May 22, 2009).

welcome relief in the event that an employer commits an inadvertent error in its compliance with the notice and consent requirements. Thus, the IRS has agreed not to challenge a failure to satisfy the notice and consent requirements if (i) the employer made a good faith effort to satisfy those requirements; (ii) the failure was inadvertent; and (iii) the employer corrects the error by the due date of its tax return for the year the contract was issued.[23] Even though this self-help mechanism provides some leeway to employers who make good faith innocent errors to avoid noncompliance with Sec. 101(j), it nevertheless puts a premium on making a prompt discovery and correction of the error.

The Notice also clarifies that: (i) the employee's consent remains valid up to the earlier of one year from the date it was obtained or the date the employment relationship ends;[24] (ii) electronic methods of providing the required notice and consent are permitted, as long as they have elements in place similar to the requirements governing electronically filed Forms W-4;[25] and (iii) the notification of the maximum face amount for which an employee could be insured must be satisfied by using either a dollar amount or a multiple of salary.[26]

Finally, under Code Sec. 6039I any employer with one or more life insurance contracts issued after August 17, 2006, must report annually the following information to the IRS for tax years ending after November 13, 2007:

- The total number of employees at the end of the year;
- The number of such employees insured under such contracts at the end of the year;
- The total amount of insurance in force under such contracts;
- The employer's name, address, taxpayer identification number, and a description of the type of business in which it engages; and
- Confirmation that the employer has obtained a valid consent for each insured employee.

Finally, Section 6039I specifies that the employer must retain documentation throughout the year demonstrating that these conditions and the requirements of Code Sec. 101(j) were met.

---

23. See Q&A-13 of Notice 2009-48.
24. See Q&A-9 of Notice 2009-48.
25. See Q&A-11 of Notice 2009-48.
26. See Q&A-12 of Notice 2009-48.

SECULAR TRUSTS

The secular trust (so named to distinguish it from a rabbi trust) is an arrangement that addresses two employee objections to deferred-compensation plans: the fear that tax savings will disappear because future tax rates will be very high, and the lack of security to the employee in relying on an unfunded plan.

A secular trust is an irrevocable trust for the benefit of the employee, with funds placed beyond the reach of the employer's unsecured creditors. The employer contributes to this trust, resulting in taxation to the employee in the year in which assets are placed in the trust, with a corresponding deduction to the employer in that year. Typically, trust assets are invested in life insurance contracts to minimize the amount of ongoing taxable income. The amounts already taxed can be distributed tax free to the employee at retirement, even if tax rates have gone up a great deal.

The secular trust arrangement provides considerable security of benefits to the employee. Also, if current tax rates are low, the employee can take advantage of these low rates. In addition, to the extent that corporate tax rates are higher than individual rates (this constantly varies as the tax law changes), the acceleration of the employer's tax deduction may provide more tax benefit than is lost by the employee in paying tax currently instead of deferring.

Secular trusts do have some problems. First, the employee has currently taxable income even though actual receipt of the compensation is deferred. Thus the employer may need to provide a source of additional compensation to the employee for paying the current tax. Second, the plan will be deemed "funded" for tax and ERISA purposes and therefore, will be subject to some of the ERISA provisions discussed in the text. In many cases, however, compliance may not be so difficult as to wipe out the benefits of the plan.

Secular trusts are generally structured as "grantor" trusts, but such structure is generally ignored for tax purposes where the trust is an employees' trust under Secs. 402(b) and 404(a)(5). That form of trust is not treated as being owned by the employer. The tax consequences of a secular trust had been somewhat unsettled prior to 2007. However, in 2007 the IRS issued a revenue ruling that for the first time clearly laid out the tax rules that apply to the various parties associated with a secular trust.[27] Pursuant to the ruling, a

---

27. Rev. Rul. 2007-48, 2007-30 I.R.B. 129 (July 2, 2007).

highly compensated employee (as defined in Sec. 414(q)) is taxed on the employee's vested accrued benefit in the trust as of the end of each tax year of the trust, reduced by the amounts remaining in the trust that were previously taxed in earlier years.[28]

The employer may deduct the deferred compensation in the year that the employee recognizes income. The deduction may not exceed the amount contributed to the trust even though an employee may recognize additional income attributable to realized and unrealized appreciation and earnings. If there is more than one employee participating in the plan, the employer may deduct contributions only if it maintains separate accounts for each employee to which employer contributions are allocated, as well as the appreciation and earnings thereon.

The secular trust is taxed on trust income. The employer is never treated as the grantor of a secular trust, even if the employer retains powers that would otherwise make it a grantor for tax purposes. However, trust earnings attributable to employee contributions are taxed to the employee. Contributions to the trust are treated as employee contributions if the employee has a right to withdraw employer contributions from the trust for a limited period of time after the contributions are made or if the employee has the option to receive cash from the employer in lieu of a contribution to the trust.

The trust may deduct from its income the distributions to the employees paid during the trust's tax year if the plan maintains separate accounts. The distribution deduction may not exceed the distributable net income allocable to each employee's separate account. Distributions from the secular trust to a highly compensated employee during a tax year are added back to the highly compensated employee's vested accrued benefit at the end of the trust's tax year. As indicated above, the highly compensated employee is then taxed on the employee's vested accrued benefit at the end of such

---

28. For purposes of Rev. Rul. 2007-48, it is assumed that one of the reasons that the trust is not tax exempt is that the plan fails to meet the minimum coverage requirements under Sec. 410(b) or if the plan has a defined benefit formula, it fails to meet the participation requirements under Sec. 401(a)(26). The vast majority of deferred compensation plans cover only highly compensated employees and thus, do not meet the requirements of Sec. 410(b). If a nonhighly compensated employee is covered by a secular trust, that employee is taxed on the amount of the employer contribution in the year that the contribution is made as long as the contribution is substantially vested and nonforfeitable at that time.

tax year, less amounts remaining in the employee's separate account that were previously taxed.[29]

Deferred compensation in a secular trust becomes subject to FICA, FUTA and Medicare taxes on the date of contribution provided that the contributions are vested on that date. In that event the employer is liable for such taxes. If not vested on the date of contribution, the FICA, FUTA and Medicare taxes are imposed once the contributions become vested. In that event, the trust is treated as the employer with respect to the payment of such taxes on those amounts. There is no further withholding of FICA, FUTA and Medicare taxes in future years on any appreciation and earnings on those contributions. Nor is there any further withholding of those taxes on amounts distributed from the secular trust.

Since a secular trust is generally associated with a funded plan, income tax withholding is required in the year of deferral (or in the year of vesting, if later). However, special rules apply to highly compensated employees. First, the deferred compensation is treated as paid on the last day of each tax year. Second, the amount subject to withholding is the fair market value of the employee's vested accrued benefit on the last day of each tax year, reduced by the fair market value of the employee's vested accrued benefit that was subject to withholding in the preceding tax year, i.e., the employee's investment in the contract. This means that if there is immediate vesting, there is no deferral for purposes of Sec. 409A. Thus, there is no reason for the plan to comply with the requirements of Sec. 409A as long as it covers only highly compensated employees. Distributions from the trust to a highly compensated employee during the tax year are added to the employee's year–end vested accrued benefit. Finally, the secular trust is treated as the employer for income tax withholding purposes.

Finally, under the tax treatment set forth in Rev. Rul. 2007-48 there is a potential for double taxation of earnings in secular trusts. The secular trust is first taxed on trust earnings at the end of each tax year. A highly compensated employee is then taxed on the vested accrued benefit under the trust as of the close of each tax year (which includes trust earnings), less previously taxed amounts. This double taxation can be avoided by paying out each year's trust income to the employee or by giving the employee the

---

29. Distributions from a secular trust to non-highly compensated employees are taxed under Sec. 72. This means that the trust must distinguish between amounts received as an annuity taxable under Sec. 72(b) and amounts not received as an annuity taxable under Sec. 72(e).

right to elect to receive a distribution of all or a part of such income. The trust then becomes entitled to a distribution deduction for the income currently distributed or made available to the employees. The latter approach enables each employee to receive a distribution of income sufficient to pay the income tax liability attributable to the annual growth in the employee's separate share of the trust. Alternatively, if the employee is given the right to withdraw trust assets for a limited period of time, for example, 30–45 days, or to receive cash from the employer in lieu of a trust contribution, the employee will be treated as the grantor of the trust and will be taxed on all of the trust income.

Left to their own devices employers generally favor using the "employer-grantor" secular trust because this allows employers to maintain control of the trust assets, a major objective in the "golden handcuffs" type of plan. However, Rev. Rul. 2007-48 confirms that the secular trust cannot be taxed as a grantor trust. This leaves trust income subject to a potential double tax. However, it is possible to structure a secular trust so that it can be initiated by the employer and include appropriate "handcuff" provisions, but at the same time it can include trust provisions that would cause the trust to be taxed as an employee-grantor trust. Such a provision might include a limited right of withdrawal by the employee. Since the secular trust represents a financing mechanism that truly secures an employer's deferred compensation obligation, something not available through a rabbi trust, many employers will continue to evaluate a secular trust as a possible financing mechanism.

DEFERRED-COMPENSATION PLANS FOR EXECUTIVES OF GOVERNMENTAL AND TAX-EXEMPT ORGANIZATIONS

For many years the classic unfunded, nonqualified deferred-compensation plan for selected executives has been a staple item for corporate planners. When the employer is a tax-exempt or governmental organization, however, the planning environment is radically different.

In the context of the for-profit business, the business owner and selected employees want to save for retirement without being subject to the requirements that apply to qualified retirement plans. In that context, the employer is entitled to an immediate deduction only if the employee is currently taxed, or conversely, the employee may defer tax only if the employer's deduction is deferred.

The tax tension that exists between employers and employees of for-profit companies is absent for employers that are tax-exempt entities. Because a tax deduction is meaningless for a tax-exempt employer, the tax-exempt employer is more inclined to allow an employee to defer compensation than its for-profit counterpart. Recognizing this difference between for-profit and tax-exempt employers, Congress established a separate tax regime applicable to deferred compensation for employees and independent contractors employed by state and local governments and tax-exempt organizations. These tax rules are found in Code Sec. 457.

There are two types of Sec. 457 deferred-compensation plans: 457(b) eligible plans and 457(f) ineligible plans. The former are similar to qualified retirement plans and are intended to ensure that tax-favored savings are used primarily for retirement purposes. The deferred compensation in a 457(b) eligible plan is taxed when it is paid or made available to the employee. A participant in a 457(f) ineligible plan will be taxed on deferred compensation if his or her right to receive those amounts is not subject to a substantial risk of forfeiture.

Employers Subject to Code Sec. 457

Code Sec. 457 applies to nonqualified deferred-compensation plans of:

1. a state, a political subdivision of a state (such as a city or township), and any agency or instrumentality of a state or political subdivision of a state (for example, a school district or a sewage authority); and

2. any organization exempt from federal income tax, except for a church or synagogue or an organization controlled by a church or a synagogue.[30]

457(b) Eligible Plans

The five principal requirements applicable to a 457(b) eligible plan are the following:

- Participation limited to service providers—Only employees and independent contractors who perform services for the employer may participate.

- Maximum annual deferral amount—The plan must provide that the maximum amount of compensation which may be deferred under the plan for the taxable year may not exceed the lesser of $16,500 (the applicable dollar amount for 2010) or 100 percent of the

---

30. IRC Sec. 457(e)(1), (13).

participant's includible compensation for services performed for the employer which is currently includible in gross income (after taking into account the deductions allowed under Section 457 and other similar income tax provisions.) Prior to 2002, amounts excluded from income under Section 403(b) and Section 401(k) plans were required to reduce the maximum allowable Section 457(b) deferral. This was a major deterrent to the use of 457(b) eligible plans. However, since 2002 this is no longer the case, and it has provided a significant impetus to the adoption of 457(b) eligible plans as supplemental plans in recent years.

- Timing of deferral election—The plan must provide that compensation will be deferred for a calendar month only if an agreement providing for such deferral has been entered into before the beginning of the month. However, with respect to a new employee, a plan may provide that compensation is to be deferred for the calendar month during which the participant first becomes an employee if an agreement providing for such deferral is entered into on or before the first day on which the participant becomes an employee.

- Timing of distributions—Amounts cannot be made available under the plan to participants or beneficiaries earlier than (i) the calendar year in which the participant attains age 70½, (ii) when the participant has a severance from employment with the employer, or (iii) when the participant is faced with an unforeseeable emergency. In addition, the plan must comply with the minimum distribution requirements of Code Section 401(a)(9). Finally, a plan may permit a distribution of benefits pursuant to a qualified domestic relations order. If an amount becomes available pursuant to one of the distribution events described in (i), (ii), or (iii) above, a participant can elect, but only once, to defer commencement of distributions, provided that payments have not yet begun. Participants in a nongovernmental 457(b) eligible plan cannot defer taxation by rolling over a distribution into an IRA or another plan.

- Property Rights—All amounts of compensation deferred under a 457(b) plan of a nongovernmental employer, all property and rights purchased with such amounts, and all income attributable to such amounts must remain solely the property of the employer, subject to claims of the employer's general creditors, until the deferred compensation is made available to the participants and beneficiaries. In contrast, the amounts deferred, including the investments made with such amounts and the income attributable to such deferrals, under a 457(b) plan maintained by a government entity must be held in a trust that is protected from the claims of the employer's creditors.

EXAMPLE

Smithtown Health System (SHS) maintains a Sec. 403(b) plan for its employees. Under this plan, employees can contribute the maximum allowable deferrals. SHS matches 50 percent of these deferrals up to 6 percent of compensation. SHS also makes a nonelective contribution equal to 5 percent of compensation. SHS can adopt a 457(b) eligible plan, which will allow the employees to supplement their 403(b) elective deferrals by making additional elective deferrals up to the $16,500 limit (for 2010).

Similar to 401(k) and 403(b) plans, 457(b) eligible plans maintained by government entities (but not by other tax-exempt employers) may allow additional salary deferrals to employees who attain age 50 prior to the end of the plan year. For 2010, this catch-up amount is $5,500. For employees nearing normal retirement, a 457(b) eligible plan may allow them to make a special catch-up contribution. However, this special catch-up contribution is limited: For one or more of the participant's last 3 taxable years ending before he or she attains normal retirement age under the plan, the applicable dollar amount under the 457(b) eligible plan for the taxable year shall not exceed the lesser of:

- twice the applicable dollar amount then in effect, or
- the sum of (i) the maximum deferral amount for the taxable year and (ii) the amount of the maximum deferral for any taxable years before the taxable year that has not previously been used under either the maximum deferral amount or the special 457(b) catch-up provision.

Coordination with ERISA

A 457(b) eligible plan can cover any group of employees or independent contractors. However, since a 457(b) eligible plan that is not maintained by a government entity must remain unfunded, it must limit its coverage to those employees who will allow the plan to qualify as an ERISA top-hat plan. A 457(b) eligible plan maintained by a tax-exempt employer must avoid ERISA coverage because if the plan becomes subject to ERISA, it would have to satisfy the ERISA trust requirement, which in turn would result in the plan no longer being unfunded. Consequently, tax-exempt employers generally structure their 457(b) eligible plans to cover a select group of management and highly compensated employees.

457(f) Ineligible Plans

If a plan does not meet the requirements for being a 457(b) eligible plan, then the deferred compensation is included in the compensation of the participant when there is no longer a substantial risk of forfeiture. These noncomplying plans are referred to as 457(f) ineligible plans. Because employees do not want to pay tax on compensation they have not yet received, almost all 457(f) ineligible plans provide for distributions when the deferred compensation vests. A 457(f) ineligible plan is broadly defined to include any agreement or arrangement that provides for a deferral of compensation.

EXAMPLE

John Donovan is an executive of a nonprofit corporation. John has earned a bonus of $100,000, payable in 3 years together with interest, provided that John remains employed for the entire 3-year period. The $100,000 amount exceeds the limit under a 457(b) eligible plan, so the arrangement must be treated as a 457(f) ineligible plan. Because John must work for 3 years to receive the bonus, it is subject to a substantial risk of forfeiture and will not be taxable until the end of the 3-year period. At that time the bonus will be paid.

The IRS has approved forfeitable deferred-compensation plans of this type for employers subject to Sec. 457,[31] and this should be considered an appropriate technique of executive compensation for governmental and nonprofit employers. Unfortunately, however, there are two major problems with forfeitable deferred-compensation plans that limit their usefulness considerably.

First of all, any risk of forfeiture must be *substantial* in order for that risk to be recognized for purposes of deferring taxes. It is easy for academic purposes to provide an illustration of a risk that will be so recognized, but not so easy to design practical provisions. For example, a provision that an executive will

---

31. See Priv. Ltr. Ruls. 88-31-022 (May 6, 1988), 90-08-059 (Nov. 29, 1989), 92-11-037 (Dec. 17, 1991). Priv. Ltr. Rul 90-08-059 involved a nonprofit (Sec. 501(c)(3)) employer that had two Sec. 457 plans, both maintained only for a select group of management and highly compensated employees (the top-hat group). Plan 1 provided benefits within the $7,500 limit (and had graduated vesting), while Plan 2 provided supplemental additional benefits that were forfeited if employment was terminated prior to normal retirement age for reasons other than death or disability.

not receive the deferred amount if he or she dies before retirement or leaves employment before retirement or expiration of his or her contract, would almost certainly pass muster with the IRS.[32]

The regulations under Sec. 83 provide some helpful examples and guidelines. For example, a forfeiture as a result of failing to meet certain incentive targets, such as a certain level of sales or profits, generally is a substantial risk of forfeiture.[33] A forfeiture provision applying if the employee goes to work for a competitor constitutes a substantial risk if the employee has scarce skills in an active job market—whatever that might mean.[34]

However, a forfeiture only as a result of some event that is relatively unlikely to occur does not constitute a substantial risk of forfeiture. For example, suppose the plan provides that the employee forfeits benefits if he or she commits embezzlement. Since this is an unlikely event and is also within the employee's control, the IRS is not likely to recognize it as a substantial risk of forfeiture.[35]

Some of the more surefire forfeiture provisions might be considered too severe by some executives. Any attempt to provide forfeiture provisions

---

32. Treas. Reg. Sec.1.83-3(c)(1). The rules in this regulation were applied in Priv. Ltr. Rul. 90-30-025 (April 27, 1990) to a plan of a Section 457 employer that involved a "continuous service" requirement to avoid forfeiture, and also in Priv. Ltr. Rul. 90-10-080 (Dec. 15, 1989) to a plan of a tax-exempt employer that provided a rolling 5-year vesting provision.

    The IRS also approved the forfeiture provisions in a public school teachers' 4-year deferral program prior to an approved leave of absence, Priv. Ltr. Rul. 92-12-006 (Dec. 19, 1991).

    The use of a rabbi-type trust in a Sec. 457(f) plan was ruled permissible (that is, it did not defeat deferral where there was substantial risk of forfeiture) in Priv. Ltr. Rul. 92-12-011 (Dec. 19, 1991).

    Priv. Ltr. Rul. 92-15-019 (Jan. 8, 1992) involved a public school superintendent with a 3-year renewable contract. Deferred-compensation benefits were designed to vest when the employee reached age 62, died, or became disabled. If the employee terminated employment before that time, the board reserved the right to vest benefits if the employee had worked for at least 3 years. The IRS held that taxation was deferred for 3 years in this case but declined to rule on the question of "fact" as to whether there was a substantial risk of forfeiture after the initial 3-year period.

    Priv. Ltr. Rul. 92-11-037 (Dec. 17, 1991) involved a risk of forfeiture (and tax deferral under Sec. 457(f)) extending to age 65, age 55 with 10 years of service, disability, or death.

33. Treas. Reg. Sec. 1.83-3(c)(2).
34. Ibid.
35. Ibid.

that are not clearly covered by these Sec. 83 guidelines leads inevitably to uncertainty regarding the result of a future IRS audit. Apart from the remote possibility of obtaining an IRS private letter ruling, there is simply no way to assure the result in this area.

The second problem relates to the taxation of benefits at retirement. Many executives would like to receive benefits in installments, over at least several years, and pay taxes on those benefits as they are received. However, if the substantial risk of forfeiture expires when the executive retires, then all benefits become taxable in the year of retirement, even if the plan provides for deferred installment payments and the executive has no current access to future installments. Workable forfeiture provisions to continue tax deferral beyond retirement are much more difficult to design than those applicable during the period of employment.

One commonly discussed way to continue tax deferral after retirement is to make each benefit installment payment contingent on the executive's continuing availability for consulting services to the employer or to impose a requirement that the executive not work for a competitor, subject to forfeiture of remaining installments. Obviously, the success of such provisions surviving a tax audit will depend on whether these provisions actually have economic reality—that is, whether they actually impose a burden on the executive and whether there is any real likelihood of forfeiture. Again, in some cases it may be possible to obtain an IRS ruling on the issue.

If the agreement provides that payments terminate on the retired employee's death, the risk of forfeiture should be substantial. For example, an arrangement that provides 10 annual $10,000 payments, with payments terminating if the executive dies before the 10-year period ends, should allow tax to be deferred. However, if there is no risk of loss, termination at death does not provide a substantial risk of forfeiture. For example, if the present value of the deferred compensation is converted at retirement to a life annuity (whether or not an annuity contract is purchased from an insurance company), the present value itself will be taxable in the year of retirement because the executive will, in fact, receive the actuarial present value of the annuity (by the definition of a life annuity) regardless of how many years he or she actually survives.[36]

---

36. These conclusions are based on the language of Sec. 457(f). Although neither the courts nor the IRS has taken a position on these issues, it is the author's opinion that it is reasonable for the IRS to take the positions stated here on audit, given the current state of the law.

Design Features

Apart from the fundamental requirement of forfeitability just discussed, 457(f) ineligible plans can be designed much like the nonqualified plans for taxable employers discussed in this and the preceding chapter. However, some 457(f) ineligible plans will also have to satisfy the Sec. 409A restrictions on the timing of distributions, acceleration of deferrals, and the making of deferral elections. However, unlike taxable employers, the penalty for failing to meet the Sec. 409A requirements is not so much the acceleration of taxation, since employees of tax exempts are already subject to tax when the substantial risk of forfeiture lapses. Rather, the real penalty is the 20-percent additional tax imposed on an employee who has violated the requirements of Sec. 409A.

On the other hand, many 457(f) ineligible plans will not be subject to Sec. 409A to the extent that those plans satisfy the exclusion available to short-term deferrals under Sec. 409A and thus, distribute the deferral compensation within 2½ months following the end of the tax year in which vesting occurs. The tax year that is used for this purpose is the later of the employer's tax year or the employee's tax year.

However, the coordination of Code Secs. 409A and 457(f) is easier said than done. There is a different concept of "substantial risk of forfeiture" under each of these Code sections and these differences can affect the tax consequences to the covered employees. For example, a 457(f) ineligible plan that provides for elective salary deferrals, a rolling risk of forfeiture, or a noncompetition provision will probably not qualify for the 2½ month exception, because Sec. 409A does not recognize any of these vesting conditions as constituting a substantial risk of forfeiture. Thus, the deferred compensation will be considered to have vested for Sec. 409A purposes, but for Sec. 457(f) purposes will not vest until some time that is later than the end of the allowable 2½ month period under Sec. 409A. Thus, care must be taken to review the provisions of a 457(f) ineligible plan in light of the requirements of both Secs. 457(f) and 409A to make sure that those requirements will not be acting at cross purposes and that the intended tax consequences can be accomplished.

ERISA

Generally, planners will want to avoid the applicability of the ERISA funding requirements to a 457(f) ineligible plan, for many of the same reasons applicable to a regular deferred compensation plan. For a governmental plan, this is not a problem, since ERISA does not apply to governmental employers. For nongovernmental tax-exempt employers, however, the funding requirements can be met only by complying with the "top-hat" restrictions of ERISA discussed earlier. Therefore, a Sec. 457(f) ineligible plan must generally be restricted to a select group of management or highly compensated employees.

Financing and Rabbi Trusts

Like regular deferred-compensation plans, a Sec. 457(f) plan will not be formally funded—that is, with an irrevocable trust fund for the exclusive benefit of employees—the employer can, and in most cases should, finance its obligations under the plan by setting aside assets in advance of the time when payments will be made. An asset reserve, or life insurance or annuity contracts are often used for this purpose. For a larger group, a COLI arrangement might be appropriate. A rabbi trust can be used in the same manner as it is for a regular nonqualified deferred-compensation plan.

If the employer purchases life insurance contracts to finance the plan, there is no current life insurance cost to employees as long as the employer retains all incidents of ownership in the policies, is the sole beneficiary under the policies, and is under no obligation to transfer the policies or pass through the proceeds of the policies. Benefits paid to beneficiaries under the plan are not eligible for the income tax exclusion for life insurance proceeds.[37]

---

37. Priv. Ltr. Rul 90-08-043 (Nov. 28, 1989).

ADDITIONAL RESOURCES

IRS Model Rabbi Trust

TRUST UNDER ————————————PLAN

OPTIONAL

(a) This Agreement made this _____day of _____, by and between_____(Company) and

_____
(Trustee);

OPTIONAL

(b) WHEREAS, Company has adopted the nonqualified deferred compensation Plan(s) as listed in Appendix _____.

OPTIONAL

(c) WHEREAS, Company has incurred or expects to incur liability under the terms of such Plan(s) with respect to the individuals participating in such Plan(s):

(d) WHEREAS, Company wishes to establish a trust (hereinafter called "Trust") and to contribute to the Trust assets that shall be held therein, subject to the claims of Company's creditors in the event the Company's Insolvency, as herein defined, until paid to Plan participants and their beneficiaries in such manner and at such times as specified in the Plan(s);

(e) WHEREAS, it is the intention of the parties that this Trust shall constitute an unfunded arrangement and shall not affect the status of the Plan(s) as an unfunded plan maintained for the purpose of providing deferred compensation for a select group of management or highly compensated employees for purposes of Title I of the Employee Retirement Income Security Act of 1974;

(f) WHEREAS, it is the intention of Company to make contributions to the Trust to provide itself with a source of funds to assist it in the meeting of its liabilities under the Plan(s);

NOW, THEREFORE, the parties do hereby establish the Trust and agree that the Trust shall be comprised, held and disposed of as follows:

Section 1. *Establishment of Trust*

(a) Company hereby deposits with Trustee in trust_____[insert amount deposited], which shall become the principal of the Trust to be held, administered and disposed of by Trustee as provided in this Trust Agreement.

ALTERNATIVES—Select one provision.

(b) The Trust hereby established shall be revocable by Company.

(b) The Trust hereby established shall be irrevocable.

(b) The Trust hereby established is revocable by Company; it shall become irrevocable upon a Change of Control, as defined herein.

(b) The Trust shall become irrevocable_____[insert number] days following the issuance of a favorable private letter ruling regarding the Trust from the Internal Revenue Service.

(b) The Trust shall become irrevocable upon approval by the Board of Directors.

(c) The Trust is intended to be a grantor trust, of which Company is the grantor, within the meaning of subpart E, part I, subchapter J, chapter 1, subtitle A of the Internal Revenue Code of 1986, as amended, and shall be construed accordingly.

(d) The principal of the Trust, and any earnings thereon shall be held separate and apart from other funds of Company and shall be used exclusively for the uses and purposes of Plan participants and general creditors and herein set forth. Plan participants and their beneficiaries shall have no preferred claim on, or any beneficial ownership interest in, any assets of the Trust. Any rights created under the Plan(s) and this Trust Agreement shall be mere unsecured contractual rights of Plan participants and their beneficiaries against Company. Any assets held by the Trust will be subject to the claims

of Company's general creditors under federal and state law in the event of Insolvency, as defined in Section 3(a) herein.

ALTERNATIVES—Select one or more provisions, as appropriate.

(e) Company, in its sole discretion, may at any time, or from time to time, make additional deposits of cash or other property in trust with Trustee to augment the principal to be held, administered and disposed of by Trustee as provided in this Trust Agreement. Neither Trustee nor any Plan participant or beneficiary shall have any right to compel such additional deposits.

(e) Upon a Change of Control, Company shall, as soon as possible, but in no event longer than_____[fill in blank] days following the Change of Control, as defined herein, make an irrevocable contribution to the Trust in an amount that is sufficient to pay each Plan participant or beneficiary the benefits to which Plan participant or their beneficiaries would be entitled pursuant to the terms of the Plan(s) as of the date on which the Change of Control occurred.

(e) Within_____[fill in blank] days following the end of the Plan year(s), ending after the Trust has become irrevocable pursuant to Section 1(b) hereof, Company shall be required to irrevocably deposit additional cash or other property to the Trust in an amount sufficient to pay each Plan participant or beneficiary the benefits payable pursuant to the terms of the Plan(s) as of the close of the Plan year(s).

Section 2. *Payments to Plan Participants and Their Beneficiaries.*

(a) Company shall deliver to Trustee a schedule (the "Payment Schedule") that indicates the amounts payable in respect of each Plan participant (and his or her beneficiaries), that provides a formula or other instructions acceptable to Trustee for determining the amounts so payable, the form in which such amount is to be paid (as provided for or available under the

Plan(s)), and the time commencement for payment of such amounts. Except as otherwise provided herein, Trustee shall make payments to the Plan participants and their beneficiaries in accordance with such Payment Schedule. The Trustee shall make provision for the reporting and withholding of any federal, state or local taxes that may be required to be withheld with respect to the payment of benefits pursuant to the terms of the Plan(s) and shall pay amount withheld to the appropriate

taxing authorities or determine that such amounts have been reported, withheld and paid by Company.

(b) The entitlement of a Plan participant or his or her beneficiaries to benefits under the Plan(s) shall be determined by Company or such party as it shall designate under the Plan(s), and any claim for such benefits shall be considered and reviewed under the procedures set out in the Plan(s).

(c) Company may make payment of benefits directly to Plan participants or their beneficiaries as they become due under the terms of the Plan(s). Company shall notify Trustee of its decision to make payment of benefits directly prior to the time amounts are payable to participants or their beneficiaries. In addition, if the principal of the Trust, and any earnings thereon, are not sufficient to make payments of benefits in accordance with the terms of the Plan(s), Company shall make the balance of each such payment as it falls due. Trustee shall notify Company where principal and earnings are not sufficient.

Section 3. *Trustee Responsibility Regarding Payment to Trust Beneficiary When Company is Insolvent.*

(a) Trustee shall cease payment of benefits to Plan participants and their beneficiaries if the Company is Insolvent. Company shall be considered "Insolvent" for purposes of this Trust Agreement if (i) Company is unable to pay its debts as they become due, or (ii) Company is subject to a pending proceeding as a debtor under the United States Bankruptcy Code.

OPTIONAL

, or (iii) Company is determined to be insolvent by _____*[insert names of applicable federal and/or state regulatory agency].*

(b) At all times during the continuance of this Trust, as provided in Section 1(d) hereof, the principal and income of the Trust shall be subject to claims of general creditors of Company under federal and state law as set forth below.

(1) The Board of Directors and the Chief Executive Officer [or substitute the title of the highest ranking officer of the Company] of Company shall have the duty to inform Trustee in writing of Company's Insolvency. If a person claiming to be a creditor of Company alleges in writing to Trustee that Company has become Insolvent, Trustee shall determine whether Company is Insolvent and, pending such determination, Trustee shall discontinue payment of benefits to Plan participants or their beneficiaries.

(2) Unless Trustee has actual knowledge of Company's Insolvency, or has received notice from Company or a person claiming to be a creditor alleging that Company is Insolvent, Trustee shall have no duty to inquire whether Company is Insolvent. Trustee may in all events rely on such evidence concerning Company's solvency as may be furnished to Trustee and that provides Trustee with a reasonable basis for making a determination concerning Company's solvency.

(3) If at any time Trustee has determined that Company is Insolvent, Trustee shall discontinue payments to Plan participants or their beneficiaries and shall hold the assets of the Trust for the benefit of Company's general creditors. Nothing this Trust Agreement shall in any way diminish any rights of Plan participation or their beneficiaries to pursue their rights as general creditors of Company with respect to benefits due under the Plan(s) or otherwise.

(4) Trustee shall resume the payment of benefits to Plan participants or their beneficiaries in accordance with Section 2 of this Trust Agreement only after Trustee has determined that Company is not Insolvent (or is no longer Insolvent).

(c) Provided that there are sufficient assets, if Trustee discontinues the payment of benefits from the Trust pursuant to Section 3(b) hereof and subsequently resumes such payments, the first payment following such discontinuance shall include the aggregate amount of all payments due to Plan participants or their beneficiaries under the terms of the Plan(s) for the period of such discontinuance, less the aggregate amount of any payments made to Plan participants or their beneficiaries by Company in lieu of the payments provided for hereunder during any such period of discontinuance.

Section 4. *Payments to Company.*

[The following need not be included if the first alternative under 1(b) is selected.]

Except as provided in Section 3 hereof, after the Trust has become irrevocable, Company shall have no right or power to direct Trustee to return to Company or to divert to others any of the Trust assets before all payment of benefits have been made to Plan participants and their beneficiaries pursuant to the terms of the Plan(s).

Section 5. *Investment Authority.*

ALTERNATIVES—Select one provision, as appropriate

(a) In no event may Trustee invest in securities (including stock or rights to acquire stock) or obligations issued by Company, other than a de minimis amount held in common investment vehicles in which Trustee invests. All rights associated with assets of the Trust shall be exercised by Trustee or the person designated by Trustee, and shall in no event be exercisable by or rest with Plan participants.

(a) Trustee may invest in securities (including stock or rights to acquire stock) or obligations issued by Company. All rights associated with assets of the Trust shall be exercised by Trustee or the person designated by Trustee, and shall in no event be exercisable by or rest with Plan participants.

OPTIONAL

, except that voting rights with respect to Trust assets will be exercised by Company.

OPTIONAL

, except that dividend rights with respect to Trust assets will rest with Company.

OPTIONAL

Company shall have the right, at anytime, and from time to time in its sole discretion, to substitute assets of equal fair market value of any asset held by the Trust.

[If the second Alternative 5(a) is selected, the trust must provide either (1) that the Trust is revocable under Alternative 1(b) or (2) the following provision must be included in the Trust]:

"Company shall have the right at anytime, and from time to time in its sole discretion, to substitute assets of equal fair market value for any asset held by the Trust. This right is exercisable by Company in a nonfiduciary capacity without the approval or consent of any person in a fiduciary capacity."

Section 6. *Disposition of Income.*

ALTERNATIVES—Select one provision.

(a) During the term of this Trust, all income received by the Trust, net of expenses and taxes, shall be accumulated and reinvested.

(a) During the term of this Trust, all, or _____[insert amount] part of the income received by the Trust, net of expenses and taxes, shall be returned to Company.

Section 7. *Accounting by Trustee.*

OPTIONAL

Trustee shall keep accurate and detailed records of all investments, receipts, disbursements, and all other transactions required to be made, including such specific records as shall be agreed upon in writing between Company and Trustee. Within _____[insert number] days following the close of each calendar year and within _____[insert number] days after the removal of resignation of Trustee, Trustee shall deliver to Company a written account of its administration of the Trust during such year or during the period from the close of last preceding year to the date of such removal or resignation, setting forth all investments, receipts, disbursements and other transactions effected by it, including a description of all securities and investments purchased and sold with the cost or net proceeds of such purchases or sales (accrued interest paid or receivable being shown separately), and showing all cash, securities and other property field in the

Trust at the end of such year or as of the date of such removal or resignation, as the case may be.

Section 8. *Responsibility of Trustee.*

OPTIONAL

(a) Trustee shall act with the care, skill, prudence and diligence under the circumstances then prevailing that a prudent person acting in like capacity and familiar with such matters would use in the conduct of an enterprise of alike character and with like aims, provided, however, that Trustee shall incur no liability to any person for any action taken pursuant to a direction, request or approval given by Company which is contemplated by, and in conformity with, the terms of the Plan(s) or this Trust and is given in writing by Company. In the event of a dispute between Company and a party, Trustee may apply to a court of competent jurisdiction to resolve the dispute.

OPTIONAL

(b) If Trustee undertakes or defends any litigation arising in connection with the Trust, Company agrees to indemnify Trustee against Trustee's costs, expenses and liabilities (including, without limitation, attorneys' fees and expenses) relating thereto and to be primarily liable for such payments. If Company does not pay such costs, expenses and liabilities in a reasonably timely manner, Trustee may obtain payment from the Trust.

OPTIONAL

(c) Trustee may consult with legal counsel (who may also be counsel for Company generally) with respect to any of its duties or obligations hereunder.

OPTIONAL

(d) Trustee may hire agents, accountants, actuaries, investment advisors, financial consultants or other professionals to assist it in performing any of its duties or obligations hereunder.

(e) Trustee shall have, without exclusion, all powers conferred on Trustees by applicable law, unless expressly provided otherwise herein, provided, however, that if an insurance policy is held as an asset of the Trust, Trustee shall have no power to name a beneficiary of the policy

other than the Trust, to assign the policy (as distinct from conversion of the policy to a different form) other than to a successor Trustee, or to loan to any person the proceeds of any borrowing against such policy.

OPTIONAL

(f) However, notwithstanding the provisions of Section 8(e) above, Trustee may loan to Company the proceeds of any borrowing against an insurance policy held as an asset of the Trust.

(g) Notwithstanding any powers granted to Trustee pursuant to this Trust Agreement or to applicable law, Trustee shall not have any power that could give this Trust the objective of carrying on a business and dividing the gains therefrom, within the meaning of section 301.7701-2 of the Procedure and Administrative Regulations promulgated pursuant to the Internal Revenue Code.

Section 9. *Compensation and Expenses of Trustee.*

OPTIONAL

Company shall pay all administrative and Trustee's fees and expenses. If not so paid, the fees and expenses shall be paid from the Trust.

Section 10. *Resignation and Removal of Trustee.*

Trustee may resign at any time by written notice to Company, which shall be effective _____[insert number] days after receipt of such notice unless Company and Trustee agree otherwise.

OPTIONAL

(b) Trustee may be removed by Company on _____[insert number] days notice or upon shorter notice accepted by Trustee.

OPTIONAL

(c) Upon a Change of Control, as defined herein, Trustee may not be removed by Company for _____[insert number] year(s).

OPTIONAL

(d) If Trustee resigns within _____ [insert number] year(s) after a Change of Control, as defined herein, Company shall apply to a court of competent jurisdiction for the appointment of a successor Trustee or for instructions.

OPTIONAL

(e) If Trustee resigns or is removed within _____ [insert number] year(s) of a Change of Control, as defined herein, Trustee shall select a successor Trustee in accordance with the provisions of Section 11(b) hereof prior to the effective date of Trustee's resignation or removal.

(f) Upon resignation or removal of Trustee and appointment of a successor Trustee, all assets shall subsequently be transferred to the successor Trustee. The transfer shall be completed within _____ [insert number] days after receipt of notice of resignation, removal or transfer, unless Company extends the time limit.

(g) If Trustee resigns or is removed, a successor shall be appointed, in accordance with Section 11 hereof, by the effective date of resignation or removal under paragraph(s) (a) [or (b)] of this section. If no such appointment has been made, Trustee may apply to a court of competent jurisdiction for appointment of a successor or for instructions. All expenses of Trustee in connection with the proceeding shall be allowed as administrative expenses of the Trust.

Section 11. *Appointment of Successor.*

OPTIONAL

(a) If Trustee resigns [or is removed] in accordance with Section 10(a) [or (b)] hereof, Company may appoint any third party, such as a bank trust department or other party that may be granted corporate trustee powers under state law, as a successor to replace Trustee upon resignation or removal. The appointment shall be effective when accepted in writing by the new Trustee, who shall have all of the rights and powers of the former Trustee, including ownership rights in the Trust assets. The former

Trustee shall execute any instrument necessary of reasonably requested by Company or the successor Trustee to evidence the transfer.

OPTIONAL

(b) If Trustee resigns or is removed pursuant to the provisions of Section 10(e) hereof and selects a successor Trustee, Trustee may appoint any third party such as a bank trust department or other party that may be granted corporate trustee powers under state law. The appointment of a successor Trustee shall be effective when accepted in writing by the new Trustee. The new Trustee shall have all the rights and powers of the former Trustee, including ownership rights in Trust assets. The former Trustee shall execute any instrument necessary or reasonably requested by the successor Trustee to evidence the transfer.

OPTIONAL

(c) The successor Trustee need not examine the records and acts of any prior Trustee and may retain or dispose of existing Trust assets, subject to Section 7 and 8 hereof. The successor Trustee shall not be responsible for and Company shall indemnify and defend the successor Trustee from any claim or liability resulting from any action or inaction of any prior Trustee or from any other past event, or any condition existing at the time it becomes successor Trustee.

Section 12. *Amendment or Termination.*

(a) This Trust Agreement may be amended by a written instrument executed by Trustee and Company. [Unless the first alternative under 1(b) is selected, the following sentence must be included.] Notwithstanding the foregoing, no such amendment shall conflict with the terms of the Plan(s) or shall make the Trust revocable after it has become irrevocable in accordance with Section 1(b) hereof.

(b) The Trust shall not terminate until the date on which Plan participants and their beneficiaries are no longer entitled to benefits pursuant to the terms of the Plan(s) [unless the second alternative under 1(b) is selected, the following must be included:], "unless sooner revoked in accordance with Section 1(b) hereof." Upon termination of the Trust any assets remaining in the Trust shall be returned to the Company.

OPTIONAL

(c) Upon written approval of participants or beneficiaries entitled to payment of benefits pursuant to the terms of the Plan(s), Company may terminate this Trust prior to the time all benefit payments under the Plan(s) have been made. All assets in the Trust at termination shall be returned to Company.

OPTIONAL

(d) Section(s)_____[insert number(s)] of this Trust Agreement may not be amended by Company for_____[insert number] year(s) following a Change of Control, as defined herein.

Section 13. *Miscellaneous.*

Any provision of this Trust Agreement prohibited by law shall be ineffective to the extent of any such prohibition, without invalidating the remaining provisions hereof.

Benefits payable to Plan participants and their beneficiaries under this Trust Agreement may not be anticipated, assigned (either at law or in equity), alienated, pledged, encumbered or subjected to attachment, garnishment, levy, execution or other legal equitable process.

(c) This Trust Agreement shall be governed by and construed in accordance with the laws of _____.

OPTIONAL

(d) For purposes of this Trust, Change or Control shall mean: [insert objective definition such as: "the purchase or other acquisition by any person, entity or group of persons, within the meaning of section 13(d) or 14(d) of the Securities Exchange Act of 1934 ("Act"), or any comparable successor provisions, of beneficial ownership (within the meaning of Rule 13d-3 promulgated under the Act) of 30 percent or more of either the outstanding shares of common stock or the combined voting power of Company's then outstanding voting securities entitled to vote generally, or the approval by the stockholders of Company of a reorganization, merger, or consolidation, in each case, with respect to which persons who were stockholders of Company immediately prior to such reorganization, merger or consolidation do not, immediately thereafter, own more than 50 percent of the combined voting power entitled to vote generally in the election of directors of the

reorganized, merged, or consolidated Company's then outstanding securities, or a liquidation or dissolution of Company or of the sale of all or substantially all of the Company's assets"].

Section 14. *Effective Date.*

The effective date of this Trust Agreement shall be

_____, 20____.

CASE PROBLEM

Charles Mann is a key employee of Essbeeco, Inc., a small publicly traded corporation. He owns no stock in Essbeeco. Mann is 50 years old and his wife is 48. They have two daughters, both of whom are happily married. Mann's current income is about $200,000; $170,000 per year is in the form of salary under a 2-year contract that expires at the end of this year, and the balance consists of dividend and rental income. He estimates his taxable income (after deductions and exemptions) to be $170,000.

Mann is considering the negotiation of a new contract for next year that would include the deferral of $20,000 annually since he is sure that he would have no problem getting along on the balance of his income. Mann feels that perhaps this would be a good way to supplement his retirement income.

Essbeeco has a noncontributory qualified pension plan under which Mann will receive a life income equal to one-third of his average salary over the last 5 years of employment. Mann is fully vested but must live to age 65 to collect benefits.

In addition, Essbeeco also provides Mann with (a) group term life insurance equal to two times his annual salary, which terminates at his retirement, and (b) a long-term disability benefit that will pay him approximately one-third of his salary beginning 6 months after a disability is incurred and continuing until he is 65.

Essbeeco is in sound financial condition and is in a 40 percent (federal and state) top tax bracket. Mann estimated that after retirement his potential top income tax bracket will be about 31 percent (taxable income of $80,000 to $90,000) not including any deferred-compensation benefits.

At present, Mann has a gross estate of about $1,600,000 that includes $100,000 of personally owned whole life insurance.

Mann has been advised by a business associate that he may be better off not deferring $20,000 annually, paying the tax now at a combined federal and state rate of 45 percent, and investing the balance after taxes in his own behalf.

Based on the facts that have been given, assume that taxation could be successfully deferred on $20,000 per year. Prepare a proposal outlining the provisions of the deferred-compensation plan you would recommend that would best overcome the argument against deferring a portion of Mann's current income. (Make any other assumptions that are appropriate and necessary.) Your proposal should include recommendations on at least the following:

1. the method by which the benefits payable to Mann at age 65 will be determined
2. the form that these benefit payments will take (for example, 10 equal installments)
3. what is to happen to Mann's benefits if he resigns, dies, or becomes disabled prior to age 65
4. the investment medium(s) for the asset reserve (if any)
5. forfeiture provision, if any
6. based on the facts given, other provisions that you deem important to protect Mann's interest

CHAPTER REVIEW

Review Questions

1. Seth Stevens, a corporate officer, is negotiating his employment contract for next year. He has been offered a contract that includes a provision for the deferral of a portion of his compensation under an unfunded nonqualified deferred-compensation plan. He is concerned about the financial soundness of the idea since he was told that, to successfully defer taxation, he must be satisfied with the unsecured promise of his employer to make the deferred-compensation payments in the future. What suggestion can you make to Stevens that would improve the likelihood that his employer will have the funds available to make the deferred-compensation payments when they become due? Explain why your suggestion should be acceptable to his employer. [1]

2. Seth Stevens's employer, Swingco, Inc., agrees with the idea of establishing an asset reserve. Under Swingco's deferred-compensation plan, Stevens will receive a fixed benefit of $10,000 per year for 10 years beginning at age 65 (20 years from now). Swingco wants to know if this means that to finance its potential obligation under the plan in equal annual payments, $5,000 must be set aside each year. Is this correct? Explain. [1]

3. Swingco, Inc., is concerned that under the deferred-compensation plan there would be no current income tax deduction for amounts set aside in the asset reserve. There would be a current deduction if the amounts deferred were paid currently. Suggest a method for overcoming this problem. [1]

4. Ira Marcs, a 58-year-old, is considering accepting employment with Swingco. He wants a current salary of $260,000 per year, plus the deferral of $10,000 per year that Swingco would invest on his behalf each year until he reaches age 65. At that time, the amount accumulated in his account would be paid to him over a 10-year period. Once again, Swingco complains that if it enters into this arrangement with Marcs, it will lose a current deduction on $10,000 per year. (Swingco is in a 35 percent top tax bracket.) Suggest a solution that is likely to overcome this objection. [1]

5. Tex Mundy, an indispensable key employee, insists on a deferred-compensation plan with a funded trusteed account for his benefit. Can this be arranged without having the plan become formally "funded" in the tax and ERISA sense? Explain. [1]

6. Describe a rabbi trust, commenting on

    a. revocability

    b. grantor trust status

    c. creditors' rights

    d. notice of insolvency [2]

7. When does an employer get a deduction for contributions to a rabbi trust? [2]

8. How is a rabbi trust income taxable? [2]

9. What are the advantages and disadvantages of a rabbi trust to the

    a. employees

    b. employer [2]

10. Popco, Inc., needs advice on how to invest the funds set aside in the reserve account to meet its future obligations under a deferred-compensation agreement. How would each of the following objectives of the plan affect your advice as to the appropriate investment of amounts contributed to the asset reserve? [3]

   a. Earnings on reserve assets should be used for the employee's benefit as a hedge against inflation.

   b. In the event of preretirement death, benefits should be subsidized so that the employee's beneficiary receives approximately the same amount the employee would have received at retirement.

   c. In the event of permanent disability prior to normal retirement age, benefits should be subsidized to equal approximately what the employee would have received at retirement.

11. Lidco, Inc., has entered into a deferred-compensation plan with Robert Rod under which Rod will receive a fixed benefit of $5,000 per year for life beginning at age 65. In addition, the plan provides the guarantee that at least 15 payments of $5,000 each will be made regardless of when Rod's death occurs. Furthermore, if Rod becomes disabled prior to retirement, payments of $5,000 each for 15 years are to begin immediately. What characteristics of either the traditional or contemporary cash value life insurance type product would make it a good choice for the investment of all or a portion of the asset reserve under this plan? [3]

12. Assume the same facts as in question 2 above except that the plan does not provide for a subsidized preretirement death benefit. Explain what your investment advice might be now. [3]

13. Ira Marcs is about to enter into a money-purchase deferred-compensation plan with his employer. He is considering requesting that the employer invest amounts deferred in either a variable annuity or a mutual fund since he would like to have an equity-based investment. Compare the characteristics of these two investment vehicles for Marcs. [3]

14. Lemco, Inc., has decided to adopt a nonqualified deferred-compensation plan covering 30 of its senior management employees. The total workforce is 400 employees. What options are available for life insurance financing for this plan? [4]

15. Comment on the use of a secular trust for Arthur Helix in objective 1 of chapter 2. [5]

16. What is the principal difference between the rules described previously and those applicable to nonqualified deferred-compensation plans for executives of tax-exempt and governmental employers? [6]

17. Quicksand Consolidated School District wants to hire Dr. Drone, aged 47, as superintendent for an annual salary in the $120,000 range, under a 5-year renewable contract. Drone has asked to receive $20,000 of this annual amount on a deferred basis, payable when he reaches age 62. What disadvantages to Dr. Drone are imposed by the tax law? [6]

18. Samuel E. Mudd, chairman of the Sewage Authority, is retiring and is eligible to receive a $300,000 deferred-compensation benefit that vests at retirement. He would like to receive this amount in 10 annual payments to minimize the tax bite. Can this be done, and if so, how? [6]

Answers to Review Questions

1. A deferred-compensation plan will be "unfunded" for income tax purposes as long as no assets are set aside for an employee so that they are no longer available to the general creditors of the employer. This requirement does not prevent the employer from financing his or her obligation by establishing an asset reserve and earmarking (by internal bookkeeping) certain amounts of the firm's assets each year for this purpose. Earmarking of assets increases the chances that the employer will be able to meet its future obligations; and psychologically, at least, it segregates the earmarked assets from the firm's operating assets. However, the deferred-compensation agreement may permit the employer to unilaterally and voluntarily convert the earmarked assets into operating assets at any time, and the agreement must provide that such assets remain available to the employee's general creditors. The establishment of such an asset reserve is in keeping with general business practice whenever a firm incurs a long-term liability. [1]

2. If a defined benefit (for example, $10,000 per year for 10 years) is payable under a salary continuation-type deferred-compensation agreement, the annual amount earmarked for the asset reserve may be invested by the employer on its own behalf during the accumulation period and the payout period. Therefore, the annual amount that must be set aside each year to fully fund the benefits may be discounted in advance at an assumed rate of return. If actual investment earnings differ from the assumed rate of return, the assumed rate can be adjusted. This, in turn, will require a corresponding change in the annual amount to be earmarked for the asset reserve. Where life insurance or annuities are to be purchased with the funds earmarked for the asset reserve, the annual contribution will be determined by the premium that would be sufficient to purchase a contract that would generate the necessary cash value to provide the promised benefits at the time

they come due. The insurance company takes future earnings into account when it calculates the premium. [1]

3. In addition to discounting the amount set aside in the asset reserve for interest earned before and during the payout period, the employer may also discount for the tax deduction the employer will receive when the deferred benefits are paid. For example, if $100,000 of benefits will be payable and the employer is in a 40 percent combined federal and state income tax bracket, the after-tax cost of paying $100,000 of deductible benefits is only $60,000. This means that the employer has to create an asset reserve of only 6/10 of its obligation ($60,000), since the other 4/10 would be provided in the form of a reduction in income taxes. That is, assuming no decrease in corporate tax brackets or rates, the employer will pay $40,000 less in income taxes as a result of paying $100,000 of deferred-compensation benefits. Hence, the $100,000 of deferred-compensation benefits is actually paid by utilizing the $60,000 accumulated in the asset reserve and the $40,000 saved on income taxes. [1]

4. Tax leverage is also available in a salary reduction arrangement based on the fact that benefits paid by the employer will be deductible. Therefore, where an employee is deferring $10,000 per year, an employer in a 40 percent combined federal and state income tax bracket may contribute only $6,000 per year to the asset reserve account and credit the asset reserve account with earnings until the time that benefit payments commence. At that point, the tax leverage created by the employer's income tax deduction may be calculated by dividing the sum accumulated in the employee's net asset reserve account by the complement of the employer's tax bracket (100 percent minus employer's tax bracket). The amount arrived at will determine the benefits under the deferred-compensation agreement. For example, if $50,000 has been accumulated in the asset reserve account, and the corporation is in a 40 percent state and federal income tax bracket, $50,000 will be divided by 60 percent (100 percent minus the employer's combined state and federal tax bracket), and the amount considered available to provide benefits for the employee will be $83,333. [1]

5. The rabbi trust type of arrangement could be considered here, as long as the parties are assured that its various tax and ERISA consequences are satisfactorily settled. Under this arrangement, a grantor trust would be established by the employer for the exclusive benefit of Tex, except that the company's unsecured creditors

would have equal access to its assets as Tex. Whether such an arrangement really provides any advantages over a nontrusteed reserve account is a matter of opinion and judgment based on all the facts of the situation. [1]

6. A *rabbi trust* is a grantor trust arrangement used to hold assets for financing a nonqualified deferred-compensation agreement. The rabbi trust is an irrevocable trust created by the employer for the benefit of the employee and is funded by assets used to finance the deferred-compensation benefits. The trust can be created as a revocable trust initially, with a provision that it becomes irrevocable on the occurrence of a later event, such as change in company ownership. The trust is treated as a grantor trust for tax purposes—that is, its income and deductions flow through directly to the grantor (the employer). The assets of the trust are subject to the claims of the employer's unsecured creditors in the event of the employer's insolvency. Insolvency cannot be defined to give the executive greater rights to the trust property than the employer's unsecured creditors. The rabbi trust must contain a timely notice requirement for notification of the trustee in the event of the employer's insolvency or bankruptcy. However, in the event of insolvency the executive can't be in a better position than general creditors. Sec. 409A no longer allows for a distribution of benefits pursuant to an insolvency-trigger provision—a provision that the trust assets will be distributed to the executive when the employer's net worth falls below a specified level. This codifies the IRS position that such provisions impermissibly create greater rights for the employee than those of the unsecured creditors. [2]

7. The employer's deduction for contributions to a rabbi trust is governed by the same rules that apply to nonqualified deferred-compensation plans financed by any other mechanism. That is, the employer is entitled to a deduction for contributions to the rabbi trust at the time the amounts are includible in the income of the executive under Code Sec. 404(a)(5). [2]

8. Since a rabbi trust is a grantor trust, income, deductions, and credits of the trust are included in computing the taxable income of the grantor-employer. In some cases this makes it advantageous to use tax-exempt investments in funding the trust. Life insurance with its tax-free inside buildup is also suitable. [2]

9. A rabbi trust provides some security to the executive that deferred compensation will actually be paid, since assets are set aside irrevocably. This prevents a new management team from denying benefits. However, it does not protect the executive in the event

of insolvency or bankruptcy of the employer. Thus, success of the plan requires the employer's continued financial success. [2]

10. The choice of a particular investment medium for the asset reserve will depend on the objectives of the parties and the benefits that are promised under the deferred-compensation agreement. For example, where the benefit at retirement age is to reflect inflation that has taken place from the time the plan was instituted as well as postretirement inflation, the asset reserve should be invested in an equity-based product. This could take the form of individual stocks; mutual funds; variable annuities; or variable, universal, or interest-sensitive life.

    Where a subsidized preretirement death benefit equal in value to the benefits that would have been payable at retirement is to be paid (as opposed to merely a benefit equal to the value of the asset reserve account at the time of death), some form of life insurance should be considered as an investment for the asset reserve. (The policy should be owned by and payable to the corporation.) Likewise, where, in the event of preretirement disability, subsidized disability benefits in excess of those that could be provided by the value of the asset reserve at the time of the disability are to be paid, some portion of the asset reserve should probably be invested in disability income insurance. [3]

11. When the employer's obligation is fixed under a deferred-compensation plan, investment in a form of cash value life insurance provides a guaranteed accumulation of assets that is not subject to current income taxation during the accumulation period. Furthermore, cash value life insurance offers guaranteed life annuity options that transfer the risk of paying lifetime benefits from the employer to the insurance company.

    When a preretirement subsidized death benefit is payable, investment life insurance will provide an income-tax-free lump-sum amount to the employer with which it can pay the required death benefit. If a waiver-of-premium benefit is added to a cash value life insurance policy, the insurance can also provide the funds necessary to pay a preretirement disability income benefit. For example, in the event of the insured's disability, the employer would be free of the obligation to pay nondeductible policy premiums. Since the payment of disability benefits would be deductible to the employer (assuming a 50 percent combined federal and state tax bracket), the employer could pay out twice the amount it was paying in nondeductible premiums each year at the same after-tax cost. In addition, the cash values of the policy will continue to grow income tax free and can be utilized through a policy loan to pay additional disability income benefits.

If the employee works until normal retirement age when he or she is entitled to a fixed income for life and the employer has utilized a cash value life insurance policy to fund its obligation, it now has substantial flexibility in meeting that obligation. The employer could cash in the policy, invest the assets as it sees fit, and utilize portions to pay the annual benefits to the employee as they fall due. Alternatively, the employer could elect a life annuity under the guaranteed settlement options of the policy and be assured that no matter how long the employee lives there would always be the funds available to pay benefits.

A third possibility would be to continue the life insurance policy in force and pay benefits out of other corporate assets. In this case, when the employee dies, the employer recoups all of its costs under the plan through the receipt of tax-free life insurance death proceeds. [3]

12. When the employer has a fixed obligation under the deferred-compensation plan but there is no subsidized preretirement death benefit, consideration could be given to utilizing a fixed-dollar annuity as an investment for the asset reserve. Specifically, an annual premium deferred annuity with guaranteed lifetime benefits equal to those promised under the deferred-compensation agreement might be purchased. Where there are guaranteed payments in the event of an early death after benefits begin, an annuity option can be selected that will guarantee a minimum number of annual payments (for example, 15). The problem with annuities is that during the accumulation period, investment earnings under the annuity contract are subject to income taxation (Code Sec. 72(u)).

However, the interest paid on corporate or U.S. government bonds will be currently taxable. Therefore, consideration should be given to the purchase of tax-free municipal bonds. Direct investments in various types of bonds have certain drawbacks, such as no guarantees as to principal, unavailability of guaranteed annuity options, and the constant requirement to make investment selection. [3]

13. Both mutual funds and variable annuities can be purchased as a hedge against inflation since they are equity-based. The following comparison chart indicates the significant differences between these two forms of investment. [3]

Comparison of Mutual Funds and Variable Annuities as an Investment Medium for Asset Reserves	
Mutual Funds	Variable Annuity
May be purchased either with a sales charge or on a no-load basis.	There is generally a sales charge.
Cannot provide a guaranteed life annuity although there are various systematic withdrawal plans available to liquidate shares over a period of time.	Does provide a guaranteed life annuity with benefits varying with the value of an accumulation unit.
No guaranteed refund of cost.	In the event of death prior to annuity starting date, will provide a death benefit equal to the greater of the current value of accumulation units or premiums paid.
Any income or capital-gains dividends declared by the fund are currently taxable to the corporation. • Income dividends will qualify for the dividend deduction. • Capital-gains dividends will be taxable as capital gains.	Current income tax to the corporation during the accumulation period under IRC Sec. 72(u). Note that since the addition of Code Sec. 72(u) under the Tax Reform Act of 1986, corporate-owned annuities are less attractive as an informal financing mechanism for a nonqualified deferred-compensation plan.
When the corporation redeems its mutual fund shares, it will incur a taxable capital gain or loss.	If cashed in, any excess surrender value over premiums paid will be taxed as ordinary income.

14. Using individual policies for this group could be cumbersome. The policies can be used in a COLI arrangement where cost recovery is projected on an overall actuarial basis. [4]

15. If Arthur is concerned with relatively long-term deferral and can expect a reasonably good rate of return on deferred amounts, the break-even analysis indicates that tax deferral is favorable from his point of view. Thus, he may not want to agree to a secular trust. For shorter term deferrals, or where a sharp increase in tax rates is expected, the secular trust could be considered. [5]

16. For an employee of a tax-exempt or governmental employer, the amount of nonqualified deferred compensation that can be provided

on an unfunded, nonforfeitable basis is subject to strict annual limits of the lesser of $16,500 (as indexed; 2010) or 100 percent of the employee's compensation. Additional rules also apply to such deferred-compensation plans. No such limit applies to employees of taxpaying employers. These rules are particularly restrictive in the design of executive compensation plans for such employers. [6]

17. The amounts Dr. Drone wants to defer in this situation exceed the Sec. 457(b) limits described in the preceding question. In order to defer $20,000 annually, Dr. Drone must rely on Sec. 457(f), which requires the amounts to be subject to a substantial risk of forfeiture in order to be deferred. It is possible for Dr. Drone to obtain full deferral by agreeing to a forfeiture risk up to age 62 (that is, if he dies prior to age 62 he forfeits the benefits). However, since it is possible or even likely that his employment relationship with the school district may be terminated before then, he may not wish to agree to such a provision. A more limited deferral to the end of his 5-year contract may be more acceptable. [6]

18. Since under Sec. 457(f) amounts deferred are taxed in the year in which the risk of forfeiture is removed, the full $300,000 will be taxed in the year of retirement unless Mudd agrees to further extend the forfeiture provision before the retirement date. Whether a forfeiture provision that the IRS will accept as "substantial" can be crafted in this situation is open to question. Moreover, since Sec. 457(f) plans are subject to Sec. 409A, any further deferral of Mudd's payment date must also satisfy the requirements of that section with regard to subsequent deferrals as well. [6]

Learning Objectives

An understanding of the material in this chapter should enable the student to

1. Describe restricted property plans in general and compare them with nonqualified deferred-compensation plans.

2. List some advantages and disadvantages of restricted property plans.

3. Explain when an employee must include the value of restricted property in income, and explain the term *substantial risk of forfeiture*.

4. Describe the election to accelerate income under Sec. 83(b) and explain when it is advantageous to the employer and the employee.

5. Explain the general rule for the amount of income to be included under Sec. 83.

6. Define *nonlapse restriction* and explain its effect on the amount to be included in the employee's income under a restricted stock plan.

7. Describe the effect of a transfer of restricted property.

8. Explain when the employer is entitled to take a tax deduction under a restricted property plan and determine the amount of the deduction.

9. Explain how income from restricted property, in particular dividends on restricted stock, is treated to employer and employee for federal income tax purposes.

10. List some nontax issues in designing a restricted property plan.

11. Explain how a restricted property plan is treated by the company for accounting purposes.

RESTRICTED PROPERTY PLANS—INTRODUCTION

This chapter focuses on restricted property plans. The objective is to analyze the advantages of these plans and the choices that can be made in designing these plans. These choices are made within the framework of the applicable federal income tax rules, and the chapter accordingly will also discuss the tax consequences to the employer and employee.

Unfunded nonqualified deferred-compensation plans rest on a contractual promise by the employer. No property is actually transferred to the employee until payment becomes due under these plans. Because there is only a promise, and not a transfer of property, taxation is deferred under the constructive-receipt doctrine, assuming that the requirements of Sec. 409A have been satisfied. Constructive receipt can be deferred merely by a substantial limitation or restriction. In an unfunded plan that complies with the requirements of Sec. 409A, there is no necessity for a risk of forfeiture in order to defer taxation.

The primary disadvantage of nonqualified deferred-compensation arrangements is that the employer's promise must effectively be unsecured in order for the arrangement to be unfunded for tax and ERISA purposes. Much planning for nonqualified deferred compensation involves attempts to improve the employee's security position, for example, by the use of a rabbi trust.

Restricted property plans, which can be used together with, or as an alternative to, nonqualified deferred compensation, involve an actual transfer of property as a form of compensation. The terms of the transfer of property are designed to defer income taxation to whatever degree is possible or desired by the participants, as well as to achieve other compensation objectives of employer and employee. This is done by applying appropriate restrictions on the employee's ownership rights in the property—that is, the employee's ownership is subject to a risk of forfeiting the ownership of the stock. Usually the property involved is stock or securities of the employer corporation (restricted stock plans), although other property can be used. For example, life insurance contracts can be transferred to an employee or the employee's irrevocable trust, subject to restrictions that defer taxation to the employee.

Typically, the risk of forfeiture is based on a provision under which the employee must give up the restricted property if he terminates employment with the company before a specified time. Transfers of employer stock under such restrictions have a high degree of incentive value since the employee's financial status is thereby tied to that of the employer.

To summarize the tax results of a properly designed restricted property plan (these are discussed in detail below):

- The employee does not pay tax on receipt of the property if it is subject to a *substantial risk of forfeiture*;
- The employee pays tax on the fair market value of the property in the year the property becomes vested; that is, the first year in which the property is no longer subject to the forfeiture risk;
- The employer gets a tax deduction equal to the amount included by the employee in the employer's tax year in which the employee includes the amount in income. However, in order to be able to claim this deduction, the employer is required by the Sec. 83 regulations to also report the employee's income on Form W-2 or Form 1099, as appropriate.

Advantages of Restricted Property Plans

From an employer's viewpoint, a restricted property arrangement is attractive for a number of reasons.

- The restriction (the possibility of forfeiting the property) discourages key individuals from terminating employment.
- The plan encourages ownership of stock by executives as an incentive—benefits from the plan are greatest when the company is most successful.
- Such plans are typically helpful in recruiting and retaining executives.
- The grant of restricted stock does not require an immediate outlay of cash, and the employer retains the use of cash that otherwise would be paid out in additional salaries, bonuses, or other forms of compensation.
- Accounting treatment is generally advantageous (see discussion below).

From the executive's viewpoint, advantages include:

- immediate (though restricted) share ownership as compared with options or phantom-stock arrangements
- no initial outlay requirement for executive (however, executive is obligated to pay tax when shares become vested)
- compensation linked to stock price

- favorable tax deferral

Although, in general, plans that provide stock to executives other than shareholder-employees are not attractive to closely held family companies that wish to restrict ownership, a restricted stock plan can be adapted to this situation by using a "first offer" or a mandatory buy-back provision. A closely held business that is allergic to outsiders owning stock can use restricted stock arrangements that give the executive only a temporary stock ownership to share in the growth of the business without diluting family ownership.

EXAMPLE

The Rogers Corporation could sell its own stock (assume a book value of $10,000) to a key nonfamily executive for $1,000. But the stock would be subject to a substantial risk of forfeiture. The stock would also be subject to restrictions that would prevent the key executive from transferring or selling it to anyone other than the Rogers Corporation or its other shareholders. The agreement could provide that if the executive is terminated within 10 years after the time the stock was issued for reasons other than death, disability, or retirement, he must sell part of the stock back at his cost. (The amount he must sell back would decrease over the 10-year span.) The part of the stock that does not have to be sold at the executive's cost must be sold back to the corporation pursuant to a formula price.

The tax implications would be the following: The employee would have no income until the stock is no longer subject to the requirement that it be repurchased at his cost. Once that restriction lapses, the executive will be taxed on the value of the stock determined pursuant to the formula price. In the year that the executive reports income, the employer-corporation would receive a deduction. The amount of the deduction would be equal to the income reported by the employee. The effect is to allow the executive to share in the corporation's growth.

TAX RULES FOR RESTRICTED PROPERTY PLANS

The tax rules that govern planning here date from the early days of the tax law, when employers frequently tried to reduce their employees' tax liability by paying them with noncash items—cars, houses, clothing, etc.—on the theory that such items were not taxable income. The courts quickly held otherwise; taxable income includes noncash as well as cash receipts from an employer, both for employees and for independent contractors. (The Sec. 83 rules governing income taxation for employees generally also apply to independent contractors, but note that withholding and employment taxes work differently for employees and independent contractors.) Moreover, if the property transferred to the employee has restrictions that temporarily eliminate or reduce its value to the employee, this does not mean that the employee need never report taxable income. The courts have held that the recipient of the property must include its value in income in the year in which the recipient becomes vested in the value of the property (*Sproull v. Commissioners*, 16 TC 244 (1951), aff'd per curiam, 194 F.2d 541 (6th Cir. 1952). The court-made rules in this area are sometimes summarized as the "economic benefit doctrine." The doctrine focuses on the vested benefits provided to the employee rather than on the type of property or the form of ownership of the property.

The economic benefit doctrine as it applies to property transferred for services is codified in Sec. 83, which provides specific rules for (1) the year in which the value of the property is included in income, and (2) the amount to be included in that year.

Year of Inclusion

Sec. 83 provides that the value of property (the excess over the amount paid by the recipient for the property) that is transferred for services is included in income "at the first time the rights of the person having the beneficial interest in such property are transferable or are not subject to a substantial risk of forfeiture...." Sec. 83(c)(1) provides that "The rights of a person in property are subject to a substantial risk of forfeiture if such person's rights to full enjoyment of such property are conditioned upon the future performance of substantial services by any individual."

EXAMPLE

Fothrex Corporation transfers 1,000 shares of Fothrex stock to employee Hanson, under the condition that Hanson may not sell the stock during a 5-year period and if Hanson leaves employment with Fothrex during the 5-year period he must return the stock to the company. Hanson pays nothing for the stock. Hanson must include the value of the stock in his income in the year in which the 5-year period expires.

Employers may wish to adopt restricted property plans that are more complex and custom-designed than the simple illustration above. Understanding the term "substantial risk of forfeiture" is the key to designing appropriate forfeiture provisions in restricted property plans. The Regulations under Sec. 83 provide some specific rules and illustrations that are helpful:

- *Discharges for cause.* The regulations state that requirements that the property be returned to the employer if the employee is discharged for cause or for committing a crime will not be considered to result in a substantial risk of forfeiture. [Treas. Reg. Sec. 1.83-3(c)(2)]

- *Noncompetition and consulting provisions.* The Sec. 83 regulations in effect create a presumption against the existence of a substantial risk of forfeiture where the forfeiture will occur only if the employee accepts a job with a competing firm. In that case, a "facts and circumstances" test will apply. Factors taken into account in determining whether the noncompetition provision constitutes a substantial risk of forfeiture include

    - the age of the employee,
    - the availability of alternative employment opportunities,
    - the likelihood of the employee's obtaining such other employment,
    - the degree of skill possessed by the employee,
    - the employee's health, and
    - the practice (if any) of the employer to enforce such covenants.

  For example, a consulting provision applicable to a majority shareholder of the employer would not generally be given much weight because there would be little likelihood of his competing with his own business and the enforcement of such a provision would be entirely at his discretion as majority owner of the company.

  The regulations also state that property transferred to a retiring employee subject to the sole requirement that the property will be returned unless he renders consulting services upon the request of his former employer will not be considered subject to a substantial risk of forfeiture unless he is in fact expected to perform substantial services. [Treas. Reg. Sec. 1.83-3(c)(2)]

- *Organizational performance and other forfeiture provisions.* The Regulations state that where an employee receives property from an employer subject to a requirement that it be returned if the total earnings of the employer do not increase, such property is subject to a substantial risk of forfeiture. [Treas. Reg. Sec. 1.83-3(c)(2)] Note that this "performance" standard does not actually involve a requirement that services be performed; it appears from this provision in the regulations that the IRS finds this acceptable although it does not strictly fit the language of Sec. 83.

The regulations state that a forfeiture provision can be valid if it is "related to the purpose of the transfer." The performance standard discussed in the preceding paragraph may be an example of this type of provision. Robinson v. Comr, 805 F.2d 38 (1st Cir. 1986), rev'g 82 TC 444, dealt with a provision under which stock was transferred to an employee under a condition that if he wished to dispose of it within one year he had to sell it back to the employer at the original cost. The court viewed this as a substantial risk of forfeiture, and noted that this provision served a substantial corporate purpose of avoiding insider trading. This is arguably also a purpose related to the transfer, though it is not specifically related.

Control Employees

The requirements necessary to defer recognition of income in the case of a stockholder-employee are more stringent than in the case of a nonowner-employee. If a corporation transfers rights and property to an employee (or to the beneficiary of an employee) who owns—directly or indirectly—in excess of 5 percent of the total combined voting power or value of all classes of stock of the employer corporation or of its parent or subsidiary corporation, the employee will not be subject to a substantial risk of forfeiture unless there is a great possibility that the employee will not satisfy the requirement claimed to result in the risk.

What are the factors used to determine whether the possibility of forfeiture is substantial? Essentially, the IRS and courts will look to the following five factors:

1. the relationship of the employee to other stockholders and the extent of their control, potential control, and possible loss of control
2. the employee's position in the corporation and the extent to which he or she is subordinate (or superior) to other employees
3. the employee's relationships to the officers and directors of the company
4. the person or persons who can fire the employee
5. past enforcement of similar restrictions in other situations

Assume 20 percent of the outstanding common stock is owned by an employee. The remaining 80 percent is owned by an unrelated individual. It is possible that rights and property transferred to the 20 percent employee-shareholder from the corporation could be considered subject to a substantial risk of forfeiture assuming all factors present indicated that he had to deal at arm's length with the other shareholders and that they continually exercised their control, that the employee did not in fact run the corporation (or if he did, that he could and would be replaced if appropriate), that the employee was subject to decisions of the corporation's directors, that he could be discharged if he didn't perform adequately, and that in similar situations, in the past, the corporation had demanded a return of its property when the conditions of the contract were breached. Conversely, even if only 6 percent of the voting power of the common stock was held by one individual—but that individual was the president of the corporation—and the remaining stock was spread so widely that no other group had power approaching control, it would be quite difficult if not impossible for the 6 percent shareholder to meet the Sec. 83 test.

In the current IRS list of "no ruling" items (published annually as a Revenue Procedure), the IRS states that, if there is a nonrecourse obligation or if the employee is a controlling shareholder, the factual situation is such that it will not give advance clearance for the transaction under Sec. 83. For many employers, this will mean that the transaction is sufficiently suspect that they will not want to enter into it, since it is highly likely that the IRS will, if it discovers the transaction on audit, challenge its treatment under Sec. 83.

Employee Election to Include in Current Income (Sec. 83(b) Election)

If an employee receives restricted property and wants to include it in income currently, rather than waiting until it is vested (perhaps because he expects the property to increase considerably in value) he can elect under Sec. 83(b) to include the current value (the fair market value at the time of transfer) in income currently. The fair market value of the property is determined without regard to restrictions (except a restriction that by its terms will not lapse).

EXAMPLE
Hott Software transfers stock in 2010 to employee Geeke, with the provision that if Geeke leaves employment during the next 10 years, his stock is forfeited. The fair market value of the stock at the time of transfer is $20,000. Geeke expects it to more than quadruple in value in 10 years, so he elects to pay taxes in 2010 on the $20,000 current value. Unfortunately, he made the wrong decision—Hott turns out to be a flash in the pan and the company is dissolved in 2013 with the stock becoming worthless. (Geeke gets no loss deduction).

Why would an employee elect to be taxed prior to a time when he or she had to? The answer is that once an employee makes an election, then any subsequent growth in the value of the assets in the trust (or held by the employee) qualifies for capital-gain treatment upon sale rather than being taxed as ordinary income. Current tax rates on capital gain are more favorable compared to those on ordinary income. Also election of current income recognition may prove advantageous by paying taxes "up front" if future tax rates are greater than current rates, as many authorities expect.

What is the disadvantage of such an election? One disadvantage is that if the employee forfeits the property (for instance, perhaps the employee refuses to perform substantial future services), the employee may not take a loss deduction. More generally, an employee making a Sec. 83(b) election as in this example is betting on the company to succeed, since if the value of the stock drops below its value at the time of transfer, no loss deduction is allowed.

The employee must therefore balance the advantage of paying tax currently on ordinary income at current rates and receiving capital-gains treatment on any appreciation from the time the corporation transfers the property until the employee reaches the specified retirement age or year of vesting against the advantage of paying no current income tax at the time of the transfer and paying ordinary income on any gain between the time the transfer and the date restrictions lapse. Factored into that decision must be the potential loss of any tax deduction if the employee makes the election but for whatever reason forfeits the property.

In addition to the tax rate difference, capital-gain treatment has some further tax impact. For sale of an asset to receive long-term capital-gain treatment, the taxpayer must have held the capital asset being sold for more than the requisite statutory holding period. The holding period for restricted property begins when the transfer becomes complete; that is, when the substantial risk of forfeiture lifts or the property becomes transferable without subjecting the transferee to a substantial risk of forfeiture, whichever is the earlier. The holding period for restricted property for which the taxpayer elects to be currently taxed under IRC Sec. 83(b) commences when the property is originally transferred by the employer.

If the Sec. 83(b) election is made, any future appreciation will be taxed to the employee as capital gain if he or she sells the stock back to the corporation. This aspect can be used in planning, with some benefit to both employer and employee. The corporation can condition its grant of restricted stock on the employee's agreement to make the special election, in order to give the business an immediate compensation deduction equal to the value of the stock. Otherwise, the employer's deduction might be deferred for many years.

EXAMPLE

Thompson, an employee of the Tiger Tankers Corporation, pays $1,000 for stock with a $10,000 value. If he makes the special election and sells the stock back to the corporation for $25,000 when he retires 10 years later, the tax results would be

1. He would report $9,000 of compensation income when he receives the stock.

2. The corporation would receive a $9,000 deduction when Thompson reports the $9,000 of compensation income.

3. When Thompson sells the stock back to the corporation, he would realize a long-term capital gain equal to the difference between the $25,000 that he receives for the stock and his $10,000 basis.

Of course, if the corporation allowed Thompson to acquire the stock without making the election, the tax results would be (assuming the stock is forfeitable prior to his retirement):

1. Thompson would have no current income at the time he acquired the stock subject to the restrictions.

2. The corporation would have no deduction in the year the stock was distributed to Thompson.

3. Thompson would report $24,000 of ordinary compensation income in the year he sells the stock back to the corporation.

4. The company would receive a $24,000 deduction in the year the $24,000 of compensation income was included by Thompson.

Amount to Be Included Under Sec. 83

The general rule under Sec. 83 is that property is included in income at its fair market value (determined without regard to any restriction other than a restriction which by its terms will never lapse) at the first time when the rights to the property are transferable or no longer subject to a substantial risk of forfeiture, as discussed above.

In other words, the amount included is the value at the time of vesting, not at the time of transfer.

EXAMPLE

In 2010, Fothrex corporation transfers 1,000 shares of Fothrex stock to employee Hanson, subject to a provision that Hanson must continue in employment for 5 years. The stock is worth $30,000 at the time of transfer. Hanson sticks it out and is still working for Fothrex on the fifth anniversary of the transfer in 2015, at which time the stock is worth $50,000. Hanson must report the $50,000 as compensation income for 2015. There is no discount to reflect the fact that the stock was restricted during the preceding 5 years.

Nonlapse Restrictions

As the example notes, the existence of a restriction that eventually lapses does not affect the valuation of the stock. However, if the stock were subject to a nonlapsing restriction, it would affect valuation. Suppose that in the example the Fothrex stock that Hanson received continued after 2015 to be subject to a provision that any shares that Hanson wanted to dispose of would have to be first offered to the company for $40 per share. (This is *not* considered to be a forfeiture provision.) This provision would affect the value of the stock in 2015 and would reduce the amount that Hanson would have to report in 2015. The actual reduction in value is an issue of facts and circumstances and some kind of independent valuation would probably have to be made for tax purposes.

A permanent limitation on the transferability of property that will require a transferee to sell the property at a price determined under a formula that would also be applied and enforced against the transferee and subsequent holders of the property is typically called a "nonlapse restriction." As discussed in Regs. Sec. 1.83-3(h) and (i), and Sec. 1.83-5, the amount included in gross income as compensation when property is substantially vested is the fair market value of the property, and no consideration is given to any restriction on the property other than a nonlapse restriction. But if the property is subject to a nonlapse restriction, for example, a restriction that requires the property to be sold only at a formula price based on book value, a multiple of earnings, or some reasonable combination of those two, the fair market value of the property for purposes of Sec. 83 will be the price as determined by that formula.

There are exceptions to the rule that a nonlapse restriction lowers the fair market value for purposes of what the employee must include as compensation. For example, if the formula price is the current book value of the stock, the value at some time in the future may be more indicative of what the stock is really worth. The example below will illustrate that a nonlapse restriction requiring a sale at a formula price based on book value or a multiple of earnings is not necessarily the deciding factor in all situations as to the fair market value of the property.

EXAMPLE

Regulation Sec. 1.83-5(c)(4) uses an illustration of an independent contractor who has been given all the shares of the outstanding common stock in a corporation in exchange for an agreement to build an office building that the corporation will own. One hundred shares of preferred stock will be owned by another individual and will have a liquidation value equal to all assets owned by the corporation. This makes the book value of the common stock zero at the time the independent contractor receives those shares. Under the terms of the transfer the contractor could dispose of the stock only to the corporation. That stock must be offered to the corporation for 150 percent of its then existing value. Until all services are performed, the contractor holds the common stock subject to a substantial risk of forfeiture.

The contractor in the above example elects to include the value of the stock in his income at the time he receives it. The restriction described above is a nonlapse restriction. Ordinarily that would mean that the book value would be used because of the formula in determining the fair market value of the common stock. But in this case logic indicates that the fair market value of the common stock at the time of the transfer has to be greater than the book value of zero since the contractor is willing to perform services in exchange for the stock. So in determining the fair market value of the stock, great weight must be given to the expected book value at the time the office building is completed. This does not deviate from the rule that it is the fair market value at the time of the transfer that must be included in gross income. But it does show that there will be situations in which the nonlapse restriction will not be determinative in setting the amount that must be included in gross income as compensation.

A common example of a restriction that will never lapse is when the employer provides by endorsement on stock transferred to an employee that the stock may only be sold to the employer and the price is set at the book value (determined as of the date of the sale). Assuming there is another restriction on the stock that prevents taxation, the first restriction will be meaningless. But as soon as there is no other restriction on the stock or as soon as that other tax-blocking restriction has lapsed, the second (value limiting) restriction will limit the fair market value of the stock to book value and therefore provide a ceiling on the amount on which the employee can be taxed.

What if, for some reason, the employer at some later date decides to lift the restriction that limits the sale of stock to the employer at book value? When a restriction that limits the market value of the stock is removed or cancelled, then the excess fair market value (any amount untaxed at this point) will become taxable to the employee at that time. The employee enters any amount not already taxed into income and the employer receives a deduction in that amount. If for some reason the parties can prove that the removal or cancellation was not compensatory in nature, the employee will not have income but the employer will not be allowed a deduction.

Two significant cases deal with how property is valued under these rules. The first case dealt with lapse restrictions. In one case, the taxpayer was an executive of a company that granted him options to purchase its stock. He exercised those options in 1971 at two separate times. In each case, the market price for the stock exceeded the option price paid. But the taxpayer took a discount on the value of the stock to account for restrictions that were imposed by an investment letter. The IRS pointed out that the language of Sec. 83 stating that "the fair market value of such property is determined without regard to any restriction other than the restriction which by its terms will never lapse" was clear. The IRS pointed out that the valuation would be made this way even if the restriction was imposed by law instead of by contract. The court conceded that the restrictions on the stock caused by the investment letter did reduce the amount that could have been received upon a sale by at least 35 percent from the potential sales proceeds if the stock was traded on an open market. But it followed the strict wording of the Code Sec. and disallowed the 35 percent discount. The court noted that the restriction on the property was one that would lapse because of the passage of time and therefore had to be disregarded for purposes of determining the fair market value of the property transferred as services. This reiterates one of the big drawbacks of restricted property arrangements: an employee could be taxed on a value that he can't actually receive if the property is sold on the date of the transfer. (Is this an unconstitutional "taking" of a citizen's wealth?)

Another case involved the effect of fraud on valuation. An option was exercised by an employee of the Mattel Company. The taxpayer reported income of $43,000 although, on the date the option was exercised, the total New York Stock Exchange value of the stock was approximately $75,000. The taxpayer claimed that on the date of the exercise, the Stock Exchange price was not the true market value because the company had perpetrated fraud on its shareholders. The company had misstated its financial condition. The true value of the shares, the taxpayer argued, should have been decreased after the misstatement by the corporation was known. But the court held that the fact that the market for the shares would have been less had the corporation's misstatements on its financial statements been known was not pertinent. The court also examined the Securities Exchange Act of 1934 (Sec. 16(b)) and noted that any profit to the corporation from the sale of stock by an "insider" was not a restriction on the stock for purposes of Sec. 83(a) and therefore did not restrict its transferability.

Transfers of Restricted Property

Can a person who receives restricted property give it to another person without triggering an income taxable event? Restricted property can be given to another person without triggering recognition of income as long as the recipient of the gift, the donee, is subject to a restriction constituting the substantial risk of forfeiture. For instance, the corporation could place a life insurance policy or annuity in the name of an employee but endorse the policy as subject to the restriction. Assuming that the restriction prevented the immediate taxation of the employee, the employee in turn could make a second transfer of the property to some other individual or trust as long as that party took the property subject to the same risk of loss. Typically, this issue is not a problem since the restricted property is usually placed in some type of trust or escrow account, but where it is not (such as the case where stock or mutual funds are placed in the hands of an employee), the restriction should be noted in bold letters on the stock certificate. Note also that there may be gift tax consequences but they would have no effect on the corporation or they would reduce the amount of compensation that the donor-employee would have to recognize.

As discussed previously, Sec. 83 provides that property distributed for services rendered is taxable as compensation. The time of recognition will occur at the earlier of (a) when it is transferable or (b) when it is no longer subject to a substantial risk of forfeiture.

Recognition may occur when the property is initially transferred or at a later time. If property is not transferable or subject to a substantial risk of forfeiture when transferred, there is no current taxation. But the taxpayer will be forced to recognize income as soon as either of these restrictions is removed. If the taxpayer does not have to recognize income immediately when property is distributed for services, and when recognition does occur at a later time, the fair market value of the property at that time is taxable (less a reduction for any amount the employee paid for it). At the same time property is includible in the employee's income, it becomes deductible in the same amount by the employer [Reg. Sec. 1.83-6(2)].

Employer's Deduction

Under Sec. 83(h), the employer's deduction is equal to the amount included in income by the employee, and is included in the year in which the employee includes the amount. (The exact rule is that the deduction is allowed in the employer's taxable year in which or in which ends the taxable year in which the amount is included in the gross income of the person who performed the services.) However, in order to be able to claim this deduction, the employer is required to report the employee's income on Form W-2 for the appropriate year.

Restricted property is a form of compensation that does not provide the employer with an "upfront" deduction—a deduction in the year the services are performed, as is the case with a qualified pension or profit-sharing plan. For compensation governed by Sec. 83 the year of deduction is tied to the year of the employee's inclusion of income. One result of this rule is that the employer's deduction is generally delayed until the employee reaches retirement, since that is the expectation with most restricted stock plans.

The amount of the employer's deduction is also tied to the amount includible in income by the employee. The employer deducts the same amount that the employee must include in income. This is advantageous to the corporation if the property appreciates between the date of the transfer to the trust or escrow account and the date the employee must enter the restricted property into income. Unfortunately, the rule also means that the employer receives a lower deduction if the property falls in value.

In summary, when an employer executes either a deferred-compensation or salary continuation plan, no deductions are allowed upon the signing of the agreement, nor is any deduction allowed when cash or other property is contributed to the plan. Not until the employee includes the benefits into his income is the employer allowed a deduction.

EXAMPLE

The Martin Satinsky Corporation contributes $50,000 to a trust in behalf of its vice president, Robert LeClair. The trust is an irrevocable trust established to accept cash or other property under a funded deferred-compensation agreement. Assuming the agreement contains a provision that places Bob LeClair under substantial risk of forfeiting the money placed into the trust by the corporation, Bob would incur no current taxable income when he signed the agreement nor would any taxable income be reportable when the corporation placed money into the irrevocable trust. The corporation would not be entitled to an income tax deduction. Assume 5 years later $50,000 has grown to $130,000. Each year the income of the trust is payable to and therefore taxable to the corporation. Assume that Bob LeClair retires at the age specified in the plan, age 60. The $130,000 in the trust is received by Bob and taxed to him at that time. The corporation would be entitled to a tax deduction in that same amount ($130,000).

There are other triggering events. Aside from retirement, death, or disability, an employee will become taxable on restricted property as soon as the substantial risk of forfeiture is removed for any reason. For instance, assume that the substantial risk will be removed upon a gift of the property or sale of the property. As soon as that event occurs, the employee recognizes income and the employer enjoys a corresponding deduction.

Taxation on Income from Restricted Property

While stock remains under restrictions, what is the effect when dividends are paid on that stock? The final regulations state that to the extent that dividends are includible as compensation in the gross income of the employee or independent contractor, they must be includible as additional compensation and are deductible at that time by the employer.

The employer generally is the "tax owner" of restricted property even if it is titled in the employee's name until the transfer is complete. Therefore, assuming income earned by trust assets either accumulates in a trust for the employee or is payable directly to the corporation, the employer pays income tax on all income generated by property subject to the risk of forfeiture.

Obviously, if income is actually paid to the employee, it is taxable to that person in the year it is actually or constructively received. At that time, the income would be deductible by the employer. Note that the treatment of income from restricted property held in a trust differs from the normal result where income-producing property is held by such a trust; in the normal case, the income is taxed to either the trust itself or to the beneficiary (if paid out). But because of the compensatory relationship involved, the Service blocks the use of the trust as an additional income-tax-paying vehicle by making either the corporation or the employee taxable on trust income.

Quite often the employer funds a plan by putting life insurance policies in the employee's name, subject to a substantial risk of forfeiture. How is the employee taxed when there is no trust? The employer will report the income and be taxed on it until the employee becomes the owner of the restricted property or until the employer directs payments to be made to the employee. At the time the employee recognizes income, the corporation can deduct it.

Who is taxed on income produced by restricted property assets? The answer is that the person who performed the services for the employer (whether that person is an individual, trust, corporation, or partnership) is the party who must recognize the income no matter who actually receives the property itself. For instance, if Herb Cheeseman performs services for the Coke Company, and consequently Herb's son Steve receives restricted property (or if Herb receives the restricted property but gives it to his son), then when the substantial risk of forfeiture is removed or lapses, Herb will be taxed on the income.

It has been mentioned a number of times in a prior objective that the employee does not incur taxable income at the time contributions are made to a restricted property plan assuming the plan has been properly created, the instrument carefully drafted, and the employee is under a substantial risk of forfeiture until retirement. But when the plan terminates at retirement, assuming no further substantial risk of forfeiture remains, the employee must recognize as compensation the entire value in the account at that time. Obviously, the income tax burden can be overwhelming and defeat the very purpose of the plan. If income averaging is available, it certainly would reduce the impact of the tax.

Can the deferral be continued beyond retirement? Employees will usually want to spread recognition of income over as many years as possible after retirement to reduce the burden imposed by the progressive income tax system. But with a deferred-compensation or salary continuation plan that imposes a substantial risk of forfeiture, this becomes quite difficult since it is only in rare cases that the employee will be able to claim that substantial services must be performed (it appears that the words "retirement" and the words "substantial services" seem to be incongruous). The employee must be able to claim that any restriction (such as the requirement of advisory services or covenant not to compete following retirement) is of real substance and much more than nominal.

The Regulations, Reg. Sec. 1.83-1(a)(i), provide some certainty as to the treatment of restricted stock dividends. The regulations provide that even though a transferee's status as owner of property may not be recognized until the transfer is complete, prior to that date income from restricted property, if paid to the transferee, would be treated as additional compensation. Therefore, dividends are characterized as additional compensation and are deductible by the employer. But the transferor (the corporation) remains the owner of the dividend until the employee is taxable on it.

If the restricted property plan consists of a restricted trust, it is not clear whether or not the income will always be taxed to the employer. A second view is that income from a restricted trust will be taxed to the trust as a separate entity as long as the grantor trust rules of the Internal Revenue Code do not apply. The income of the trust paid to the employee would be taxable to the employee as compensation, and the employer would get a corresponding deduction.

DESIGNING A PLAN

The employer and employee have complete freedom to design a restricted property plan as long as it has the desired tax results under the tax law rules discussed above. Some typical choices in design include:

- Type of property. Employer stock is most often used, but other property such as life insurance contracts can also be part of a restricted property plan. For a nonprofit or a partnership with no employer stock, stock of other corporations or other types of investment assets can be used.

- Actual shares or restricted stock units. The plan can involve actual shares of stock or alternatively, *restricted stock units (RSUs)*. RSUs are certificates that provide for no transfer of shares initially, but there is a transfer of actual shares to the employee after the forfeiture provision lapses. RSUs are generally nonvoting, but may provide for value increases equivalent to the dividends paid on actual stock. RSUs generally do not "dilute" the stock of existing shareholders until shares are actually issued, while regular restricted stock plans using actual shares can produce dilution at the time transferred to the employee. Similarly, there is a difference in earnings per share impact between the issuance of actual shares and RSUs, with an actual-share plan generally producing lower earnings per share during the restriction period.

- Restriction period. The parties may wish to use a relatively short-term restriction period, such as 5 years. This approach might often be used as a method of attracting a key employee for near-term requirements, such as an expert in a high-technology business. Other plans might focus on long-term incentives and provide a forfeiture of benefits for any termination other than death, disability, or retirement.
- Plan documentation and administration. The plan might involve issuance of shares to the employee directly, or to an escrow agent or trust for the employee's benefit.

ACCOUNTING FOR RESTRICTED PROPERTY PLANS

Under current accounting standards, (FAS 123) the amount recognized as an expense by the company is the fair market value on the date of the award. This amount is charged to earnings over the period during which the employee performs the services for which the compensation amount relates. For example, if the restriction period is 5 years, and the benefit is considered to be for future services after which the employee is fully vested in the shares, then the initial fair market value is accrued by the employer as an expense ratably over 5 years.

With regard to dividends on restricted stock, many practitioners treat them like other dividends for accounting purposes. That is, they are not considered a compensation expense despite the tax treatment. However, the rule is not clear.

The following table shows the differences in accounting between restricted share plans and RSU plans.

Table 4-1 Accounting Treatment of Restricted Shares or Share Units			
	Income Statement Share Value	**Dividends**	**Earnings per Share**
Re-stricted shares	Accrued as compensation expense ratably during the employment period; gain or loss in share value *during* period is not recorded as compensation expense even though tax deductible.	No clear accounting rulings but majority opinion is that dividends on restricted shares are *not* recorded as compensation expense even though deductible.	Restricted shares are outstanding shares during employment period for EPS-calculation purposes.
RSUs	Same as restricted shares except changes in share value *during* the period will be recorded as compensation expense for the share units, which will be paid in cash.	Dividend equivalents recorded as compensation expense when paid.	Share units to be paid in actual shares are treated as common stock equivalents, as determined under the treasury stock method, during the employment period for EPS-calculation purposes.

CASE PROBLEM

The board of directors of Shapeco Corporation recognizes that a large measure of the corporation's previous successes is due to the competent management of the operational vice president, Joe Koval. Koval is 45, married, and earns $60,000 annually but finds it difficult to save anything. Koval's marginal tax bracket is 50 percent.

The board of directors has recently heard rumors that Koval is considering a move to a rival corporation. Apparently, Koval is concerned about the financial drain caused by certain interest-rate problems. As a result of these interest-rate problems, the Shapeco Corporation's earnings per share have dropped sharply. The current market value of the stock is $75 per share. The corporation's combined state and federal tax bracket is 50 percent.

The Employee Benefit Subcommittee of the board of directors has been directed to design some type of arrangement to align Koval's long-term interests with the interest of the corporation. The plan described below has been suggested to the board of directors. Answer the questions following the plan description, specifically considering the goals of Shapeco Corporation and Joe Koval. Be sure to include the following in your analysis:

1. For Koval: (1) benefit security (likelihood of receiving some benefits), (2) timing of income tax inclusion, (3) character of income for tax purposes, (4) the effect of stock market conditions, and (5) out-of-pocket costs of Koval to receive his deferred compensation.

2. For Shapeco: (1) ability of Shapeco to control Koval's business conduct, (2) the plan as an incentive to Koval, (3) the timing of Shapeco's income tax deduction, and (4) the cost of the plan to Shapeco.

Recommended Plan

A benefit analyst whom the subcommittee consulted favors a restricted stock arrangement. He recommends that the company place $50,000 of stock in Koval's hands. Koval would have to pay the stock back to the firm unless he works for the corporation for 10 more years. In the event that he terminated his employment in any of the next 10 years, he would keep nothing.

1. Analyze and discuss this approach with reference to (a) and (b) above.

2. If Koval did receive restricted stock, what factors would you suggest to help him determine his choice of when to declare income from receipt of the stock?

CHAPTER REVIEW

Review Questions

1. What is the most fundamental difference between nonqualified deferred compensation and executive compensation in the form of restricted stock? [1]

2. Describe a typical executive who might benefit from a restricted stock plan, from the viewpoint of employer and employee. [2]

3. Can a restricted stock plan be designed that would be suitable for a closely held family business? [2]

4. Harry Horrock is a participant in Playman's restricted stock plan. Five years ago Horrock received certificates of Playman stock with the following legend stamped on them:

    The rights in this stock shall be forfeited in the event that the employee named herein leaves the employ of the corporation at any time during a 10-year period commencing with the receipt of the stock. [3]

    a. Briefly describe the Code Sec. that applies in this situation.

    b. Under this section of the Code, is Horrock required to include an amount in income during the restricted period? Explain.

    c. What advantages are there for an employer who pays compensation in the form of restricted property? Why might an employee dislike such restrictions?

5. If Horrock makes a gift of his restricted stock to his son: [3]

    a. How will the restricted stock be treated for income tax purposes if the son, as donee, is still subject to a substantial risk of forfeiture as required by the restricted stock plan?

    b. How will the restricted stock be treated for income tax purposes if the son, as donee, is not subject to a substantial risk of forfeiture, and such a transfer is permitted by the restricted stock plan?

6. John Jacob, the skilled operations vice president of Playman Corporation, recently retired at age 55 because of poor health. Upon announcing his retirement, he received stock certificates of the corporation with the following legend stamped on them:

    In the event that at any time within 3 years from date hereof, Jacob either (a) accepts a job with a competing firm or (b) refuses to render consulting services to Playman, there shall be an automatic forfeiture of this stock. [3]

    a. What factors must be taken into consideration in determining whether restrictions on receipt of stock amount to a substantial risk of forfeiture?

    b. Discuss whether the restrictions on Jacob's stock are sufficient to defer taxation.

    c. What effect, if any, would the fact that Jacob was already a 30 percent shareholder prior to his receipt of the restricted stock have on your deliberations in (b) above?

7.   Robert Rough received 100 shares of stock from his employer, Comet Corporation, 3 years ago today, when the fair market value of each share was $100. He paid nothing for the stock. The terms of the agreement state that Rough will forfeit the stock unless he works for the company for 3 more years. Today, when there are no longer any applicable restrictions, the stock is worth $150 a share. [4]

a. Did Rough have a choice of including or not including income from the restricted property plan in his taxable income for the year in which he received the stock? Explain.

b. If Rough did decide to include income from the restricted property plan as taxable income in the year he received the stock, how much time did he have to make the election?

8.   Given the same facts as in the previous question, assume that Rough did make an election to be taxed in the year he received the stock. [4]

a. What amount must be included in taxable income this year?

b. What will be the tax consequences if Rough sells his stock for $150 a share (i) 15 months after the restrictions lapse or (ii) 10 months after the restrictions lapse?

c. If Rough left the employ of Comet one year after receiving the stock and, thus, forfeited the stock, can he take a deduction for his loss? Explain.

9.   Sam Silver received 100 shares of stock from his employer, Bullet Corporation, 2 years ago today, when the fair market value of each share was $200. He paid nothing for the stock. The terms of the agreement he made with his employer when he received the stock state that Silver will forfeit the stock unless he works for the company for 2 more years. Today, when there are no longer any applicable restrictions, the stock is worth $250 a share. [5]

a. What amount is Silver required to include in gross income (i) in the year he first received the stock and (ii) this year, as a result of the above transaction?

b. Will the amount that Silver includes in income be treated as ordinary income or capital gain?

10.   Last year, Dave Retzel, vice president of Eggnog Corporation, purchased 100 shares of stock from his corporation for $10 a share. The sole terms of purchase were that if he desired to sell or dispose of the stock, he must sell the stock to the corporation at its then existing book value. Assume that the book value per share at the time he received the stock of Eggnog was $15 and the fair market value per share was $100. [6]

   a. Did the restrictions imposed on Dave's stock amount to a substantial risk of forfeiture so that Dave did not have taxable income from this transaction last year? Explain.

   b. If Dave did have taxable income last year, what would that amount have been? Explain.

   c. Would the includible amount be treated as ordinary income or capital gains? Explain.

11.   Can the recipient of restricted property transfer the property without triggering taxation? [7]

12.   What is the amount of the employer's deduction and in what year is the deduction permitted? [8]

13.   Harry Horrock is a participant in Playman's restricted stock plan. Five years ago Horrock received certificates of Playman stock with the following legend stamped on them:

   The rights in this stock shall be forfeited in the event that the employee named herein leaves the employ of the corporation at any time during a 10-year period commencing with the receipt of the stock.

   During the 10-year period that Horrock may forfeit his stock, dividends paid on Playman stock are paid directly to Horrock. [9]

   a. Who pays taxes on undistributed income, if any, generated by restricted property until the end of the restriction period?

   b. Is Horrock required to pay tax on the dividends? Explain.

   c. Is Playman entitled to a deduction for the dividends received by Horrock? Explain.

14.   How might a nonprofit organization use a restricted property plan to compensate executives? [10]

15.   What is a restricted stock unit (RSU) plan? [10]

16. How is the cost of a restricted stock plan treated by the company under current accounting standards? [11]

Answers to Review Questions

1. A nonqualified deferred-compensation plan is an unsecured promise by the employer to pay a deferred-compensation benefit at some future time. A restricted stock plan is an actual transfer of property from the employer to the employee, subject to a risk of forfeiture. The difference between a benefit based on a contractual promise, as opposed to a benefit based on an actual current transfer of property, is the source of the differences in the tax and design issues that apply to the two types of plans. [1]

2. A restricted stock plan is a good type of benefit for an executive who wishes to gain the benefits of growth in the company stock through ownership of an equity interest in the company, and can benefit from a plan that provides deferral of income taxation. From the employer's standpoint, the plan will be used to attract and retain executives with desired skill, and provide incentives through sharing in company stock growth. Generally if the company does not want to expand ownership to outsiders, a restricted stock plan, like other equity-based compensation arrangements, is not desirable. [2]

3. Some of the advantages of a restricted stock plan can be gained by a company that does not want to provide stock to outsiders by including a buyback or first-offer provision in the plan, whereby the stock is ultimately returned to the company. [2]

4. The general rule for taxation of restricted property plans stated in Sec. 83 of the Internal Revenue Code is that the employee is not taxed as a result of having received restricted property from his employer until the property is "substantially vested." In other words, an employee will be subject to tax (a) at the time the substantial risk of forfeiture is removed or (b) at the time the property becomes "transferable," whichever occurs first. Transferability in this context refers to a transfer free of the risk of forfeiture. If the property can be transferred but the transferee remains subject to the same risk of forfeiture as the employee, there is no taxation until the risk of forfeiture is removed.

   The employee is taxed on the fair market value at the time the restrictions are removed. The advantage of restricted property to the employer is that the employee only gets paid if he continues employment. The employee dislikes the restrictions because he cannot sell the property to realize his gain. [3]

5. An employee who gifts his restricted property does not have income at that time as long as the donee of the stock remains subject to a substantial risk of forfeiture. The employee does not have income because the transfer from the employer to the employee is still considered incomplete. On the other hand, if the donee of the restricted stock takes the stock without being subject to a substantial risk of forfeiture, then the employee (not the donee) has income at the time of the gift because the compensation payment from the employer is considered complete at that time. Note that it is always the employee and not the donee of the property who is taxed when the substantial risk of forfeiture is removed or the property becomes transferable without being subject to a substantial risk of forfeiture. [3]

6. The term substantial risk of forfeiture refers to the employee's rights in the property being conditioned upon either performance or refraining from performance of substantial services by any individual at some future time. Property is considered substantially vested when it is either transferable or not subject to a substantial risk of forfeiture.

    Whether such services are substantial depends on the facts and circumstances of each case. A requirement that an employee must return property if he does not complete an additional period of substantial service would cause such property to be subject to a substantial risk of forfeiture. A requirement that an employee forfeit his stock if he commits a crime would not be considered a substantial risk of forfeiture (mainly because such an act is entirely within the employee's control). The requirements of consulting services after retirement or refraining from entering into competition would, in all likelihood, not be considered substantial risks of forfeiture unless there is actually an expectation of either the rendering of substantial consulting services or entering into competition with the corporation.

    Similarly, the employee who holds more than 5 percent of the stock of a company is also subject to a "facts and circumstances" test regarding his control of the corporation to determine whether his restricted property is subject to a substantial risk of forfeiture. For such an employee-shareholder, there is a question of whether his employment can be involuntarily terminated. Therefore, the following factors must be considered in order to determine if a substantial risk of forfeiture is present in this situation: [3]

- employee's relationship to the other stockholders and the extent of their control
- position of employee in the corporation
- employee's relationship to the officers and directors of the corporation
- persons who must approve the employee's discharge
- **past actions of the employer in enforcing such restrictive provisions**

7. Within 30 days of the receipt of the restricted property, an employee can elect to be taxed on the fair market value of the property at the date of grant (less any consideration paid by the employee) at ordinary income rates. Subsequent appreciation will be taxed as long-term capital gains upon disposition if the property is held for the requisite statutory holding period after the transfer to the employee (as opposed to the time when the restriction lapses). The disadvantage to the election is that, in the event the property is later forfeited, Sec. 83(b) provides that no loss deduction is permitted. That election cannot be revoked unless the IRS consents. (Consent will be given only if the transferee is under a mistake of fact as to the underlying transaction.)

An employee should elect to be currently taxed under a restricted property plan within certain circumstances. The employee should consider the potential growth of the company, whether he can afford to pay taxes currently, his estimated tax rate this year, and his estimated tax rate when the restrictions lift. Further, since the employee may not deduct his loss if he forfeits the stock after the election, he should consider whether he is likely to stay in the employ of the corporation for the restricted period. [4]

The answers to this question are as follows:

a. Yes, he can so elect.
b. 30 days from receipt of the restricted property

8. [4]

a. $10,000
b.

(1) $50 per share long-term capital gain

(2) $50 per share long-term capital gain

 c. No

9. As previously stated, an employee who receives restricted property has taxable ordinary income equal to the fair market value of the property at the time of either the removal of the substantial risk of forfeiture or when the property becomes transferable (without the transferee being subject to a substantial risk of forfeiture). The fair market value of the stock (but not the timing of taxation) will be affected by restrictions on the stock that, by their terms, will never lapse. (This concept is discussed below.)

As long as the employer appropriately reports the amount of the employee's ordinary income to the IRS, the employer is permitted to deduct the value of Sec. 83 property when it is includible in the employee's income. Subsequent appreciation in the value of the property (appreciation occurring after the employee reports the receipt of compensation income) will be taxed as capital gain to the employee upon disposition of the property. [5]

 a. As a consequence of the substantial risk of forfeiture, Silver is not required to report any amount in gross income in the year that he receives the stock. Once the substantial risk of forfeiture lapses in year 2, silver must report $25,000 (100 x $250) as additional income in that year.

 b. The amount that Silver includes in income in year 2 is taxed as ordinary income.

10. The amount to be included in income is affected by a restriction that, by its terms, will never lapse. If the employee receives property restricted only in that he must dispose of the property by selling the property back to the employer at a formula price such as book value, then the amount to be included in income is the formula price (the book value) at the time of the grant less any consideration paid by the employee. Note that since such a restriction is not considered a substantial risk of forfeiture, the nonlapse restriction by itself does not defer the timing of taxation. Therefore the answers to this question are as follows: [6]

 a. No

 b. $5 per share or $500 total

 c. The includible amount is ordinary income.

11. Section 83 provides that taxation occurs in the first year in which the property is (a) transferable or (b) no longer subject to a substantial risk of forfeiture. However, if an employee transfers the property along with the substantial risk of forfeiture, there is not necessarily a taxable event. For example, a donation of restricted stock where the stock would continue to be forfeited if the employee failed to meet the restriction would not be a taxable event. However, if restricted stock at any time becomes freely transferable (where the transfer terminates the restriction), then the value of the stock is taxable to the employee when the stock becomes freely transferable, even if the employee does not actually transfer the stock. [7]

12. The employer's deduction is equal to the amount included in income by the employee. The deduction is allowed in the employer's taxable year in which or in which ends the taxable year in which the income is includible by the employee, as long as the employer appropriately reports the amount of the employee's ordinary income to the IRS. [8]

13. The employer pays taxes on income from the restricted property during the restriction period, even if the employee holds full legal title to the property. If income from the property during that period is actually paid out to the employee (for example, as dividends from restricted stock), the employee has additional taxable compensation and the employer obtains a tax deduction in the same amount. The dividends received are subject to Social Security tax and other employment taxes. For years prior to 2011, the employee is not eligible for the special 15 percent tax rate for dividends, since the amount paid is treated as extra compensation.

    If the employee made the Sec. 83(b) election, however (see below), for years prior to 2011, the dividends are eligible for the 15 percent rate (and the employer cannot deduct the dividend payment). The answers to the questions are as follows: [9]

    a. the employer
    b. yes
    c. yes

14. An organization that does not have company stock, such as a partnership or nonprofit organization, can use other types of property for a restricted property plan. For example, life insurance contracts can be used, or stock of other corporations or mutual funds can be used. Such plans provide some of the benefits of restricted stock plans as such, although there is no inherent

incentive function when company stock is not used. Incentives can be built into the forfeiture conditions in plans for nonprofits or partnerships. [10]

15. An RSU plan uses paper "units" rather than actual shares during the restriction period. When the forfeiture condition lapses, actual shares can then be transferred to the employee. [10]

16. The amount recognized as an expense is the fair market value of the stock on the date of the award. This amount is charged to earnings ratably over the period during which the restriction on the stock is in effect. [11]

Learning Objectives

An understanding of the material in this chapter should enable the student to

1. Describe an incentive stock option (ISO) and explain its advantages and disadvantages.

2. Explain the applicability of nonstatutory (nonqualified) stock options.

3. Explain how a stock bonus plan is used in executive compensation.

4. Evaluate the use of nonstatutory stock purchase plans in executive compensation.

5. Describe the characteristics of a stock appreciation right (SAR) plan of executive compensation.

6. Distinguish phantom-stock plans and performance unit plans from SARs.

7. Describe the requirements of Sec. 409A as they apply to stock option plans, phantom stock plans, performance unit plans, and SARs.

Incentive-based compensation related to the value of the employer company's stock—often referred to as equity-type compensation—is an important element in current techniques of executive compensation. A compensation plan based on company stock values can help to attract and retain talented key employees. It is attractive to employees because there is the potential for future growth in the amount the executive will receive where the company is successful. From the company's point of view, it helps to tie the executive to the company by creating a common interest between shareholders and executives.

Equity compensation arrangements are increasingly common in large companies with stock traded on a stock exchange, where the employee can track future compensation based on stock growth that will accrue to him or her eventually. Equity-based compensation is also used in smaller startup companies in technology or other growth areas; there it is used to supplement relatively low cash salaries in the company's early years. The benefit it provides to the executive is the potential of large future benefits if the company is successful and is then sold or makes a public stock offering.

This chapter covers the two types of such compensation:

- Equity compensation—compensation arrangements by which the employee receives actual shares of stock of the company under certain circumstances. These can be stock option plans (plans that provide the executive with a right to buy shares at a specified price) or direct grants or purchases of stock.

- Cash-based equity-like plans—nonqualified deferred-compensation plans. The distinctive feature of the plans discussed here is that the benefits from the plans are based on the value of company stock or some comparable measure. In this type of arrangement, the executive does not have the benefits or burdens of actual ownership of the company.

STOCK OPTIONS

A *stock option* is the grant of a right to purchase stock at a specific price on or after a specified date. When provided as executive compensation, the grant is part of a compensation contract and may be subject to various terms and restrictions designed to meet the interests of the employer and employee. Typically the option remains open for a number of years and thus allows the employee to defer taxation of the option's compensation element beyond the year in which the compensation was earned.

An option is considered to be *granted* on the date when the company gives the right to the employee to purchase the stock at a stated price within a stated time window—that is, the date on which the company transfers the option to the employee. No stock is transferred on the date of the grant. The option is *exercised* by the employee when he or she purchases stock subject to the option at the option price. Naturally, options will be exercised only when the market value of the stock covered under the option agreement exceeds the option price—that is the purpose of the option as a form of compensation.

Options can be divided into two types for tax purposes: statutory and nonstatutory. A statutory option is one that receives favorable tax treatment under the Internal Revenue Code. Congress has long believed that it's a good thing for the country if employees have an ownership share in their employer, and the tax laws reflect that policy. Various benefits for stock options have been provided over the years; the benefit currently available for stock options applies to option plans that meet the definition of *incentive stock options* or ISOs, under Code Sec. 422.

A nonstatutory option (sometimes called a nonqualified option) is basically any type of option other than an ISO. Nonstatutory options have no specific tax benefits but are taxed under general principles of tax law. For example, a nonstatutory stock option generally is not taxable when received since its value is not ascertainable; however, if the option is traded on an exchange, it does have an ascertainable value and may be taxable when received.

Incentive Stock Options

An ISO is a stock option plan that meets the following requirements of Code Sec. 422:

- After exercising the option the employee must hold stock for at least 2 years after the date the options were granted and for at least one year after exercise.
- The grantee of the option must be an employee of the company or related entity at all times during the period from the date of grant until 3 months before the date of exercise.
- Options must be granted pursuant to a plan approved by shareholders within 12 months of the plan's adoption stating the aggregate number of shares covered under the plan.
- Options must be granted within 10 years from the earlier of (1) the date of the plan's adoption or (2) the date of the plan's approval by shareholders.
- Options must be exercisable within 10 years from the date of the grant.
- The option price may not be less than the fair market value of the shares involved at the time the option is granted.
- Options must be nontransferable other than at death and must be exercisable only by the employee during the employee's life.
- The employee-grantee must not own more than 10 percent of the total combined voting power of the company and related companies (directly or indirectly) at the time of the grant.
- The aggregate fair market value of stock that can be purchased by the employee pursuant to options exercisable for the first time during any calendar year under all ISO plans of the company,

parent, and subsidiaries must not exceed $100,000 (determined as of the date of the grant).

EXAMPLE

Grand Prix Corporation grants an option to purchase 20,000 shares of the corporation's common stock to Peter Driver in 2010. On the date of grant the fair market value of Grand Prix Corporation's common stock is $100 per share. The option is exercisable in the following installments: 20% (4,000 shares) in 2011, 20% (4,000) in 2012 and 60% (12,000 shares) in 2013. Due to the fact that in 2013 shares having a fair market value of $120,000 initially become exercisable, the option as a whole does not qualify as an incentive stock option. However, the portions of the option exercisable in 2011 and 2012 do qualify for incentive stock option treatment. Similarly, in 2013 the portion of the option covering 10,000 shares will qualify for incentive stock option treatment, but the portion of the option covering the remaining 2,000 shares must be treated as a nonqualified stock option.

Apart from the above-referenced statutory requirements, many of the design issues described with respect to NSOs may apply to ISOs.

Tax Treatment of ISOs

The tax treatment of ISOs is significantly more beneficial than the treatment of options under the general rules of tax law. If an option qualifies as an ISO, an employee who exercises an option and does not dispose of the stock within (a) at least 2 years of the date the option was granted and (b) at least one year after the date the option was exercised, will be entitled to the following income tax treatment:

- At the time the incentive stock option is granted, there will be no tax consequence to the employee.
- At the time the incentive stock option is exercised, there will be no tax consequence to the employee or to the employer.
- At the time the stock (that was received as a result of the exercise of the option) is sold, the employee will be taxed on the gain as a capital gain. The amount taxable is the difference between the option price and the sale price of the stock.

When the employee is taxed under the above rules, the employer will receive no business-expense deduction with respect to the incentive stock option at any time.

EXAMPLE

Frank Opp, an employee of Flam Co., participated in an ISO plan under which he was granted an option in November 2009 to buy 100 shares of Flam stock for $100 per share, exercisable through 2018. In March 2010, Opp exercises the option, paying $10,000 for 100 shares. The fair market value of the 100 shares at the time of exercise is $25,000. Opp reports no regular taxable income in 2010 resulting from the exercise of the option. The $15,000 of benefit Opp receives in 2010 is an item of tax preference that could subject Opp to alternative minimum tax (AMT). Flam Co. gets no tax deduction in 2010 for this transaction, even if Opp has to pay some AMT.

In 2012 Opp sells the 100 shares of Flam stock for $30,000. His basis for this stock is $10,000, and he therefore has $20,000 of resulting capital gain in 2012. Flam receives no resulting deduction in 2012.

If the employee does not meet the holding requirements for the stock outlined above, tax will nevertheless be deferred until the sale of the stock. However, the difference between the option price and the fair market value of the stock on the date of exercise will be ordinary income rather than capital gain. Under this circumstance, as long as the employer reports the ordinary income to the IRS, the employer will be allowed a business expense deduction in the year in which the employee receives ordinary income. Any portion of the sales proceeds in excess of the ordinary income component will be taxed as capital gain to the employee, but the employer will not be entitled to any further deduction.

The difference between the option price and the fair market value of the stock on the date of exercise of the option is considered an item of tax preference to the executive and is potentially subject to the alternative minimum tax (AMT). This difference will not be an item of tax preference if a disqualifying disposition of the option shares occurs in the same year as the incentive stock option is exercised.

EXAMPLE

If in the preceding example, Opp sells the 100 shares of Flam stock for $30,000 in May, 2011, Opp will not have held the shares for the requisite two years from the date of grant. Consequently, the stock sale is a disqualifying disposition. Opp's exercise price is $10,000 and the difference between the exercise price and the fair market value of the Flam stock on the date of exercise is $15,000. Opp must report this gain as ordinary income. Assuming Flam properly reports this income to the IRS, it can deduct this amount in 2011. The difference between the sale proceeds of $30,000 and the $25,000, representing the sum of Opp's exercise price and ordinary income, is $5,000. Opp can treat this $5,000 as a capital gain in 2011. Flam is not entitled to any deduction for this amount in 2011.

Advantages and Disadvantages of ISOs

Executive Advantages. The principal advantage of an ISO to the executive is, of course, the potential (applicable as well to nonstatutory options) for considerable gains if the company is successful. In addition, a specific benefit of an ISO is the beneficial tax treatment afforded. The executive does not have any taxable ordinary income on the value of the benefit (the difference between the stock's value at the time of exercise and the option price), but AMT could apply. Gains above the option price are generally treated as capital gains (taxed at 15 percent if the maximum holding period requirement for long-term capital gains is met).

Company Advantages. From the company's point of view, the existence of the ISO and the holding period requirement of the ISO create an incentive for the executive to remain with the company and contribute to its growth. And, as with all forms of option compensation, the company benefits by providing a form of valuable compensation without a cash outlay.

Executive Disadvantages. Although stock options of any type are generally beneficial to executives, the ISO restrictions are more burdensome than those that typically are applicable to nonstatutory options. For example, the holding period requirement can restrict the employee's ability to take advantage of market fluctuations. The nontransferability restriction can limit the executive's estate or financial planning options, for example, by limiting his ability to transfer the options to family members or trusts to reduce estate taxes.

Company Disadvantages. The ISO limitations can hamper the company's planning options as well. The $100,000 restriction, for example, limits the usefulness of ISOs for highly paid executives. The requirement that the option price not be less than fair market value at the time of grant also limits the company's flexibility, since it indicates that no compensation opportunity can be granted to the executive unless stock prices rise. (However, under Code Sec. 409A, discussed below, a similar market value restriction also applies to nonstatutory options.) ISOs also have the general disadvantages of all option plans from the company's perspective, such as diluting the value of stock held by existing shareholders and also diluting their voting power.

Nonstatutory Stock Options

A nonstatutory stock option plan, or NSO plan, is an option plan that is taxed under generally applicable tax law principles; there is no specific Code (statutory) provision for these plans, such as the provision for ISOs (Code Sec. 422). NSOs are also sometimes referred to as *nonqualified* stock option plans.

NSOs encompass a very broad category of plans for employees. Because there are no specific restrictions like those for ISOs, NSOs can be designed to meet a relatively unlimited spectrum of employer and employee needs.

NSOs are not limited to salaried employees; they can be used to compensate service providers in general, including commissioned employees and independent contractors.

There are no legal restrictions on the terms of NSOs, so almost any grant formula, vesting provision, and so on, can be used (of course, general provisions of civil rights, sex and age discrimination, and similar employment laws would apply). Typically, terms and provisions are used that provide a performance incentive for the executive. Some of the design issues include the following:

- Exercise price—very flexible under NSOs. However, the use of exercise prices below the fair market value at the date of grant, so the option is "in the money" immediately is precluded by the provisions of Code Sec. 409A. As discussed below, options are exempted from the requirements of Sec. 409A only if the exercise price is at least equal to the FMV at the date of exercise. However, within the limits of the 409A rules, a NSO can provide a variable exercise price based on company performance targets such as sales, profits, earnings per share, or cost reductions in the executive's area of responsibility.

- Vesting—the executive's nonforfeitable right to the option can be deferred for a specified period of time such as 2 years or 5 years, or deferred until the attainment of specified performance targets. A vesting provision is an example of the type of "handcuff" provision often provided in executive compensation arrangements as a method of tying the executive to the company for at least a minimum period of time. These provisions should be realistic and targeted to specific needs of the company and the executive.

- Holding period—there are no statutory holding period requirements for NSOs, but to meet employer or employer concerns an NSO can provide a requirement that stock purchased through the exercise of an option be held for a specified period. In effect, the stock purchased would be treated as restricted stock under the rules described in the preceding chapter.

- Transferability—unlike ISOs, NSOs can be transferred to others for estate and financial planning purposes. They could be transferred to family members, trusts, or family partnerships. For gift tax purposes, the valuation is the FMV of the option itself at the date of the gift. The gift is not treated as complete until the option becomes exercisable. There is no further estate or gift tax even if the option increases in value because the underlying stock increases in value. However, if the stock decreases in value, there is no way to reclaim any gift tax exemption that has been used up as a result of the transfer. There is no income tax consequence at the date of the gift of the option to either the executive or the recipient. When the recipient exercises the option during the executive's lifetime, the executive who transferred the option will recognize income as if the executive had exercised the option. Thus, in effect, the executive has made a tax-free gift to the recipient in the amount of the income taxes paid as a result of the exercise. If the option is exercised after the executive's death, the recipient will incur ordinary income at the time of exercise equal to the difference between the fair market value of the underlying stock and the exercise price. In either case the employer is entitled to a corresponding tax deduction.

Tax Treatment of NSOs

The tax treatment of NSOs is governed by general principles of tax law relating to compensation income and transfers of property, rather than specific rules such as those that apply to ISOs. Generally, the tax treatment is as follows:

- There is no tax to the executive at the time of the grant unless the option has a "readily ascertainable fair market value." Options rarely will be considered to have an ascertainable FMV unless the options (not the stock, the options themselves) are traded on an established market. If options have an ascertainable FMV, the executive will have immediate taxable compensation income equal to the fair market value of the options granted. In a small, closely held business the options will rarely have an ascertainable fair market value.

- When the option is exercised, (assuming the grant was not taxable), the executive has taxable income equal to the difference between the fair market value of the stock purchased under the option and the option price paid by the executive.

- At exercise of an option by an executive, the company has a corresponding income tax deduction in the amount includible by the executive. Like all deductions for compensation paid, this deduction is limited by the "reasonableness" test discussed in chapter one.

- The executive's basis for stock received upon exercise of an option under an NSO plan is the amount paid, plus the additional amount included as compensation income. (For basis purposes, this additional amount is in effect deemed to have been paid to the company as additional payment for the stock).

- Any gain on subsequent sale of the stock by the executive is capital gain, eligible for favorable tax rates if the stock meets the long-term gain requirements of the Code.

- If the stock is purchased by the executive subject to a substantial risk of forfeiture, the executive's taxation (along with the company's deduction) is postponed until the risk of forfeiture lapses.

EXAMPLE
Bill Pims, an employee of Netz Co., participates in an NSO plan under which he is granted an option in 2008 to buy 100 shares of Netz stock for $100 per share, exercisable through 2018. Netz options are not traded on an established market and their exercise price is the stock's fair market value on the date of grant. Pims reports no regular taxable income in 2008 resulting from the grant of the option. In 2010, Pims exercises the option, paying $10,000 for 100 shares. The fair market value of the 100 shares in 2010 is $25,000. In 2010 upon exercise of the option, Pims reports $15,000 of ordinary compensation income reflecting the benefit that Pims receives in 2010. Netz can deduct this $15,000 amount in 2010.   In 2012 Pims sells the 100 shares of Netz stock for $30,000. His basis for this stock is $25,000, and he therefore has $5,000 of resulting capital gain in 2012. Netz receives no deduction in 2012.

Generally, if the issuance of an NSO does not satisfy the requirements of Sec. 409A, the tax treatment is as follows:

- There is no tax to the executive at the time of the grant unless the option has a readily ascertainable fair market value.

- Once the option becomes exercisable (assuming the grant was not taxable), the executive has taxable income equal to the difference between the fair market value of the underlying stock on the date the option is first exercisable and the option's exercise price (the "taxable Sec. 409A spread"). This taxable Sec. 409A spread will also be subject to the 20 percent penalty tax and the increased underpayment interest rate, if the taxable amount is not included in the executive's gross income in the first year that it arises. This tax calculation must be reported in each of the executive's subsequent taxable years, except that the taxable Sec. 409A spread is reduced by the amounts previously included in income. Thus, if an option does not meet the requirements of Sec. 409A at grant, the executive is best advised to exercise the option as soon as it becomes exercisable in order to avoid any further adverse tax consequences under Sec. 409A.

- Once the executive has to recognize income under Sec. 409A, the company is entitled to a corresponding income tax deduction for the amount recognized as income. The deduction is limited by the "reasonableness" test discussed in Chapter 1.

- The executive's basis for the stock received upon exercise of the option is the amount paid, plus the additional amounts included as compensation income under Sec. 409A.

- Any gain on subsequent sale of the stock by the executive is capital gain, eligible for favorable tax rates if the stock is held for the long-term capital gain holding period.

- If the underlying option stock is subject to a substantial risk of forfeiture, the executive's taxation (along with the company's deduction) is postponed until the risk of forfeiture lapses.

Advantages and Disadvantages of NSOs

For the most part, the advantages and disadvantages of ISOs discussed earlier also apply to NSOs. However, from both employer and employee standpoints, the additional major advantage of NSOs is their flexibility due to the less stringent statutory restrictions. NSOs can provide a variety of formulas, are not specifically limited in amount, and can even cover nonemployees such as directors, legal counsel, and other independent contractors.

The tax treatment of NSOs is favorable, even though it is somewhat less favorable than ISOs. The chief disadvantage of the NSO tax treatment is that the executive must pay taxes at exercise of the option but does not receive a cash asset to pay the taxes. This situation can be alleviated by providing a bonus to the employee to pay the taxes upon exercising an NSO.

STOCK BONUS PLANS

A stock bonus is simply a grant of stock to an employee as a bonus. Much the same rules are involved as in the case of a cash bonus, discussed in chapter one. A stock bonus plan, as discussed here, should be distinguished from a qualified stock bonus plan, a form of qualified retirement plan similar to a qualified profit-sharing plan, with participant accounts in the form of employer stock.

Stock granted to an executive as a bonus may be vested, but usually the shares are granted subject to a substantial risk of forfeiture (that is, unvested), typically with vesting occurring after several more years of employment, as a way of encouraging the executive to remain or to perform well. As discussed in the preceding chapter, with a grant of restricted stock, the executive is subject to ordinary income tax on the fair market value of the stock in the year it becomes substantially vested—that is, when the stock is no longer subject to a substantial risk of forfeiture. If stock is granted to the executive without restrictions (is vested immediately), then its fair market value is taxable to the executive in the year received.

In the case of restricted stock, the executive can elect under Code Sec. 83(b) to include the value in an earlier year (see discussion of this issue in the preceding chapter).

The employer gets a tax deduction in the year the executive includes the amount in income for tax purposes; and the deduction is the same amount as the employee includes.

Stock bonus plans are attractive to employer and employee like other forms of equity-based compensation, and they have the advantage of relative simplicity. However, from the company's standpoint, stock bonus plans are harder to design with real incentive features, and they require that executives actually own stock, which may be undesirable for other shareholders or potential shareholders.

STOCK PURCHASE PLANS

For purposes of executive compensation, a stock purchase plan is similar to a stock bonus plan except that shares are sold to the executive rather than granted as a bonus. Generally, after the shares are purchased there is no provision for forfeiting the shares. However, there may be a formula that requires resale of the shares to the company at a price specified in the purchase agreement.

Like option plans, stock purchase plans can be divided into statutory and nonstatutory versions. The current form of statutory plan is an "Employee Stock Purchase Plan" under Sec. 423 of the Code, sometimes referred to as a "Section 423 Plan." A Sec. 423 plan is designed for compensating a broad group of employees by allowing them to buy stock of the employer company at a specified price. These plans are not generally used for compensating higher paid executives because of their restrictions. For example, benefits are limited to $25,000 per year per employee, and more-than-5 percent owners of the company can't participate in a Sec. 423 plan. So in this chapter we will focus on nonstatutory plans—arrangements for executive stock purchase that are taxed under general rules of tax law, not under any specific code provisions.

In a stock purchase plan for executives, shares are generally sold at a price less than or equal to their fair market value. If the price is a bargain price, the difference between the fair market value and the price actually paid by the executive is taxable ordinary income to the executive. The company can deduct any amount included as income by the executive as a result of the purchase.

The fact that the executive must invest his or her own money in the company under a stock purchase plan is an excellent way to tie the executive to the company. However, the downside is that some executives may be reluctant or unable to find the necessary dollars.

STOCK APPRECIATION RIGHT (SAR)

So far, the plans discussed in this chapter have involved situations in which actual property was given to the executive as compensation. The next group of plans involves not a current transfer of property rights (or a transfer within a few years after the current year), but a long-term contractual commitment by the employer to provide a cash benefit, typically at retirement or termination of employment. Thus, these equity-based cash benefit plans—SARs, phantom-stock plans, and performance unit plans—are actually types of nonqualified deferred compensation rather than transfers of property. As a type of nonqualified deferred compensation, SARs are subject to Code Sec. 409A. This means that in order to avoid the Sec. 409A requirements, the SAR must use the fair market value of the underlying company stock as the initial value of the SAR. If the initial SAR value is less than the fair market value of the underlying company stock, the tax consequences are similar to those applicable to the issuance of a discount NSO. However, because the ultimate payment is based on company stock values, SARs serve some of the same incentive purposes as actual equity-transfer plans.

Because there is only a corporate contractual promise to pay rather than an actual transfer of valuable property, if the SAR is issued at the fair market value of the underlying company stock, SARs will be taxed under the rules applicable to nonqualified deferred-compensation plans rather than under the restricted property (Code Sec. 83) rules. Also, there is a possibility that these plans are covered under ERISA, thus affording the executive the protections of ERISA. One significant advantage of an ERISA plan is that the executive may be able to sue for benefits in the federal courts. However, some courts have held that when these plans cover only a few highly-compensated executives and when there is no ongoing burden of plan administration, there is no ERISA plan.

An SAR agreement provides that the employer will provide the executive with additional cash compensation at retirement or other specified future time, with the payout measured by the increase in value of a specified asset, generally the stock of the employer company from the date of grant until the SAR is exercised. The payout from an SAR may also be in actual shares of stock or some other form of valuable property.

Under the agreement, payout from an SAR, as in the case of regular nonqualified deferred-compensation plans, takes place on the occurrence of certain specified events, such as the passage of a specified time or retirement or termination of employment. The distribution provisions of Section 409A will apply to SARs that are not issued at the fair market value of the underlying stock.

As with any other deferred-compensation plan, vesting provisions may be included to preclude payouts to short-term employees. SARs may be combined with option plans to provide executives with cash to exercise their options.

Generally, assuming that Sec. 409A is not applicable, the cash or property received under an SAR is taxed when received by the executive under the rules otherwise applicable to nonqualified deferred-compensation plans. The company receives a corresponding deduction in the year in which the executive includes the compensation in income.

SARs are more appropriate for closely held companies than are actual equity-transfer plans, since SARs do not dilute the stock or bring in new ownership to the company.

PHANTOM-STOCK PLANS AND PERFORMANCE UNIT PLANS

A phantom-stock plan is, in principle, almost exactly the same thing as an SAR. However, the term phantom-stock plan is generally used to refer to a plan where the benefit is based on actual specified shares of stock set aside for the employee, with the employee receiving a future benefit equal to the value of the shares at that time or the actual shares themselves. An SAR by comparison generally provides a benefit based on the appreciation in the stock price as determined on a particular date, rather than on the total value of a share of stock. Generally, these arrangements are used interchangeably, but a phantom-stock plan has the disadvantage that it could be misleading to the executive, giving the impression of actual equity ownership and the possibility of ultimate capital gains, when this is not usually the case. Agreements should be drafted carefully to make clear the actual nature of the benefit.

A performance unit plan is a plan of deferred compensation where the benefit is based, not on the value of the company stock, but on a more specific measure of the executive's performance. Units earned can be based on such things as earnings, sales, growth, production, return on equity or investment, profit margin, or other measures that the executive can specifically affect.

Code Sec. 409A provides rules for nonqualified deferred-compensation plans. To the extent that a performance share plan or performance unit plan is structured such that shares are issued or cash paid in settlement of the award immediately upon vesting, such plans will fit within the "short-term deferral rule" and will be able to avoid the requirements of Sec. 409A. However, to the extent that the award structure includes any form of additional deferral feature, for example, an opportunity to defer distribution for a period beyond the vesting date, then this deferral feature will cause the award to become deferred compensation that must be structured to satisfy the requirements of Sec. 409A.

SEC. 409A AND STOCK PLANS

Code Sec. 409A defines the term nonqualified deferred-compensation plans broadly[38] so as to cover many of the plans discussed in this chapter. There are specific exclusions for stock options and other plans that planners must review carefully, since the applicability of Sec. 409A to a stock plan can be disadvantageous.

Exemptions

Fortunately, there are exemptions from the Sec. 409A rules for certain stock plans. First, ISOs under Code Sec. 422 and Sec. 423 employee stock purchase plans are generally exempt.[39] But nonstatutory stock options will be treated as deferred compensation for Sec. 409A purposes unless all of the following conditions are met.

- The exercise price may never be less than the fair market value of the stock on the date the option is granted.
- The option is subject to taxation under Sec. 83.
- The option does not include any feature for the deferral of compensation other than the deferral of recognition of income until the later of the exercise or disposition of the option.

A nonstatutory option plan that does not meet the above requirements—that is, one that is subject to Sec. 409A—probably would fail the distribution requirements of Sec. 409A and be subject to the penalty tax and early income taxation, thus "killing" the plan. This is because the significant benefit of most stock option plans is that the option holder is able to determine when to exercise the option and receive taxable income. This distribution possibility is not on the list of permitted distributions under Sec. 409A. Consequently, a nonstatutory option plan must meet the conditions discussed in Chapter 2 in order to avoid the application of Sec. 409A. This factor materially reduces the flexibility that stock option plans formerly enjoyed.

Many stock-option holders have options that are about to expire and would like to defer the taxable compensation element of the option plan beyond the date on which the option expires. The employer and employee can agree to extend the option, but this negotiation probably will be treated as

---

38. Treas. Reg. Sec. 1.409A-1(b)(1).
39. Treas. Reg. Sec. 1.409A-1(b)(5)(ii).

the creation of a new option[40] and if the new option price is below the fair market value at the date of the extension, the plan will become subject to Sec. 409A. Therefore, extension of options, a common practice in the past, is impracticable under current law. However, the Sec. 409A regulations permit a limited extension: an option can be extended to the end of the calendar year or for 3 months, if later.[41]

In recent years, especially during recent bull markets, some executives holding options have wanted to renegotiate their option agreements prior to exercise and convert the option agreement into a conventional deferred-compensation plan of equivalent value, thus deferring taxation beyond the expiration date of the option. There has been some difference of opinion as to the tax treatment of this "swap," with some commentators and the IRS arguing that a taxable constructive receipt occurs on the termination of the option agreement thereby changing its nature; while others argue that the option has been changed to a benefit that is based purely on an unsecured corporate promise, and that there is no constructive receipt and no tax-abusive situation involved at all.[42] The Sec. 409A regulations have negative provisions relating to this type of transaction,[43] but Congress specifically deleted a provision penalizing option swaps as part of the American Jobs Creation Act of 2004. The treatment of such swaps remains to be clarified.

Exemption for SARs

SARs and similar arrangements are subject to Sec. 409A, since they are essentially nonqualified deferred-compensation plans. However, plans that are called "SARs" can vary tremendously in nature, so the Sec. 409A regulations provide an exemption for an SAR that meets the following conditions (conditions that make the plan appear similar to an option plan rather than deferred compensation):

- the SAR has an exercise price that is never less than the fair market value of the stock subject to the SAR on the date the SAR is granted,

---

40. Treas. Reg. Sec. 1.409A-1(b)(5)(v)(A).

41. Treas. Reg. Sec. 1.409A-1(b)(5)(v)(E).

42. See Kroll, "Deferring Tax on Gain from the Exercise of Stock Options," *Journal of Deferred Compensation*, Vol. 8, Issue 2 (2003).

43. Treas. Reg. Sec. 1.409A-1(b)(5)(v)(I).

- the SAR does not include any feature for the deferral of compensation (other than the deferral of recognition of income until the exercise of the SAR), and

- the number of shares subject to the SAR must be fixed on or before the grant date.[44]

Valuation

The Sec. 409A exemption requirement that a stock option have an exercise price equal to the fair market value of the underlying stock on the date of grant puts a premium on proper valuation, particularly for private companies. The Sec. 409A regulations provide very detailed guidance with regard to how stock subject to rights must be valued. This guidance is provided with regard to both private company and publicly traded stock. These acceptable valuation methodologies are a very important element of the Sec. 409A regulatory regime. The fair market value of public company stock is usually to be determined based on the last sale before (or the first sale after) the grant, the closing price on a trading day near the grant date, or any other method using actual transactions.[45]

The Sec. 409A regulations recognize that the valuation of private company stock cannot be as precise as the valuation of publicly traded stock. Consequently, the fair market value of private company stock must be determined, based on the private company's particular facts and circumstances, by application of a reasonable valuation method. For this purpose for a valuation method to be considered reasonable, it must take into account all available information material to the valuation of the private company. In the typical case the factors to be taken into account, as applicable, under a reasonable valuation method include: (i) the value of tangible and intangible assets; (ii) the present value of future cash flows; (iii) the readily determinable market value of similar entities engaged in a substantially similar business; (iv) other relevant factors such as control premiums or discounts for lack of marketability; and (v) whether the valuation method is used for other purposes that have a material economic effect on the service recipient, its stockholders, or its creditors.

The valuation of a private company remains current as long as the value was calculated within 12 months earlier than the date for which the valuation is

---

44. Treas. Reg. Sec. 1.409A-1(b)(1)(v).

45. Treas. Reg. Sec. 1.409A-1(b)(5)(iv)(A).

being used. However, this general rule does not apply in circumstances where the initial valuation fails to reflect information available after the initial valuation date that materially affects the value of a private company, for example, the resolution of a material income tax audit or the value of a private company, the resolution of a material income tax audit or the grant of a material patent. Thus, if during the usual 12-month reliance period, there is a material change in financial circumstances, the old valuation must be revised in order for it to continue to be reasonable under the Sec. 409A regulations.[46]

The Sec. 409A regulations also offer three circumstances where a private company's determination of fair market value will be presumed to be reasonable, as long as the method is consistently used. The IRS may rebut this presumption of reasonableness only on a showing that either the valuation method or the application of such method was grossly unreasonable.[47]

One of the circumstances which is presumed reasonable is where the valuation is determined by an independent appraisal that meets the employee stock ownership plan requirements of Code Sec. 401(a)(28) and is no more than 12-months old. The second circumstance is where the valuation is determined pursuant to a formula that produces the fair market value of the stock under Treas. Reg. 1.83-5 (applicable to stock subject to a nonlapse restriction under Treas. Reg. 1.83-3 (h)), provided that the valuation is consistently used for this purpose.

Finally, reasonableness will be presumed where the valuation is of "illiquid stock of a start-up corporation" and is made reasonably in good faith, takes into account the relevant valuation factors for privately held corporations described above and is evidenced by a written report. Stock will be considered to have been issued by an "illiquid start-up corporation" if the following factors are satisfied:

- The company has not conducted (directly or indirectly through a predecessor) a trade or business for a period of 10 years or more;
- The company has no class of securities that is traded on an established securities market;
- The stock is not subject to put or call rights or other obligations to purchase such stock (other than a right of first refusal or other

---

46. Treas. Reg. Sec. 1.409A-1(b)(5)(iv)(B)(1)
47. Treas. Reg. Sec. 1.409A-1(b)(5)(iv)(B)(2)

"lapse restriction" such as the right to purchase unvested stock at its original cost.

- The company is not reasonably expected, as of the time the valuation is applied, to undergo a change in control within 90 days or to make a public offering within 180 days of the date the valuation is used; and

- The valuation is performed by a person or persons "with significant knowledge and experience or training in performing similar valuations." This means at least 5 years of relevant experience in business valuation or appraisal, financial accounting, investment banking, private equity, secured lending, or other comparable experience in the line of business or industry in which the service recipient operates.[48]

CASE PROBLEM

The Ajax Corporation is a small but well-run corporation. Its stock is traded on the American Exchange and, at the current time, it has 2,000,000 shares authorized with 1,000,000 of these shares issued and outstanding. Shareholder equity amounts to $1,500,000. The current market value of a share is $4.

Important information about Ajax's key employees is as follows:

Name	Title	Compensation	Shares Now Owned
I. M. Clean	Chairman, Board of Directors	$ 10,000*	$150,000
D. Tergent	President	150,000	150,000
A. Powder	Exec. Vice President	120,000	60,000
C. Foam	Vice President	100,000	7,000
Cass Cade	Vice President	84,000	4,000

*Director's fees

In addition, Ajax employs three other vice presidents who earn between $90,000 and $96,000 a year, nine department heads who earn between

---

48. Treas. Reg. Sec. 1.409A-1(b)(5)(iv)(B)(2)(iii)

$60,000 and $80,000 a year, and six other key employees who earn between $50,000 and $60,000 a year. No one in this group owns any Ajax stock.

Growth in the soap industry in recent years has been at an annual rate of 10 percent. Ajax hopes to increase its earnings at an annual rate of 12 percent.

Based on the foregoing information, you are asked to design an incentive stock option plan. How would you determine eligibility for the plan? Explain.

CHAPTER REVIEW

Review Questions

1. What is a stock option? [1]

2. List the requirements that a stock option must meet in order to qualify under the Code's ISO provisions. [1]

3. Gene Splicer is covered under his employer's ISO plan. Three years ago he was granted options to buy company stock at $50 per share. This year he exercises the option and buys 500 shares. The market price of the shares at the time of exercise is $75 per share. How is this transaction treated for tax purposes? [1]

4. What are the advantages and disadvantages of ISOs? [1]

5. What is a nonqualified or nonstatutory stock option (NSO)? [2]

6. What type of formulas are typically used for exercise price, holding periods, and vesting? [2]

7. Describe the tax treatment of NSOs. [2]

8. List some advantages and disadvantages of NSOs. [2]

9. Describe the general structure of a stock bonus plan. [3]

10. What is the federal income tax treatment of a stock bonus plan? [3]

11. Assess the motivational impact of a stock bonus plan. [3]

12. What are the differences between a stock purchase plan and a stock bonus plan? [4]

13. Executive Bob is covered under Enterprise, Inc.'s stock purchase plan, which allows him to purchase stock this year for $50 per share. He purchases 100 shares. The fair market value at time of purchase is $75 per share. How is this transaction treated for federal income tax purposes to Bob and to Enterprise? [4]

14. Phil Cratchit, a promising executive, comes from a poor family and, prior to employment by your company, worked for the government. Is he a good prospect for a stock purchase plan? [4]

15. Explain the major contractual difference between an SAR and the plans discussed in the preceding questions of this chapter. [5]

16. What is the formula for the benefit provided for an SAR? [5]

17. How are SARs taxed? [5]

18. Why are SARs appropriate for closely held companies? [5]

19. Explain the similarities and differences between SARs and phantom-stock plans. [6]

20. How do performance unit plans operate in contrast with SARs and phantom-stock plans? [6]

21. Holosystems, Inc., proposes a nonstatutory stock option for executive Len. The exercise price is $100 per share. Holosystems, Inc., recently sold stock to a group of investors for $150 per share. Comment on this plan. [7]

22. Larry Flint holds stock options in Stonewalls, Inc.'s stock at $100 per share that are due to expire on the first of next month. Stonewalls' stock is now trading at $350 per share. Larry unfortunately has no money to exercise the options but expects a cash windfall next year at the death of a very sick relative. He wants to ask Stonewalls to extend the option for an additional year at the original price of $100. Should Stonewalls agree to this plan? [7]

Answers to Review Questions

1. A stock option is the grant of a right to purchase stock at a specific price on or after a specified future date. When provided as executive compensation, the grant is part of a compensation contract and may be subject to various terms and restrictions. For income tax purposes, a stock option generally is not taxable when received since its value is not ascertainable; however, if the option is traded on an exchange, it does have an ascertainable value and may be taxable when received. [1]

2. An ISO is a "statutory" plan based on a specific statutory provision in the Internal Revenue Code. ISO requirements include the following: [1]

   • Employee must hold stock for 2 years from date of grant and for one year from date of exercise.

   • Grantee must be an employee of the company or related entity at all times during period from date of grant to 3 months before date of exercise.

- Options must be granted pursuant to a plan approved by shareholders within 12 months of adoption stating aggregate number of shares.
- Options must be granted within 10 years from earlier of date of adoption or date of approval by shareholders.
- Options must be exercisable within 10 years from date of grant.
- Option price may not be less than fair market value at time option is granted.
- Options must be nontransferable other than at death and must be exercisable only by employee during employee's life.
- Employee-grantee must not own more than 10 percent of company (directly or indirectly) at time of grant.
- Aggregate fair market value of stock under ISO plan for options that initially become exercisable during any calendar year must not exceed $100,000.

3. The tax treatment of an ISO is as follows: [1]

- If an option qualifies as an incentive stock option, an employee who exercises an option and does not dispose of the stock within (a) 2 years of the date the option was granted and (b) one year after the date the option was exercised, will be entitled to the following income tax treatment:
- At the time the incentive stock option is granted, there will be no tax consequence to the employee.
- At the time the incentive stock option is exercised, there will be no tax consequence to the employee or to the employer.
- At the time the stock (that was received as a result of the exercise of the option) is sold, the employee will be taxed on the gain as a capital gain. The amount taxable is the difference between the option price and the sale price of the stock.

  When the employee is taxed under the above rules, the employer will receive no business expense deduction with respect to the incentive stock option at any time.

If the employee does not meet the holding requirements for the stock outlined above, tax will nevertheless be deferred until the sale of the stock. However, the spread between the option price and the fair market value of the stock on the date of exercise will be ordinary income rather than capital gain. Under this circumstance, as long as the employer reports the ordinary income to the IRS, the employer will be allowed a business expense deduction in the year in which the employee receives ordinary income. Any portion of the sales proceeds in excess of the ordinary income component will be taxed as capital gain to the employee, but the employer will not be entitled to any further deduction.

The difference between the option price and the fair market value of the stock on the date of exercise of the option is considered an item of tax preference to the executive and is potentially subject to the alternative minimum tax (AMT).

Therefore, Gene Splicer has no regular taxable income this year upon exercise of the ISO, and the company has no tax deduction. However, Gene will have an item of tax preferences that is potentially subject to the AMT.

4. A major advantage of ISOs is the tax treatment as described above—there is no recognition of income by the executive either at the grant of the option or upon its exercise, although there may be an AMT at exercise. (However, correspondingly, the employer does not have a tax deduction at any time.) Furthermore, upon eventually selling the stock, the executive's gain (difference between amount he paid for stock and amount realized) is taxed as capital gain.

   From the corporation's viewpoint, although it gets no tax deduction, the ISO is a form of compensation requiring no cash outlay. Moreover, the holding period requirement creates an incentive for the executive to stay.

   The major disadvantage of an ISO is the number of strict statutory requirements summarized above. These can make the ISO unfeasible in certain circumstances. [1]

5. An NSO is an option plan that is taxed under generally applicable tax-law principles; there is no specific Code (statutory) provision for these plans, such as the provision for ISOs (Code Sec. 422). [2]

6. Apart from the requirement under Sec. 409A that the exercise price of the NSO must be at least equal to the fair market value of the underlying stock on the date of grant, there are no other legal restrictions on the terms of NSOs, so almost any grant formula, vesting provision, and so on, can be used (of course, general provisions of civil rights and similar employment laws would apply). Typically, terms and provisions are used that provide a performance incentive for the executive. [2]

7. Generally, there is no tax to the executive at the time of grant unless the option has a "readily ascertainable fair market value." At exercise (assuming the grant was not taxable), the executive has taxable income equal to the difference between the fair market value of the stock purchased under the option and the option price paid by the executive. The company has a corresponding income tax deduction in that amount. Any gain on subsequent sale of the stock is capital gain. If the stock is purchased by the executive subject to a substantial risk of forfeiture, the executive's taxation (along with the company's deduction) is postponed until the risk of forfeiture lapses. [2]

8. The major advantage of NSOs is their flexibility due to the lack of statutory restrictions. Even nonemployees can be covered. The tax treatment is favorable, even though somewhat less favorable than ISOs. The chief disadvantage of the NSO tax treatment is that the executive must pay taxes at exercise of the option but does not receive a cash asset to pay the taxes. This can be alleviated by providing a bonus to the employee to pay the taxes upon exercising an NSO. [2]

9. A stock bonus plan is an outright grant of stock to an executive as a bonus. The shares may be vested, but usually are granted subject to a substantial risk of forfeiture as a way of encouraging the executive to stay on or to perform well. [3]

10. The executive is subject to ordinary income tax on the amount of the value of the stock in the year it is received (if vested immediately) or in the year in which the stock becomes vested (no longer subject to a substantial risk of forfeiture). However, the executive can elect under Code Sec. 83(b) to include the value in an earlier year (see discussion of this issue in the preceding chapter). The employer gets a tax deduction in the year the executive includes the amount

in income for tax purposes; and the deduction is the same amount as the employee includes. [3]

11. Stock bonus plans are attractive to employer and employee like other forms of equity-based compensation, and they have the advantage of relative simplicity. However, from the company's standpoint, stock bonus plans are harder to design with real incentive features, and they require that executives actually own stock, which may be undesirable to other shareholders or potential shareholders. [3]

12. A stock purchase plan is similar to a stock bonus plan except that shares are sold to the executive rather than granted as a bonus, and after the shares are purchased there is generally no provision for forfeiting the shares. However, there may be a formula that requires resale of the shares to the company. [4]

13. In a stock purchase plan, shares are generally sold at a price less than or equal to their fair market value. If the price is a bargain price, the difference between the fair market value and the price actually paid by the executive is taxable ordinary income to the executive. The company can deduct any amount included as income by the executive as a result of the purchase.

    Therefore, Executive Bob has an additional $2,500 of ordinary compensation income as a result of purchasing the shares in the question. Enterprise is allowed a deduction of $2,500. [4]

14. While the fact that the executive must invest his own money in the company under a stock purchase plan is an excellent way to tie the executive to the company, the downside is that some executives may be reluctant or unable to find the necessary dollars. Thus, poverty-stricken Phil in the example would not be motivated by a stock purchase plan. [4]

15. All the plans discussed in the preceding objectives of this chapter involved situations in which actual property was given to the executive as compensation. SARs, phantom-stock plans, and performance unit plans involve not a current transfer of property rights but a long-term contractual commitment by the employer to provide a cash benefit, typically at retirement or termination of employment. Thus, SARs, phantom-stock plans, and performance unit plans, are actually types of nonqualified deferred-compensation plans, rather than transfers of property (with or without restrictions). [5]

16. An SAR agreement states that the employer will provide the executive with additional cash compensation in the future (based

on the value of current services) measured by the value of a specified asset, generally the stock of the employer company. The payout from an SAR may also be in actual shares of stock. Payout takes place on the occurrence of certain events, such as the passage of a specified time, new ownership of the company, or simply retirement or termination of employment. Vesting provisions may be included to preclude payouts to short-term employees. SARs may be included with option plans to provide executives with cash to exercise the options. [5]

17. Generally, the cash or property received under an SAR is taxed when received by the executive under the rules for nonqualified deferred-compensation plans. The company receives a corresponding deduction in the year in which the executive includes the compensation income. [5]

18. SARs are more appropriate for closely held companies than are actual equity-transfer plans since SARs do not dilute the stock or bring in new ownership to the company. [5]

19. The term phantom-stock plan is generally used to refer to a plan where the benefit is based on actual specified shares of stock set aside for the employee, with the employee receiving a future benefit equal to the value of the shares at that time or the actual shares themselves. An SAR, by comparison, is generally a formula based on stock prices or values, not the value of specific shares. [6]

20. A performance unit plan is a plan of deferred compensation where the benefit is based not on the value of the company stock but on a more specific measure of the executive's performance. Units earned can be based on such things as earnings, sales, growth, production, return on equity or investment, profit margin, or other measures that the executive can specifically affect. [6]

21. If a stock option is issued "in the money" with an exercise price below the FMV at the date of the grant, the option plan does not qualify for the exemption from Sec. 409A coverage. Thus, if the option does not satisfy the distribution requirements under Sec. 409A, Len will have a taxable event when following the exercise of the option, the option stock vests. Each year thereafter Len will have to recognize taxable income equal to the excess of the stock's fair market value over the exercise price, less any prior amount included in income. Len will also be subject to a 20 percent penalty tax. This is not a favorable result for either Len or Holosystems. [7]

22. An extension of an option is tested for 409A coverage as if it is a new option. The proposed extended-option price of $100 would be

less than the current FMV of $350, so the 409A exemption would not apply. [7]

1. Explain how a split-dollar life insurance plan operates and state its purpose in the executive-compensation context.

2. Describe generally the applications of split-dollar life insurance in providing an executive benefit.

3. Explain policy ownership in split-dollar plans.

4. Compare the forms of premium split in split-dollar plans.

5. Describe how cash values and proceeds are split, and define an equity plan.

6. Explain federal income tax treatment of split-dollar plans regarding the employer and the employee.

7. Determine income and estate taxation of death benefits.

8. Explain what is meant by reverse split-dollar plans.

9. Understand combinations of split-dollar plans and deferred-compensation plans and their tax consequences.

INTRODUCTION

Preretirement death benefits are common benefits for employees. Generally they are provided for a broad group of employees, up to certain maximum levels, such as a multiple of annual compensation. Where an employer wishes to provide an additional death benefit to selected executives, split-dollar plans have been one of the favored techniques.

A split-dollar life insurance plan is not a specific form of life insurance, but rather is a formal or informal arrangement, typically between an employer and an employee, in which there is a sharing of the costs and benefits of a life insurance policy. In other words, it is an arrangement whereby a taxpayer with a need for life insurance and a taxpayer with the resources to pay premiums join together in purchasing a life insurance contract in which there is a substantial investment element.[49] In the employment context, the purpose is to provide a benefit to the employee as an additional form of compensation from the employer. Split-dollar plans can be used for purposes other than compensating employees; for example, as a gift or estate planning arrangement between a parent and a child or in-law. However, the emphasis in this chapter will be on employer/employee-split-dollar arrangements.

For a period of almost fifty years before September 18, 2003, split-dollar arrangements offered a particularly taxpayer-friendly approach to financing premium payments on whole life insurance policies. For historical reasons, the IRS had been of the view that split-dollar arrangements were not loans, even though they were structured as interest-free loans, but rather constituted an investment in the policy by the employer. Accordingly, the economic benefit to the employee was the term insurance premium for the cost of the life insurance coverage. When this characterization was combined with life insurance policies whose cash values in a short period of time exceeded the total premiums paid for the coverage, the employee benefited from such cash value growth which the employee could count on using to keep the policy in effect without further premium payments after the employer was repaid following the termination of the split-dollar arrangement.

As life insurance policies became more efficient over the years and the cash value buildup was able to exceed the employers' aggregate premium payments in a shorter period of time, there was a continuing debate among tax practitioners as to whether the equity buildup in a split-dollar arrangement should be taxable to the employee as an additional economic benefit. For post-September 17, 2003 split-dollar arrangements, the debate is settled with either the equity being protected from tax if the applicable federal interest rate is paid (loan/collateral assignment regime) or the equity being subject to tax as an economic benefit (economic benefit/endorsement regime).

Under the post-September 17, 2003 rules, collateral assignment split-dollar arrangements are generally treated as loans subject to Sec. 7872. Alternatively, post-September 17, 2003 endorsement split-dollar arrangements are treated as a transfer of property and the equity buildup in the cash value owned by the employee becomes subject to income taxes. This chapter will review split-dollar planning in its entirety in light of the

---

49. Rev. Rul. 64-328, 1964-2 CB 11.

post-September 17, 2003 regulations promulgated by the IRS. Transitional or "grandfathering" provisions for older plans are also discussed in connection with the discussion of the new regulations. The primary effect of the new rules is that split-dollar life insurance plans, while not dead, are now just more expensive than before.

APPLICATIONS OF SPLIT DOLLAR FOR EXECUTIVE COMPENSATION

Fundamentally, the purpose of a compensatory split-dollar plan is to provide an executive with a life insurance benefit at low cost and low outlay to the executive. Executive insurance needs include either or both (1) life insurance protection for the family or (2) estate liquidity. Split-dollar plans are an alternative to other methods of providing death benefits (as a reward or incentive to selected executives), such as an insurance-financed nonqualified deferred-compensation plan or life insurance in a qualified plan.

Split-dollar plans can also help provide business continuity by providing funds for shareholder-employees to finance a buyout of stock under a cross purchase buy-sell agreement or make it possible for non-stockholding employees to affect a one way stock purchase at an existing shareholder's death. This helps establish a market for what otherwise might be unmarketable stock while providing an incentive for employees to stay with the company.

A split-dollar plan is a selective executive benefit. An employer can provide the benefit only for a selected group of employees and can treat each covered employee differently. The coverage, amounts, and terms of a split-dollar arrangement are not subject to the nondiscrimination rules that apply to qualified pension plans and certain other benefit arrangements.

Generally the employer's cost for a split-dollar plan is fully secured by the insurance contract. At the employee's death or termination of employment, the employer is reimbursed from policy proceeds for its premium outlay. The employer receives no tax deduction for its payments, but because of the reimbursement the net cost to the employer for the plan is limited to the loss of the net after-tax income which could have been earned on the amount paid by the employer during the period in which the plan was in effect.

In order for the employer to receive the full benefit of a split-dollar plan, it must remain in effect for a reasonably long time—10 to 20 years—so that policy cash values have time to rise to a level sufficient to maximize plan benefits. Nonetheless, the plan must generally be terminated at approximately age 65, since the employee's tax cost for the plan, the Table 2001 cost or equivalent, rises sharply at ages beyond age 65.

A current issue, discussed further below, is that the current tax rules discourage plans that provide the employee with an interest in policy cash values (equity plans). Before 2003, these equity plans had become extremely popular as a means of providing savings, investment, and retirement benefits to executives. The market for split-dollar plans has been substantially diminished due to the less favorable tax treatment accorded to equity plans.

PLAN DESIGN—POLICY OWNERSHIP ISSUES

The two common methods of arranging split-dollar policy ownership are discussed below.

Endorsement Method

- The employer owns the policy and is primarily responsible to the insurance company for paying the entire premium.
- The beneficiary designation provides for the employer to receive a portion of the death benefit equal to its premium outlay (or some alternative share), with the remainder of the death proceeds going to the employee's designated beneficiary.
- An endorsement to the policy is filed with the insurance company under which payment to the employee's beneficiary cannot be changed without consent of the employee (or, in some cases, a designated third person where the employee wishes to avoid incidents of ownership for estate tax purposes).

Advantages of the endorsement method are as follows:

- greater control by the employer over the policy
- simpler installation and administration; the only documentation required (except for possible ERISA requirements described below) being the policy and endorsement
- avoidance of any formal arrangement that might be deemed to constitute a "loan" for purposes of state laws prohibiting corporate loans to officers and directors
- that if the company owns an existing key employee policy on the employee, it can be used directly in the split-dollar plan without

change of ownership. (Using an existing policy may be important if the employee has developed health problems since the policy was issued.)

- that under the regulations (see below) the plan will be taxed under the economic benefit rules (participant reports income based on value of pure insurance coverage under Table 2001 or equivalent), which may be more advantageous from a tax standpoint than the alternative loan treatment

Collateral Assignment Method

- The employee (or a third party) is the owner of the policy and is responsible for premium payments.
- The employer then makes what are in effect interest-free loans of the amount of the premium the employer has agreed to pay under the split-dollar plan.
- This arrangement is treated for tax purposes as a series of loans unless the plan is a *nonequity plan* (see below).
- To secure the loans the policy is assigned as collateral to the employer.
- At the employee's death, the employer recovers its aggregate premium payments from the policy proceeds, as collateral assignee. The remainder of the policy proceeds is paid to the employee's designated beneficiary.
- If the plan terminates before the employee's death, the employer has the right to be reimbursed out of policy cash value; the employee continues as the owner of the policy.

Some advantages of the collateral assignment method are as follows:

- It arguably gives more protection to the employee and the employee's beneficiary.
- It is easier to implement using existing insurance policies owned by the employee.
- It is easier for the employee to keep the policy out of the estate for federal estate tax purposes. Typically this is done by having the policy owned from the outset by a third party chosen by the employee to funnel insurance proceeds to the desired beneficiary—for example, the employee's irrevocable life insurance trust.

Joint Ownership

If, in connection with a split-dollar arrangement, two or more persons are named as policyowners of a life insurance contract, the person who is the first named policyowner is treated as the owner of the entire contract if each person does not have all of the incidents of ownership with respect to an undivided interest in the contract.[50] Thus, if employee and employer are listed as joint owners in that order, the split-dollar loan regime applies, but if the policy lists them in reverse order, the economic benefit regime applies and it is not a loan.

If each co-owner has all of the incidents of ownership with respect to an undivided interest in the contract, each person is treated as the owner of a separate contract to the extent of such person's undivided interest. Neither contract would be a split-dollar arrangement. The regulations state that an undivided interest consists of an identical fractional or percentage interest or share in each right, benefit, and obligation with respect to the contract.

The preamble to the regulations states that a purported undivided interest will be disregarded, and the entire arrangement will be treated as a split-dollar life insurance arrangement, if the employer and the employee agree to enter into a split-dollar life insurance arrangement with respect to what otherwise would have been treated as separate contracts. The IRS will consider all of the facts and circumstances of an arrangement to determine whether the parties have appropriately characterized the arrangement as one involving undivided interests. In summary, the regulations effectively negate any advantage that might be obtained from joint ownership.

PREMIUM COST SPLIT

There are four major categories of premium split. In designing the plan, these provide flexibility to meet the needs of the employee. However, the tax treatment under the regulations also must be considered, as discussed later.

These four categories are as follows:

- *classic or standard* split-dollar plan under which the employer pays a portion of the annual premium equal to the increase in cash surrender value of the policy for the year, or the net premium due, if lower. The employee pays the remainder of the annual

---

50. Treas. Reg. Sec. 1.61-22(c)(1)(i)

premium. This arrangement minimizes the employer's risk, since the policy's cash value is enough to fully reimburse the employer's cumulative payments even if the plan is terminated in the early years. However, the employee's outlay is very high in the initial years of the plan, when cash values may increase slowly.

- *level premium* plan, under which the employee's premium share is leveled over an initial period of years, such as 5 or 10. This avoids the objection to the standard arrangement that the employee's initial premium share is too large. If the plan continues in effect long enough, the employee and employer eventually pay about the same total amount as under the standard arrangement. One disadvantage of the level premium plan is that if the plan is terminated in the early years, the policy cash value has not increased to a level that will fully reimburse the employer for its cumulative payments. In drafting the split-dollar agreement, some consideration should be given to providing the employer a remedy in this situation, although it is difficult to do this satisfactorily.

- *employer-pay-all* arrangement under which the employer pays the entire annual premium. This arrangement is used when the employee's financial resources are limited. As with the level premium plan, if the plan is terminated early, the policy cash value will not fully reimburse the employer outlay; again, the agreement between the employer and employee should address this problem.

- *offset or zero-tax* plan, under which the employee pays an amount equal to the term insurance cost for the coverage (or if less, the net premium due) each year. The employer pays the balance of the premium. The purpose of this arrangement is to zero out the employee's income tax cost for the plan, as discussed below. As a further refinement, the employer can reduce the employee's out-of-pocket cost for this arrangement by paying a tax deductible bonus to the employee equal to the employee's payment under the split-dollar plan. The employer might want to go a step further and pay an additional amount equal to the tax on the first bonus as a tax gross-up.

CASH VALUE AND DEATH PROCEEDS SPLIT

The first goal of the plan provision relating to the split of cash value or death proceeds is to reimburse the employer, in whole or in part, for its share of the premium outlay, if the employee dies or the plan is terminated. At the employee's death, any policy proceeds not used to reimburse the employer go to the employee's designated beneficiary. This provides a significant death benefit in the early years of the plan, one of the principal objectives of a split-dollar plan. If the plan provides cash value growth that is in excess of the employer's share and benefits the employee, it is regarded as an *equity plan* under the regulations, and the annual growth in the employee's equity will be taxed each year.

TAX TREATMENT

Prior Tax Treatment

Because split dollar has long been an important financial planning tool, it is useful to briefly review the prior tax treatment. Before 1964, the treatment was unsettled. Then the IRS ruled (in Rev. Rul. 64-328)[51] that the tax consequences of a split-dollar plan would be the same regardless of whether the collateral assignment or the endorsement arrangement was used. In effect this ruling held that after 1964 the IRS would not claim that a split-dollar plan was an interest-free loan.

Under Rev. Rul. 64-328 (as under the current regulations in the case of an endorsement-type plan or nonequity collateral assignment plan), the employee is considered to be in receipt each year of an amount of taxable "economic benefit." Under prior law, this taxable amount for the basic insurance coverage was equal to the PS 58 rate for the insurance protection under the plan less the premium amount paid by the employee. As an alternative, the annual renewable term insurance rates of the company issuing the split-dollar policy could under prior law be substituted for the PS 58 rates in calculating the employee's reportable economic benefit if the term rates were lower than the PS 58 rates.[52] The application of policy dividends further affects the employee's income tax consequences.

Prior law did not provide any specific treatment of equity-type plans. In the absence of specific IRS rules, many practitioners took the position that increases in the employee's share of the cash value were not taxable to the employee, or taxable only when the plan was terminated and the policy rolled out to the employee.

---

51. Rev. Rul. 64-328, 1964-2 CB 11.
52. Rev. Rul. 66-110, 1966-1 CB 12.

Under both current and prior law, the employer cannot deduct any portion of its premium contribution. The IRS does not allow a deduction even for the part of the employer's contribution that results in taxable compensation income to the employee.[53]

Current Regulations (Post-September 17, 2003)

These regulations significantly changed the tax treatment of split-dollar plans. Transitional rules discussed under this heading are important for plans existing before the effective date of the current regulations, September 17, 2003.

A. Definition of Split Dollar

Under the current regulations, a split-dollar arrangement is "any arrangement between an owner and a nonowner of a life insurance contract" that satisfies three criteria: (1) either party pays premiums including a payment by means of a loan secured by the life insurance contract; (2) one of the parties can recover a portion of the premiums paid from the contract (or payment is secured by the contract); and (3) the arrangement is not part of a Sec. 79 group term life insurance plan.

The current regulations provide that if (a) the plan is a *compensatory arrangement* (essentially one in which the beneficiary is one the employee "would reasonably be expected to designate as the beneficiary") and (b) the employer pays any part of the premium, then the plan is deemed a split-dollar plan, regardless of the criteria listed above. There is a similar provision for split-dollar plans for shareholders and corporations.[54]

This is a broad definition and covers most normal compensation-planning split-dollar arrangements between an employer and employee. It also covers the types of plans sometimes referred to as *private split-dollar* that individuals use for business continuation or estate planning purposes.

The following discussion focuses primarily on compensatory arrangements.

B. In General—Mutually Exclusive Regimes for Taxation

The Preamble states that the regulations provide two "mutually exclusive regimes for taxing split-dollar life insurance arrangements."

---

53. IRC Sec. 264(a)(1).

54. Reg. Sec. 1.61-22(b).

1. Under the *economic benefit regime* (set forth in the Regulations Sec. 1.61-22) "the owner of the life insurance contract is treated as providing economic benefits to the nonowner of the contract." This approach is similar to the old rules governing split-dollar plans under Rev. Rul. 64-328, with some significant differences. In particular, the value of the life insurance coverage or other benefit provided to an employee under a split-dollar plan subject to the economic benefit regime is valued and taxed to the employee as additional taxable income. Under the regulations, the economic benefit regime essentially applies to two types of plans:

   a. an *endorsement-type* plan under which the employer is the owner of the life insurance contract and endorses a portion of the death benefit to the employee

   b. any split-dollar plan entered into in connection with the performance of services, where the employee or service provider is not the owner of the contract. (Similar provisions apply to donor-donee plans.)[55]

2. Under the loan regime, (set forth in Regulations Sec. 1.7872-15) the nonowner of the life insurance contract is treated as loaning premium payments to the owner. The loan regime is the default treatment for split-dollar plans that don't meet the specified requirements for the economic benefit regime. Thus, loan treatment will apply to plans of the type that have been referred to as "collateral assignment plans" where the employee or the employee's trust or beneficiary is the owner of the contract. It appears that loan treatment would not apply to a nonequity collateral assignment contract (see "Special rule," however, under "Who Is the Owner?" below).

C. Who Is the Owner?

1. General rules

   a. The person named as the policyowner is generally treated as the owner for purposes of the regulations.

   b. If two or more persons are named as owners and all named owners have all the incidents of ownership with respect to an undivided interest in the contract, each person is treated as the owner of a separate contract.

---

55. Reg. Sec. 1.61-22(b)(3).

    c. If two or more persons are named as owners and each person does not have all the incidents of ownership, the first-named owner is considered the owner for purposes of the regulations.

2. Special rule—If the arrangement is a *nonequity plan* (one where the only benefit to the employee or service provider is current life insurance protection), then the employer or service recipient is treated as the owner of the life insurance contract.[56] This would appear to place nonequity collateral-assignment plans under the economic benefit regime, as well as endorsement nonequity plans.

D. Economic Benefit Treatment

Under the economic benefit regime, economic benefits must be fully and consistently accounted for by the owner and nonowner and the "value of the economic benefits, reduced by any consideration paid by the nonowner to the owner, is treated as transferred from the owner to the nonowner." In the case of an employment relationship, this amount is treated as compensation. Other types of relationships result in a different tax treatment.[57]

If the plan is a nonequity arrangement, that is, the economic benefit consists only of current life insurance protection, this economic benefit is valued in accordance with a table or method to be furnished in the future. For many years, the "PS 58" table was used for this purpose. This was a table based on 1940s mortality rates that generally provided relatively high insurance costs. A new Table 2001 has been adopted for this purpose. The Table 2001 rates are much lower than the PS 58 rates.

EXAMPLE
Employer R owns a $1,000,000 policy that is part of a split-dollar arrangement with Employee E. Employer R pays all premiums and is entitled to receive the greater of its premiums or the cash surrender value of the contract when the arrangement terminates or E dies. In year 10 the cost of term insurance for E is $1.00 per $1,000 of insurance and the cash surrender value of the contract is $200,000. In year 10, E must include in compensation income $800, that is, $1,000,000 − $200,000 (payable to R) or $800,000 multiplied by .001 (E's premium rate factor [1/1000]). If E had paid $300 of the premium, E would include $500 in compensation income.

---

56. Reg. Sec. 1.61-22(c), (d)(2).
57. Reg. Sec. 1.61-22(d)(1).

If the plan is an equity-type arrangement (a plan providing the nonowner something other than just current life insurance protection), then "any right in, or benefit of, a life insurance contract (including, but not limited to, an interest in the cash surrender value) provided during a taxable year to a nonowner . . . is an economic benefit."[58]

In other words, taxable compensation includes the value of current life insurance protection as well as any other benefit received by the employee during the year including any increase in the amount of policy cash value to which the nonowner (the employee) "has current access." Current access in general means that the employee has access or either the employer or the employer's creditors do not have access.

Rollout (Transfer of Contract). The regulations specifically provide that when a contract is transferred to a nonowner (transferee), the transferee has income equal to the fair market value of the contract over the sum of

- the amount paid by the transferee to the transferor and
- the amount that the transferee took into income as an economic benefit under an equity split-dollar arrangement, less (a) the economic benefit attributable to current life insurance protection and (b) any amount paid by the transferee for the pure equity element.[59]

Fair market value for this purpose is the cash surrender value and the value of all other rights under the contract, other than current life insurance protection. The possibility of an artificially low cash value—the "springing cash value" issue—is not alluded to in the regulations.[60]

Unlike prior rules for split-dollar plans, no amounts paid by the employee toward the premium are includible in the employee's basis.[61] These amounts are included in the owner's (employer's) gross income and included in the owner's basis for the contract.[62] This treatment discourages the use of contributory plans.

Policy Valuation at Rollout. Rollouts often involve the springing cash value issue. Insurance policies can be designed to specify very low cash values for a period of time, followed by a rapid increase in cash value. If rollout

---

58. Reg. Sec. 1.61-22(d)(3).
59. Reg. Sec. 1.61-22(g)(1).
60. Reg. Sec. 1.61-22(g)(2).
61. Reg. Sec. 1.61-22(g)(4)(D)(iii).
62. Reg. Sec. 1-61(f)(3).

occurs when the cash value is low, the argument can be made that the tax consequence to the employee on distribution of the policy (or the cost for the employee to buy the policy) is low because of the low cash value at that time. However, the IRS position in general is that the tax consequences are based on the policy's fair market value and not the stated cash value alone. The fair market value is based on what the policy would be worth to a buyer or recipient in an arms-length transaction. Policy reserves used for purposes of insurance company income taxation can be used for this purpose.[63]

Sec. 83. For a compensatory arrangement (employer-employee) the rules under this heading (Rollout) do not apply until the amount is taxable under Sec. 83 of the Code. That is, taxation to the employee could be delayed to a year later than the year of rollout if the contract is subject to a substantial risk of forfeiture. The amount would not be taxable until the year in which the contract is no longer subject to a risk of forfeiture (becomes substantially vested).[64]

E. Loan Treatment

A payment under a split-dollar arrangement is treated as a loan for federal tax purposes if the arrangement is like the traditional collateral assignment arrangement, specifically if (1) the payment is made by the nonowner directly or indirectly to the owner or the insurance company; (2) the payment is a loan under general principles of federal tax law or if a reasonable person would expect the payment to be repaid in full to the nonowner; and (3) the payment is made from or secured by either the death benefit or the cash surrender value.[65]

If the loan is an interest-free or below-market loan (as it generally would be), Sec. 7872 applies to determine the amount of resultant additional compensation that is taxed to the employee. Generally, except possibly where the employee is very old, Sec. 7872 will result in more income inclusion than the application of the economic benefit approach; although this determination will depend on the final IRS table replacing PS 58 and Table 2001.

---

63. Notice 89-25, 1989-1 CB 662.

64. Reg. Sec. 1.61-22(g)(3).

65. Reg. Sec. 1.7872-15.

If the arrangement carries no stated interest rate and is considered a *demand loan* (an issue that needs IRS clarification), it would be treated under Code Sec. 7872 as follows:

- Employer is treated as if it paid additional compensation income to the employee equal to the "applicable federal rate." This amount is taxable to the employee and deductible by the employer.

- Employee is treated as if he or she paid this additional amount back to the employer. This amount is additional taxable income to the employer and is generally not deductible to the employee (unless it can be characterized as some kind of deductible interest, such as home mortgage interest).

F. Transitional Rules from Notice 2002-8

The transitional rules from Notice 2002-8 (a precursor of the current regulations) are as follows:

- Arrangements entered into before September 17, 2003, have no current tax on the equity buildup. This provision removes a threat that was implicit in earlier IRS pronouncements.

- Arrangements entered into before September 17, 2003, will not be treated as terminated with a rollout and transfer of property subject to Sec. 83 as long as life insurance protection continues to be treated as an economic benefit to the employee.

- For arrangements entered into before September 17, 2003, the parties had the option of treating premium payments as loans under any reasonable effort to comply with Sec. 7872.

- For a split-dollar arrangement entered into before January 28, 2002, and which was terminated with a rollout before January 1, 2004, there was no Sec. 83 taxation of the rollout. This grandfathering provision was particularly welcome, since it recognized that many of these arrangements had been sold to clients with representations that the rollout would not be a taxable event.

Notice 2002-8 retained new Table 2001, which replaced the PS 58 table for valuing economic benefit. This change also includes a series of transitional rules:

- Arrangements entered into before January 28, 2002, can continue to use the PS 58 table. Since the Table 2001 rates are lower than the PS 58 rates, this is useful only for limited purposes.

- Arrangements entered into before September 17, 2003, can use Table 2001.

- Arrangements entered into before September 17, 2003, can use an insurer's lower term premium rate in lieu of PS 58 or Table 2001 rates. However, after December 31, 2003, the published insurer rates can't be used "(i) unless the insurer generally makes the availability of such rates known to persons who apply for term insurance coverage from the insurer, and (ii) the insurer regularly sells term insurance at such rates to individuals who apply for term insurance coverage through the insurer's normal distribution channels."

G. Effective Date

The regulations apply to arrangements entered into or materially modified after the effective date of the final regulations, September 17, 2003.

The regulations provide that the transitional rules in Notice 2002-8 will continue to apply for arrangements entered into on or before September 17, 2003. Alternatively, taxpayers are allowed to apply the new regulations immediately to existing and new arrangements if all parties treat the arrangement consistently.

H. Impact of Sec. 409A

The IRS has published Notice 2007-34, which generally describes the circumstances under which split-dollar life insurance arrangements can qualify under, or be exempt from, Sec. 409A. The notice provides that any split-dollar life insurance arrangement (i) that only provides a death benefit, that is, a so-called nonequity arrangement that only provides for short-term deferrals, or (ii) where premium payments are made as loans are exempt from Sec. 409A as long as in the latter situation the service recipient has not agreed to waive, cancel, forgive or eliminate all or any portion of the loan after a stated period of time.

If certain conditions are satisfied, the notice also allows split-dollar life insurance arrangements entered into on or before September 17, 2003 and not materially modified since that date ("grandfathered SDLI") to be amended to the extent necessary to comply with Sec. 409A without foregoing their grandfathered status under the tax rules applicable to split-dollar life insurance arrangements. Generally, the principal conditions require that the service provider's benefits not be materially enhanced by the modification to comply with Sec. 409A and that the such modifications only apply to the provisions relating to the payment timing requirements, the forfeitability of benefits or the definitions under the grandfathered SDLI arrangement, to the extent required to bring such arrangement into compliance.

Moreover, under the notice an equity economic benefit form of split-dollar life insurance arrangement will be treated as deferred compensation for Sec. 409A purposes to the extent that the service provider has a legally binding right to access a policy's cash value so that it becomes payable in a year later than the current year and does not qualify as a short term deferral. A nonequity economic benefit form of split-dollar arrangement, that is, one in which the service provider has no rights in the policy, other than to a portion of the death benefit, is generally not affected by Sec. 409A. Thus, if a service provider has any nonforfeitable right to the policy's cash value, it will become taxable as deferred compensation under Sec. 409A, unless the requirements of Sec. 409A are satisfied by the arrangement.

Finally, if a grandfathered SDLI arrangement becomes subject to Sec. 409A, the Notice provides a safe harbor allocation method for determining the portion of the increases in a policy's cash value after December 31, 2004 that is properly attributable to the Sec. 409A grandfathered benefit and which portion is attributable to the Sec. 409A non-grandfathered component of the cash value.

OTHER TAX AND REGULATORY ISSUES

The IRS has published Notice 2007-34, which generally describes the circumstances under which split-dollar life insurance arrangements can qualify under, or be exempt from, Sec. 409A. The Notice provides that any split-dollar life insurance arrangement (i) that only provides a death benefit, i.e., a so-called non-equity arrangement, that only provides for short-term deferrals, or (ii) where premium payments are made as loans are exempt from Sec. 409A as long as in the latter situation the service recipient has not agreed to waive, cancel, forgive or eliminate all or any portion of the loan after a period of time.

If certain conditions are satisfied, the Notice also allows split-dollar life insurance arrangements entered into on or before September 17, 2003 and not materially modified since that date ("grandfathered SDLI") to be amended to the extent necessary to comply with Sec. 409A without foregoing their grandfathered status under the tax rules applicable to split-dollar life insurance arrangements. Generally, the principal conditions require that the service provider's benefits not be materially enhanced by the modification to comply with Sec. 409A and that the such modifications only apply to the provisions relating to the payment timing requirements, the forfeitability of benefits or the definitions under the grandfathered SDLI arrangement, to the extent required to bring such arrangement into compliance.

Moreover, under the Notice an equity economic benefit form of split-dollar life insurance arrangement will be treated as deferred compensation for Sec. 409A purposes to the extent that the service provider has a legally binding right to access a policy's cash value so that it becomes payable in a year later than the current year and does not qualify as a short term deferral. A non-equity economic benefit form of split-dollar arrangement, that is, one in which the service provider has no rights in the policy, other than to a portion of the death benefit, is generally not affected by Sec. 409A. Thus, if a service provider has any nonforfeitable right to the policy's cash value, it will become taxable as deferred compensation under Sec. 409A, unless the requirements of Sec. 409A are satisfied by the arrangement.

Finally, if a grandfathered SDLI arrangement becomes subject to Sec. 409A, the Notice provides a safe harbor allocation method for determining the portion of the increases in a policy's cash value after December 31, 2004 that is properly attributable to the Sec. 409A grandfathered benefit and which portion is attributable to the Sec. 409A non-grandfathered component of the cash value.

Income Taxation of Death Benefits

Generally the death benefits from a split-dollar plan are income tax free only to the extent they are allocable to current life insurance protection that was taken into account for tax purposes by the employee.[66] That is, only the pure insurance element received by the beneficiary is tax free. The tax-free nature of the death proceeds is lost if the policy has been "transferred for value" in certain situations. This result should be avoided in designing split-dollar plans.[67] The following transfers of insurance policies are exempt from the transfer-for-value rules—in other words, they will not destroy the tax exemption for death proceeds: (a) a transfer of the policy to the insured, (b) a transfer to a partner of the insured or to a partnership of which the insured is a partner, (c) a transfer to a corporation of which the insured is a shareholder or officer, and (d) a transfer in which the transferee's basis is determined in

---

66. Reg. Sec. 1.61-22(f)(3).

67. IRC Sec. 101(a)(2).

whole or in part by reference to the transferor's basis (that is, a substituted or carryover basis).

Estate Taxes

If the employee had no *incidents of ownership* in the policy, the death benefit is not includible in the employee's estate for federal estate tax purposes unless the policy proceeds are payable to the employee's estate.[68] If an employee is potentially faced with a federal estate tax liability, all incidents of ownership in the policy should therefore be assigned irrevocably to a third party—a beneficiary or a trust. Proceeds generally should be payable to a named personal beneficiary and not to the employee's estate. If the employee is a controlling shareholder (more than 50 percent) in the employer corporation, the corporation's incidents of ownership in the policy will be attributed to the majority shareholder. The current IRS position is that even if the corporation has only the right to make policy loans against its share of the cash value, this is an incident of ownership that will be attributed to the controlling shareholder and cause estate tax inclusion of the policy death proceeds.[69] For a majority shareholder, the only way to avoid estate tax inclusion is for not only the employee but also the employer to get rid of the incidents of ownership. The corporation can avoid such incidents by retaining no rights of ownership in the policy, including any policy contract provisions or riders relating to the split-dollar agreement. One method is for the employee's personal beneficiary to be the original purchaser of the policy, and the beneficiary to enter into the split-dollar agreement with the corporation on a collateral assignment basis. This is a common arrangement for split-dollar plans that primarily are intended to provide estate liquidity to a highly compensated executive.

Gift Taxes

The transfer of the policy from the employee to another party (such as a relative or the employee's irrevocable life insurance trust) is a gift subject to tax. In addition, there is a continuing annual gift if the employee pays premiums on the policy. There is also a continuing annual gift by the employee if the employer pays premiums, because this employer payment represents compensation earned by the employee that is indirectly

---

68. IRC Sec. 2042.

69. Rev. Rul. 82-145, 1982-2 CB 213.

transferred to the policyowner.[70] Such potentially taxable gifts may avoid taxation if they qualify for the $13,000 (2010) annual gift tax exclusion. Gifts made directly to beneficiaries generally qualify, while gifts to insurance trusts may be considered future interests that do not qualify for the $13,000 (2010) exclusion.

ERISA

A split-dollar plan where the employer is the owner of the policy is considered an *employee welfare benefit plan* and is subject to the ERISA rules applicable to such plans. Generally, a welfare plan can escape the ERISA reporting and disclosure requirements, including the Form 5500 filing and the summary plan description (SPD) requirement, if it is an insured plan maintained for "a select group of management or highly compensated employees."[71] Most split-dollar plans where the employer is the owner of the policy qualify for this exception. If the split-dollar plan is structured so that the executive owns the policy, the employer is providing financing, but is not providing any of the enumerated benefits under the definition of welfare benefit plan in ERISA. Consequently, those plans are not covered by ERISA.

Sarbanes-Oxley Act

As part of the wave of corporate governance regulations arising out of the Enron collapse and similar events in 2001 and 2002, Congress enacted the Sarbanes-Oxley Act, which contained a range of corporate accountability provisions. Among them was a provision banning publicly traded corporations from making personal loans to any director or executive officer. The applicability of this provision to split-dollar plans is unclear. It could be argued that if applicable, it would apply only to split-dollar plans taxed under the loan regime. In any event, the law does not apply to split-dollar plans for employees who are not directors or officers, nor does it apply to any plan of a corporation that is not publicly traded.

REVERSE SPLIT-DOLLAR PLANS

A *reverse split-dollar* plan is one characterized as follows:

---

70. Rev. Rul. 78-420, 1978-2 CB 67

71. Labor Reg. Sec. 2520.104-24

- The employee has the right to policy cash values up to the aggregate of his or her premium payments.
- The employer is beneficiary of the death proceeds in excess of the employee's share.

The benefits of reverse split-dollar are as follows:

- It maximizes the investment benefit of the plan to the employee.
- Policy cash values provide a substantial investment return over the years as they build up (presumably free of tax under prior law). At retirement or when the plan terminates, the cash value is substantial and the policy is generally substantially funded.
- The closely held corporation reverse split dollar can be used to fund a stock redemption buy-sell agreement with the employee paying part of the cost with personal funds.

The disadvantage to the employee of a reverse split-dollar arrangement is that the death benefit for the employee's beneficiaries is very low in the early years, since the corporation, not the employee, is the beneficiary of the amount at risk (pure term life insurance element) of the arrangement.

The premium is split so that the executive pays a share equal to the cash value build up, while the corporation pays the remainder of the premium.

Most tax planners have advised that the corporation should include something in income to reflect the economic benefit of the amount at risk or insurance coverage that will benefit the corporation if the employee dies. Prior to the final regulations, there was no IRS guidance on this issue, but the practice was to use the old PS 58 rates, rather than the insurance company's lower term rates, since using the higher PS 58 rates reduces the employee's share of the premium.

Under the regulations, the status of reverse split dollar is uncertain; there is no specific provision for reverse plans in the regulations. The regulations would seem to mandate substantial ongoing taxation of the employee's equity-type benefits. Also, the IRS has ruled against the use of artificially high PS 58 rates in determining the employee premium share.[72]

In addition, if the employee is a majority shareholder, there is a risk of federal estate tax inclusion, as discussed above under "Other Tax and Regulatory Issues."

---

72. Notice 2002-59, 2002-2 CB 481.

COMBINING SPLIT-DOLLAR PLANS WITH NONQUALIFIED DEFERRED-COMPENSATION PLANS

Double-Duty Split-Dollar Plan

For executives and key employees who are compensated in the middle ranges, classic life insurance financing of deferred compensation may encounter some employer and employee objections. Employees may object to the fact that the preretirement death benefit is taxable to their beneficiaries even though life insurance is used (that is, the corporation, not the employee, benefits from the tax-free nature of the death proceeds). Employees with estate planning concerns may also object that the plan's death benefit cannot be excluded from their estates for federal estate tax purposes. In other words, during the employment period these employees essentially need a life insurance plan more than a retirement savings plan, while they still need some degree of supplemental retirement income.

From the employer point of view, the degree of cost recovery using the cost-recovery approach may be an issue. The corporation's deduction for benefit payments is taken against a corporate tax rate that generally does not exceed 35 percent. Years ago, when corporate tax rates were higher, this deduction coupled with tax-free receipt of the death benefit provided more tax leverage than it does with the current 35 percent top rate. Therefore, the cost-recovery aspect of the traditional plan may not be particularly compelling to the corporation under current circumstances.

Combining a split-dollar life insurance plan with a deferred-compensation plan, using a single policy to finance both plans may be an attractive approach in these situations. The split-dollar/deferred-compensation approach works as follows:

- The company provides two separate benefits for the covered executives—a split-dollar life insurance plan that operates only during the preretirement period, and a nonqualified deferred-compensation plan that applies only at retirement—a retirement-only salary continuation plan.
- The split-dollar insurance policy is typically owned by the employer under the endorsement method, so the employer has control of the cash values. The employee's share of the premium is negotiated; typically this involves little out-of-pocket cost for the employee.

- During the preretirement period, the employee pays taxes on the economic benefit of the pure insurance amount (the death benefit payable to his or her beneficiaries) less his or her share of the premium payments. In return for this small ongoing tax cost, however, if the employee dies during the preretirement period the death benefit is tax free to his or her beneficiaries. For estate tax purposes, if the marital deduction is not available, the death benefit can be kept out of the employee's estate (if he or she is not a controlling shareholder) by making an irrevocable gift of his or her interest in the split-dollar plan to an irrevocable life insurance trust for the benefit of his or her heirs.

- At retirement, the split-dollar plan is terminated. The employer retains the full value of policy cash values at this point. The policy is used to finance the benefits under the nonqualified deferred-compensation plan. This is done either by currently making use of cash values to pay retirement benefits, or by paying retirement benefits out of current assets and holding the policy until the employee dies, thus receiving the death proceeds as cost recovery. The income tax deferral of the deferred-compensation benefits is unaffected—that is, tax is paid by the executive or beneficiary when benefits are received.

Deferred-Compensation Plan Converted to Insurance Plan (SERP Swap)

For the highest compensated executives, the predominant life insurance need arises as the executive gets older and then retires. These executives need life insurance in order to preserve liquidity in their estates and transfer wealth in a tax-efficient manner. It is very difficult, or impossible, to design a deferred-compensation benefit that can be excluded from the executive's estate, but a split-dollar or other life insurance benefit can be excluded from the estate under a variety of well-known techniques, such as making a gift of the contract to an irrevocable life insurance trust or having the trust as the owner of the contract from the outset.

For executives in this situation, it may be beneficial to switch, swap, or exchange an existing nonqualified deferred-compensation benefit for a life insurance benefit, typically a split-dollar arrangement. This is sometimes referred to as a "SERP swap," because of the common terminology that describes NQDC plans for groups of executives as SERPs (supplemental executive retirement plans).

Technically, what happens in this type of planning is that the executive agrees with the employer to modify the existing NQDC contract to convert it to a life insurance contract of equivalent value. From an economic point of view there is an exchange: the executive gives up the present value of the NQDC plan and receives a commitment by the employer to make equivalent payments into an insurance contract owned by the employee's irrevocable life insurance trust for his or her beneficiaries.

If this exchange is deemed to be taxable at the time it is made, the SERP swap will incur a loss of tax deferral that may make it unattractive. There appears to be no specific case law or stated IRS position as to whether these transactions are taxable at the time of the swap.

Analyzing the exchange under general principles of tax law, one possibility is that the exchange could be treated as a Sec. 83 transfer of property in exchange for services. The issue here is, what property is being transferred from the employer to the employee? It can be argued that if the life insurance contract is owned from the outset by the employee or by the employee's life insurance trust (using the collateral assignment method), no property in the form of a life insurance contract is transferred from the employer. However, the employer will make a premium payment to the insurance company on behalf of the policyowner. Whether this constitutes property within the meaning of Sec. 83 is unclear. If it is deemed to be property, then it will be taxable to the employee in the year in which it is *substantially vested*. Generally, in a SERP swap the employee will want immediate vesting of his or her rights in the successor split-dollar plan, so this might imply immediate taxation of amounts paid by the employer toward the policy.

There is another tax principle that could result in taxation at the time of the swap: the principle of constructive receipt. The argument would be that the executive's modification of the NQDC contract (in exchange for some other benefit such as a life insurance plan) constitutes constructive receipt of the benefits of the NQDC plan. There are no relevant cases or other authority strictly on point. However, the leading court cases in this area give little support to an IRS attack based on this theory of constructive receipt. In particular, the case of *Martin v. Commissioner* 96 TC 814 (1991) stands for the proposition that an executive's renegotiation of an NQDC contract, before the time that benefits are due under the original contract, does not in itself cause constructive receipt of those benefits. See also PLR 199901066. However, the principles of Sec. 409A have undercut the precedential authority of the *Martin* decision with respect to NQDC arrangements entered into after 2004.

Finally, the SERP swap needs to be analyzed under the requirements of Sec. 409A. It must be determined whether the swap has indirectly resulted in a prohibited acceleration of benefits or whether the swap has deferred the payment of benefits in a manner that is inconsistent with the requirements of Sec. 409A. Moreover, if the swap can be characterized as a termination of the NQDC arrangement, such termination must be consistent with the requirements of Sec. 409A.

In summary, there are reasonable grounds to take the position that a SERP swap does not result in taxable income at the time of the swap, if planning is done carefully. However, there is no specific authority to this effect, and there are numerous unresolved tax questions involved in making this determination. Clients and advisors should be aware of the risks, particularly those associated with the application of Sec. 409A.

ADDITIONAL RESOURCE

Table 6-1 TABLE 2001 Interim Table of One-Year Term Premiums for $1,000 of Life Insurance Protection					
Attained Age	Sec. 79 Extended and Interpolated Annual Rates	Attained Age	Sec. 79 Extended and Interpolated Annual Rates	Attained Age	Sec. 79 Extended and Interpolated Annual Rates
0	$0.70	35	$0.99	70	$ 20.62
1	0.41	36	1.01	71	22.72
2	0.27	37	1.04	72	25.07
3	0.19	38	1.06	73	27.57
4	0.13	39	1.07	74	30.18
5	0.13	40	1.10	75	33.05
6	0.14	41	1.13	76	36.33
7	0.15	42	1.20	77	40.17
8	0.16	43	1.29	78	44.33
9	0.16	44	1.40	79	49.23
10	0.16	45	1.53	80	54.56
11	0.19	46	1.67	81	60.51
12	0.24	47	1.83	82	66.74
13	0.28	48	1.98	83	73.07

Attained Age	Sec. 79 Extended and Interpolated Annual Rates	Attained Age	Sec. 79 Extended and Interpolated Annual Rates	Attained Age	Sec. 79 Extended and Interpolated Annual Rates
14	0.33	49	2.13	84	80.35
15	0.38	50	2.30	85	88.76
16	0.52	51	2.52	86	99.16
17	0.57	52	2.81	87	110.40
18	0.59	53	3.20	88	121.85
19	0.61	54	3.65	89	133.40
20	0.62	55	4.15	90	144.30
21	0.62	56	4.68	91	155.80
22	0.64	57	5.20	92	168.75
23	0.66	58	5.66	93	186.44
24	0.68	59	6.06	94	207.70
25	0.71	60	6.51	95	228.35
26	0.73	61	7.11	96	250.01
27	0.76	62	7.96	97	265.09
28	0.80	63	9.08	98	270.11
29	0.83	64	10.41	99	281.05
30	0.87	65	11.90		
31	0.90	66	13.51		
32	0.93	67	15.20		
33	0.96	68	16.92		
34	0.98	69	18.70		

1. Under the type of life insurance contract involved in Rev. Rul. 66-110, the cash surrender value of paid-up additions purchased with dividends was separate and distinct from the cash surrender value of the life insurance contract under which the dividends were paid.

2. For income or gift ax purposes outside of the compensation context, transfers of beneficial interests in the cash surrender value of life insurance contracts may similarly be treated as transfers of property interests in accordance with general tax principles.

3. The table is limited to insureds below age 100.

CHAPTER REVIEW

Review Questions

1. Apex corporation would like to provide a life insurance benefit to three of its key employees. Explain how a split-dollar plan would work to accomplish this and what its economic advantages would be. [1]

2. What are the basic employee needs addressed by a life insurance benefit? [2]

3. What are the advantages of split dollar with regard to design flexibility and financing? [2]

4. List some disadvantages of split-dollar plans as an executive-compensation tool. [2]

5. Ariel Corporation has expressed an interest in providing extra compensation to two of its executives. The executives would like a life insurance form of benefit for purposes of increasing liquidity in their estates. A split-dollar plan is being investigated. [3]

   a. Describe the two possibilities for ownership of policies in the split-dollar plan.

   b. Recommend a form of split-dollar policy ownership, giving advantages and disadvantages of your choice.

6. Executive Sam Katz is eligible for a split-dollar plan provided by his employer. The plan offered requires the employer to pay premiums each year up to an amount equal to the increase in the policy's cash value, with Sam paying the remainder. Sam protests that this arrangement will cost him a disproportionate amount in the early years of the plan. Why is this the case? [4]

7. List several alternatives that would reduce Sam's expenditure in the early years of the plan. [4]

8. Describe disadvantages (to Sam or to the employer) to the alternatives listed in the preceding question. [4]

9. Executive Maxine has a need for supplemental insurance but would also like some help from her employer with her investment and retirement savings programs. Explain how a split-dollar plan could meet these needs. [5]

10. What specifically is the definition of an equity split-dollar plan? [5]

11. What are the disadvantages of an equity plan under the regulations? [5]

12. Describe how split-dollar plans are taxed under prior law (that is, Rev. Rul. 64-328). [6]

13. Under the current regulations, what are the two *mutually exclusive regimes* for taxing split-dollar plans? [6]

14. Who is considered the *owner* of a split-dollar plan under the current regulations, and what is the significance of being considered the owner? [6]

15. Describe how pure insurance elements and increases in the participant's share of the cash value in an equity plan are taxed under the economic benefit regime of taxation. [6]

16. How is a split-dollar policy that has been taxed under the economic benefit regime treated when it is distributed or rolled out to the employee? [6]

17. Under what circumstances is a split-dollar plan taxed under the loan regime? [6]

18. If a split-dollar plan is taxed under the loan regime and the arrangement carries no stated rate of interest, how is the plan taxed to the employer and to the employee? [6]

19. How are the death benefits from a split-dollar plan taxed to the beneficiaries for federal income tax purposes? [7]

20. Under what circumstances are death benefits includible in the deceased employee's estate for federal estate tax purposes? [7]

21. How can benefits described in question 2 be excluded from the employee's estate? [7]

22. What is a reverse split-dollar plan? [8]

23. What are the problems related to reverse plans under current law? [8]

24. What is a *double-duty split-dollar plan*? [9]

25. How does a *SERP swap* work, and what are the federal income tax consequences? [9]

Answers to Review Questions

1. A split-dollar plan adopted by Apex Corporation would have the advantage of bringing together parties needing insurance (the executives) with another party having the funds to provide the insurance plan (Apex). The employer provides part or all of the premium costs, with its outlay secured by the policy's cash value. The employee's beneficiary receives a death benefit equal to the amount remaining after the employer has been reimbursed. This provides a death benefit at favorable cost to the employee. [1]

2. Employees need life insurance generally either for current income protection or estate liquidity, or for a combination of both. Higher

paid executives (who are the market for the largest policies) generally tend toward the estate-liquidity motivation for life insurance planning. Split dollar can also help finance the buyout of the company by a key executive. [2]

3. A split-dollar plan is a selective plan for executives; it is not subject to any kind of rules relating to nondiscrimination against the highly compensated. Therefore it can be designed to meet specific employee and employer needs. Also, there are no rules or restrictions as to what share of the premiums the parties must pay, or how the arrangement should be structured. (However, income tax rules, especially the current regulations, will influence planning significantly.) [2]

4. In order to receive full benefits, the plan must remain in effect for a reasonable period of time. However, continuing the plan at advanced ages becomes expensive for the executive under the economic benefit regime (see below); although the loan regime might remain advantageous. Equity-type plans that provide a savings element to the executive are very beneficial, but under the regulations they may be limited in usefulness. [2]

5. [3]

   a. Generally, ownership can be through the collateral assignment method (employee or trust or other party designated by the employee is the owner) or the endorsement method (employer is the owner).

   b. Since the Ariel executives are interested in split-dollar planning primarily to provide estate liquidity, the collateral assignment method should be investigated. This method provides the easiest way to keep the policy out of the employee's estate for tax purposes. Generally, the practice is to have the policy owned from the outset by an irrevocable life insurance trust set up by the employee, or other third party designated by the employee. However, if application of the new tax rules makes this disadvantageous, it might still be possible to use the endorsement method.

6. Policy cash values tend to increase slowly in the early years. Therefore the employer's share of the premium is relatively small; Sam's share is large and generally larger in the initial years than the economic benefit (Table 2001 or equivalent) cost of the life insurance protection. [4]

7. As an alternative to the *standard plan*, the parties could investigate the level-premium plan, an employer-pay-all arrangement, or an *offset arrangement* whereby the employee would pay an amount equal to the economic benefit cost each year, with or without a bonus to cover the income tax. [4]

8. From the employer's viewpoint, the disadvantage in reducing Sam's share in the early years is that if Sam quits to run for elective office or for another reason, there might not be enough cash value in the policy to reimburse the employer for its outlay. It could be difficult to recover this amount from an employee who has terminated employment, even if there was an employment agreement requiring repayment by the employee. [4]

9. Generally, cash values in current life insurance policies tend to increase faster than the sum of the premiums paid. Therefore, the employer may not need to claim an interest in the entire cash value in order to preserve its security for its payment. The plan can be designed so that the excess cash value is credited to the employee. This increasing "equity" fund can be a valuable element of the employee's savings and retirement program. [5]

10. Under the regulations, an equity plan is any plan under which the benefit to the employee is something more than current life insurance protection. [5]

11. Under the regulations, an equity plan of the collateral assignment type (employee or employee's designee is owner) results in current taxation of the equity buildup (that is, annual taxation of the increase in the equity), to the extent that the employee has current access to the equity buildup. In an endorsement-type equity plan, the loan regime applies. At this point the full implications of the loan regime are not entirely clear, but they are thought to be relatively unfavorable in most situations. [5]

12. Until 1964, the tax treatment of split-dollar was unsettled. Rev. Rul. 64-328 provided that current life insurance protection in a split-dollar plan would be taxed to the employee at specified rates (the PS 58 table or the insurance company's term rates in certain situations), regardless of whether the collateral assignment or endorsement method was used. The law was silent on the treatment of equity plans. [6]

13. The two mutually exclusive methods of taxation are the *economic benefit* regime (under which the employee is taxed on the economic benefit of the life insurance coverage plus equity buildup if any) and the *loan* regime, under which the arrangement is treated as a

series of loans from the employer to the employee corresponding to the employer's payment of premiums. [6]

14. Generally the owner is the person named as the owner of the insurance contract, or the first named owner, if more than one owner is named. If two persons are named as owners and all have all incidents of ownership, each person is treated as owner of a separate contract. This is rarely the case in a split dollar plan. The identity of the person who is the policy owner is significant since this plays a large part in determining whether the economic benefit or loan regime applies. [6]

15. The economic benefit regime applies if (1) the plan is an endorsement-type arrangement (employer is owner) and (2) more broadly, any split-dollar plan entered into in connection with the performance of services where the employee is not the owner. Under the regulations, an endorsement-type plan is treated somewhat as under Rev. Rul. 64-328; that is, the current life insurance protection is taxed currently to the employee under Table 2001 (which was issued as an interim table). Equity buildup is also currently taxed to the employee. [6]

16. When a policy is rolled out, under the regulations, the transferee (employee) has income equal to the fair market value of the contract over the employee's basis. Basis does not include the employee's premium share, so this rule is unfavorable to contributory plans. [6]

17. The loan regime applies to all cases in which the economic benefit regime does not apply (described in question 4 above). Under the loan regime, the plan is treated as a series of loans to the employee from the employer. [6]

18. If the arrangement is treated under the loan regime, and there is no stated rate of interest payable by the employee, or if the interest is below the market rate, the bargain loan rules of Code Sec. 7872 apply. If the arrangement is treated as a demand loan (no schedule for repayment), then the employer is treated as if it paid additional compensation income to the employee equal to the "applicable federal rate." This amount is taxable to the employee and deductible by the employer. The employee is treated as if he or she paid this additional amount back to the employer. This amount is additional taxable income to the employer and is generally not deductible to the employee (unless it can be characterized as some kind of deductible interest, such as home mortgage interest). [6]

19. Generally, death benefits to an employee's beneficiary are income tax free as life insurance proceeds under Code Sec. 101. However,

under the regulations only the pure insurance element is received tax free. The tax exclusion can be lost for the same reasons that generally apply to life insurance proceeds (transfer for value and so on). [7]

20. As with life insurance in general, policy proceeds are includible in the decedent employee's estate for federal estate tax purposes when the decedent had incidents of ownership in the policy. [7]

21. Split-dollar planning for estate liquidity therefore focuses on avoiding incidents of ownership. With the collateral assignment method, the policy is transferred to (a 3-year waiting rule applies) or owned from the outset by a third party related to the beneficiary, such as an irrevocable life insurance trust. With the endorsement method, the incidents of ownership can generally be avoided by an irrevocable beneficiary designation. However, if the decedent employee is a controlling shareholder, the corporation's incidents of ownership can be imputed to the employee. In this situation the corporation should avoid all rights of ownership in the policy except the right to be reimbursed out of its share of the death proceeds. [7]

22. A reverse split-dollar plan is one in which the usual arrangement is reversed: the employee owns the cash value and the beneficiary of the life insurance protection is the employer. [8]

23. There is considerable uncertainty under the regulations and other current IRS positions as to the tax treatment of reverse split dollar. [8]

24. Under a double-duty split-dollar plan, the split-dollar plan covers the employee before retirement, where insurance protection for the employee's family is significant. The employer retains policy values after the employee's retirement for purposes of financing a nonqualified retirement benefit. This arrangement is suitable for an employee whose primary insurance need is something other than estate liquidity. [9]

25. Under the SERP swap (a SERP is a term occasionally used to refer to a nonqualified deferred-compensation plan with a salary-continuation (defined-benefit) formula), an executive with a substantial accrued benefit under a nonqualified plan would like to exchange this for an insurance benefit, generally for estate liquidity purposes. It is unclear whether this swap can be arranged without income tax consequences at the time of the swap, but arguments to this effect can be made. [9]

1. Define "fringe benefits" and explain the role of Code Sec. 132 in determining the taxation of fringe benefits.

2. Describe qualified employee discounts and comment on their practicality as an executive compensation tool.

3. Explain the rules for executive dining rooms.

4. Describe how qualified parking can be used as an executive benefit.

5. Explain the rules for security-related executive benefits.

6. Explain the benefits and tax treatment of company cars provided to executives.

7. Describe how reimbursed moving expenses are treated by companies and executives.

8. Comment on the advantages and tax treatment of athletic tickets, skyboxes, and similar perks for executives.

9. Explain the tax treatment of company-provided or reimbursed club memberships for executives.

10. Show how the tax rules for executive loans work.

11. List some other potentially useful executive benefits that are generally taxable to executives.

TAXATION OF FRINGE BENEFITS IN GENERAL

Executive compensation typically includes both cash and noncash elements. The category of noncash compensation is comprised of an almost unlimited list of benefits (large and small) that can be provided by an employer to augment compensation. These benefits are generally referred to as "fringe benefits." The term fringe benefits is not a precise term; and it is often used for major benefits like pensions and health insurance as well as lesser items. This chapter will deal with a number of specific, generally smaller scale fringe benefits and how they can be used in executive-compensative planning.

From the viewpoint of the tax law, any property or service that an executive receives in lieu of or in addition to regular taxable wages is a fringe benefit that may be subject to taxation. The Internal Revenue Code includes the term "fringe benefits" in the definition of gross income found in Sec. 61. A fringe benefit provided in connection with the performance of services, regardless of its form, must be treated as compensation includible in income under Sec. 61.

Whether a particular fringe benefit is taxable depends on whether there is a specific statutory exclusion that applies to the benefit. For example, when Code Sec. 61 was amended to include the term "fringe benefits", Code Sec. 132 was added to provide exclusions for a list of certain commonly provided fringe benefits that had previously not been covered specifically in the Code (see next section below). Executive benefits that are not on this list are either covered under other specific provisions of tax law (such as qualified retirement plans, split-dollar, etc.) or are presumed to be taxable income to the executive.

FRINGE BENEFITS COVERED UNDER SEC. 132

Under Sec. 61 of the tax law all fringe benefits are taxable to the employee and therefore subject to income and employment taxes, unless specifically exempted by statute. The IRS is given the authority to determine the manner of collecting these taxes.

Earlier chapters have discussed specific provisions of tax law dealing with qualified and nonqualified deferred-compensation arrangements, restricted property plans, equity-based compensation, and life insurance plans. Code Sec. 132 provides further rules under which the following types of fringe benefits are generally not subject to income tax, income tax withholding, FICA, FUTA, or RRTA:

- no-additional-cost services
- qualified employee discounts
- working condition fringes
- *de minimis* fringes
- qualified transportation fringes

In reviewing the provisions of Sec. 132 as described here, the executive compensation planner should note that some of the fringe benefits covered under this section can be provided tax free as an executive-only benefit, while others require coverage of a broader group of employees.

No Additional Cost Service

A no-additional-cost service is any service provided by an employer to an employee for the employee's use. The service must be one offered by the employer for sale to customers, and the employee must be performing services in that line of business. For example, a flight attendant for an airline that also provides hotel services could fly free on a vacation and exclude the value of the airfare but could not exclude the value of the hotel room from income. However, the chief executive officer of the airline—being involved in both lines of business—could exclude the value of a free flight and the value of a free hotel room. The employer must incur no additional cost (including forgone revenue) in providing the service to the employee.

Qualified Employee Discount

A qualified employee discount is any discount allowed on "qualified property or services" (defined as property or services—with the exception of real property or personal investment-type property—that is offered for sale to customers in the ordinary course of the employer's line of business in which the employee is performing services). The discount is the difference between the customer price of the property or services and the price paid by the employee. In the case of property the exemption is limited to the gross profit percentage at which the property is offered by the employer to the customers. So if the gross profit percentage was 50 percent, then an employee discount would be excludible to the extent it did not exceed 50 percent of the selling price of the merchandise to regular consumers. If a firm gave its employees an 80 percent discount, they would have to report the 30 percent difference. When the discount is given on a qualified service, the excludible amount can't exceed 20 percent of the price at which the service is offered by the employer to nonemployee customers in the ordinary course of business. (This exclusion does apply to insurance policies provided to employees of insurers, but it does not apply to loans provided to employees of banks.)

As the IRS states the rules in its audit guide:

> This exclusion applies to a price reduction an employer gives an executive on qualified property, Sec. 132(c)(4), or services offered

to customers in the ordinary course of the line of business in which the employee performs substantial service. It does not apply to discounts on real property or discounts on personal property of a kind commonly held for investment (such as stocks and bonds) Sec. 132(c). There are specific rules that must be followed if the employee is highly compensated (see Notice 2002-71, 2002-45 I.R.B. 830). Treasury Regulation Sec. 1.132-1(b)(1) does not allow company discounts for directors and independent contractors. It has become quite common for former officers to be retained on a contractual basis by the corporation upon retirement and continue to receive discounts. Qualified employee discounts must be provided on a nondiscriminatory basis. See generally Regulations Sec. 1.132-8. This regulation incorporates Sec. 410(b) nondiscrimination standards, and the Sec. 414(q) definition of HCE. See Regulations Sec. 1.132-8(d) and (f).

Working Condition Fringe

A working condition fringe is defined as any property or services provided to an employee that would have been deductible by the employee if the employee had paid for it. Examples of such fringes include (1) company cars or planes used for business purposes, (2) subscriptions to business-related magazines, and (3) on-the-job training or travel expenses—assuming such employer costs are ordinary and necessary business expenses. Some of these are significant enough that they are discussed below under separate headings.

De Minimis Fringe

De minimis fringe benefits are defined as any property or service with the value so small that it would be administratively unreasonable or impractical to account for it. Examples of *de minimis* fringe benefits include (1) typing of personal letters by a company secretary, (2) occasional personal use of the company copying machine, (3) occasional parties or company picnics, (4) occasional supper money or taxi fare necessitated by overtime work, (5) tickets to shows, sports events, and the like, and (6) coffee and doughnuts for employees.

Athletic Facilities for Employees or Executives

The value of athletic facilities provided by an employer can be excluded from an employee's income as a *de minimis* fringe if (1) the facility is located on the employer's premises, (2) the facility is operated by the employer, and (3) the facility is mainly used only by employees, their spouses, and dependent children.

There are no nondiscrimination requirements for tax-free athletic facilities under Sec. 132. That is, it is possible to provide this benefit for a selected group of executives only. As long as the athletic facility meets the requirements in the preceding paragraph, it will be tax free to the executives.[73] This makes the athletic facility a useful tool for a planner designing an "executive fitness" program.

Executive Dining Room

In the case of an employer-operated eating facility, the rules of IRC Sec. 132(e)(2) must be met in order for the income to be excludible from the employee's income as a *de minimis* fringe. Under Reg. Sec. 1.132-7(a)(2), an employer-operated eating facility must meet the following conditions:

- The facility must be owned or leased by the employer.
- The facility is operated by the employer.
- The facility is located on or near the employer's business premises.
- The meals furnished at the facility are provided during, or immediately before or after, the employee's workday.

In addition, the "direct operating cost" test of Reg. Sec. 1.132-7(a)(1)(i) must be satisfied; under this test, the revenue derived from the facility must normally equal or exceed the direct operating costs involved.

Finally, in order for an employer-operated eating facility to be treated as a tax-free *de minimis* fringe for highly compensated employees, the facility must not discriminate in favor of highly compensated employees. For purposes of applying these nondiscrimination rules, a highly compensated

---

73. Treas. Reg. Sec. 1.132-1(e)(5).

employee is defined the same as for qualified plan purposes.[74] This rule has tended to discourage the use of traditional "executive dining rooms" on company facilities.

Note that meals for employees can still be tax free to employees and fully deductible by the employer even if they do not meet these tests—if the meals are served on business premises for the employer's convenience (Code Secs. 119 and 274(e)). If more than 50 percent of the employees receiving on-premises meals are receiving them for the convenience of the employer, then all on-premises employee meals will be treated as for the convenience of the employer. A facility might be considered for the employer's convenience if there are no alternative eating facilities in the vicinity; it's a facts and circumstances test.

Qualified Transportation Fringe

A qualified transportation fringe is a plan that provides one or more of the following benefits for employees:[75]

- transportation in a "commuter highway vehicle"
- a transit pass for use on a mass transit system (public or private)
- "qualified parking"

Advantages

1. The value of these benefits can be considerable in some cases and they are provided tax free to employees, while the cost is fully deductible to employers.

2. Qualified transportation fringes, unlike other fringe benefits, can be provided to employees on a cash-option (salary reduction) basis.[76] For example, the employer can offer a group of employees the choice of receiving a monthly transit pass worth $50 or $50 more in cash that month. Those who choose the transit pass do not pay

---

74. Code Sec. 414(q); a highly compensated employee is one who meets either of the following tests.

   (1) the employee was a 5 percent owner at any time during the year or the preceding year; or

   (2) the employee received more than $110,000 in pay (2010 figure as indexed) for the preceding year. The employer can elect to ignore test (2) if the employee was not also in the top 20 percent of employees when ranked by pay for the preceding year. The definition of HCEs for fringe benefit purposes incorporates the standard under Sec. 414(q).

75. IRC Sec. 132(f)(1)

76. IRC Sec. 132(f)(4)

federal income taxes on its value; only those who choose the cash option must pay taxes on the $50 monthly benefit.

By contrast, if an employer offered another fringe benefit on this basis, all employees would be taxable on the value of the benefit, whether they took cash or not. For example, if a department store offered employees a choice between $50 worth of monthly discounts on store merchandise or $50 monthly in cash, all employees covered by the plan would have $50 of taxable income each month, whether or not they chose the cash option. Fringe benefits other than qualified transportation fringes must be offered as an employer-paid extra only, not under a cash option—otherwise they will lose their tax-free status.

3. There are no nondiscrimination requirements for qualified transportation fringes. For example, parking can be provided tax free (up to the monthly limit described below) even if it is available only to selected executives. Planners of executive compensation programs, particularly for executives working in downtown office buildings, should make note of the compensation opportunity potentially available.

Benefits

Commuter Highway Vehicle. This benefit is available for transportation in vans seating at least six passengers and running on commuting trips when it is at least half full. (This half-full provision is evidently designed to exclude chauffeured executive limos.) The van can be operated by the employer or a contractor hired by the employer.[77] Tax-free benefits are limited to an aggregated per-employee monthly limit of $120 (2010) worth of transportation in commuter highway vehicles and transit passes.[78]

Transit Pass. A transit pass applied to mass transit as normally understood, as well as costs for a van operated as a business by a third party (not the employer or a contractor hired by the employer) and having at least a six-passenger capacity.[79] As indicated, a $120 monthly aggregate limit (2010) applies for transit passes together with commuter highway vehicle benefits.

---

77. IRC Sec. 132(f)5(B)

78. IRC Sec. 132(f)(2)(A).

79. IRC Sec. 132(f)(5)(A)

Parking. Although many employees probably do not think of parking as an employee benefit, particularly if they work in suburban locations, the value of parking to employees can be considerable.

Under the tax law, parking provided to employees is excludible from their taxable income up to $175 per month (as adjusted for inflation; 2010: $230).[80] To qualify, the employer must provide the parking arrangement on or near the employer's place of business or near a location from which the employee can board some type of commuter vehicle.[81]

Although it is relatively easy to determine the value of a parking space in a commercial lot or garage, valuing spaces at suburban office or plant facilities may be a problem. The IRS has simplified this somewhat by taking the position that the value of the parking is zero if nobody but an employee would pay to park in the lot or garage.[82]

Security-Related Transportation and Other Security Expenses

Some companies provide transportation to executives and others in order to deal with security concerns such as crime and terrorism. The IRS position on these issues is set forth at length in their audit guidelines:

> Regulations Sec. 1.132-5(m)(1) provides that if both a bona fide business-oriented security concern and an overall security program exist, then the employee may exclude the excess of the value of the transportation provided by the employer over the amount that the employee would have paid for the same mode of transportation absent the bona fide security concern. With respect to air transportation, the phrase "same mode of transportation" means comparable air transportation.
>
> A bona fide business-oriented security concern exists only if the facts and circumstances establish a specific basis for concern regarding the safety of the executive (Sec. 1.132-5(m)(2)(i)). A generalized concern for the executive's safety will not trigger application of the security exclusion (Sec. 1.132-5(m)(2)(i)). Under Sec. 1.132-5(m)(2)(i), the employer must demonstrate the existence

---

80. IRC Sec. 132(f)(2)(B), 132(f)(6)
81. IRC Sec. 132(f)(5)(C).
82. Notice 94-3, 1994-1 CB 327, Q-10

of a bona fide security concern. A bona fide security concern exists if the facts and circumstances demonstrate a specific basis for concern regarding the safety of the employee. Examples of specific bases for a bona fide security concern include a specific threat to harm the employee or a recent history of violent terrorist activity in the geographic area in which the transportation is provided.

Sec. 1.132-5(m)(2)(ii) provides that an overall security program must be established. In order to establish the existence of an overall security program, the employer must generally establish that security is provided to the employee on a 24-hour basis.

However, under Sec. 1.132-5(m)(2)(iv), an overall security program is deemed to exist if the following conditions are satisfied:

- A security study is performed with respect to the employer and the employee (or a similarly situated employee of the employer) by an independent security consultant;
- The security study is based on an objective assessment of all facts and circumstances;
- The recommendation of the security study is that an overall security program is not necessary and the recommendation is reasonable under the circumstances; and
- The employer applies the specific security recommendations contained in the security study to the employee on a consistent basis.

An independent security study could conclude, for example, that security during air travel is necessary, but security on a 24-hour basis is unnecessary.

The expenses incurred for security services will normally be deducted under "Other Deductions." A review of the W-2/1099 forms and employment agreements may provide information related to security services.

Upon examination it has been found that homes of executives have been fortified with special rooms or other security devises. It is important to evaluate the level of security afforded top executives and their families to determine that security studies are being followed.

WORKING CONDITION FRINGES—REIMBURSEMENT OF DEDUCTIBLE ITEMS

Car Expenses

If an employer provides a car or other road vehicle for an executive's use, the amount excludible as a working condition fringe benefit is the amount that would be allowable as a deductible business expense if the executive paid for its use (Sec. 1.132-5(b)). The executive's personal use of the vehicle is taxable. The value is generally determined by reference to fair market value unless one of the special valuation methods is used (Sec. 1.61-21(b)(4)). The three special valuation rules for automobiles are as follows:

1. Automobile lease valuation rule—Sec. 1.61-21(d)(2);
2. Vehicle cents-per-mile rule—Sec. 1.61-21(e); and
3. Commuting valuation rule—Sec. 1.61-21(f).

There are specific requirements that must be met in order to use these special valuation rules. For example, the employer must provide the employee with a vehicle for commuting for bona fide noncompensatory business reasons in order to use the commuting valuation rule.

Reporting of car expenses is discussed in detail in IRS Publication 463. The current version of this publication is available on the IRS website. The following table copied from IRS Publication 463, is helpful in summarizing the rules.

Table 7-1 Reporting Travel, Entertainment, Gift, and Car Expenses and Reimbursements		
If the type of reimbursement (or other expense allowance) arrangement is under:	**THEN the employer reports on Form W-2:**	**AND the employee reports on Form 2106:***
An accountable plan with:		
Actual expense reimbursement: Adequate accounting made <u>and</u> excess returned	No amount.	No amount.
Actual expense reimbursement: Adequate accounting and return of excess both required <u>but</u> excess not returned	The excess amount as wages in box 1.	No amount

If the type of reimbursement (or other expense allowance) arrangement is under:	THEN the employer reports on Form W-2:	AND the employee reports on Form 2106:*
Per diem or mileage allowance up to the federal rate: Adequate accounting made <u>and</u> excess returned.	No amount.	All expenses and reimbursements only if excess expenses are claimed. Otherwise, form is not filed.
Per diem or mileage allowance up to the federal rate: Adequate accounting and return of excess both required but excess not returned	The excess amount as wages in box 1. The amount up to the federal rate is reported only in box 12—it is not reported in box 1.	No amount.
Per diem or mileage allowance exceeds the federal rate: Adequate accounting up to the federal rate only <u>and</u> excess not returned	The excess amount as wages in box 1. The amount up to the federal rate is reported only in box 12—it is not reported in box 1.	All expenses (and reimbursements reported on Form W-2, box 12) only if expenses in excess of the federal rate are claimed. Otherwise, form is not filed.
A nonaccountable plan with:		
Either adequate accounting or return of excess, or both, not	The entire amount as wages in box 1.	All expenses.
required by plan		
No reimbursement plan:	The entire amount as wages in box 1.	All expenses.
*You may be able to use Form 2106-EZ. See Completing Forms 2106 and 2106-EZ.		

Moving and Relocation Expenses

The value of relocation benefits may be includible in gross income. Sec. 82 provides that there shall be included in gross income (as compensation for services) any amounts received as payment for or reimbursement of expenses of moving from one residence to another which is attributable to employment. However, Sec. 132(g) provides an exclusion for qualified moving expense reimbursements. Under Sec. 132(g), an employee may exclude the amount paid or reimbursed by the employer that would be deductible as a moving expense under Sec. 217 if the executive paid the moving expense directly. Under Sec. 217, only the costs of moving personal belongings and traveling to the new location are deductible. Costs such as meals and lodging in temporary quarters are not deductible under Sec. 217. In addition, other costs paid by the employer, such as brokerage fees, property taxes, insurance, fix-up expenses, and reimbursement for losses with respect to the sale of the prior home are includible in gross income.

Moving expense rules are covered in detail in IRS Publication 521, available on the IRS website, www.IRS.gov. The following flow chart summarizes the rules:

Can You Deduct Expenses for a Non-Military Move Within the United States?[1]

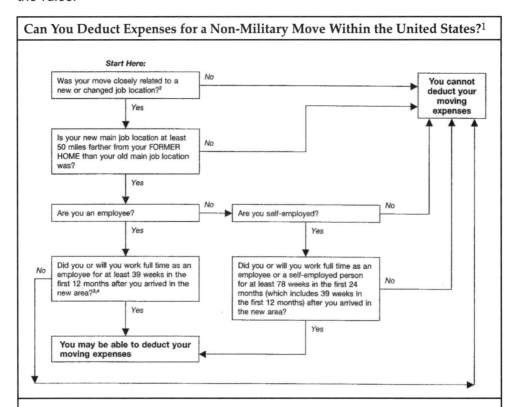

1. Military persons should see *Members of the Armed Forces* for special rules that apply to them.

2. Your move must be closely related to the start of work at your new job location. See Related to Start of *Work*.

3. If you deduct expenses and do not meet this test later, you must either file an amended tax return or report your moving expense deduction as other income. See T*ime test not yet met*.

4. If you became self-employed during the first 12 months, answer YES if your time as a full-time employee added to your time as a self-employed person equals or will equal at least 78 weeks in the first 24 months (including 39 weeks in the first 12 months) after you arrived in the new area.

Some companies subsidize an executive's mortgage payments by paying the differential based on old and current interest rates. Three to five years of such assistance is common. Also, an employer might agree to buy the old home or provide the executive with a "gap loan" while the executive is between houses.

It may be advantageous for the employer to use the services of a professional relocation-assistant consulting firm. The relocation firm might give the employee cash now for his old home and take over the burden of finding the buyer. Several letter rulings state that fees paid by the employer to a relocation company are (a) tax free to the employee and (b) tax deductible by the employer. In one of the rulings, the corporation hired a relocation company to help its employees relocate if they were transferred for business reasons. The relocation company agreed to purchase the home of an employee and resell the home within one year. The relocation company paid the employee cash for an amount up to the amount of the employee's equity (value of the home less the outstanding mortgage). The value of the home was ascertained based on at least two appraisals. The relocation company then had complete control over the subsequent sale. In the same ruling, the executive's company paid the relocation company a fee for buying the home and also reimbursed the relocation company for the closing costs it incurred on the purchase and resale of the home. (If there was a loss on a resale, the relocation company would be reimbursed by the executive's firm in the amount of the loss.) The Service stated that payments by the executive's firm to the relocation company are tax free to the employee. (See Private Letter Ruling 8016098 and Revenue Ruling 72-339, 1972-2 C.B. 31.) Furthermore, the fees are deductible by the employer company as an ordinary and necessary business expense because the services purchased (the relocation company's services) minimized the disruptive effect of the employee having to relocate his home. This, in turn, helps promote the prompt assumption of new job duties by the executive. (See Private Letter Ruling 8113020.)

Athletic Skyboxes and Cultural Entertainment Suites

As with most working condition fringe benefits, reimbursements for business entertainment expenses can be excluded if the entertainment amount would be deductible as a business expense if paid directly by the executive. Generally, only 50 percent of business meals and entertainment expenses can be deducted under Code Sec. 274.

In the case of a skybox or other private luxury box leased for more than one event, the amount allowable as a deduction under Code Sec. 274(l)(2) with respect to such events may not exceed the sum of the face value of a non-luxury box seat ticket(s) for the number of seats in the luxury box. Luxury boxes rented by related parties or individuals are treated as a single lease in determining whether a luxury box is leased for more than one event. See Notice 87-23, 1987-1 C.B. 467, 469. The remaining amount for attendance at the event is limited to ordinary and necessary business expenditures that also satisfy all the requirements under Sec. 274(a), (d), and (n) for deducting entertainment expenses. Similarly, a purchase of a skybox is the purchase of a facility subject to Sec. 274(a). Catered events may need examination to verify that the deduction limitations of IRC Sec. 274(n) have been correctly applied. If the purchased or leased skybox is used personally by the top executives of the corporation, the value of the benefit may be taxable income to the executives.

Tickets

Deductions for tickets to entertainment events that qualify as business expenses are limited to the face value of the tickets. The face value limitation will make the premium paid to a scalper, as well as the premium paid to a legitimate ticket agency, nondeductible. The deduction, of course, is then further reduced by the 50 percent limitation.

Club Memberships

Reimbursements by a company to an executive for dues for organization membership, business entertainment, etc., can be excluded from income by the executive (as working condition fringes), if the expenses would be deductible as business expenses under Sec. 274 if paid directly by the executive.

With regard to club dues, Sec. 274(a)(3) provides that no deduction is permitted. This includes all types of clubs, including social, athletic, sporting, luncheon clubs, airline and hotel clubs and "business" clubs.

Regulations defining the term "club" for purposes of Sec. 274(a)(3) have been issued (Reg. Sec. 1.274-2). Clubs organized for business, pleasure, recreation, or other social purposes include any membership organization if a principal purpose of the organization is to conduct entertainment activities for members of the organization or their guests or to provide members or their guests with access to entertainment facilities. Clubs organized for business, pleasure, etc. include, but are not limited to, country clubs, golf and athletic clubs, airline clubs, hotel clubs, and clubs operated to provide meals under circumstances generally considered to be conducive to business discussion (Reg. Sec. 1.247-2(a)(2)(iii)(a)). Membership business lunch clubs are included in the latter category.

Specific business expenses at a club are deductible to the extent they otherwise satisfy the rules for deductibility. For example, 50 percent of allowable meal and entertainment expenses are deductible. Thus, while membership dues for a business lunch club are not deductible, 50 percent of qualifying meal expenses can be deducted.

The regulations clarify that the purposes and activities of a club, and not its name, determine whether it is covered under the disallowance provision. The employer has the choice of either including the value of the club membership in the employee's income or forgoing any deduction for the club dues. IRC Sec. 274(e)(2). Put another way, the company can deduct the cost if it treats the club dues as compensation includible in gross income and wages. However, if the employer's deduction for club dues is disallowed by Sec. 274(a)(3), Regulations Sec. 1.132-5(s) provides that the amount, if any, of an employee's working condition fringe benefit relating to the employer-provided membership in the club is determined without regard to the application of Sec. 274(a) to the employee. To be excludible as a working condition fringe, however, the amount must otherwise qualify for deduction by the employee under Sec. 162(a). Note that the requirements of Sec. 274(d) must still be met (that is, time, place, and business purpose must be established. See Regulations Sec. 1.132-5(s)(3) for examples applying these rules.

Planners should take note of the IRS view as discussed in its Audit Guide:

> Although many corporations are aware of the law regarding the deductibility of club dues and membership fees, they will often make such expenditures and disguise the deduction. Club memberships have been distributed to departing executives through severance agreements. The value of a club membership distributed to executives upon departure is wages. Close scrutiny should be afforded employment contracts and severance agreements for executives.

Although membership dues and fees for social or country clubs are not deductible, membership fees for *professional and civic organizations* may be deductible if they qualify as ordinary and necessary business expenses.[83] But note that out-of-pocket expenses for entertaining at any club, such as food and beverages, fall within the general rules for business entertainment.

Professional and Civic Organizations

Under the regulations, the following organizations would not be treated as organized for business, pleasure, etc., and absent a principal organizational purpose to conduct entertainment activities for members or their guests or to provide members or their guests with access to entertainment facilities:

- professional organizations (such as bar associations and medical associations),
- business leagues,
- trade associations,
- chambers of commerce,
- boards of trade,
- real estate boards, and
- civic or public service organizations (Reg. Sec. 1.274-2(a)(2)(iii)(b)).

Accordingly, dues and similar payments to these organizations could be deductible as business expenses. The IRS identifies Kiwanis, Lions, Rotary, and Civitan as examples of such civic or public service organizations.[84]

EXECUTIVE LOAN PROGRAMS

Like the benefits described in Code Sec. 132 and discussed above, loans to employees are a form of benefit that are governed by specific tax rules. An executive loan program can be an attractive benefit as a supplement to an executive's compensation. Typically, loans are offered either interest free or at a rate of interest below the market rate. Most programs are limited to loans that provide cash to the executive for specific needs, such as

- purchase of company stock under a restricted stock plan or stock option plan
- mortgage loan or bridge loan in connection with the hiring of a new executive or the executive's move from one business location to another

---

83. Treas. Reg. Sec. 1.274(e)(3)(ii) (based on pre-1993 law).

84. Preamble, TD 8601.

- life insurance purchases including split-dollar plans
- expenditures for college or private school tuition for dependents, or for personal or family emergencies

Generally the federal income tax rules for below-market-rate loans provide no tax advantage for loans to executives. However, the plans can still be attractive for nontax reasons such as making cash available where other sources are unavailable or available only at very high rates of interest.

The tax rules are complicated and the requirements of monitoring and complying with them increase the company's administrative costs in setting up and maintaining a loan program. It is also possible that the paperwork and other requirements of the Federal Truth In Lending Act[85] may apply.

The Sarbanes-Oxley Act, enacted in the wake of the Enron scandals and similar events in 2001 and 2002, prohibits a publicly traded corporation from making a personal loan to any director or executive officer. The act does not prohibit loans to other types of employees and does not apply to corporations that are not publicly traded.

Tax Treatment of Below-Market Loans

Code Sec. 7872 governs the tax treatment of a "compensation-related"[86] loan that carries interest at a "below-market" rate. For purposes of Sec. 7872, below market means that the interest is below the "applicable federal rate" (AFR). The AFR is published monthly by the IRS as a Revenue Ruling in the Internal Revenue Bulletin.[87] The general effect of Sec. 7872 is to impose tax on the bargain element of the interest as if it was paid as additional compensation income. The details are somewhat complex as indicated below.

---

85. Title I of the Consumer Protection Act, as amended, 15 USC 1601 et seq. The Truth in Lending Act applies if more than 25 loans or more than five loans secured by dwellings are extended in a calendar year.

86. A loan is compensation related if it is directly or indirectly between (1) an employer and an employee or (2) an independent contractor and the person for whom the independent contractor provides services. Code Sec. 7872(c)(1)(B).

87. For demand loans, the AFR is the short-term semiannual rate. For term loans, the AFR is the short-term, mid-term, or long-term rate (depending on the term of the loan) in effect on the day the loan was made. See Rev. Rul. 86-17, 1986-1 CB 377.

Demand Loan

A demand loan is a loan payable in full at any time upon demand of the lender. Under Code Sec. 7872, a loan is also a demand loan if (1) the interest arrangements are conditioned on the future services of the employee, and (2) the interest benefits are not transferable by the employee.[88]

Interest on a below-market compensation-related demand loan is treated as a combination of three transactions: the actual transaction plus two "deemed" transactions. These are

1. Interest that is actually paid by the borrowing executive is treated as income to the company (the lender). This interest may be deductible by the executive if it falls into some category of deductible personal indebtedness interest—for example, investment interest. Otherwise, it is nondeductible.

2. The employee is treated as receiving additional compensation from the employer equal to the difference between the actual rate of interest and the AFR. This additional amount is taxable to the employee. It is also deductible by the employer to the extent it meets the "reasonable compensation" test for deductibility.

3. The employee is deemed to have paid the additional amount in (2) above back to the employer. This amount is taxable income to the employer. The employee can deduct this amount but only if it falls within a category of deductible interest payments.

EXAMPLE

Employee Adam Smith receives a demand loan of $100,000 from his employer, Wealth, Inc. In the first year of the loan, assume that interest at the AFR would be $6,000. Actual interest required by the loan agreement is $2,000. The result of this loan is additional taxable compensation income to Smith in the first year of the loan equal to $4,000 ($6,000 less $2,000). If Smith can deduct the interest—say it's investment interest—he can deduct $6,000, that is, the actual $2,000 he paid plus the deemed additional amount of $4,000. Wealth, Inc., has $6,000 of interest income as a result of this transaction, and it can deduct $4,000 as compensation paid, regardless of whether Smith can deduct any interest on the loan.

---

88. Code Sec. 7872(f)(5). The IRS has the authority to issue regulations treating any loan with an indefinite maturity as a demand loan.

Term Loan

Under Code Sec. 7872, a term loan is defined as any loan that is not a demand loan. Generally a term loan is a loan payable after a specified term of years. Under Sec. 7872, a term loan is considered to be a below-market loan if the amount loaned is more than the present value of all payments due under the loan. The present value is determined using a discount rate based on the AFR.

Under Sec. 7872, a below-market compensation-related term loan results in the employee being treated as if he immediately received an amount equal to the excess of (1) the amount of the loan over (2) the present value of all payments required to be made under the loan. This is generally an unfavorable result, that is, the rules of Sec. 7872 tend to discourage such loans.

EXAMPLE

Employer Baubles, Inc. lends employee Bijou $50,000 interest free, payable in 5 years. Based on the AFR for the year of the loan, the present value of this loan is $24,000. Bijou is treated as receiving additional compensation income of $26,000 ($50,000 less $24,000) in the first year of the loan. Baubles, Inc. can deduct this $26,000 as additional compensation paid, assuming that total compensation meets the reasonable compensation test. Over the loan's 5-year term, Bijou is deemed to pay additional interest each year to Baubles, Inc. at the AFR applied to the deemed unpaid amount of $24,000; Baubles, Inc. must include this amount in its income.

Exceptions to Application of Code Sec. 7872

There are exceptions to the applicability of Code Sec. 7872. If these exceptions apply, the loan transaction is treated as it appears on its face with no deemed or imputed features. The existence of these exceptions is important to the executive benefit planner, because executive loan programs can be designed to fit the exceptions and can thus provide benefits to the executive without the unfavorable tax consequences of Code Sec. 7872.

There are three exceptions:

- mortgage and bridge loans
- *de minimis* loans
- no-tax-effect loans

The following must be met in order to qualify for the mortgage loan exception:

- The loan is a compensation-related term or demand loan.
- The borrower's principal residence is acquired in connection with the transfer of the employee to a new principal place of work (which meets the distance and time requirements for a moving expense deduction under Code Sec. 217).
- The executive certifies to the employer that he or she reasonably expects to be entitled to and will itemize deductions while the loan is outstanding.
- Under the loan agreement, loan proceeds may be used only to buy the executive's new principal residence.
- The loan is secured by a mortgage on the new principal residence of the employee.

A *bridge* loan must satisfy all the requirements for a mortgage loan listed above as well as the following:

- The loan must be payable in full within 15 days after the old principal residence is sold.
- The aggregate principal of all bridge loans must not exceed the employer's reasonable estimate of the equity of the executive and his or her spouse in the old residence.
- The old residence must not be converted to business or investment use.

A *de minimis* loan is a compensation-related loan for any day on which aggregate loans outstanding between the company and the executive do not exceed $10,000, provided that tax avoidance is not one of the principal purposes of the interest arrangements. A husband and wife are treated as one borrower for this purpose.

A loan with *no tax effect* is exempt from Sec. 7872 if the taxpayer can show that the interest arrangements will have no significant effect on any federal tax liability of the lender or borrower. In making this determination the IRS considers the following:

- whether items of income and deduction generated by the loan offset each other
- the amount of such items
- the cost to the taxpayer of complying with the below-market loan rules
- any nontax reasons for structuring the transaction as a below-market loan

Other issues often noted by the IRS are summarized in the IRS Audit Guidelines on executive compensation:

> Some loans to executives are essentially disguised compensation based on the terms of the loan. Secs. 61(a)(1) and 61(a)(12) define gross income to include compensation for services and income from discharge of indebtedness. Reg. Sec. 1.61-12(a) provides that if an individual performs services for a creditor, who in consideration for the services, cancels the debt, the debtor realizes income in the amount of the debt as compensation for services. Discharge of indebtedness income by an employee from an employer under these circumstances is payment in the nature of compensation, and thus is includible in gross income and wages for employment tax purposes.

> Issues have been raised regarding loan forgiveness (remain in the employ of the corporation for a period of four years), unusual repayment methods (stock in lieu of cash), and extreme repayment dates (repayment by the executive's trust upon the death of the executive and his spouse). Loans are often used to disguise compensation; therefore, the underlying intent must be examined and addressed.

Summary

An executive loan program providing loans that avoid Sec. 7872 (that is, loans that fall within the exceptions to Sec. 7872) will produce significant tax and nontax benefits to the executive. The only cost to the employer is the cost of the money (to the extent not recovered by interest payments from the employee) and the cost of administration.

If the plan includes loans that fall within Sec. 7872, the benefits to the executive are less and the costs of administration are greater. It is not necessarily the case, however, that the plan is not beneficial at all from the executive's point of view.

To illustrate the advantage, using the earlier Adam Smith example, suppose the worst—that Smith can't deduct any interest. In the first year of the loan, Smith has additional taxable income of $4,000; tax at 35 percent would be $1,400. Smith's total cost for the loan would therefore be the $2,000 of interest he actually paid plus the $1,400 of tax on the deemed additional taxable income for a total cost of $3,400. Without the executive loan program, his first-year interest cost for this loan would be approximately $6,000, the AFR amount that presumably is about the same as the market rate of interest.

There are alternatives to below-market loans if the company wants to help an executive deal with cash needs. For example, the company can lend at market rates and "bonus" the cost of the interest to the executive as additional compensation (deductible to the company). Another alternative is for the company to guarantee loans made by a local bank to the executive for specific purposes.

FRINGE BENEFITS THAT ARE GENERALLY TAXABLE

A company can provide an almost unlimited program of taxable fringe benefits for executives. Some of the types of benefits that have been frequently used are listed here and briefly discussed.

Wealth Management and Financial Counseling

A wealth management program is advantageous for selected executives because it can relieve time pressures on executives and provide skilled advisors for executive financial planning. Benefits typically include estate planning, tax planning (annual return preparation), and life insurance planning.

Qualified Retirement Planning

Although financial planning services for employees are generally taxable to the employees, there is an exception for qualified retirement planning services under Code Sec. 132. The services are limited to explaining terms of the employer's qualified plans, and they are taxable to highly compensated employees unless the services are available to employees in general. Consequently, qualified retirement planning is not generally a useful benefit for selected executives.

Corporate Credit Card

Companies often provide credit cards to employees to cover business-related expenses. The amount paid by the employer to the credit card company is generally taxable to the employee except to the extent that the employee files a report with the employer indicating the number of business expenses charged on the card. Any personal amounts remaining will be taxable as compensation income to the employee. Executive cards sometimes do not require accounting, for the convenience of the executive, but then the entire amount paid by the employer is taxable income to the executive.

Outplacement Services

Companies can cushion the impact of retrenchment decisions for both the company and the employee by providing outplacement services—helping an employee due for separation to find another job. The value of these services is, in general, taxable to the recipient. However, the IRS has ruled[89] that if outplacement services are provided to all classes of employees, the value of the services can be excluded as a working condition fringe benefit, even if the services provided to executives are different from those provided for other employees.

Life Insurance for Spouse and Dependents

In general, if a company provides life insurance for an employee's spouse or dependents, the value of the coverage is taxable to the employee as additional compensation income. The method of valuation may differ depending on the method of coverage—group term, split dollar, or life insurance in a qualified plan.

Travel in Company Aircraft

If an executive (or family member) uses the employer's aircraft for personal reasons, under the Regulations the use must be valued and included in taxable wages.[90] The valuation depends on whether the flight is primarily business or personal and whether the executive is a "control employee." The value of the flight is determined by reference to fair market value unless the special valuation rules, known as the Standard Industry Fare Level formula ("SIFL") are elected. There is a lower SIFL inclusion amount if the air travel is a security-related benefit meeting the requirements discussed earlier under Objective 5. The amount deductible by the employer may be limited to the amount included by the executive, if Code Sec. 274(e)(2) applies (where the executive is an officer of a listed company under SEC rules). Sec. 274

---

89. Rev. Rul. 92-69, 1992-2 CB 51.

90. Reg. Sec. 1.61-21(g).

also limits or disallows deductions by the company for the cost of travel by a spouse or dependent of the executive.

HOW THE IRS IDENTIFIES EXECUTIVE FRINGE BENEFITS

The following excerpt from the IRS Audit Guide illustrates how the IRS looks for executive compensation items in general. The IRS view should be helpful for benefit planners in properly documenting compensation arrangements:

"Because the tax treatment of fringe benefits can vary depending on the facts and circumstances under which they are provided, the IRS tends to follow a 3-step analysis when examining a particular item an employer gives or makes available to an executive.

- First, identify the particular fringe benefit and start with the assumption that its value will be taxable as compensation to the employee.
- Second, check to see if there are any statutory provisions that exclude the fringe benefit from the executive's gross income.
- Third, value any portion of the benefit that is not excludible and include it in the executive's gross income. Fringe benefits are generally valued at the amount the employee would have to pay for the benefit in an arm's-length transaction.

"SEC Items such as Form 10-K (Items 10, 11, and 12) and Form 4 can be used to identify executive compensation issues. The Form 4, Statement of Changes in Beneficial Ownership, may indicate whether stock was used for loan repayments. (Sarbanes-Oxley Act restricts the use of loans after July 30, 2002.)

The following line items on the income tax return frequently contain taxable fringe benefits; the list is not all-inclusive:

- Other Deductions
- Cost of Goods Sold
- Depreciation
- Employee Benefits
- Schedule M-1
- Travel and Entertainment

- Rent

Request a listing of the executives and officers from the taxpayer to identify the highly compensated executives. A representative group of executives may be selected for an in-depth examination. At a minimum the selection should include the SEC Sec. 16b executives (CEO, CFO and the other three highest compensated officers) for publicly traded companies.

The following steps should aid in the examination of Executive Fringe Benefits:

- Determine the department responsible for approving and processing payments to executives and officers.
- Review the Executive Compensation Committee Minutes, reports, etc.
- Review loan agreements between the corporation and executives/ officers.
- Identify all payments to, or on behalf of, the executives/ officers.
- Inspect the employment contracts and/or severance agreements to identify salaries and benefits paid to the executives.
- Sample monthly expense reports submitted by executives. Determine if there is an Accountable Plan and if the plan meets the requirements of IRC 62(c).
- Search for the executive's name, SSN, or title in Accounts Payable. This search may identify payments to executives that were not included on a Form W-2 or Form 1099.
- Request a listing of the specific Payroll Codes or other accounting codes that relate to expenses/expenditures for executives. These codes can be used to identify payments to the executives/officers that may be taxable as compensation."

CHAPTER REVIEW

Review Questions

1. What is a fringe benefit? [1]

2. List the fringe benefits excluded from tax under Code Sec. 132. [1]

3. Forota Co. manufactures automobiles. It proposes to offer its top 50 executives a 75 percent discount on its luxury automobile, the Lexion. Comment on the tax treatment of this proposed plan. [2]

4. Jensen Products Company has a company dining room for its employees. Lunches actually cost the company $8.00, and each employee eats about 230 lunches per year. There is, however, no charge to the employee for these lunches. All employees eat in the dining room. [3]
   a. What are the requirements for the company to be able to deduct the cost of this program?
   b. How much is taxable to the employee?
   c. What are the advantages to a company of having dining arrangements on the premises?

5. Fiduciary Company has a plan to pay employees $5.00 as supper money on those nights when they work 2 hours overtime. What are the tax consequences of this practice (a) to the employee and (b) to the company? [3]

6. What executive-compensation opportunities are available as a result of the "qualified transportation fringe" provisions of the Code? [4]

7. Ulam, an executive for Merchants o' Death, Inc (MOD), often travels to a MOD facility in a country where there is thought to be crime and terrorism.

   What steps, if any, can be taken to allow MOD's expenses for bodyguards, armored vehicles, and private jets for Ulam to be excluded from Ulam's income? [5]

8. What are the three major types of employer/employee arrangements for car expense sharing? Summarize their tax consequences. [6]

9. Which of the three arrangements from question 1 above generally provides the best tax results? Why? [6]

10. Briefly describe how reimbursed car expenses (employee business expenses) are handled by (a) an employee and (b) a self-employed person. [6]

11. Elmer Brown was transferred by his company from one plant to another plant in the same region. He had commuted 15 miles to the old plant from his home in Pleasant Valley; the new plant, however, is 30 miles from his Pleasant Valley home, so he moves to a new house in Plush Hills. He has the following moving expenses: [7]

    direct moving: $1,500

    direct travel: $400

    home search: $200

    temporary living costs for 10 days in new location: $200

    residence sale cost: $1,500

    residence purchase cost: $600,000

    a. If the company reimburses Brown for all of the above costs, what will be the income tax treatment to (i) the company and (ii) Brown?

    b. Given the same facts as above except that Brown is transferred to a location 100 miles from his current home, what will be the income tax treatment to (i) the company and (ii) Brown?

12. When Harold McMullan was promoted by the Rover Company, he was required to move from Pittsburgh, Pennsylvania, to Hartford, Connecticut, a distance of approximately 400 miles from his former home. McMullan used to commute 10 miles to his office in Pittsburgh. McMullan has the following moving expenses: [7]

    direct moving costs: $3,000

    direct travel costs: $1,500

    home search trips: $700

    temporary living cost for 25 days in Connecticut: $1,000

    residence sale costs: $1,000

    residence purchase costs: $1,200,000

    If the Rover Company reimburses McMullan for all his moving expenses, what will be the income tax consequences to McMullan?

13. Upscale Co. would like to provide executive Vandergraft with a box at the opera to entertain the company's wealthy and sophisticated clients. Describe the probable tax consequences. [8]

14. Ralph Smith, sales manager of Rarity Company, has joined the Gulph Hills
     Country Club and the Midday Downtown Lunch Club.

     Gulph Hills requires an initiation fee and annual dues. Smith plans to play
     golf with business prospects there, and 60 percent of his use of the club
     will be for business purposes. Smith also uses the lunch club to entertain
     business prospects. Rarity Company is willing to pay for the memberships
     (initiation fees and dues) in both of these clubs. What would be the income
     tax treatment of these benefits to the company and to Ralph? [9]

15. Byron Williams, Esq., general counsel for Effortless Experts Company,
     belongs to the local, state, and national bar associations. He is also a CLU
     and belongs to The American College Alumni Association. Effortless pays
     his annual dues to all these organizations. What is the tax status of such
     payments for the company and Williams? [9]

16. James Wilson is considering an offer from Failsafe Investments, Inc., to be its
     chief financial officer. If James accepts the position, he will have to relocate.
     At the present time, interest on mortgage money and loans for home repairs
     average about 10 percent. Failsafe has offered to lend Wilson $75,000
     interest free to encourage him to make the move and to enable him to buy
     the $250,000 home he is interested in. [10]

     a. What is the tax treatment of such an interest-free loan to Wilson and to
     Failsafe?

     b. What advice would you give Failsafe concerning the structuring of the
     loan?

     c. If Failsafe had not offered to lend James the money, what else could it do
     to help him in his search for mortgage money?

17. What are the corporate reasons for adopting a wealth management or
     financial planning program for executives? [11]

18. What financial planning benefits, if any, can be excluded from tax by the
     executive? [11]

19. Comment on a company's providing (a) private jet travel for executive
     business trips; (b) air travel for an executive's family to remote business
     locations in order for the executive to live there more comfortably and be
     more productive. [11]

Answers to Review Questions

1. Fringe benefit is not a precisely defined term and can cover almost all forms of noncash compensation. However, generally it refers to relatively minor benefits such as those discussed in this chapter. [1]

2. Code Sec. 132 provides a tax exclusion in some cases for working condition fringes, *de minimis* fringes, no additional cost services, qualified employee discounts, qualified moving expenses, qualified transportation fringes, and qualified retirement planning services. These are generally discussed in more detail below. [1]

3. A qualified employee discount is a discount allowed to an employee for property or services that is offered for sale to customers by the company. The discount is tax free to the employee only up to the company's "gross profit percentage" in a sale to a regular customer. In addition, discounts must be made on a basis that does not discriminate in favor of highly compensated employees.

   Therefore, Forota's discount program is vulnerable on two points: (a) the discount appears to exceed the company's likely gross profit percentage, and (b) since it is limited to executives, it appears to be discriminatory in favor of highly compensated employees. [2]

4.

   a. An eating facility operated by an employer for the benefit of employees is fully deductible so that the after-tax cost to most companies is about 60 percent of the total paid. The subsidy to employees is considered a *de minimis* fringe if the revenue equals or exceeds the direct operating costs of the facility. Therefore (assuming nondiscrimination rules are met), the excess of the value of meals over the fees charged to employees is excludible from income. If the company does not have space for such on-premises dining, use of private facilities at another nearby location has been permitted.

   b. The employee is not subject to tax for the value of free or subsidized meals if nondiscrimination rules are met.

   c. Employee dining rooms are frequently set up if the company is located in an area where there are no suitable dining facilities. In any event, it is a time-saving arrangement for employees to have on-premise luncheon facilities. They also serve as a way of controlling alcoholic consumption since they are usually liquor free. [3]

5. When employees work late, a company can have a policy of paying a specified amount as supper money after a certain amount of overtime has been worked. If the amount is reasonable, it should be deductible to the company and, if paid occasionally and on a nondiscriminatory basis, can be excluded from the taxable income of the employee. [3]

6. Planners should not overlook the possibility of executive parking spaces or allowances not available to other employees. [4]

7. Security expenses can be excluded from the executive's income as a working condition fringe if a "bona fide business-oriented security concern" exists involving a specific basis for concern for the executive's security. In this case, the recent history of violent terrorist activity in the area of travel could justify the security. [5]

8. The three major types of arrangements are as follows:

   - A corporate business can provide a car for the employee.
   - A business can reimburse the employee for expenses.
   - An employee can assume all business expenses for the car, with his or her salary (perhaps) reflecting this.

   With the first arrangement, it is possible for all business-related car expenses to be nontaxable to the employee, since the employer can report only the employee's nonbusiness use of the car. The employee need not then deduct any employee business expenses, which are subject to a 2 percent of gross income floor. In the second and third arrangements, the employee must deduct employee business expenses on his or her tax returns, and the floor may prevent full deduction of these amounts. [6]

9. Because the floor for deductions is avoided, the company car can be the best arrangement taxwise. However, if the employee uses the car extensively for nonbusiness as well as business purposes, the employer must ascertain the nonbusiness use and report it on the employee's W-2. This is burdensome, and many employers will not want to do it. Alternatively, the employer can simply report the full value of the car on the employee's W-2; however, this means that the employee must deduct employee business expenses and become subject to the 2 percent floor. [6]

10. Reimbursed car expenses are reported on an employee's Form W-2 and the employee is eligible for an offsetting employee business expense deduction, subject to the 2 percent floor. Form 2106 must be filed by an employee. A self-employed person

does not file Form 2106 but instead deducts all car expenses on Schedule C, without a 2 percent floor. [6]

11. When a company requires an employee to move, it usually pays for all expenses connected with the transfer so that the employee will not suffer monetary loss because of the relocation. Such payments are taxable to the employee and deductible to the company as compensation expense if reasonable in amount when taken together with all other forms of compensation. However, if the following requirements are met, the employee will be entitled to an offsetting deduction within certain limits. To the extent that reimbursement of deductible moving expenses is deductible by the employee, it is not subject to withholding tax. (See IRS Form 4782 Employee Moving Expense Information for the form the employer uses to provide the employee with this information.)

When a permanent move is made at the employer's command to a principal place of work requiring 50 more miles of commuting than to the former place of employment, the following categories of moving expenses are deductible to the employee: all reasonable expenses of moving household goods and personal effects from the employee's former residence to his new residence, and reasonable expenses of traveling from the former residence to the new residence, including lodging but not meals, are deductible without limitation as moving expenses. (IRS Form 3903 Moving Expense Adjustment is the form used by the employee to calculate deductible moving expenses.) [7]

The answers to the question therefore are

    a. (i) fully deductible and subject to withholding tax

       (ii) taxable with no offsetting moving expense deduction

    b. (i) fully deductible and not subject to withholding tax

       (ii) taxable but with an offsetting deduction for the direct moving and direct travel costs

12. Reimbursement is taxable income, but an amount equal to items (a) and (b) is deductible. Items (c) through (f) are not deductible. [7]

13. If the night at the opera qualifies as business entertainment under Code Sec. 274, the company's deduction is limited to the value of a non-luxury box seat at the opera house, which may be difficult to determine. Generally, the value of the box is not taxable income

to the executive to the extent it would be deductible as a business expense under Sec. 162 if the executive had paid for it himself. [8]

14. Fees paid to any social, athletic, or sporting club or organization are not deductible. However, 50 percent of the cost of business meals is deductible, whether at a club or a regular restaurant.

    Dues to a professional association are not subject to the entertainment facility rules and are deductible if they qualify as ordinary and necessary business expenses. These items are not taxable income to the executive to the extent they would qualify as business expenses if the executive had paid for them himself. [9]

15. Company payments of dues for an employee's membership in business or professional organizations are deductible by the company and tax exempt to the employee as working condition fringes. [9]

16. Companies sometimes will provide a benefit to executives in the form of loans that are either interest free or at a rate lower than prevailing interest rates.

    a. Under Code Sec. 7872, "compensation-related" loans may generate taxable income for the employee who is given such a loan, and there are generally no adverse tax consequences to the corporation. Technically, the interest on the loan is deductible by the corporation, taxable to the employee, and then offset by any interest deduction allowed to the employee for the interest the employee is deemed to pay. However, the interest generally is not deductible unless the loan is secured by a home mortgage and the loan meets the requirements for deductibility of home mortgage interest (Code Sec. 163(h)). The amount of interest the employee saves is thus a benefit that may be tax free, although current law limits this to the "mortgage interest" situation. The benefit to the corporation is that it is another inducement to an employee to either join the company or stay with it.

    b. Any loan made to an employee should be made formally with the written agreement specifying the provision for a fixed repayment date or installment payments. The loan should be secured. This could be by the property the employee intends to purchase with the loan. (Note that the employee cannot assign his or her vested interest in the company's qualified retirement plan as collateral for a company loan. This practice is prohibited by Code Sec.

401(a)(13) unless the loan is made by the retirement plan itself.) In the case of a low-interest loan, the amount of interest should be stated. Loans should be made only for certain specified purposes, and the reason for the loan should be included in the agreement.

It is advisable that repayment be required before the executive leaves the company. Provision should be made for what is to occur in the event of death. State law must be checked with respect to possible restrictions on loans to officers or directors.

c. If a company does not wish to provide favorable loans, it could encourage its bank to make the loan—perhaps even at a favorable rate. This approach avoids the troublesome situation that can result if the executive defaults on loan payments to his or her own company. [10]

17. From the company's point of view, financial counseling and wealth management services are desirable benefits because such a plan allows the executive to devote more time to the company by alleviating the necessity of finding time for arranging financial affairs on a piecemeal hit-or-miss basis. In many cases, the company is better able to locate qualified people to perform this service and the company might be able to secure such services at a lesser fee than an individual would. It is also hoped that use of these services will result in the executive getting the most value from the compensation received from the company.

The company may not wish to offer this service because it does not want to be involved in an employee's personal affairs, does not want to be responsible for bad advice, and does not wish to endorse the service that is provided when it is not satisfied with the quality of services available.

For these reasons, if financial counseling is offered, it is advisable to have an independent consulting firm, which will assure confidentiality, perform this service. [11]

18. Under Code Sec. 132 (a)(7), the value of qualified retirement planning services are excluded from gross income. Qualified retirement planning services are any retirement planning provided to an employee by an employer that maintains a qualified retirement plan. The benefit is tax free to an executive only if the services are

available to all employees who are normally provided education and information regarding the employer's qualified plan. [11]

19. The value of personal air travel furnished to the executive is valued in accordance with the Sec. 61 regulations and included in his income. The expense is deductible to the employer as a business expense, limited under Code Sec. 274(e)(2) to the amount included by the employee.

   The company can't deduct the value of air travel for a family member or other person who accompanies the executive on a business trip, unless the cost for the family member or other person is treated as compensation income to the executive as indicated above. [11]

Learning Objectives

An understanding of the material in this chapter should enable the student to

1. Describe and analyze basic provisions of an insured long-term disability (LTD) plan.

2. Describe and analyze special features of LTD plans that can be used to meet specific needs of employees or employers.

3. Describe the issues involved in underwriting an insured LTD plan.

4. Explain the applicability of individual LTD plans in planning.

5. Describe the design and applications of self-insured short-term sick-leave plans.

6. Explain the applications of short-term insured disability plans.

7. Explain the income tax treatment of disability plans.

8. Explain the issues in determining the most efficient use of the tax benefits of LTD plans.

Loss of income is a principal consequence of disability. Even a brief period of disability can mean loss of wages or salary. Most people rely primarily upon current earned income to meet their usual living expenses as well as the added medical care bills. Consequently, there is a need to assure the employee of a continuation of income despite the inability to work. Disability income insurance, the oldest of all group health insurance coverages, has been designed to meet this need.

Disability income benefits tend to be included under many different programs rather than a single one. For example, sick-leave or salary continuation practices, short-term and long-term disability income plans, disability pensions, group life benefits, Social Security, and workers' compensation may provide income benefits to the employee whose earned income ceases because of disability. This chapter covers formal and informal sick-leave programs and short-term and long-term disability income plans.

To properly design a disability income plan, one must take into account all sources of disability income and integrate them to provide an appropriate level of benefits during the various periods of disability. Factors that determine the appropriate level of benefits include the employer's objectives to meet the income needs of its employees while not encouraging malingering. The employer's ability to pay for benefits is, obviously, another important factor.

Private insurance and government benefit plans are concerned with helping individuals face retirement, death, and disability. Of these, disability is potentially the most serious in its economic consequences. A program of financial security that does not provide adequate protection against disability cannot be considered complete. Disability income protection, therefore, is an important element in designing compensation plans for executives and other employees.

In discussing disability income plans, it is useful to distinguish three elements of this type of planning, since these three all work somewhat differently:

- Short-term disability plans typically provide benefits for a limited period of time, generally 6 months or less. Short-term benefits can be provided through a sick-leave or salary continuation plan, without any formal financing mechanism (benefits are provided through payroll on a pay-as-you-go basis) or an insured plan can be adopted (generally referred to as an "accident and sickness" plan). Most absences from work covered under these plans last much less than 6 months.

- Long-term disability (LTD) plans provide benefits for employees who are disabled for several months or longer. Generally, an LTD plan begins paying benefits after a waiting period (generally 6 months, but a lesser period can be used), and benefits continue until retirement age. Thereafter, the company's retirement plan, if any, provides benefits to the employee. LTD plans are generally insured.

- Social Security provides benefits beginning with the sixth month of disability. Benefits are provided to an employee who is "totally and permanently disabled," a more stringent definition than is generally used in private LTD plans. Benefits are also provided to the employee's family. In designing an employer's plan, avoiding duplication of Social Security disability benefits is important in reducing employer costs.

BASIC FEATURES OF AN INSURED LONG-TERM DISABILITY (LTD) PLAN

A long-term disability plan is intended to provide benefits during a long absence from work because of disability. Plan design for an LTD plan involves four broad features:

- determination of when benefits begin
- the definition of what constitutes a disability
- the duration of benefit payments and termination of payments
- the amount of the disability benefit

Elimination Period

Before any long-term disability benefits will be payable under a plan, the employee will have to be disabled for a stated period of time known as the elimination period. The purpose of the elimination period is to avoid the administrative costs of beginning coverage for an employee who turns out to have only a short-term disability.

The typical elimination period is 6 months, although some more liberal plans have only a 3-month elimination period. Some elimination periods are coordinated with the Social Security beginning date (commencement on the first day of the sixth calendar month after disability begins).

The elimination period may require some disabled employees to be without substantial income for a matter of months. If a plan is designed for selected executives, it is common to provide some kind of benefit during this period. Reducing the elimination period in an insured plan is generally a costly way to accomplish this goal, because of the way insurance premiums are determined, so other methods are generally used. Short-term plans are discussed further below.

Successive Disabilities

An employee may return to work after a disability and then be absent again because of a relapse. In such a case, the question arises whether the employee must meet another elimination period before benefits are payable as the result of the relapse. Most plans will not require a second elimination period if successive disabilities for the same or related conditions occur within a 3-month period. Some liberal plans use a 6-month period in place of 3 months.

Definition of Disability

The definition of disability in the LTD plan is an important factor in the cost of the plan, whether insured or not, because it limits the class of employees who will receive benefits. From an employee's point of view, however, disability coverage that denies benefits as long as the employee is able to perform menial employment is not much of a benefit. For executive plans, the definition is usually liberal. Otherwise, it is a matter of cost-benefit analysis for the company. There are generally three types of definitions:

- The Social Security definition of "total and permanent" disability (unable to engage in any substantial gainful employment) is the most stringent.
- The "reasonable qualification" definition specifies that benefits are payable if the employee is unable to engage in any occupation for which the employee is reasonably qualified by education, training, or experience.
- The "own occupation" definition states that benefits are payable if the employee is unable to engage in his or her occupation.

It is typical for an LTD plan to ensure that benefits are provided initially under the "own occupation" definition, with the plan shifting to the "reasonable qualification" definition after some period such as 2 years. In an insured plan, insurance companies typically monitor the status of employees and perform periodic audits of disability payments to determine compliance with the disability status provisions of the LTD contract.

Many LTD plans provide a separate benefit limit for disabilities that are mental in nature rather than physical. For example, benefits for a mental disability may be limited to a 24-month period with an extension for hospital confinement. The trend in recent years has been to liberalize such plans.

Note that under the more liberal definitions used in private plans as opposed to Social Security, it is possible that an employee may recover from the disability sufficiently to be ineligible for the Social Security benefit, but may still be eligible for the employer's LTD benefit. Employers' LTD plan benefit formulas must take account of this possibility.

Benefit Payment Periods

The typical long-term disability plan written by most insurance carriers provides for benefits to be paid until the earliest of death, recovery, or attainment of age 65 regardless of whether the disability is a result of sickness or accident. A few plans are even more liberal and provide lifetime benefits for disabilities because of accidents. Furthermore, where benefits are payable until age 65, many plans provide for a minimum of 12 monthly payments where disability occurs within one year of age 65.

If an employer is covered under the age discrimination law (discussed below and in chapter 10), benefit payments can't generally be denied for employees who are older than some specified age (such as 65) when they become disabled. However, because of the "equal cost" rule of the age discrimination law, the payment period may be adjusted for older employees; for example, an employee aged 61 or under at disability might be eligible for payments up to age 65, but an employee who is 61 or over at disability might be restricted to a lesser number of years of payments rather than payments up to age 65. But note the comments below in connection with age discrimination as applied to benefit payment formulas.

Benefit Payment Formulas

The level of disability benefits payable to an employee should be significant in amount but not so great as to encourage malingering. Taking into account the fact that a disabled employee will not incur the same transportation expenses and expenses for meals away from home, plus the fact that a portion of disability benefits may be received income tax free, implies that disability benefits from all sources should be considerably less than 100 percent of pay. Benefit consultants typically recommend 60 percent to 70 percent of pay as an appropriate disability benefit from all sources.

Plans for selected groups of executives might be designed to provide a greater percentage in order to allow the full maintenance of the executive's pre-disability lifestyle. Executive disability plans might even provide additional benefits for house remodeling, special vans, or similar items since it often requires more income rather than less to maintain lifestyle and comfort in a condition of disability. Such add-ons would probably have to be paid directly by an employer, since most insurance companies would not cover insurance for these items, at least not for very extensive or costly facilities.

Offsets

In addition to the insured LTD plan, disability benefits may also be payable from a number of other sources including

- Social Security
- workers' compensation

- qualified pension and profit-sharing plans
- nonqualified deferred-compensation plans
- state statutory disability income plans
- individual plans

The benefit formula under an LTD plan generally includes an "offset" so that total benefits do not exceed the target percentage of income. An offset can be either direct or indirect. A direct offset is a formula under which a specific amount is subtracted from the amount otherwise payable, in order to avoid duplicating the subtracted benefit. With an indirect offset, instead of subtracting actual benefit amounts to avoid duplicating specific other sources of income, the benefit formula itself provides a lower benefit to reflect the existence of other sources of income. For example, for a group of participants who all have Social Security coverage, the target benefit of 60 percent of compensation might be reduced to 40 percent of compensation for all participants. Direct offsets are more commonly used, especially for a group of executives.

Of all the alternative sources of disability income, Social Security is generally the most significant, providing a primary benefit for the employee and a family benefit for eligible dependents. The typical Social Security offset is a direct offset.

EXAMPLE

Participant Jack Delafon earns $9,000 per month before becoming disabled. Under the company's LTD plan, he is entitled to a benefit of 60 percent of his compensation, with an offset for Social Security. Jack is entitled to a Social Security disability benefit of $1,800 per month. Jack's benefit from the company LTD plan is $3,600 (60 percent of $9,000 or $5,400, less the Social Security benefit of $1,800).

If the disabled employee is entitled to workers' compensation, note that there is an 80 percent "cap." Social Security benefits are reduced so that Social Security plus workers' compensation together equal 80 percent of the employee's earnings prior to the disability.

In addition to a percentage of pay limit from all sources, an insured plan will also provide a maximum dollar limit from all sources. An insured group LTD plan might typically provide for maximums of $4,000 to $6,000 per month, not to exceed 60 percent (or some similar percentage) of pre-disability income.

This maximum might be reduced by full family Social Security and other employer-sponsored benefits with a specified dollar maximum of all such benefits including benefits from the insured LTD plan. A plan for a selected group of executives would, of course, have a much higher maximum benefit in general.

Some plans use two percentage factors, one applicable when benefits are payable only under the insured LTD plan and the other when there are also benefits from other sources. For example, the plan may provide a maximum benefit of 60 percent of earnings up to $4,000 per month when there are no other benefits and 70 percent of earnings up to $4,000 per month when there are disability benefits from other sources. Another approach is to use a schedule of maximum monthly benefits for different earnings brackets. These are examples of indirect offset formulas. Their complexity tends to make planners wary, and direct offsets are more common.

Social Security Freeze

Most long-term disability income plans provide a fixed income for a disabled employee. The result will be a decrease over a period of time in the buying power of a disabled employee because of the effect of inflation. To combat inflation the federal government has built into Social Security disability benefits an automatic cost-of-living increase based on increases in the Consumer Price Index.

In order not to defeat the purpose of the Social Security cost-of-living increase, an insured LTD plan will freeze any Social Security offset at the level of Social Security benefits at the time disability first occurs. Therefore, subsequent increases in Social Security benefits will increase overall disability benefits even if they exceed the limits stated in the plan. Some insured LTD plans have their own built-in cost-of-living increase. For example, the benefits payable under the plan may increase automatically 2 percent per year with the maximum benefit payable under the plan also increasing by 2 percent per year.

When an insured LTD plan offsets its benefit by benefits provided from Social Security and other employer-sponsored sources, it may be that for a relatively low-paid employee no benefits will be payable from the insured LTD plan. Although the employee will be receiving the desired percentage of pay from other sources, the fact that in his or her perspective a benefit promised by the employer has not materialized may make the employee resentful. To overcome this, some LTD plans provide a minimum benefit (such as

$50 per month or 25 percent of the amount that would be payable absent any offset) that is payable even though total benefits exceed the maximum stated by the plan.

Discrimination in Coverage

Disability coverage is one of the only executive benefits for which there are no nondiscrimination requirements for tax purposes. An employer can provide disability insurance benefits on a completely discriminatory basis. It can discriminate as to who will be covered and the amount of the coverage as well.

Gender Discrimination in Disability Plans

In general, the Civil Rights Act of 1964, or applicable state civil rights law, prohibits discrimination on the basis of sex or gender in an employer's compensation programs, including employee benefit plans. This is discussed further in chapter 10. An amendment to the Civil Rights Act prohibits employment discrimination because of pregnancy, childbirth, or related medical conditions. The essence of this legislation is that employee benefit programs must treat women affected by these conditions in a manner equal with other employees, that is, on the basis of their ability to work. An employer may not terminate or refuse to hire or promote a woman solely because she is pregnant. It also prevents mandatory leaves for pregnant women that are arbitrarily set at a certain time in their pregnancy and not based on their inability to work. The amendment also protects the reinstatement rights of women who are on leave for pregnancy and gives them credit for previous service, accrued retirement benefits, and seniority that they have accumulated. (An employer is not required to pay for health insurance benefits related to abortions unless the life of the mother would have been endangered had the abortion not been performed.)

It is important to note that the law does not require an employer to provide disability benefits or paid sick leave to employees or to pregnant workers. However, if the employer generally provides such benefits, pregnant workers must receive the same benefits. Benefits must be paid on the same terms applicable to other employees (other employees receive benefits only when they are medically unable to work), but an employer will not have to allow a pregnant woman to use paid sick leave or receive disability benefits merely because she is pregnant.

Age Discrimination

If a plan is provided by an employer with more than 20 employees, the age-discrimination provisions of federal law may be applicable. These provisions generally would prohibit the plan from denying disability benefits to employees who become disabled after age 65 or some other age specified in the plan. However, for disability programs, an "equal-cost" rule applies, so that benefits for employees who are disabled at older ages can be scaled back in amount or duration as long as the cost of these benefits is the same as that for younger employees.[91]

EXAMPLE

The Compliance Manual of the Equal Employment Opportunity Commission (EEOC) gives the following example. Two employees, A and B become disabled on the same day. Employee A is aged 30 with 10 years of service, and Employee B is aged 55 with 10 years of service. Under the employer's disability plan, disabled employees receive payments based on the number of years they would have worked had they worked until normal retirement age (age 60 in this plan). Employee A will receive a disability benefit based on 40 years of service, while Employee B will receive a disability benefit based on 15 years of service. Since A's disability benefit would be almost three times the size of B's, even though they worked for the employer for the same number of years, the EEOC Manual regards the benefits as unequal. However, if the employer can show that the benefit for the 55-year-old employee actually costs as much as or more than the benefit for the 30-year-old, the age-discrimination law would not be violated.

There are still many issues in age-discrimination law being currently litigated, so no bright-line set of rules can easily be set out. Insurance companies offering disability coverage under their own contract language should have supporting legal opinions stating that the benefit structure complies with age-discrimination rules.

SPECIAL FEATURES OF LTD PLANS

Rehabilitation Provision

A special feature found in some LTD plans is a rehabilitation provision that is intended to encourage a disabled individual to return to work. The provision accomplishes this simply by reducing the individual's disability benefit by some percentage (such as 70 percent) of the compensation received at his

---

91. See EEOC Compliance Manual, Oct. 3, 2000

or her new work rather than disqualifying the person entirely from any further LTD plan benefits. The rehabilitation provision is generally applicable for up to 24 months after the return to work.

Insurers generally find that efforts at rehabilitation can be cost-effective. One recent company study found that for every dollar spent in rehabilitation, there had been a return to employers of more than $10. Because employees adjust quickly to disability income and lifestyle, early identification and early referral of LTD claims are important. Also important in the rehabilitation process is the spouse of the disabled employee.

Rehabilitation efforts are particularly important where LTD claims were filed for reasons other than total disability. This frequently happens where the insured's job was in jeopardy (a layoff was imminent), the insured was close to retirement, or there was litigation pending where the insured wanted another benefit that hinged on "disabled" status.

Pension Supplements

Some qualified pension plans utilize an accrued benefit formula whereby an employee accrues a percentage of pay as a retirement benefit each year (such as 2 percent of final 5-years average pay for each year of employment). Under such a plan, if an employee becomes disabled after only a few years of employment, the retirement benefit, which will be payable beginning at age 65, will often be substantially less than the long-term disability benefit that the employee was receiving up to age 65.

It is increasingly common for employees to be covered only under a defined-contribution plan. In this case, benefits are based on the total amount contributed to the employee's account in the plan over the employee's working career, plus earnings on the account. Thus the cut in benefits as a result of early disability can be particularly severe.

To overcome this problem, an employer may add a pension accrual provision to the LTD or qualified retirement plan. Under this provision, if an employee becomes disabled before accruing the maximum benefit, the individual will still be considered to be an employee for pension plan purposes after the disability, and the insurer will make the necessary contributions to the retirement plan each year. If the pension plan is fully insured, this can be accomplished by a waiver-of-premium provision in the pension plan policy. In the case of a defined-contribution plan, the pension accrual provision would provide for an annual addition to the plan comparable to the amount that would have been added if the employee continued working.

Not all pension plans lend themselves to the use of a pension accrual provision as part of the LTD plan. For example, some pension plans utilize contributions that are not allocated to a specific participant's account each year. Under such a plan, it would be difficult to determine how much had to be contributed for a specific participant in a given year.

Survivor Benefits

Once in a while, an insurer will not be notified of a disabled employee's death, and LTD benefit checks will continue to be sent by the insurer for several months after death has occurred. This problem would be obviated if the LTD coverage and the group life insurance were written in the same company. Another device for encouraging the reporting of a disabled employee's death is to add a modest survivor's benefit (equal to 3 months of benefits) to the LTD plan with the survivor's benefit payable to the decedent's spouse if living, otherwise to the children.

Exclusions and Limitations

No matter how liberal an employer may want to be in providing long-term disability benefits, disabilities arising from certain causes are generally excluded (or limited) from coverage. Exclusions are generally more stringent for small groups. Typical examples include:

- disabilities that result from alcoholism or drug addiction
- disabilities from self-inflicted wounds
- disabilities from war, riot, or the commission of a felony
- disabilities that occur within a stated period of time after the effective date of coverage (such as 12 months) that are the result of a preexisting condition for which treatment was rendered within a stated period before the effective date of the LTD coverage (for example, 3 months)
- disabilities attributable to pregnancy for small employers (fewer than 15 employees) not covered under the Civil Rights Act

UNDERWRITING THE LTD PLAN

Long-term disability coverage is highly volatile. Claims are infrequent but can be very large. For this reason, most employers seek to insure their LTD plans with a private insurance company. Before an insurer will decide to underwrite an LTD case, the characteristics of the firm will be analyzed. This is also necessary in order to determine the premium to be charged.

Negative Employer Characteristics

For certain types of employers, insurers will refuse to provide disability insurance or provide only limited insurance because the nature of the employer's business activities is likely to make claims more frequent or more costly than usual. For example:

- If a firm is in a hazardous industry, the insurer may be willing to underwrite only nonoccupational disabilities under the LTD plan because of the great frequency of occupational disabilities.

- Companies with seasonal employment or high layoff frequencies are avoided by insurers since out-of-work employees are more likely to file claims for disability benefits than individuals who are able to find work.

- Insurers try to avoid companies whose employees perform precision work such that even a minor ailment will result in a disability that will make them unable to perform their jobs.

- Insurers hesitate to provide LTD coverage for production-line employees because experience shows that they may have a poor work attitude that makes it difficult for them to return to work after an absence resulting from disability.

Employee Characteristics

Employees who are to be covered for the first time under an insured LTD plan are generally required to meet certain underwriting criteria. These include

1. Full-time employment (that is, at least 30 hours per week) is required.

2. A specified minimum wage (sometimes used to exclude employees who would receive no benefits because of a Social Security offset) or a certain job classification (that is, salaried employees only) is necessary.

3. An eligibility period for coverage, such as 6 months, serves to eliminate preexisting conditions.

4. In small groups (less than 25 lives), employees may have to provide satisfactory evidence of good health, usually by completing a health questionnaire.

INDIVIDUAL LTD PLANS

There are some instances when an employer should consider the use of individual as opposed to group long-term disability insurance to fund its LTD plan. For example, where only one or two key employees are to be covered, it may not be possible to purchase group LTD coverage.

Where an employer wants to provide long-term disability benefits for only one or two key employees or where the employer is interested in providing LTD benefits for a small group of executives in excess of the amounts generally available through group LTD policies, it should consider the use of individual long-term disability insurance. Generally, individual LTD policies will not be issued without evidence of insurability. However, if the individual is insurable the maximum amount of coverage can sometimes be quite high (but generally not in excess of approximately 67 percent of earned income). Furthermore, individual LTD policies can be purchased that are noncancellable by the insurer.

Individual policies also provide flexibility in design. It is possible to purchase an individual LTD policy that defines disability as being unable to perform in the employee's regular occupation until age 65 (instead of his or her occupation for 2 years, any occupation thereafter).

As an approach when the employer wants to provide maximum benefits in excess of the amounts generally available under a group LTD policy, the employer can consider first instituting an individual LTD plan. Then it sets up a group LTD plan, which in establishing its maximum benefits, will not take into account the benefits provided by the individual LTD policy.

EXAMPLE

Standard Company wants to set up a plan that provides disability benefits of up to two-thirds of pay with a maximum overall benefit of $10,000 per month. It is unable to do so through a group LTD policy alone. Standard does, however, find a provider for a group LTD policy that provides a maximum benefit of up to $6,000 per month. Standard sets up individual LTD plans for its key class of employees that provide disability benefits equal to two-thirds of pay with a maximum of $4,000 per month; and then it adopts a group LTD plan that provides maximum benefits of two-thirds of pay up to $6,000 per month.

Note that before issuing an individual LTD policy, the insurer looks into the existence of any group LTD coverage in order to determine the maximum amount of individual LTD insurance that will be issued. However, applications for group LTD coverage do not inquire about existing individual LTD coverage. Therefore, if maximum coverage is desired, an employer should set up the individual LTD plan before it sets up the group LTD plan.

SICK-LEAVE PLANS

The long-term disability income plan of an employer generally has an elimination period of at least one month and most often 6 months. Therefore, there is a need to provide disability income from another source during this elimination period. One method that is often used for salaried employees is for the employer to provide sick-leave benefits out of the general assets of the company. Such plans may be informal with full salary continued for an undesignated period of time, or the plan may be formalized. In larger organizations, it is always advisable to commit employee plans to writing and communicate them to employees, in order to provide the best position for possible future litigation as well as to satisfy the requirements of ERISA if for some reason the plan is not considered a payroll practice.

Some formal self-insured sick-leave plans simply provide that an employee is entitled to a stated number of days of sick pay per year (for example, 12 days per year). The sick pay received is generally equal to the regular salary of the employee. Such plans often provide for a carryover of unused sick-leave days up to a specified maximum number, such as 75 days. Another approach to a formal self-insured sick-leave plan is to gear the number of weeks of sick pay to the employee's number of years of service in accordance with a specified schedule. Under this approach, depending upon the years of service, full salary is generally paid for a specified number of weeks (or days) after which half salary may be payable for an additional specified number of weeks (or days).

One problem with many self-insured formal sick-leave plans is that they often cease to provide benefits before the long-term disability benefit plan begins to pay benefits. This leads to the next topic, short-term insured disability plans.

SHORT-TERM INSURED DISABILITY PLANS

An insured short-term disability income (accident and sickness) plan can fill the gap between the end of coverage under a sick-leave plan and the beginning of LTD payments. Historically it has been most often used for hourly employees, but some companies also use it for salaried employees.

Benefits

Short-term disability plans generally provide benefits for a maximum of from 13 (or more commonly, 26) to 52 weeks. To select the appropriate number of weeks of benefits, an employer should determine when benefits will begin to be payable under its long-term disability income plan. The short-term disability income plan should then be designed accordingly. Benefits could start from the first day of absence from work due to accident or sickness; but since the determination of when an individual is sick is highly subjective, most plans provide benefits from the first day for absences resulting from accident and from the 8th day for absences resulting from sickness. This design also helps to control the premium cost of the plan, which would be much higher if a shorter elimination period was used for sickness.

Few insured short-term disability income plans provide a weekly benefit in excess of the lesser of a stated dollar amount per week or 70 percent of earnings. The actual benefit can be determined in several different ways. Benefits can be based on an earnings schedule with the weekly benefit increasing as the weekly earnings bracket increases. Another approach is to provide different amounts of benefits for different classes of employees. Still another approach is to provide that benefits will be equal to a stated percentage of earnings, such as 60 percent, but in no event in excess of a stated dollar amount per week, for example $300.

Some insured short-term disability income plans reduce the benefits otherwise payable under the plan by any benefits received under workers' compensation. An alternative approach is not to provide any short-term disability benefits for work-related accidents or sicknesses. Furthermore, some insurers will not write short-term disability plans in those states that have statutory short-term wage-replacement benefits (California, Hawaii, New Jersey, New York, and Rhode Island).

Most short-term disability income plans pay benefits on a per-disability basis. That is, once a disabled employee returns to work on a full-time basis for a stated period of time, for instance, 2 weeks, he or she is again eligible for a maximum number of weeks of disability benefits even for a disability in the same calendar year. For example, in a plan providing a maximum of 26 weeks of benefits per disability, an employee may receive 26 weeks of benefits, return to work for 2 weeks, and then become disabled again and receive additional disability benefits for up to another 26 weeks. To keep plan costs down, many plans modify this provision for employees aged 60 or over by providing only one period of 26 weeks of benefits per 12-month period.

Exclusions

Short-term disability income plans once excluded benefits for pregnancy-related disabilities or limited such benefits, for example, to a 6-week maximum. A justification that was given is that most women do not return to their former jobs after the birth of a child. Such practices are now confined to smaller employers who are not covered under any state or federal civil rights laws prohibiting gender discrimination. At the federal level, EEOC regulations now require disabilities resulting from pregnancy to be treated like any other disability for purposes of coverage under a short-term disability income plan. Furthermore, the laws of many states are more specific and require that the insurer (and not the employer) be responsible for such coverage. Obviously, both federal and state laws must be considered by the employee benefit counselor.

Most insurers will exclude from a short-term disability income plan any disabilities not treated by a physician, any disabilities resulting from self-inflicted injuries, riots, wars, or injuries that result from committing an illegal act.

TAX CONSEQUENCES OF DISABILITY PLANS

Income tax consequences must be taken into account in determining whether to establish a disability income plan and what the design features of a plan should be. There are specific rules for plan contributions (or premium payments) and for plan benefit payments.

Premium payments in an insured plan that are paid by the employer are deductible by the employer and not taxable to covered employees. Premium payments by employees are not deductible. In other words, the tax law favors employer-pay-all premium arrangements, but the economics of the situation may lead employers to require employee copayment arrangements nevertheless.

Disability benefits are taxed based on the source of the benefit:

- Disability benefits received by an employee from Social Security are partly or entirely income tax free, in the same manner as Social Security retirement benefits.
- Disability benefits that are attributable to employer contributions to the plan are includible in taxable income.

- Disability benefits that were paid for by the employee with after-tax dollars (for example, from a personal disability income policy or attributable to employee contributions to an employer-sponsored disability income plan) are receivable free of income tax.

- Where both employer and employee contribute toward the premiums for the plan, benefits are split in the same proportion between taxable and nontaxable amounts. The time period used to calculate this proportion varies, depending on the type of disability income plan and the length of time that the disability plan has been in effect. Under group insurance polices, the time period used to calculate the premiums paid by the employee is the three policy years ending prior to the beginning of the calendar year in which the employee is disabled. If coverage has been in effect for a shorter period, then the premiums paid for the policy years during that shorter period are used. If benefits are provided under individual disability income policies, the proportion is determined on the basis of the premiums paid for the current policy year.

- Taxable benefits are subject to a limited tax credit under Code Sec. 22, if the employee is retired on account of permanent and total disability. (See below.)

Disability benefits (if taxable) are subject to income tax withholding. If benefits are paid directly by the employer to an employee under an employer plan, they are treated like any other wages for withholding purposes. If they are paid by a third party (such as an insurance company or a trust), they are subject to withholding only if the employee requests that taxes be withheld.

Disability income benefits attributable to employer contributions (but not those attributable to employee contributions) are also subject to Social Security taxes, but only for a limited period of time in the case of long-term disabilities; Social Security taxes are payable from the time an employee ceases work because of disability until the end of the 6th calendar month following the last calendar month in which the employee worked.

Tax Planning Issues

The disparity in tax treatment between company-paid and employee-paid disability plans creates an incentive to try to gain the best tax result through creative design of a disability plan. The opportunity to do such planning works best for individual policies and primarily affects smaller companies or plans covering a small group of executives, since the administrative burden can be significant. Essentially, the idea is to provide a plan in which the premiums are paid most years by the company (and are therefore nontaxable to the employee), but in the year in which an employee becomes disabled, the employee is covered under a plan for which the employee paid the premium. Generally employees who are risk-averse, particularly those who are older and consider themselves more likely to become disabled, will lean toward the choice of after-tax payment for disability benefits since they can foresee the need for tax-free benefits.

First, consider how not to do it. The following approach probably will not work, at least if the "lights are on" when the IRS happens by: The company pays the premium in all years, but if an employee becomes disabled, the premium for that year is recharacterized retroactively by some means as an employee payment.

By contrast, the following approach probably will work:

- Flush, Inc., adopts a plan under which each employee has the choice, before the beginning of the year, to elect to pay premiums or to allow the employer to pay premiums.

- If employee Armitage Shanks is in bad health at the time of this election, or has been given a forecast of doom by his neighborhood crystal-ball reader, he will probably elect to pay premiums.

- Because there was no advance certainty to the arrangement, and Armitage has assumed the risk of paying taxes on the premiums (that is, not getting a deduction), the arrangement has economic substance and will not be challenged by the IRS.

- If Armitage becomes disabled during the ensuing year, his benefits will be tax free if he is covered by an individual policy. If Armitage is covered by a group policy, only a proportion of the benefit will be tax free.

Disability Tax Credit

For individuals "retired on disability," there is a very limited tax credit, a dollar-per-dollar reduction in the tax liability (Code Sec. 22) for an individual who is totally and permanently disabled. This is defined (similar to the Social Security disability benefit) as the inability to engage in any substantial gainful activity by reason of physical or mental impairment that can be expected to last at least 12 months or result in death. A formula is used that makes the credit unavailable for taxpayers who receive significant amounts of nontaxable income (such as Social Security) or who have significant adjusted gross income.

How much is the credit? Of course, Congress would never do something as simple as giving you a flat amount you could easily deduct. Instead, you have to use the following formula:

Formula for Computing Disability Retirement Income Credit

1. State "initial base amount" ($5,000 for either a single individual or a joint return where only one spouse is permanently disabled) $_____

2. State amount of Social Security disability or other nontaxable pensions or annuities received. $_____

3. Subtract #2 from #1 $_____

4. State adjusted gross income. $_____

5. State designated figure ($10,000 if filing jointly, $7,500 if single, or $5,000 if married filing separately). $_____

6. Subtract #5 from #4. $_____

7. Compute 1/2 of #6. $_____

8. Subtract #7 from #3. (If this number is negative, no credit is allowed.) $_____

9. Multiply #8 by 15 percent to determine credit. $_____

For example, if a married client had a $12,000 adjusted gross income and received $2,000 of Social Security, the credit would be $300.

The credit cannot exceed either the disability payment the taxpayer receives or the tax due. It's a "use it or lose it" credit; there is no carryover to future years. Worse yet, the higher the taxpayer's adjusted gross income, the less the credit helps, and consequently most estate and financial planning clients will receive no benefit at all from the credit.

TAX EFFICIENCY IN PLAN DESIGN

Disparate Employee Interests

As was just discussed, if any portion of the premiums for an LTD plan is paid for by the employee out of after-tax income, the benefits attributable to that portion of the payment are tax free. By contrast, employer-paid premiums are not currently taxable to employees, but benefits to disabled participants are taxable to the extent premiums are employer-paid. This disparity in tax consequences creates a conflict of interest between the relative minority of disabled participants (who want the maximum amount of wage replacement, that is, benefits without tax burden) and the majority of employees who will not become disabled and want to maximize their current take-home pay.

It appears that the latter interests (those of nondisabled employees) outweigh the former in most cases. In one study, for every $100 on which the disabled did not pay income taxes, the active employee had $117.50 in taxable income.[92] However, an employer may still wish to emphasize wage replacement in designing the plan depending on the degree of paternalistic concern that underlies the employer's benefit planning.

Loss of Social Security Benefits

Social Security taxes are not payable on LTD premiums that are paid directly by the employer or by the employee under a Sec. 125 cafeteria plan. Another way of putting this is that these amounts—non-Social-Security taxable premiums—represent income to the employee that doesn't appear in the Social Security tax or earnings base. Nevertheless, if the employee takes these amounts as cash compensation and pays the premiums himself, the amounts paid do appear in the Social Security tax and earnings base.

As a result of the differences in the earnings base for Social Security purposes, when the employer pays LTD premiums rather than providing them as a bonus or extra salary, the employee's ultimate Social Security benefit is theoretically reduced, at least for employees who earn less than the taxable wage base.[93] However, in practice, the amount of this reduction is generally negligible. The same study referenced above also showed that the

---

92. Luecke and Blair, "Designing Long-Term Disability Plans: Tax Efficiency vs. Maximizing Wage Replacement," Benefits Quarterly, 2003.

93. For an employee receiving the maximum Social Security benefit because his earnings were always above the taxable wage base for the year, there will be no effect on benefits.

reduction in benefits was less than $100 annually for most employees, less than the value of the income tax savings resulting from employer payment of the LTD premiums.

CASE PROBLEMS

Case Problem 1

The Midway Corporation has 77 employees; 17 are management level and 60 are hourly. Salaries of management employees range from $50,000 per year ($4,166 per month) to $160,000 per year ($13,333 per month). Wages of hourly employees range from $14,000 per year ($1,167 per month and $270 per week) to $30,000 per year ($2,500 per month and $576 per week). At this time, Midway Corporation does not have an insured disability income (wage continuation) plan. The company utilizes a self-insured sick-leave plan by the terms of which hourly employees with at least 6 months service are paid full salary for up to 10 sick days per year. Unused sick days may be carried over to later years, but such carryover days may not exceed 20. Management employees are not subjected to a probationary service period. A management employee who is absent from work because of disability receives full pay for up to 6 months and half pay for an additional 6-month period.

At this time, Midway Corporation is interested in revising its disability income plan. It would like to provide some benefits for all employees for as long as the disability lasts or until age 65, whichever comes first. However, the corporation does not want to unduly encourage malingering. The corporation feels that many of its hourly employees make sure to use up their paid sick days whether they are really sick or not. The new plan should discourage this behavior. The corporation indicates that it believes that total disability benefits from all sources of 70 percent of pay is a sufficient benefit. However, the corporation does feel some commitment to its management employees to continue its policy of full pay for the first 6 months of disability. The corporation indicates that it would like to insure the bulk of its liability under a disability income plan.

Design a disability income plan or plans for the management and hourly employees of Midway Corporation that is in keeping with the objectives of the corporation. Be sure to include a description of the benefit provisions you would recommend that relate to each of the following:

    1. the initial period of absence (for example, first week)

2. intermediate period of absence (for example, second week to 6 months)
3. long-term absence (beyond 6 months)
4. definition of covered disability
5. occupation-related disabilities
6. maternity disabilities
7. elimination periods
8. minimum benefit provisions
9. probationary periods

You may assume any other facts that are necessary for the design of a plan as long as they are consistent with those given.

Case Problem 2

The Davis Corporation has 76 employees with salaries ranging from $14,000 to $150,000. The employees are currently covered under Social Security, but the board of directors feels that adequate coverage is not provided for many of its employees should a long-term disability prevent them from working for Davis Corporation. Consequently, Davis Corporation is interested in establishing an insured long-term disability income plan that will meet the following objectives:

1. provide an overall disability benefit from all sources equal to 70 percent of salary from Davis Corporation until normal retirement age
2. encourage an employee to return to work when physically able
3. define a covered disability in a reasonable fashion
4. protect any disabled employee against the adverse effects of inflation

    a. For each of the above objectives, (i) describe the provisions (acceptable to most insurance companies) that should be included in Davis Corporation's disability income plan, and (ii) explain how each provision would accomplish that objective.

    b. Discuss the need, if any, for including a pension accrual provision in the disability income plan.

CHAPTER REVIEW

Review Questions

1. The Apex Corporation's long-term disability contains a 3-month elimination period and treats successive disabilities as the same disability if separated by 3 months or less. [1]

    a. Would you consider these provisions to be liberal when compared to the typical LTD plan? Explain.

    b.Tom Jones, an employee of the Apex Corporation, was away from work for 6 months because of a disability arising from an auto accident. He returned to work for 4 months but then had a relapse and was out of work for 2 more months. For how many months will Tom Jones receive disability benefits? Explain.

2. The Nadir Corporation's group long-term disability insurance plan provides for the payment of benefits up to age 65, but benefits will not be paid for more than 5 years if the disability is a result of sickness as opposed to accident. To be eligible for benefits, an employee must be unable to engage in any substantial gainful employment. Nadir is interested in liberalizing these provisions of its LTD plan. What recommendations would you make that would be acceptable to most insurance carriers? [1]

3. The Apex Corporation is interested in establishing a long-term disability income plan for its 77 employees. Apex would like the plan to provide significant benefits to its employees but at the same time does not want to discourage employees from returning to work. What recommendations would you make concerning the amount of LTD benefits? Explain the rationale for your answers. [1]

4. The Apex Corporation is concerned about the effects of inflation on its employees who retire on the fixed income provided by its LTD plan. What provisions can you suggest that will help combat the effects of inflation? [1]

5. The Apex Corporation notes that under its insured LTD plan, because of the offset for Social Security, some of its lower paid employees who become disabled may find that they receive no benefits from the insured plan because full Social Security benefits will equal or exceed 70 percent of earnings. Although Apex does not want to encourage malingering, it also does not want to be accused of promoting a mythical employer-provided benefit. What can you suggest to overcome this problem? [1]

6. The Apex-insured LTD plan provides for benefits to be payable during the first 2 years of disability if an employee is unable to engage in his or her occupation, and thereafter if unable to engage in any occupation for which the employee is reasonably qualified by education, training, or experience. Apex is concerned that after the first 2 years of disability an employee will be reluctant to try to reenter the labor market for fear of losing LTD benefits. Suggest a provision that could be added to the LTD plan that would tend to encourage a disabled individual to return to work. [2]

7. The Apex Corporation's qualified pension plan provides that an employee will accrue a retirement benefit for each year of service of 2 percent of the final 5-years' average salary with payments beginning at age 65, with a maximum retirement benefit equal to 50 percent of final 5-years' average pay less 50 percent of the primary Social Security retirement benefit. Apex is concerned that an employee who becomes disabled after only a few years of employment will receive a retirement benefit beginning at age 65, which will be substantially less than the LTD benefit that was payable until age 65. For example, an employee who began working for Apex at age 30 and becomes disabled at age 40 will have accrued a retirement benefit of only 20 percent of final-average pay less one-half of his or her primary Social Security benefit. What can you recommend to avoid this drastic reduction in benefits after age 65? [2]

8. In the past, Apex Corporation has had a few instances when an employee who was disabled several years earlier died without the death being reported to the insurer, so that disability benefits continued for several months after death. Suggest a provision that can be added to the Apex-insured LTD plan to reduce the chance of this happening again. [2]

9. Disabilities that arise from certain stated causes are generally excluded from coverage under an insured long-term disability plan. What are some of these causes? [2]

10. Explain why each of the following characteristics of a company will tend to either make an insurer reluctant to underwrite an LTD plan or result in an additional premium charge: [3]

    a. a company in a hazardous industry (a professional football team)

    b. a company with seasonal employment or a high layoff frequency (building trades)

    c. a company that engages in precision work (watchmakers)

    d. a company with many production-line employees

11. What underwriting requirements are frequently imposed on employees who are to be covered for the first time under an insured LTD plan? [3]

12. When might an employer want to utilize individual LTD policies in lieu of or in addition to group LTD policies to fund an LTD plan? [4]

13. The Apex Corporation has had an informal sick-leave plan under which it simply continues to pay, out of the general assets of the corporation, the full salary of an employee who is absent for a short period of time. Several employees have complained about not knowing how long Apex would continue to pay salaries during sick leave. Suggest to Apex the terms of some formal self-insured sick-leave plans that it could consider instituting. [5]

14. The Apex Corporation would like to institute an insured short-term disability income (accident and sickness) plan for its hourly employees. [6]

    a. How would you determine the benefit payment period that would be most appropriate for Apex?

    b. Should benefits be payable from the first day of absence from work? Explain.

15. What is the maximum short-term disability income benefit that most insurers will underwrite, and what alternative methods are used for determining the benefits that will be payable to a covered employee? [6]

16. a. The Apex Corporation short-term disability income (accident and sickness) plan has a maximum 26 weeks per disability provision. Is it possible under this plan for a covered employee to receive disability benefits for more than 26 weeks in any one calendar year? Explain.

    b.The Apex Corporation plan further provides that the maximum benefit period for employees aged 60 or more is 26 weeks per 12-month period. How would this affect your answer to (a) above for an employee aged 60? [6]

17. The Apex Corporation's short-term disability income plan provides no benefits for a disability that results from pregnancy. Is such an exclusion lawful? Explain. [6]

18.   The Topp Corporation has a contributory insured disability income plan under which the company contributes 75 percent of the premium cost and a covered employee must contribute 25 percent. Georgia Green, aged 45 and an employee of Topp Corporation, is permanently and totally disabled. For this tax year she receives $2,000 from Social Security as a disability benefit and $4,000 from the Topp disability income plan in 52 equal weekly payments. Georgia has adjusted gross income of $14,000 for the year. [7]

a. What is the income tax treatment of the premium payments made by

   i. Topp Corporation

   ii. Georgia Green

b. What is the income tax treatment of the disability benefits received by Georgia Green? Explain.

19.   Describe the trade-off between maximizing overall tax benefits to all employees and maximizing wage replacement to disabled employees under an LTD plan. [8]

20.   If employees are given a choice between pretax (employer contribution) or after-tax (employee contribution) funding for their company's LTD plan, what decisions are employees likely to make, given their personal circumstances? [8]

21.   What are the differences in FICA (Social Security) benefits and taxes between an after-tax plan and a pretax plan? [8]

Answers to Review Questions

1.

   a. Before any long-term disability benefits will be payable under a plan, the employee will have to be disabled for a stated period of time known as the elimination period. The typical elimination period is 6 months, although many of the more liberal plans have only a 3-month elimination period.

   b. Sometimes an employee will return to work after a disability and then be absent again because of a relapse. In such a case, the question arises whether the employee must meet another elimination period before benefits are payable as the result of the relapse. Most plans will not require a second elimination period if successive disabilities for the same or related conditions occur within a 3-month period. Some liberal plans use a 6-month period in place of 3 months. [1]

2. Although some LTD plans use the Social Security definition of disability (unable to engage in any substantial gainful employment) to be eligible for benefits, most plans provide that benefits will be payable if the employee is unable to engage in his or her occupation during the first 2 years of disability and unable to engage in any occupation for which the employee is reasonably qualified by education, training, or experience thereafter.

   Many LTD plans provide a separate benefit limit for disabilities that are mental in nature rather than physical. For example, benefits for a mental disability may be limited to a 24-month period with an extension for hospital confinement. The trend in recent years has been to liberalize such plans. [1]

3. The level of disability benefits payable to an employee should be significant in amount but not so great as to encourage malingering. Most benefit consultants recommend 60 percent to 70 percent of pay as an appropriate disability benefit from all sources.

   In addition to the insured LTD plan, disability benefits may also be payable from Social Security, workers' compensation, qualified pension and profit-sharing plans, nonqualified deferred-compensation and salary continuation plans, and state statutory disability income plans, as well as individual plans. [1]

4. Most long-term disability income plans provide a fixed income for a disabled employee. To combat inflation the federal government has built into Social Security disability benefits an automatic cost-of-living increase based on increases in the Consumer Price Index. In order not to defeat the purpose of the Social Security cost-of-living increase, an insured LTD plan will freeze any Social Security offset at the level of Social Security benefits at the time disability first occurs. Therefore, subsequent increases in Social Security benefits will increase overall disability benefits, even if they exceed the limits stated in the plan. [1]

5. To avoid having all benefits eliminated by an offset, some LTD plans provide a minimum benefit (such as $100 per month or 25 percent of the amount that would be payable absent any offset) that is payable even though total benefits exceed the maximum stated by the plan. [1]

6. A special feature found in some LTD plans is a rehabilitation provision that is intended to encourage a disabled individual to return to work. The provision accomplishes this simply by reducing the individual's disability benefit by some percentage (such as 70 percent) of the compensation received at his or her new work rather than disqualifying the person entirely from any further LTD plan benefits. [2]

7. To overcome the problem of loss of pension accruals by a disabled employee, an employer may add a pension accrual provision to the LTD or qualified retirement plan. Under this provision, if an employee becomes disabled before accruing the maximum benefit, the individual will still be considered to be an employee for pension plan purposes after the disability, and the insurer will make the necessary contributions to the retirement plan each year. [2]

8. The inclusion of a survivor benefit may encourage reporting of the death of the disabled employee. [2]

9. Disability insurance contracts exclude coverage for such items as disabilities that result from alcoholism, drug addiction, self-inflicted wounds, war, riot, and the commission of a felony. Also, disabilities that occur within a stated period of time after the effective date of coverage (such as 12 months) that are the result of a preexisting condition for which treatment was rendered within a stated period before the effective date of the LTD coverage (for example, 3 months) may be excluded from coverage. [2]

10. A disability insurer may decide not to cover certain types of company/employer, or cover them only at a higher premium level. [3]

    a. In a hazardous industry, the insurer may be willing to underwrite only nonoccupational disabilities under the LTD plan because of the great frequency of occupational disabilities.

    b. Companies with seasonal employment or high layoff frequencies are often avoided by insurers since out-of-work employees are more likely to file claims for disability benefits than individuals who are able to find work.

    c. Insurers may try to avoid companies whose employees perform precision work such that even a minor ailment will result in a disability that will make them unable to perform their jobs.

d. LTD coverage for production-line employees may be difficult to underwrite because the insurer's experience shows that production-line employees have a poor work attitude that makes it difficult for them to return to work after an absence resulting from disability.

11. Employees who are to be covered for the first time under an insured LTD plan are generally required to meet certain underwriting criteria. These include [3]

  - full-time employment (that is, at least 30 hours per week)
  - a specified minimum wage (sometimes used to exclude employees who would receive no benefits because of a Social Security offset) or a certain job classification (that is, salaried employees only)
  - an eligibility period for coverage, such as 6 months (that tends to eliminate preexisting conditions)
  - in small groups (less than 25 lives), employees that may have to provide satisfactory evidence of good health, usually by completing a health questionnaire

12. An employer might consider the use of individual as opposed to group long-term disability insurance to fund its LTD plan when the group is small-for example, where only one or two key employees are to be covered, it may not be possible to purchase group LTD coverage. Also, where the employer wants to provide maximum benefits in excess of the amounts generally available under a group LTD policy, it should consider first instituting an individual LTD plan and then setting up a group LTD plan. In addition, an individual LTD policy may also provide more design flexibility. For example, a "his occupation" definition of disability may apply up to age 65, or the individual policy may be noncancellable and guaranteed renewable. [4]

13. The gap between sick-leave and LTD benefits can be covered in various ways: [5]

  - The employer could provide sick-leave benefits out of the general assets of the company. Such plans may be informal with full salary continued for an undesignated period of time, or the plan may be formalized, providing a specific number of sick days.
  - Another approach is to determine the number of weeks of sick pay according to the employee's years of service under a specified schedule. Depending on years of

service, full salary is generally paid for a specified number of weeks (or days) after which half salary may be payable for an additional specified number of weeks (or days).

14. [6]

    a. These plans generally provide benefits for a maximum of from 13 (or more commonly, 26) to 52 weeks, depending on when benefits will begin to be payable under its LTD plan.

    b. Benefits could start from the first day because of accident or sickness, but since the determination of when an individual is sick is highly subjective, most plans provide benefits from the first day for absences resulting from accident and later (for example, 8 days) for absences resulting from sickness.

15. Most insured plans provide a weekly benefit up to the lesser of a stated dollar amount per week or 70 percent of earnings. Benefits can be based on [6]

    • an earnings schedule with the weekly benefit increasing as the weekly earnings bracket increases

    • different amounts of benefits for different classes of employees

    • a stated percentage of earnings, such as 60 percent, but in no event in excess of a stated dollar amount per week, for example $300

16.

    a. Most short-term disability income plans pay benefits on a per-disability basis. That is, once a disabled employee returns to work on a full-time basis for a stated period of time (for instance, 2 weeks), he or she is again eligible for a maximum number of weeks of disability benefits even for a disability in the same calendar year. For example, in a plan providing a maximum of 26 weeks of benefits per disability, an employee may receive 26 weeks of benefits, return to work for 2 weeks, and then become disabled again and receive additional disability benefits for up to another 26 weeks.

    b. To keep plan costs down, many plans modify this provision for employees aged 60 or over by providing only one period of 26 weeks of benefits per 12-month period. [6]

17. For a company subject to the civil rights laws, EEOC regulations now require disabilities resulting from pregnancy to be treated like any other disability for purposes of coverage under a short-term disability income plan. State law provisions may also apply. [6]

18. [7]

    a. i. Disability plan premium payments made by the corporation are deductible by the corporation.

      ii. The premium payments made by the corporation are not taxable to the employee. However, premium payments made by the employee are not tax deductible.

    b. Green's Social Security disability benefits are taxable, but only to the extent that Social Security retirement benefits are taxable. With Georgia's low AGI, there probably is no tax on the Social Security benefit. For federal income tax purposes, the $4,000 of disability income from the company's plan is split the same way as the premium payments—that is, 25 percent of the amount is nontaxable (the employee-paid share) and 75 percent is taxable (the employer-paid share). Georgia may also be eligible for the limited tax credit for disability income (Sec. 22). [7]

19. Because of the tax treatment of disability benefits (taxable benefits for employer-paid premiums) there is a conflict of interest between the relative minority of disabled participants (who want the maximum amount of wage replacement, that is, benefits without tax burden) and the majority of employees who will not become disabled and want to maximize their current take-home pay. [8]

20. Generally employees who are risk-averse, particularly those who are older and consider themselves more likely to become disabled, will lean toward the choice of after-tax payment for disability benefits since they can foresee the need for tax-free benefits. [8]

21. When the employer pays LTD premiums rather than providing them as a bonus or extra salary, the employee's ultimate Social Security benefit is theoretically reduced, at least for employees who earn less than the taxable wage base. However, in practice, the amount of this reduction is generally negligible. [8]

Learning Objectives

An understanding of the material in this chapter should enable the student to

1. Summarize the nondiscrimination benefit and coverage requirements currently applicable to employee benefit plans other than qualified pension and profit-sharing plans and describe the changes to these nondiscrimination rules that will be effective after 2010.

2. Describe the options available for designing executive life insurance plans and the relationship of such plans.

3. Describe the basic features of health reimbursement arrangements (HRAs).

4. Explain how health savings accounts (HSAs) can be provided for executives.

5. Describe and evaluate the methods available for providing health insurance to retired executives.

6. Describe the limitations applicable to payments received in connection with a change of control.

7. Describe the factors that must be taken into account in determining the compensation structure and level for executives who are being transferred to a foreign country.

8. Explain what provisions of the tax law can be used to mitigate the double taxation of income earned while an employee is working abroad.

This chapter covers several benefit topics that are "advanced" in the following sense: (1) they involve complicated tax-law issues that are subject to frequent legislative, regulatory, and judicial change and (2) they typically involve a desire to provide particularly favorable benefits for a professional, an executive, or a group of selected executives. In other words, they involve sophisticated planning that requires close attention to the current tax-law climate.

The chapter first discusses the current status of nondiscrimination rules for executive benefits. The chapter then discusses the concept of "carving out" executive coverage in connection with an employer's Sec. 79 plan, medical expense plans, and health insurance coverage for retired executives.

NONDISCRIMINATION RULES FOR EXECUTIVE BENEFITS

As most financial planners are aware, qualified pension and profit-sharing plans must be established for a "nondiscriminatory" group of employees. That is, the plan must not discriminate in favor of highly compensated employees. The term *highly compensated* for qualified plan purposes is specifically defined in Code Sec. 414(q) as a more than 5 percent owner of the employer business in the current or preceding year, or an employee earning more than $110,000 (2011 figure; annually adjusted for inflation) in the preceding year (referred to in Code Sec. 414 (q) as the "look-back" year). The question in this section of chapter 9 is, are there comparable nondiscrimination rules for other types of employee benefits? This issue obviously is important in designing benefit plans for selected executives.

HEALTH BENEFIT PLANS

Health Care Reform

On March 23, 2010, the Patient Protection and Affordable Care Act (H.R. 3590) was signed into law by President Obama. As a result of the reconciliation process, this law was subsequently amended by the Health Care and Education Reconciliation Act of 2010 (H.R. 4872) which was signed into law by President Obama on March 30, 2010. Both pieces of legislation (the "Acts") collectively encompass a comprehensive system of health care reform that when fully implemented will significantly affect nearly every aspect of health care in the United States, including employer-provided group health plan coverage. The Acts are structured so that the new provisions become effective in stages, that is, from the date of enactment to 2018. Thus, many of the mandates imposed by the Acts do not become effective until 2014 and much of the implementation of the Acts' provisions must await issuance of regulatory guidance. Nevertheless, there are some provisions that are effective immediately or in the next couple of years. While a comprehensive summary of the Acts is beyond the scope of this chapter, this section will focus on those changes that are most imminent for employers and their plans.

The health reform legislation contains special exemptions for "grandfathered plans," which require employers to carefully examine the new law to determine which provisions apply to their plans and to evaluate the advantages and disadvantages of maintaining grandfathered status. For this purpose, a grandfathered group health plan is a plan in which an individual was enrolled on March 23, 2010. A grandfathered plan can be a single employer plan, a multiemployer plan or a multiple employer plan. It can also be an insured or a self-insured arrangement. The addition of new employees (and their families) should not adversely affect a plan's grandfathered status. Changes to plan costs and benefits within certain acceptable percentage limits (related to medical cost inflation) will be allowed, but changes in excess of those limits will result in the plan's loss of its grandfathered status. The extent to which a plan amendment may cause a forfeiture of a plan's grandfathered status will have to be determined under the applicable regulatory guidance. Until that guidance is finalized, employers have to be cautious about making plan design changes (beyond those required by the Acts).

The Acts initial impact will be felt in plan years beginning after September 23, 2010. This means that calendar year plans must begin to comply with the changes described below on January 1, 2011. The changes that apply to both new and grandfathered plans for plan years beginning after September 23, 2010 are as follows:

- **Prohibition of Exclusions for Pre-Existing Conditions for Children Under Age 19.** Employer group health plans will no longer be permitted to exclude coverage of preexisting conditions for any period of time for children under age 19. (For all other participants, the elimination of preexisting condition limitations under employer group health plans will take effect for plan years beginning on or after January 1, 2014.)

- **Prohibition of Lifetime Benefit Limits on "Essential Health Benefits".** Lifetime limits on certain "essential health benefits" under employer plans will be prohibited. A definition of "essential health benefits" is not provided in the legislation, but is left to future regulations from the United States Department of Health and Human Services. These regulations are to be informed by a survey to be conducted by the U.S. Department of Labor as to what is typically offered under employer-sponsored plans, including collectively-bargained plans.

- **Restriction on Annual Benefit Limits.** Between 2010 and 2014, employer group health plans may only establish a "restricted annual limit" – to be determined in subsequent guidance – on the scope of benefits that are "essential health benefits." After January 1, 2014, those limits will be prohibited. Annual limits on what will eventually be determined to be nonessential health benefits will not be affected.

- **Expanded Availability Coverage for Adult Children.** For new group health plans that cover dependent children, all children under the age of 26 must be offered coverage under the plan. This coverage will be available to an adult child regardless of the adult child's income, marital status, or lack of status as a dependent for federal tax purposes. For plan years beginning prior to January 1, 2014, grandfathered plans are required to offer coverage to such adult children only if they are not eligible for coverage under another employer's group health plan. The Internal Revenue Code was also amended to provide for an exclusion from income related to the cost of such coverage provided to the adult child. This tax fix is effective as of March 23, 2010.

- **Prohibition on Rescinding Coverage.** Group health plans will be prohibited from rescinding coverage with respect to an enrollee once that enrollee becomes covered under the plan, except in the case of fraud or intentional misrepresentation of material fact as stated in the plan document.

The principal changes effective for plan years beginning after September 23, 2010, that apply only to new group health plans and not to grandfathered plans are as follows:

- **Required Coverage of Preventive Care Without Cost-Sharing.** A new group health plan will be required to cover—and without cost-sharing—certain preventive care benefits, including but not limited to: recommended immunizations, preventive care for children, and additional preventive care and screening for women.

- **Prohibition of Preauthorization for Emergency Services.** A new group health plan may not require prior authorization for emergency services, regardless of whether such services are provided in-network or out-of-network.

- **Prohibition of Certain Preauthorization or Referrals.** A new group health plan will be prohibited from requiring preauthorization or referral by the plan for a patient who seeks certain coverage, including coverage for obstetrical or gynecological care, regardless of whether such services are provided in-network or out-of-network.

- **Expanded Prohibition on Discrimination in Favor of Highly Compensated Employees.** Insured group health plans will be prohibited from discriminating in favor of highly compensated individuals. This requirement previously applied only to self-insured group health plans. Thus, the ability of employers to offer new insured executive-only group health plan coverages that benefit highly compensated executives will be severely restricted.

- **Improvement of Appeals Procedures.** A new group health plan will be required to have a new effective appeals process for appeals of coverage determinations and claims, with clear and easily understood processes and notice requirements.

Additional changes affecting FSAs, HSAs and HRAs are as follows:

- **New Restrictions on What Expenses are Reimbursable.** Certain expenses will no longer be eligible for reimbursement under health flexible spending accounts, health savings accounts or health reimbursement accounts. Among these new disallowed expenses will be over-the-counter medications purchased without a prescription. Thus, for example, employees will not be able to spend down the remaining balances of their health flexible spending accounts to purchase common pain relievers or cold medicines at the end of the year. Plan sponsors should notify employees of this change before they make their elections for the 2011 taxable year.

- **Increased Penalties for Non-Medical Distributions.** Distributions from health savings accounts and Archer medical savings accounts that are not used for qualified medical expenses will be subject to a 20 percent excise tax, up from 10 percent under current law. These increased penalties apply to distributions made after December 31, 2010.

Numerous other provisions, beyond the scope of the preceding discussion, will take effect in later years. These include rules regarding the individual mandate, health insurance exchanges, broader preexisting condition exclusions, Medicare tax changes, guaranteed availability, guaranteed renewability, wellness plan reward increases and employer "pay or play" penalties. These changes will be addressed in later editions of this text, as their effective dates draw nearer.

Insured Plans

For plan years beginning before September 23, 2010, there is *no* nondiscrimination test for health benefits—neither coverage nor benefits—under an *insured* plan (Code Secs. 105 and 106). This means that if the benefits are provided under an insurance contract; the following are permissible:

- The plan can cover only selected executives.
- The plan can cover a large group of employees but provides larger benefits to executives (higher limits, lower deductibles, more covered conditions and procedures, lower copay requirements, etc.).
- The plan can subsidize executives' benefits while requiring other employees to pay part or all of the premium.

For plan years beginning after September 23, 2010, a fully-insured group health plan will be subject to the same nondiscrimination requirements as apply to self-funded plans under Sec. 105(h). The current nondiscrimination requirements applicable to self-insured plans are discussed below. It remains to be seen how these nondiscrimination requirements will be applied to insured plans under the regulatory guidance that has yet to be issued under this new requirement. However, the penalty applicable to discriminatory insured group health plans will be different than the income inclusion required of highly compensated individuals under discriminatory self-funded plans. The statutory penalty imposed on insured plans that violate the nondiscrimination requirements is an excise tax equal to $100 per participant per day. This penalty is imposed on the employer. This form of penalty may affect how discriminatory provisions are addressed in an insured plan. Under self-insured plans, one of the steps taken to avoid the application of the penalty under Sec. 105(h) is to require the highly compensated individuals to pay for the cost of the discriminatory coverage that they receive with after-tax dollars. This avoids the income tax inclusion because the benefit is not employer-provided. However, where the penalty is an excise tax imposed on the employer, this same approach will not work due to the fact that the benefit will continue to be discriminatory and thus, will continue to be subject to the excise tax. This change is not applicable to grandfathered plans.

Self-Insured Plans

Self-insured plans (medical reimbursement plans) are subject to nondiscrimination rules in coverage and benefits. Failure to meet such rules results in taxation of part or all of a medical reimbursement to a highly compensated individual. (Code Sec. 105(h).)

Highly compensated individual has a special definition in Sec. 105(h)—it is *not* the Sec. 414(q) definition. (Unfortunately, there are multiple "bad guys" in the various Code rules for nondiscrimination; congressional action to make the definition uniform has often been suggested but forever ends up on the back burner.) For medical reimbursement plans under Sec. 105(h) a highly compensated individual is an individual who is

- one of the 5 highest paid officers
- a shareholder who owns more than 10 percent in value of the employer's stock (attribution rules of Sec. 318 apply)
- among the highest paid 25 percent of all employees, excluding employees not counted in the discrimination head count (see below)

Coverage Test

The plan must benefit at least one of the following classifications:

- 70 percent or more of all employees
- 80 percent or more of all employees who are eligible to participate in the plan
- a nondiscriminatory group of employees, as approved by the IRS

Benefits Test

All benefits provided under the plan for highly compensated individuals, including dependent coverage, must be provided for all plan participants. Maximum reimbursement limits are permitted (same limit for all participants); benefits may not be in proportion to compensation.

Who Can Be Excluded

In applying the coverage tests, the following employees can be excluded:

- employees who have not completed 3 years of service
- employees who have not attained age 25
- part-time or seasonal employees
- employees in a collective-bargaining agreement if there has been bargaining on the health plan issue and the unit has agreed to exclude these employees from the plan in question
- nonresident alien employees

Design Issues

Prior to 2011, most employers who wished to provide special health insurance benefits for executives simply paid for additional individual health insurance for the executive. Generally, the cost of this insurance was deductible to the corporation and tax free to the executive like other company-provided health insurance. And, this approach did not require any broadening of coverage for rank-and-file employees because the plan was "insured" and therefore not covered by any nondiscrimination rules. After 2010, this will no longer be the case, as nondiscrimination rules will be extended to new insured health benefit plans.

Prior to 2011, if health benefits other than traditional health insurance were considered, the question was whether the additional coverage constituted a "self-insured" plan for these purposes. The IRS position was that if the "risk was shifted" to an insurer, the plan was insured; if not, it was self-insured. This issue as well as a more comprehensive explanation of the tax consequences of self-insured plans is discussed further below under "Health Reimbursement Arrangements."

For health savings accounts (HSAs), there are no traditional nondiscrimination rules, but there is a "comparability" requirement that is discussed below in the section relating to HSAs.

GROUP TERM LIFE INSURANCE

The rules for group term life insurance under Sec. 79 include certain nondiscrimination rules. If the plan violates these rules, (1) the $50,000 exclusion is lost to "key employees" and (2) the cost of insurance over $50,000 for key employees is the greater of Table I or actual cost.

Key employee is defined in Code Sec. 416(i), the qualified plan top-heavy rules. Note that this is not the Sec. 414(q) definition; there's yet another bad-guy definition here. Under current Sec. 416(i), a key employee is any participant in the plan who at any time during the plan year or any of the 4 preceding plan years is

- an officer of the employer having an annual compensation greater than $160,000 (as indexed for 2010)
- a more-than-5-percent owner of the employer
- a more-than-one-percent owner of the employer having an annual compensation greater than $150,000

Coverage Rules

The plan must

- benefit at least 70 percent of all employees; or
- benefit a group of which at least 85 percent are not key employees; or
- benefit a nondiscriminatory classification of employees, as determined by the IRS; or
- in a cafeteria (Sec. 125) plan, meet the Sec. 125 nondiscrimination rules.

Benefit Rules

These rules are as follows:

- Benefits must not discriminate in favor of key employees.
- All benefits available to key employees must be available to other plan participants.
- Life insurance coverage equal to the same percentage of compensation for all participants will not violate the benefit nondiscrimination rule.

Do all employees of the company have to receive the same percentage of compensation? Not necessarily. The company can set up two or more plans, having different benefit formulas, as long as each plan meets the coverage rules.

EXAMPLE
An employer has 600 employees; 500 of them are non-unionized hourly employees and 100 are salaried; of the 100 salaried, 10 are key employees. Plan 1 provides group insurance equal to 1 times compensation for all hourly employees. Plan 2 provides group insurance equal to 2 times compensation for all salaried employees. Both plans meet the coverage requirements (Plan 1: 100 percent of participants are not key employees; Plan 2: 90 percent of participants are not key employees). Both percentages are greater than 85 percent.

Who Can Be Excluded

In applying the percentage tests, the following employees may be excluded:

- employees who have not completed 3 years of service
- part-time or seasonal employees
- employees not included in the plan who are part of a collective-bargaining unit that has engaged in good-faith bargaining on the issue of death benefits

The Limit on Compensation for Plan Purposes

Unlike the Sec. 401(a)(17) limit on compensation applicable to qualified plans ($245,000 for 2010), there is no compensation limit for most types of benefits. That is, the benefit formula can be applied to total compensation rather than the first $245,000 only. However, benefits provided through a VEBA (Sec. 501(c)(9) organization) are subject to the Sec. 401(a)(17) limit (see Code Sec. 505), except that if Sec. 79 coverage is provided through a VEBA, the compensation limit does not apply in determining whether the requirements of Sec. 79 are met. (H.J.Res. 280, Sec. 204(c)).

CAFETERIA PLANS

If the cafeteria (flexible spending) plan provides health benefits, prior provisions of Code Sec. 125 are reinstated. The health benefit under the cafeteria plan will not be considered discriminatory if

1. contributions on behalf of each participant include an amount that equals either 100 percent of the cost of health benefit coverage under the plan of the majority of highly compensated persons who are similarly situated (family size, etc.) or at least 75 percent of the cost of the most expensive health benefit coverage elected by any similarly situated participant; and
2. contributions or benefits in excess of those described above bear a uniform relationship to compensation.[94]

---

94. Effective for expenses incurred on or after January 1, 2011, health flexible spending accounts in cafeteria plans may no longer reimburse for over-the-counter drugs unless they are prescribed. The precise meaning of "drugs" and "prescribed" is unclear and will have to be determined under regulatory guidance. The same rule will apply to health reimbursement arrangements and health savings accounts.

DISABILITY PLANS

Employer-paid disability benefits (insured or otherwise) can discriminate in coverage or benefits in favor of a select group of executives without endangering the employer's tax deduction (as long as total compensation is reasonable). Benefit payments are taxable to the employee in any event.

DEPENDENT-CARE-ASSISTANCE PROGRAMS

Dependent-care-assistance programs under Sec. 129 have specific nondiscrimination rules. Failure to meet the nondiscrimination requirements results in taxation of benefits only for highly compensated employees (Sec. 129(d)(1)). A 55-percent test, Sec. 129(d)(7), requires average benefits to nonhighly compensateds to be at least 55 percent of benefits to highly compensateds.

EXECUTIVE LIFE INSURANCE PLANS

If an employer wants to provide life insurance benefits for selected executives, many approaches are available. Other options can be listed here:

1. Group Life Carve-out for Executives (discussed further in the next section of this chapter)

    a. *The carve-out concept.* An executive now covered under a company's group term life insurance plan (Sec. 79 plan) can often obtain a better benefit if the executive is taken out of the group plan and given a separate individual policy plan provided by the employer. (A group of selected executives can be similarly treated.) Removing these executives does not affect the qualified status of the group term plan for the remaining employees.

    b. *Advantages of carve-out coverage over group term*

        • Executives can be provided with more insurance than would be available under a group term plan; a group term plan requires the same multiple of salary for all employees. Carve-out plan formula can be selective and discriminatory.

        • The plan can provide cash growth that is a "portable" benefit for the executive. In a group term plan, coverage after retirement can be provided only by an expensive policy conversion or purchasing new individual coverage.

- Cost to the employer can be favorable.
- Carving out discriminatory benefits in a group term plan can save an otherwise discriminatory plan.

c. *How to structure the carve-out coverage.* All the methods used to finance executive life insurance are generally available for carved-out benefits. They are

- bonus or "Sec. 162" plans
- split-dollar plans
- DBO plans

d. *Comparison of group term vs. carve out—see chart that follows.*

GROUP TERM VERSUS CARVE-OUT		
	Group Term	**Carve-Out**
Income tax to employee	a. First $50,000 is income tax free b. Coverage over $50,000 is taxed at Table I rates (can't use insurer's lower term rate)	a. All coverage is taxable (except for DBO arrangement) b. Coverage is taxed at PS 58/Table 2001 rate
Premium deductibility to corporation	Fully deductible	Varies; bonus-type plan is fully deductible, nondeductible if corporation is beneficiary
Cost to corporation	Rises if group ages; experience-rated (rises if group mortality or incidence of policy conversion at 65 increases)	Most plans involve level-premium insurance contracts with guaranteed premium
Nondiscrimination coverage requirements	Sec. 79 coverage requirements apply; if not met, highly compensated employees lose part or all of $50,000 exemption	None

GROUP TERM VERSUS CARVE-OUT		
	Group Term	**Carve-Out**
Benefit nondiscrimination requirements	Sec. 79 requirements apply; generally benefits must be uniform percentage of compensation for all participants	None; coverage can vary from executive to executive
Underwriting	Group, with guaranteed issue	Generally individual
Treatment at retirement	Coverage usually terminates or is reduced sharply because of increasing employer cost; also, Table I extension past age 64 will increase cost to employee	Can be continued beyond retirement with no increased employer cost; employee cost is PS 58/Table 2001 cost
Use of cash value or permanent insurance	May result in unfavorable taxation to covered employee	Enhances planning flexibility

2. Life Insurance in a Qualified Plan

    a. A defined-benefit plan can adopt an incidental life insurance benefit. The additional cost of this benefit may allow additional deductible contributions to an otherwise overfunded plan. The deductibility of the premiums produces a net benefit to the participant's estate that generally is greater than if insurance is purchased out of after-tax personal funds outside the plan. An incidental benefit is also possible in a defined-contribution plan, but the insurance premium payments must come out of otherwise deductible plan contributions—the insurance does not increase the employer's deductible contribution limit.

    b. The amount of insurance is governed by the "incidental benefit" limitations set out in Reg. Sec. 1.401-1(b)(1)(i) and IRS rulings. The basic rule is that no more than 25 percent of aggregate deductible contributions to the plan may be used to purchase pure life insurance. Variations of the rule for various policy types and for different plans are provided in rulings discussed, for example, in *Tax Facts* (National Underwriter Company). For an existing plan, this may permit substantial amounts of insurance.

    c. The "pure insurance amount" (the amount of the death benefit less the cash surrender value of the policy immediately prior to death) is exempt from federal income taxes under Code Sec. 101(a).

d. The insured death benefit can arguably be kept out of the participant's estate for federal estate tax purposes on the same basis as personally owned insurance. This requires avoiding "incidents of ownership" in the life insurance contracts. However, it is not clear whether it is possible to avoid incidents of ownership where the life insurance is provided in connection with a qualified plan. As an alternative, in some cases estate taxes can be minimized if the life insurance is second-death coverage on the participant and his or her spouse.

Carve-out Life Insurance Plans

A group term life insurance plan is a popular employee benefit offered by many employers. However, tax-law changes have made this benefit less favorable for owner-employees and executives who desire substantial coverage.

First, complex nondiscrimination rules make it difficult to provide substantial benefits to key executives while excluding or providing minimal coverage for regular employees. The nondiscrimination rules applicable under Sec. 79 generally permit a carefully designed plan to provide somewhat higher benefits to owner-employees and other key executives of a business, but the restrictions are significant.

The tax treatment of the benefits provided by group term life insurance plans creates additional problems. The taxation of group term life insurance under Sec. 79 is rather straightforward. The employer may provide up to $50,000 of group term life coverage in a nondiscriminatory plan without the employee incurring taxable income for such benefits. The employee is taxed on covered amounts in excess of $50,000. The value of such excess coverage for income tax purposes is determined by the so-called Table I rates provided by the Treasury Regulations. The cost of coverage under the Table I rates for the employee's attained age is multiplied by the amount of coverage in excess of $50,000 to determine the employee's taxable income from the plan.

Owner-employees and key executives often desire substantial continuing coverage beyond normal retirement age. Current law and accounting requirements make it difficult to fund postretirement group term life coverage in excess of $50,000 to these retired key owner-employees. (See discussion below). This is unfortunate because these individuals are likely to have substantial estates and need continuing coverage for estate liquidity purposes. However, in 1999 the Table I rates were lowered overall, making coverage for older retirees somewhat more affordable.

EXAMPLE

Suppose a retired executive has $150,000 of postretirement group term life coverage. Since $100,000 of this coverage is subject to tax, the executive would have to include $792 in income annually at age 64 using the current rates. Under these rates, the annual taxable income incurred by the executive jumps to $1,524 at age 65 and $2,472 at age 70.

A comparison of the older Table I rates with the current Table I rates is presented in the following table:

Table 9-1 Cost per Month per $1,000			
5-Year Age Bracket	Pre-1985 Table	1985–99 Table	Effective 7/1/99
Under 25	$.08	$.08	.05
25 to 29	.08	.08	.06
30 to 34	.09	.09	.08
35 to 39	.11	.11	.09
40 to 44	.17	.17	.10
45 to 49	.29	.29	.15
50 to 54	.48	.48	.23
55 to 59	.75	.75	.43
60 to 64	1.17	1.17	.66
65 to 69	1.17	2.10	1.27
70 and above	1.17	3.76	2.06

As the example demonstrates, the Table I costs dramatically increase the cost of excess coverage above age 64. Thus any continuing coverage to these employees above $50,000 will begin to become a tax burden to the retiree, particularly if the retiree's income is otherwise fixed.

The postretirement increases tend to diminish the usefulness of Sec. 79 group term life insurance for providing substantial postretirement group coverage for shareholder-employees and key executives. Since these individuals typically desire some type of continuing substantial life protection, this presents a problem. One solution is the executive bonus carve-out life insurance plan. The following characteristics make this approach appealing:

- The plan is refreshingly simple and easy to present to corporate officers.
- The corporation can be used as a vehicle to provide individually owned permanent life insurance for shareholder-employees and key executives.
- The plan avoids the complex and costly nondiscrimination rules.
- The premium amounts bonused to the participants are deductible as an ordinary business expense under Sec. 162.
- Tax leveraging may be possible since the corporate deduction may be greater than the taxable income incurred by the participants in the plan.

The executive carve-out plan does not necessarily sound the death knell for Sec. 79 group insurance plans. In fact, the Sec. 79 coverage is still quite favorable. The corporation receives deductions for all contributions to a nondiscriminatory Sec. 79 plan. Participants in the plan receive no taxable income to the extent coverage does not exceed $50,000. Since the Sec. 79 plan is a relatively inexpensive benefit and is popular with plan participants, the corporation could continue the coverage under the Sec. 79 plan up to the $50,000 benefit limit. The shareholder-employees and other key executives will, of course, desire coverage in excess of $50,000. These excess coverages are "carved out" of the Sec. 79 plan.

The participants in the carve-out plan are provided additional compensation from the corporation through a simple executive bonus plan. The bonus arrangement should be adopted by the board of directors of the corporation through formal resolution at the board meeting. The bonus amounts will be either (1) paid directly to the insurer for individual coverage on the lives of the participants or (2) provided directly to the employee as compensation to be used by the participants to provide life insurance premiums. An additional feature of the carve-out plan is the flexibility available to the participants. The participant could choose either term or permanent life insurance coverage. The use of permanent insurance is particularly favorable since a primary purpose of the carve-out arrangement is to avoid the higher taxable cost of Sec. 79 group term life insurance in the retirement years of the employee. The permanent insurance can be selected with level or vanishing premiums reducing (1) the bonus cost to the corporation and (2) the taxable income to the executive in the later years.

There are several considerations with respect to providing the bonus to the participating executives. First, any bonus must meet the test for reasonable compensation when the remainder of the executive compensation package is taken into account. Any amount in excess of reasonable compensation will not be deductible by the corporation. This risk should be relatively minor since the cost of the bonus plan should be insignificant when compared to the substantial benefit packages offered to shareholder-employees and other key executives. The board of directors should provide justification for offering such bonuses when passing the resolution to adopt the carve-out plan. The justification could include the need to attract and retain these key executives and the realization that similar benefits are offered to key executives in other firms. In addition, the bonuses could be provided to the executives on a zero-tax basis. Under this arrangement, the corporation provides the executive with a bonus large enough to pay the premium amounts *and* the additional income tax caused by the receipt of a taxable bonus.

The work sheet below helps to calculate the total amount needed for a zero tax approach.

Zero Tax Bonus Approach Work Sheet	
Step 1: State the target premium amount.	
Step 2: Specify the applicable tax rate (including federal, state, local and other applicable taxes).	
Step 3: Subtract the step 2 amount from 1.00.	
Step 4: Divide the step 1 amount by the step 3 amount to find the amount of the zero tax bonus.	

EXAMPLE

JANCO wants to provide executive Kathy Beamer with a $10,000 nontaxable bonus to pay the premium under her cash-value life policy. JANCO will have to provide Kathy with a zero tax bonus of $16,666.67, determined as follows:

Step 1: State the target premiums.	$10,000
Step 2: State the individual's tax rate	.40
Step 3: Subtract the step 2 amount from 1.00	.60
Step 4: Divide the step 1 amount by the step 3 amount to find the amount of both bonuses.	$16,666.67

Note that the 40 percent tax rate used in the example includes a 31 percent federal tax rate, a 4 percent state tax rate, city taxes of 3.55 percent and Medicare taxes of 1.45 percent. In lieu of the work sheet, the following formula can be used:

$$\frac{\text{Amount of premium}}{1 - \text{tax rate}} = \text{Amount of zero tax bonus}$$

The zero-tax approach is particularly favorable when the corporation is in a higher tax bracket than the executive. In that circumstance the corporation's greater tax benefit will shelter more of the gross-up amount paid to the executive. Thus, the executive bonus plan can provide the life insurance for the shareholder-employee and other key executives at a lower tax cost than if the participants purchased the insurance individually.

The executive carve-out plan is an exciting method to provide substantial life insurance coverage on a discriminatory basis to shareholder-employees and other key executives. The plan is particularly favorable since the tax laws and the IRS Table I rates have increased the cost of providing Sec. 79 group term life insurance. The tax changes have been particularly unfavorable to postretirement group term coverage. The bonus arrangement provides the key executives with a substantial employee benefit without the cost of compliance associated with either the nondiscrimination rules or the reporting and disclosure requirements applicable to formal benefit arrangements. The participants in the qualified plan will retire with substantial individually owned life insurance coverage provided by deductible corporate dollars.

The IRS recently took a position that could create problems with the carve-out concept. In a Technical Advice Memorandum (TAM),[95] the IRS concluded that the insurance for the carved-out group in question was itself a group-term plan subject to Sec. 79 rather than a split-dollar plan as the designers intended. The Service concluded that the carve-out split-dollar plan actually had all four of the characteristics of Sec. 79 group-term insurance set forth in the Sec. 79 regulations. Accordingly, it was governed by Sec. 79 and taxation to employees was based on Table 1 (see below).

It would appear that in order for carve-out programs to work as intended, the carve-out coverage will have to be actively designed to avoid Sec. 79 status. If the carve-out coverage involves a split-dollar plan, it may be possible to avoid Sec. 79 status if the plan provides more than a pure insurance benefit—that is, if the split-dollar plan is an equity-type plan. However, the full implications of the current IRS position on carve-outs as described in the TAM are not completely clear at this time.

HEALTH REIMBURSEMENT ARRANGEMENTS

A health reimbursement arrangement (HRA), sometimes called a medical expense reimbursement plan (MERP) is an employer plan that provides for reimbursement to covered employees for medical, dental, or other similar expenses. The plan can provide reimbursement for any medical expense that is eligible for an itemized medical deduction under Code Sec. 213. (The 7 1/2 percent of AGI "floor" does not apply, and the HRA participant does not have to itemize deductions.) This is a very broad category of medical expenses, much broader than generally provided by health insurance. (See the list that appears later in this chapter.) Typically, an HRA provides reimbursement of medical expenses not covered under the company's health insurance that are incurred by the employee and the employee's spouse and dependents. Unless an HRA itself is insured, which almost never happens, it is basically a form of self-insured medical plan discussed earlier in this chapter.

If properly designed, the HRA provides benefits that are tax free to the employee and tax deductible to the employer. Any form of business

---

95. TAM 2000-02047, 1/18/2000. However, this TAM predated the current Split-Dollar taxing regime described in Chapter 6 and is probably no longer valid. Moreover, TAMs are technically applicable only to the specific taxpayer in question in the TAM situation, but as indications of IRS positions they command considerable deference in planning.

entity—a regular corporation, professional corporation, LLC, partnership or proprietorship—can adopt an HRA.

HRAs are particularly advantageous for closely held corporations where family members are the primary or only employees. The adoption of an HRA makes personal medical expenses 100 percent tax deductible where otherwise they would be deductible only as itemized deductions subject to a 7.5 percent of gross income floor.

Design Requirements

If the plan is not insured (see below), the HRA must meet rules intended to prevent discrimination in favor of highly compensated individuals in self-insured plans.[96] The plan must not discriminate either in eligibility or benefits.[97]

The penalty for a plan that is considered discriminatory is that all or part of the reimbursements to highly compensated employees will be included in their income.[98] Nonhighly compensated employees, however, will be entitled to the income tax exclusion in any event.

Eligibility Tests

There are two alternative tests for eligibility and coverage:

- the plan must benefit 70 percent or more of all employees, or if 70 percent of all employees are eligible to be covered, 80 percent of those individuals must in fact participate in coverage,[99] or
- the plan must cover a nondiscriminatory classification of employees.[100] Since this is not a definite mathematically determinable test, the IRS will determine on a case-by-case basis under this alternative whether there has been discrimination.

Definition of Highly Compensated Individuals

A highly compensated individual for purposes of an HRA is the same as highly compensated individual described above with respect to self-insured

---

96. IRC Sec. 105(h)
97. IRC Sec. 105(h)(2).
98. IRC Sec. 105(h)(2).
99. IRC Sec. 105(h)(3)(A)(i).
100. IRC Sec. 105(h)(3)(A)(ii).

medical plans. Note that this definition is different from the definition of highly compensated employee for qualified retirement plan purposes.

Excludible Employees

The following employees don't have to be counted in applying the eligibility tests (and therefore can be excluded from the plan): (1) employees with less than 3 years of service; (2) employees under age 25; (3) part-time employees whose customary weekly employment is less than 35 hours; (4) seasonal employees whose customary annual employment is less than 9 months; (5) union employees who are covered by a collective-bargaining agreement, but only if accident and health benefits were the subject of good-faith bargaining.

If a plan discriminates in eligibility, a fraction of payments received will be includible.[101] That fraction is

$$\frac{\text{Amount reimbursed to highly compensated } \textit{individuals}}{\textit{Total amount } \text{reimbursed to } \textit{all} \text{ employees}} \times \begin{array}{c} \text{Payment received by the particular} \\ \text{highly compensated individual} \end{array}$$

Inclusion, in other words, depends on the proportion of total payments that went to highly compensated individuals. This percentage will then be multiplied by each highly compensated individual's reimbursement. There is no consequence to nonhighly compensated employees.

EXAMPLE
Suppose Graf Corporation's plan fails the eligibility requirements. The corporation paid out $20,000 in medical reimbursements, $5,000 of which went to highly compensated individuals. Of that, $4,000 went to Ginger Steinhart, a company vice president. Ginger must include $1,000 in income ([$5,000/$20,000] x $4,000 = 1/4 x $4,000 = $1,000).

Benefits Test

Highly compensated individuals may not have greater benefits than other individuals. For example, benefit levels cannot be based on a percentage of compensation. The test is applied to benefits available under the plan rather than amounts actually paid. (The mere fact that highly compensated employees submit more claims than other employees will not *per se* make the plan discriminatory.)

---

101. IRC Sec. 105(h)(7)(B).

If the plan fails the benefits test, a highly compensated individual who receives an excess benefit must include in income the entire amount of reimbursement for the excess benefit. For example, suppose Graham Finlay, president of Recycling Co., receives a $1,000 reimbursement for orthodontia benefits, a benefit provided only for him and his family. The entire $1,000 is taxable compensation income to Graham.

Year of Inclusion

Generally, the amount of the excess reimbursement is included in the income of the highly compensated individual for the taxable year of that individual in which the plan year ends. Thus, if a corporation has a plan year end of June 30, and the highly compensated individual receives an excess reimbursement on November 1 of that year, he or she will include that amount in his or her gross income in the next taxable year.

Insured Plans—Definition

The nondiscrimination rules do not apply to insured plans, so the meaning of this term is a key aspect of HRA design. An insured plan is one in which risk has been shifted to and accepted by an insurer.[102] For an example of what this means, consider the following situation:

EXAMPLE
Allon Industries purchases a policy from Slippery Rock Insurance Company, a licensed insurance company, that provides an exact reimbursement of 100 percent of each covered employee's medical expenses. The premium for such a policy is equal to the amount of the expenses reimbursed plus a certain percentage (presumably to provide for the administration costs).

---

102. The Treasury has issued Reg. Sec. 1.105-11(b)(1)(ii) for determining what an insured medical plan is. That regulation specifically states that a "plan underwritten by a policy of insurance or a prepaid health care plan *that does not involve the shifting of risk to an unrelated third party* is considered self-insured for purposes of the section" (emphasis added). Thus, a plan that has been underwritten by a policy of insurance that contains no shifting of risk, or merely provides administrative or bookkeeping services, will be considered self-insured under this section.

However, a regular health insurance program, with risk shifted to the insurance company, is not affected by the law.

This arrangement appears to be an attempt to avoid the pre-2011 intent of Congress when it excluded insured plans from the nondiscrimination requirements. According to Committee Reports relating to the provisions for HRAs, Congress felt that underwriting considerations generally preclude or effectively limit abuses in insured plans so the nondiscrimination rules were not necessary in insured plans. The Allon plan is therefore not what Congress meant by an "insured" plan since there is no shifting of the risk to an insurer.

Eligible Medical Expenses

Here is a list of expenses that typically are eligible to be paid for with funds from an HRA (as long as they are not covered under the employee's health or dental care plan).

Dental Care Expenses

- Braces and retainers, if medically necessary
- Dentures
- Extractions
- Exams and cleaning
- Fillings, crowns, bridges
- Fluoridation—cost to fluoridate home water supply if recommended by physician
- X rays

Handicapped/Disabled Care Expenses

- Artificial limbs
- Braille publications
- Car controls—excess cost over cost of an ordinary automobile
- Care for mentally handicapped child
- Costs for special home for retarded persons
- Device for lifting handicapped person into automobile
- Devices such as a tape recorder or typewriter for a blind person
- Equipment and plumbing—special for the handicapped
- Household visual alert system for deaf person
- Seeing Eye dog and its upkeep
- Schools—special for the disabled
- Telephone—special for the disabled
- Television audio display equipment for the deaf

- Tutoring by licensed school or therapist for a child with severe learning disabilities
- Wheelchairs or other equipment for the handicapped

Hearing/Vision Expenses

- Hearing aids
- Batteries for operation of hearing aids
- Contact lenses
- Eye exams
- Fees of optometrist or ophthalmologist
- Lenses and frames
- Sunglasses—prescription

Medical Fees/Services

- Anesthesiologist's fees
- Chiropractor's fees
- Christian Science practitioner's fees
- Dermatologist's fees
- Gynecologist's fees
- Nursing fees
- Osteopath's fees
- Physician's fees
- Diagnostic fees
- Surgical fees
- Lab fees
- Life fee to retirement home for medical care
- Membership fees connected with furnishing medical services, hospitalization, and clinical care
- Abortion
- Ambulance expenses
- Cosmetic surgery, if medically necessary
- Electrolysis, if medically necessary
- Hair transplant, if medically necessary
- Hospital expenses
- Obstetrical expenses
- Organ donation—expenses of services connected with donating

- Oxygen
- Physicals—routine, school, work
- Sterilization
- Vaccinations
- X rays

Medical Equipment

- Artificial limbs
- Capital improvements to your home—if recommended by a physician (ramp for wheelchair, for example)
- Crutches
- Orthopedic shoes—excess cost over ordinary shoes
- Syringes, needles
- Wheelchairs

Expenses Related to Health Insurance

- Coinsurance amounts for which you are responsible
- Deductible amounts for which you are responsible

Prescription Drugs

- Birth control pills
- Laetrile
- Prescription drugs
- Insulin
- Vitamins prescribed by a physician
- Smoking cessation

Psychiatric Care Expenses

- Fees of licensed psychotherapist, psychologist, psychiatrist
- Halfway house—to help adjust from life in a mental hospital to life in the community
- Legal fees directly related to committing of a mentally ill person

Therapy Treatment

- Acupuncture
- Fee for using swimming pool for exercise—if prescribed by a physician to treat a specific medical condition
- Hypnosis for treatment of an illness
- Kinescotherapy—for cardiovascular and coronary rehabilitation only
- Physical therapy
- Speech therapy
- Treatment for chemical dependency
- Treatment for drug abuse, alcoholism
- X-ray treatments

Miscellaneous

- Special diet if prescribed by a doctor to relieve or treat a diagnosed illness
- Transplants

For a more complete list of eligible expenses, consult Internal Revenue Publication 502 or a tax adviser.

Beware—Disallowed Expenses

These expenses have been specifically disallowed by the Code, the IRS, or by the courts. This list is not intended to be all-inclusive.

- Premiums paid for health plan coverage
- Auto insurance providing medical coverage for all persons injured in or by the taxpayer's automobile, where amounts allocable to taxpayer and dependent are not stated separately
- Contributions to state disability funds
- Cosmetic surgery
- Dental procedures that are not medically necessary
- Diaper service
- Distilled water bought to avoid drinking fluoridated city water supply
- Divorce expenses, even if doctor or psychiatrist recommends divorce

- Domestic help, babysitter, or similar person who provides services of a primarily nonmedical nature
- Installation of power steering in a car
- Marriage counseling provided by a clergyman
- Maternity clothes
- Mechanical exercise device not specifically prescribed by a physician
- Membership fees for an exercise, athletic, or health club where there is no specific medical reason for needing the membership
- Mobile telephone used for personal calls, as well as calls to physician
- Nonprescription or over-the-counter drugs or medicines
- Nursemaid or practical nurse who renders general care for a healthy infant
- Physical treatments unrelated to a specific health problem
- Psychoanalysis undertaken to satisfy the curriculum requirements of a student
- Premiums for insurance against loss of income, loss of life, limb, or sight
- Premiums—any portion of a premium charge that represents a tax
- Religious cult deprogramming
- Smoking cessation program for general well-being
- Special foods taken as a substitute for a regular diet when the special diet is not medically necessary or taxpayer cannot show cost in excess of cost of normal diet
- Toiletries, cosmetics, and sundry items (soap, toothbrush, etc.)
- Union dues for sick benefits for members
- Vacuum cleaner for a person with dust allergy
- Weight loss program

HEALTH SAVINGS ACCOUNTS FOR EXECUTIVES

Health Savings Accounts (HSAs) provide participants with a tax exemption or deduction for amounts accumulated in an IRA-like fund to pay health care expenditures. The requirement for eligibility is that the individual must be covered under a *high-deductible health plan* (HDHP). The HDHP can be provided by an employer, but HSAs do not have to be linked to a business at all and can be adopted by any individual who qualifies.

An HDHP is a plan (it can be insured or noninsured) that has (1) an annual deductible of at least $1,200 (2010) for an individual or $2,400 (2010) for a family, and (2) an annual out-of-pocket limit (deductibles, copayments, etc., not including premiums) not exceeding $5,950 for an individual or $11,900 for a family.

The individual covered under a HDHP is not eligible if he is also covered under a non-HDHP, such as that of his spouse. The individual can be eligible for an HSA even though covered by certain types of "permitted insurance" that don't have high deductibles; these include coverage for accidents, disability, dental care, vision care, long-term care, workers' compensation, hospitalization insurance paying a certain sum per day of hospitalization, insurance for a specified disease or illness, and preventive care. An individual who may be claimed as a dependent on another person's tax return is not eligible for his own HSA, but can be covered under a family plan.

HSAs are an extension and expansion of the existing Archer Medical Savings Account (MSA) provisions, which expired after 2003 for new MSAs (existing MSAs are grandfathered).

Contributions

The maximum contribution to an HSA is a monthly limit. For coverage during the full year 2011, the maximum annual monthly limits add up to $3,050 for an individual and $6,150 for a family. The aggregate annual contribution limit is the *lesser* of (a) the above dollar amount or (b) the HDHP plan's annual deductible. There is a "catch-up" addition of $1,000 (for 2011) for individuals aged 55 or older which apparently applies even if it brings the total above the plan's annual deductible.

Contributions to an HSA can be made by an individual, or by an employer as part of an employee benefit plan. Contributions made by an individual are deductible "above the line" (that is, regardless of whether the individual itemizes deductions). Contributions by an employer are deductible by the employer, not taxable to the employee, and not subject to FICA and FUTA taxes (Social Security and federal unemployment).

HSA contributions generally must cease after the attainment of age 65 and eligibility for Medicare.

Distributions

Distributions from the plan are not taxable if participants use the distribution to pay for qualified medical expenses for themselves, their spouses, and dependents. "Qualified medical expense" means any expense eligible for an itemized medical expense deduction under Code Sec. 213(d), which includes many items not usually provided by health insurance. See the discussion above in connection with HRAs, and the previous charts.

Unlike cafeteria arrangements like FSAs, HSA plan funds can't be withdrawn tax free to pay the employee's share of health insurance premiums (copayments). However, HSA qualified medical expenses include (1) qualified long-term care insurance; (2) COBRA continuation payments; (3) health care while receiving unemployment compensation, and (4) Medicare Part A or B and certain other post-65 payments including employer-sponsored retiree health insurance premiums.

Distributions that are not for qualified medical expenses are taxable and subject to a 10 percent penalty; but there is no penalty if the distribution is made after the account beneficiary's death, disability, or attainment of age 65. This is not as flexible as the regular IRA rules. However, a participant in an employer's qualified plan can contribute to an HSA (but not an IRA) regardless of his or her income.

Funding of HSAs and the Savings Element

HSA contributions must be held in a tax-exempt IRA-like plan with a qualified trustee or custodian. Contributions must be in cash and the fund may not be invested in life insurance contracts. Amounts in the account can accumulate without limit; unused amounts are not forfeited. Also, unused amounts do not reduce the participant's contribution limit in the future. Whatever amount remains in the HSA account when the participant reaches age 65 is treated much like an IRA accumulation thereafter, except that it can be used tax free to pay medical expenses in the future.

Because the benefits of HSAs involve savings or deferral of income taxes, HSAs provide their greatest benefits for highly compensated employees in higher tax brackets. Also, higher-compensated employees are in a better position to defer part of their compensation since they have more discretionary income and can therefore take maximum advantage of tax-favored benefits in general.

HSAs for Selected Executives

An HSA can be structured as an employee benefit plan—as an alternative to traditional health insurance—and this may become the most common form of HSA. The employer provides the employees covered under the plan with HDHP coverage, and makes contributions to the HSA up to the limits applicable for the year. With this structure, the employee pays no income, FICA, or FUTA taxes on either the premium for the HDHP or the amount the employer contributes to his HSA.

Can the employer provide an HSA only for selected executives? Within limits, this is possible. There are no nondiscrimination rules such as those applicable to uninsured HRAs, as discussed above. Therefore, there is no requirement that a plan must cover all employees or a specified percentage of employees. However, there is a "comparability" rule. If an employer makes a contribution to an employee's HSA plan, the contributions must be "comparable" for all "comparable participating employees.[103]" Comparable participating employees are eligible individuals who have the same category of HDHP coverage.

It appears that an employer could adopt a plan for a selected group of executives that would comply with this rule. The employer would have to make the same contribution for all executives in the group with a given HDHP in order to meet the comparability rule; certain participants could not be favored with a higher level of contributions.[104] It may even be possible to create different groups of executives with different HDHPs, as long as contributions are comparable within the HDHP group. It's important, however, to make sure that the Regulations are followed closely.

FUNDING OR FINANCING OF RETIREE HEALTH INSURANCE

Continuing health insurance coverage after retirement is an attractive benefit for employees. This type of benefit provides full health insurance for a retiree under 65, and supplemental insurance after the retiree reaches age 65 and is eligible for Medicare. This is an expensive benefit under current conditions in the health insurance industry, and the employer may wish to limit the benefit to selected employees or executives.

---

103. Code Sec. 223.

104. See Reg. Sec. 54.4980G-5. Q&A 8(b) Example (3).

In retiree health plans covering broad groups of employees, the employer typically reserves the right to eliminate the coverage at its discretion, even for employees who are already retired. Court cases on this issue stress the importance of making this reservation of the right to terminate the plan as clear as possible to employees so that there are no misunderstandings. If the plan covers a selected group of executives, however, the executives might have enough bargaining power to get the employer to agree to maintain the coverage for the executive's lifetime, perhaps within certain reasonable limits to protect the employer. It would definitely be in the executive's interest to explore this issue carefully.

Since the adoption of FAS 106, discussed in the next chapter, the accrued liability for this benefit must appear on the company's balance sheet, so a key issue is how to responsibly fund or finance this liability.[105] There is no one best way to design the plan's financing arrangement, so planners must look at the alternatives and evaluate them in light of the employer's objectives and financial situation. Some alternatives include:

- *Pay-as-you-go.* Under this alternative there is no advance funding or financing. Instead, health insurance premiums are paid each year after the employee retires. This alternative is the simplest and provides the lowest upfront costs. Since the plan is insured, it can be limited to selected executives only, as discussed above. The approach has disadvantages. Costs can be unpredictable in light of current well-known trends in the health insurance marketplace. Also, this method does not reduce the FAS 106 liability, so it has maximum balance-sheet "visibility."

- *Asset reserve.* This approach is basically the same as pay-as-you-go, but an asset reserve is set aside to indicate the company's financial responsibility. This does not reduce the balance-sheet liability nor does it control future costs.

- *Corporate-owned life insurance (COLI).* This approach is a variation on the asset-reserve approach, with the reserve in this case dedicated exclusively or primarily to life insurance contracts on the lives of the covered employees. The corporation is owner and beneficiary of the life insurance contracts. The cash values and death benefits from the policies allow the company to recover its

---

105. For a detailed discussion of the legal aspects of these various alternatives, see *Prefunding Retiree Health Benefits: An Overview of Current Alternatives and Their Pros and Cons,* Colleen Hutchison, *BNA Pension Reporter,* Vol. 18, No. 51, pp. 2299–2308 (Dec. 23, 1991). Copyright 1991 by The Bureau of National Affairs, Inc. (800-372-1033).

costs from the plan. An actuarial study can be used to determine the amounts of insurance required, much like a nonqualified deferred-compensation plan financed through COLI.

- *Increase in pension benefits.* Health insurance premiums can be paid by the employee, with pension benefits increased to cover the cost. If the pension plan is qualified, the employer can deduct the cost of the increased pension benefits as they are accrued. If the plan is limited to the top-hat group and is nonqualified, then the employer's cost is deferred to the year in which the employee receives the benefits. This approach is simple, but there is no certainty that the increased benefits will actually cover the costs of the health coverage in the future.

- *Incidental benefit in qualified plan (Sec. 401(h) account).* A qualified pension or profit-sharing plan can provide health coverage as an incidental benefit (limited to 25 percent of the aggregate plan contributions). The total plan cost is tax deductible to the employer in the year the employer makes the plan contribution. Under Code Sec. 401(h), the fund for health insurance must be kept in a separate individual account for each participant. As with direct furnishing of health insurance by the employer, neither the health insurance costs to the employer nor the benefit payments are taxable to the employee. This approach is not particularly useful to provide health coverage for executives, however. First of all, the qualified plan rules require the health option (Sec. 401(h) account) to be available to all participants. Furthermore, there are additional Sec. 415 limits applicable to 401(h) accounts of "key employees." Finally, the 25 percent incidental limit is viewed by many actuaries as inadequate to fund health insurance benefits.

- *Trust Fund or VEBA.* Setting aside funds in a trust fund, which can be a regular taxable trust or a tax-exempt VEBA (Sec. 501(c)(9) organization, has the advantage that the dedicated fund can reduce the balance-sheet liability to the extent it covers accrued benefits for the retiree health plan under FAS 106. Contributions are limited by Code Secs. 419 and 419A, which significantly limit the amount of prefunding permitted for welfare benefits in general. The use of a VEBA has disadvantages, primarily the fact that VEBAs have nondiscrimination rules and therefore are difficult to use for funding a plan for selected executives. The tax-exempt nature of the VEBA sounds attractive, but in fact the rules for unrelated business taxable income (Code Sec. 512) would result in taxation of most of the VEBA's income in this situation.

LIMITATIONS ON GOLDEN PARACHUTE PAYMENTS

One of the elements of many executive compensation packages is some form of arrangement that addresses what happens if the employer undergoes a change of control. These so-called change-of-control agreements provide that designated executives will receive substantial compensation and benefits if they lose their jobs under certain circumstances after control of their company has changed hands. These change-of-control agreements are found in both privately held and publicly traded corporations.

It is argued that change-of-control agreements protect the interests of employees, particularly senior executives, when a potential change of control could affect the employees' job security, authority, or compensation. Such arrangements also promote the interests of shareholders by mitigating executives' concerns about such personal matters and thereby assuring that the management provides guidance to the board and shareholders that is divorced from such concerns. Moreover, such arrangements can help insure that the management team stays intact before, during, and after a change of control, thereby protecting the interests not only of the company's shareholders, but also of any acquirer.

Typically, change-of-control arrangements arise under employment or severance agreements with senior executives. These are sometimes called "golden parachutes" because they provide generous protection for executives who "bail out" of the company involuntarily or voluntarily—after a change of control. The severance benefits typically include severance pay for 2 or 3 years of compensation (sometimes including bonuses as well as salary), plus medical benefits for a like period and outplacement services. They may also include continued or accelerated vesting of restricted stock, stock options, deferred compensation, or supplemental or excess retirement benefits. Finally, they may provide for reimbursement of legal fees and costs that the executive may have to incur in enforcing the agreement.

Sometimes, the executive is entitled to the severance benefits if his or her employment terminates for any reason during a certain period after the change of control (say, 1 to 3 years)—even if the employee simply quits the job; these are called "single-trigger" arrangements. Under "double-trigger" arrangements, the executive is entitled to the severance benefits only if the company terminates the executive involuntarily or the executive resigns for a good reason within a certain period after the change of control. (Good reason to resign usually includes a reduction in the executive's duties, responsibilities, authority, title, compensation, or benefits, or relocation beyond a certain distance.) Under a modified double-trigger arrangement, a double trigger exists for a certain period (say, one year) and then a single trigger exists for a window period (say, 30 days), during which the executive can resign for any reason and collect the severance benefits. Such an arrangement provides economic incentives for an executive to stay for a transition period after the change of control and allows the company and the executive to negotiate for continued employment thereafter if they so choose.

In the 1980s there was a significant increase in the number of mergers and acquisitions which typically provided senior executives with substantial golden parachute payments under change-of-control agreements. This caused Congress to become concerned about abusively large payments made to executives when a corporation was acquired. In response to this perceived abuse, Congress enacted a pair of provisions designed to reduce or eliminate these payments. Code Secs. 280G and 4999, both entitled "Golden parachute payments," are punitive tax provisions designed to discourage corporations from making, and executives from receiving, abusively large payments when a corporation is acquired.

With Sec. 280G, Congress attacked corporations by disallowing a corporate income tax deduction that was intended to discourage parachute payments to executives. With Sec. 4999, Congress attacked executives receiving excess golden parachute payments by imposing a new 20 percent excise tax that was intended to discourage the executive's receipt of these payments.

Parachute Payments

A "parachute payment" results when the payments received by an employee that are contingent on a change of control equal or exceed an amount based on the employee's prior earnings from the employer, referred to as the "base amount." The employee's "base amount" is the average of the employee's annual taxable compensation (that is, the W-2 amount) paid by the employer for the 5 years (or any shorter period of employment) before the year of the change of control; this includes, for example, gain recognized from the exercise of nonqualified stock options, but does not include deferred compensation. The total parachute payment is the amount by which the payments made that are contingent on the change of control exceeds three times the employee's base amount. These payments include not only cash payments, such as severance pay and bonuses triggered by the change of control, but also the economic value of benefits, such as the accelerated vesting of stock rights and deferred compensation. A parachute payment also includes any payment in the nature of compensation to an individual if the payment is pursuant to an agreement that violates any generally enforced securities laws or regulations.

Once it has been determined that parachute payments have been made, whether it be a dollar or more, Code Sec. 4999 imposes a 20 percent excise tax on the executive. The amount subject to the excise tax is not just imposed on the parachute payment. Rather the existence of the parachute payment merely serves as a triggering event. The excise tax is imposed on the excess parachute payment which is the amount by which the total parachute payments exceed the base amount.

EXAMPLE

Richard Lionhart is Chief Financial Officer of Epic Corporation, a publicly traded corporation. All of the assets of Epic Corporation have recently been sold to Jupiter Software Corporation, another publicly traded corporation. Richard has a change of control agreement that pays him $1,750,000 if Epic has a change of control. Immediately prior to the change of control Richard had a base amount of $430,000. Richard's parachute payment is $460,000 ($1,750,000 – (3 x $430,000)). However, the excise tax that is imposed by Sec. 4999 on Richard is $264,000 (20% x ($1,750,000 – 430,000)).

Disqualified Individuals

A corporation may pay severance and other benefits to a large number of its employees following a change of control. However, the excess parachute payment restrictions only apply to "disqualified individuals" (DIs). DIs include certain officers, shareholders, or highly compensated individuals who are employees or independent contractors of the acquired corporation or of any corporation connected to the corporation by a parent-subsidiary relationship through 80 percent or more ownership (an "affiliated group member"). The regulations clarify the DI definition so that fewer individuals will fall within that definition. The definition of a DI as interpreted by the Sec. 280G regulations, include the following:

Shareholders

A shareholder is considered a DI if he or she owns stock with a fair market value that exceeds 1 percent of the total fair market value of the outstanding shares of all classes of the corporation's stock.

Officers

Whether an individual is an officer of the corporation is determined on the basis of all the facts and circumstances of the individual's situation, such as his or her authority and the nature of his or her duties. An officer generally means an administrative executive who is in regular and continuous service with the corporation or an affiliated group member. No more than 50 employees (or, if less, the greater of three employees or 10 percent of the employees) will be treated as officers who are DIs.

Highly Compensated Individuals

A highly compensated individual is an individual (1) whose compensation, on an annualized basis, is at least equal to the limit set forth in the definition of "highly compensated employee" under Code Sec. 414(q) and (2) who was part of the group consisting of the highest paid 1 percent of the employees (or, if less, the highest paid 250 employees) of the corporation and its affiliated group members.

An individual is considered a DI with respect to a corporation during the 12-month period prior to and ending on the date of the change of control. For example, if a corporation incurs a change of control on July 31, 2010, the DI determination period would begin on August 1, 2009, and end on July 31, 2010. Thus, the determination period for any change of control will be the 12 months immediately preceding the change of control, regardless of when the change occurs during a year.

Small Business Exemption

Code Sec. 280G(b)(5) contains an exemption for a "small business corporation," which includes any corporation that, immediately before the change of control:

1. is a small business corporation under Code Sec. 1361(b); or
2. has no stock that is readily tradeable on an established securities market or otherwise, and that satisfies certain shareholder approval requirements with respect to the payments to the DIs.

Code Sec. 280G(b)(5)(B) provides that a corporation satisfies the shareholder approval requirements if: (1) the payment was approved by a vote of the persons who owned, immediately before the change of control, more than 75 percent of the voting power of all outstanding stock of the corporation, and (2) there was adequate disclosure to shareholders of all material facts concerning all payments that, but for this exception, would be parachute payments to a DI. Stock held by a DI is disregarded in determining whether the "more than 75 percent" approval requirement has been met.

Change-of-control agreements typically address the tax issues raised by Sec. 280G in one of three ways: (1) "grossing up" the payment so that the DI receives the full value of the package net of the excise tax; (2) capping the parachute payments at $1 less than the safe harbor amount, that is, 3 x the base amount; or (3) reducing the parachute payment to the safe harbor if doing so would put the DI in a better position than doing nothing, In other words, an excess parachute payment cap is applied only if the net after-tax payment to a DI is greater by applying the $1 less than the safe harbor amount limit than would result if the $1 less than the safe harbor amount limit was not applied. The first approach is the most generous to the DI, but may be perceived as expensive for the employer, though the amount might be small relative to the amount of the underlying transaction. The second approach restricts the value of the package to the DI, sometimes effectively nullifying the value of such enhancements as accelerated vesting of stock interests and deferred compensation. The third approach balances these interests somewhat.

INTERNATIONAL ASPECTS OF EXECUTIVE COMPENSATION

As a consequence of the ever increasing globalization of the United States economy, more and more United States businesses have established foreign subsidiaries, offices and facilities that employ both United States citizens and citizens of one or more foreign countries. For these multinational companies there are generally three scenarios that involve foreign transfers: (1) sending a United States citizen to work in a foreign country; (2) importing a foreign national to live and to work in the United States; and (3) sending a foreign national or resident to live and to work in a third country for the United States company.

Each of these scenarios has several considerations in common, but this section will only focus on the first scenario and look at the factors that are involved in compensation planning for employees who will be taking an overseas assignment (hereinafter referred to as an "expatriate"). Typically, it is appropriate to reach an agreement with the expatriate, prior to transfer, on a compensation arrangement that addresses those unique problems that are associated with foreign service. Of necessity, this arrangement will go beyond the usual subjects of salary, bonuses and benefits that are covered in domestic employment agreements. It must cover various allowances and reimbursements that are intended to ensure that the expatriate does not incur expenses beyond those that would have been incurred had the expatriate continued to be employed in the United States.

Moreover, the expatriate's agreement should enable the expatriate to make as smooth a transition to and from the foreign location as possible, to maintain his standard of living while on the foreign assignment and to ensure that the expatriate will be able to handle the difficulties inherent in relocating and living in a foreign locale. In particular, some of the factors that should be taken into account include the following: (i) the intended duration of the foreign assignment; assignments of more than a year will generally require a complete move by the expatriate and her family; (ii) the location of the assignment; the greater the hardship involved in living in a particular location, the greater may be the incentive provided to take the assignment; (iii) the expatriate's position in the United States company (hereafter referred to as the "employer"); the more senior the position, the more individualized the arrangements may be; (iv) immigration and residency rules; and (v) the tax treatment of compensation under applicable tax laws and treaties; the potential for double taxation will affect the expatriate's compensation levels.

The employer must also decide whether the expatriate's compensation level and structure will be determined in accordance with the compensation policies in effect in one of three locations—the home country, the host country or the headquarters company, if different. Under the home country approach, the expatriate's compensation level and structure will be determined in accordance with the same criteria as are used to determine the salary and bonuses of domestic executives who have comparable positions in the expatriate's home country. On the other hand, the host country and the headquarters approaches determine compensation levels and structures based in the expatriate's host country and at the employer's headquarters, respectively. Each of these approaches is then modified to incorporate the special incentives, allowances and reimbursements that the expatriate has specifically negotiated into the compensation arrangement associated with her particular assignment.

The home country approach is most typically used where the transfer involves only a few expatriates and the employer anticipates their return within a few years. This approach is also followed where an expatriate transfers from a country with a high level of executive compensation and standard of living to a country where such levels are lower. Alternatively, the host country approach may be a better fit when it is anticipated that a foreign assignment will last a significant number of years; the expatriate is not expected to return home; or the host country's compensation levels and standard of living are higher than those of the home country.

Finally, there is no question that the after-tax value of the compensation paid to an expatriate while on foreign assignment is one of the principal elements in deciding whether to accept employment in a foreign country that will last for an extended period of time. The goal of the expatriate is to ensure that her after-tax position is comparable to the position she would have been in had she remained in the United States. In order to preserve such after-tax value, the employer must adopt an appropriate tax policy. Generally, this is accomplished by means of providing some form of "tax equalization" reimbursement to the expatriate. The concept of tax equalization requires that a comparison be made of the expatriate's "hypothetical tax," determined by looking at the tax that she would have incurred had she continued to be employed in the United States, and the expatriate's total tax incurred while on foreign assignment. If based on this comparison the expatriate's actual tax burden is greater than her hypothetical tax, the employer will usually reduce the expatriate's compensation by the amount of her hypothetical tax and then will reimburse the expatriate for the amount of the home country and host country taxes actually incurred. The determination of the hypothetical tax is clearly a crucial element in any viable tax equalization policy. The employer must decide (i) the specific types of taxes that will be taken into account under the policy, for example, federal, state, local and Social Security taxes; (ii) whether bonuses and other incentive pay will be taken into account in calculating gross income; (iii) whether a certain amount of itemized deductions will be assumed; (iv) whether income from sources outside the employer will be considered; and (v) whether the expatriate's actual filing status will be used or whether a predetermined status will applied to all expatriates.

Income Tax Treatment of U. S. Citizens Working Abroad

As a consequence of the fact that the United States taxes its citizens and residents on their worldwide income regardless of the country in which it is earned or in which the taxpayer resides, such citizens and residents will usually be subject to double taxation on income earned while working abroad. Such income will initially be taxed by the host country and then will be taxed again by the United States on the basis of the taxpayer's citizenship or residency. A number of provisions in the Internal Revenue Code and provisions under tax treaties have been adopted for the purpose of mitigating such double taxation. The Code provisions include the foreign earned income exclusion, the foreign housing expense exclusion and the foreign tax credit. The financial services professional should be familiar with the availability and effect of each of these statutory provisions.

Income and Housing Exclusions

United States citizens and residents working in a foreign country may be able to exclude all or a portion of their foreign earned income, as well as certain employer-provided housing amounts, in determining taxable income under the Code. To be eligible for the foreign earned income and the foreign housing exclusions individuals must:

1. maintain their "tax home" in a foreign country;
2. satisfy either a "bona fide residence" or "physical presence" test; and
3. receive foreign earned income or employer-provided housing.

An expatriate's "tax home" is generally located at her place of business or employment. It is generally not located at the expatriate's "abode", that is, residence, dwelling, domicile or family home. An expatriate will not be considered to have a tax home in a foreign country if the expatriate is permanently or indefinitely engaged to work as an employee or self-employed individual. Having a "tax home" in a given location does not necessarily mean that the given location is the expatriate's residence or domicile for tax purposes.

EXAMPLE

Adam Ross is employed on an off-shore oil rig in the territorial waters of Great Britain. Adam works a 28 day on/28 day off schedule. He returns to his family residence in Texas during his off periods. Adam is considered to have an abode in the United States, but he does not have a tax home in Great Britain. The result would be different if Adam went to a residence in Great Britain on his off days.

An expatriate must also meet either the "bona fide residence" test or the "physical presence" test to qualify for the foreign earned income and housing exclusions. The bona fide residence test involves a determination of the nature and duration of the foreign assignment and living arrangements. To satisfy this test, the expatriate must reside in a foreign country for an uninterrupted period that includes at least one full taxable year. Once a bona fide residence has been established for the minimum uninterrupted period, the actual period of such residence will be deemed to start on the first day of such residence and end on the date the residence is abandoned.[106]

EXAMPLE 1
Christie Blankley has a domicile in Cleveland, Ohio. Christie goes to work in Edinburgh, Scotland. The fact that Christie goes to Scotland does not automatically make Scotland her bona fide residence. She could be going for only a temporary period of time. However, if Christie is going to work for an extended period of time and she sets up permanent quarters there for herself, she probably will have established a bona fide residence in Scotland, even though she may intend to return eventually to Cleveland.
EXAMPLE 2
Peter Woods becomes a resident of a foreign country for a continuous period of 22 months from February 1, 2009 to December 1, 2010. He does not meet the bona fide residency test, since he is not a resident of a foreign country for an uninterrupted period coinciding with an entire taxable year, that is, a calendar year.
EXAMPLE 3
Mona Jones transfers to France on July 15, 2009, immediately establishes a residence and then on March 15, 2011, abandons it and returns to the United States. Mona would have established a bona fide residence in France for the 2010 tax year and the period of such residence would then include the period from July 15, 2009, through March 14, 2011. For these purposes, temporary visits to the United States will not be considered an interruption of the residency period.

The physical presence test may involve some degree of recordkeeping, depending on the business and personal travel requirements of the expatriate. To satisfy this test, the expatriate must be present in a foreign country or countries for 330 full days during a period of twelve consecutive months. Any twelve consecutive month period may be utilized and the applicable period does not have to start on the first day or end on the last day of the expatriate's assignment. In addition, one twelve consecutive month

---

106. This test is available to all United States citizens, but is only available to a United States resident alien if she is a citizen or national of a country which has entered into a tax treaty with the United States.

period may overlap with another twelve consecutive month period, provided that the 330 day requirement is satisfied within each such period.

For this purpose, "full" means a continuous twenty-four hour period which commences at midnight and ends on the following midnight. Any time spent in the United States or over international waters will prevent a day from counting toward the 330-day requirement.

Foreign Earned Income and Housing Expenses

"Foreign earned income" is income that is received from foreign sources for services performed during the period the expatriate (i) has established a tax home in the foreign country and (ii) satisfies either the bona fide residence test or the physical presence test. Earned income, for this purpose, includes wages, salaries, professional fees, bonuses and commissions for services performed in the foreign country. The fair market value of noncash compensation items, for example, a house or a car, and any allowances received by the expatriate would also constitute earned income.

Reimbursements for moving expenses for outbound moves from the United States are considered foreign source income and thus are eligible for exclusion. Conversely, reimbursements for moving expenses associated with inbound moves to the United States are not eligible for the foreign earned income exclusion, unless paid pursuant to a written agreement entered into prior to the initial move from the United States. Consequently, it should be a routine practice for the initial agreement governing any transfer overseas to specifically commit the employer to providing a moving expense reimbursement for the eventual move back to the United States.

The foreign housing expense exclusion is available only for amounts that are paid by an employer for reasonable foreign housing expenses of an expatriate. Moreover, an amount will qualify for the housing expense exclusion only if it is attributable to the period during which the expatriate has a tax home in a foreign country and satisfies either the bona fide residence test or the physical presence test. Qualifying housing expenses include rent, the fair rental value of housing provided in-kind by an employer, repairs, utilities (other than telephone), real and personal property insurance, nondeductible occupancy taxes, rental cost of furniture and fees for residential parking. Expenses that do not qualify for the housing exclusion include deductible interest and taxes, the cost of purchasing a home, mortgage payments, pay television subscriptions, real property improvements, purchases of furniture and depreciation and amortization expense.

Amount of Exclusions and Effect of Election

The foreign earned income and foreign housing expense exclusions can be elected separately, but if both are elected the foreign housing expense exclusion is generally calculated first. An expatriate may claim a foreign housing expense exclusion in an amount equal to her qualifying foreign housing expenses that exceed a base amount. The base amount is 16% of the annual salary of a United States government employee at a salary level of GS-14, step 1. This establishes the base amount at approximately $15,000.

The maximum foreign earned income exclusion that may be claimed is $80,000 which beginning in 2007 is adjusted for inflation ($92,900 for 2011). The expatriate may not, however, exclude more than the amount of the expatriate's foreign earned income for the year in excess of the amount of her foreign housing exclusion. If an expatriate qualifies under the bona fide residence test or the physical presence test for only part of a tax year, the maximum foreign earned income exclusion is adjusted based on the number of days during which those tests are satisfied during the year.

EXAMPLE
Timothy Edgar qualified for the foreign earned income exclusion under the bona fide residence test for 75 days in 2011. Tim can exclude a maximum of 75/365 of $92,900, or $19,089, of his foreign earned income for 2011. If Tim can qualify under the bona fide residence test for all of 2012, he can exclude his foreign earned income up to the 2012 limit.

Once the foreign earned income and foreign housing expense exclusions are elected, the elections remain in effect until revoked. Any revocation prevents the expatriate from making a new election for the next five tax years unless the IRS consents to the new election.[107]

The decision to make the election to take advantage of the foreign earned income and foreign housing expense exclusions will depend on several factors. If the expatriate is working in a foreign country that has little or no income taxes on wages, then it is probably advisable to make the election and forego the deductions and foreign tax credit. On the other hand, if the

---

107. An election to take the foreign earned income exclusion or the foreign housing expense exclusion will be deemed revoked if the expatriate claims a foreign tax credit for amounts that would qualify for the exclusions.

expatriate is working in a foreign country with a tax rate higher than the United States tax rate, then it may be advisable to forego the exclusion and take the deductions and the foreign tax credit. The foreign tax credit will offset any United States taxes owed and any excess foreign tax credit may be carried forward.

Foreign Tax Credit

The foreign tax credit is another statutory provision intended to mitigate the adverse effects of double taxation of the same income by both the United States and the foreign host country. The credit is available to United States citizens and resident aliens and, unlike the foreign earned income and foreign housing expense exclusions, the credit may be elected on an annual basis. While the expatriate is also permitted to deduct certain taxes paid to the host country instead of taking a credit, the credit is generally considered more advantageous because it is a dollar-for-dollar reduction of the United States tax liability and can be carried back two years and forward for five years if not fully utilized in the year it arises.

The foreign tax credit is limited to income taxes paid or accrued to a foreign country on foreign source income and, consequently, it does not reduce United States taxes on United States source income. While the computations involving the credit can be somewhat complicated, there is a limit on the amount of foreign taxes that may be used as a credit. Generally, if the expatriate has only compensation income, the credit limitation is determined by multiplying the expatriate's United States tax liability for the year by a fraction, the numerator of which is taxable income from foreign sources and the denominator of which is total worldwide income, as indicated below:

Tenative U.S. tax limitation = Foreign source taxable income ÷ Worldwide taxable income (determined before credit) x U.S. tax liability

EXAMPLE
Sam Elliot, a U.S. taxpayer, has worldwide taxable income of $1 million and owes U.S. taxes of $200,000 prior to the foreign tax credit. The effective U.S. tax rate is 20% ($200,000 divided by $1 million). Sam earned $100,000 from foreign sources and $900,000 from U.S. sources. The maximum amount of foreign tax credit is $20,000 (20% of $100,000) even though Sam may have paid more than $20,000 in foreign taxes on the $100,000 of foreign source income.

There is a second limitation after the maximum tax credit is determined under the above formula. The foreign tax credit can never exceed the actual amount of foreign taxes paid on foreign source income.

CHAPTER REVIEW

Review Questions

1. Briefly describe the nondiscrimination requirements applicable to Code Sec. 105/106 health and accident plans after 2010. [1]

2. Describe the coverage and benefit nondiscrimination rules applicable to group term life insurance. [1]

3. Under current law, what types of employee benefit plans (other than qualified retirement plans, health and accident plans, and group term life insurance) involve nondiscrimination requirements? [1]

4. What are the specific benefits of a group term life insurance plan, and how relevant are these benefits to highly compensated executives? [2]

5. Arnold Wormwood, a key executive of Alpha Company, expects to have considerable need for life insurance protection after retirement for estate liquidity and other reasons. What is the best way to provide substantial postretirement life insurance for an executive in this situation? [2]

6. Describe the "carve-out" concept for executive life insurance. [2]

7. How can "carve-out" life insurance coverage be structured? [2]

8. Refuse Processors, Inc., is a closely held corporation with 30 employees. The company has an insured comprehensive major medical plan that covers all 30 employees. The plan has substantial deductible and coinsurance provisions. For calendar year 2011, Milo Refuse, the company's president, is investigating two proposals: (1) a plan under which the company would directly reimburse the president and three other executives for deductibles and coinsurance payments and (2) a plan under which the company would provide more favorable health insurance with limited deductibles and coinsurance for the president and three other executives. Under both proposals, the remaining employees would continue to be covered under the existing plan. [3]

   a. Can either of these plans provide tax-free benefits to the covered executives?

   b. What are the consequences to the other employees of Refuse Processors, Inc., if the company adopts the reimbursement plan for Milo and the three executives?

9. For what type of employer does a direct (uninsured) medical reimbursement plan provide significant tax benefits? [3]

10. In calendar year 2010, Gamma Company entered into an agreement with an insurance company under which the insurance company will reimburse selected executives for medical expenses, in return for an annual premium paid by Gamma Company equal to the amount reimbursed during the year plus an administrative charge. Is this plan subject to the nondiscrimination rules for medical reimbursement plans? [3]

11. How can an HSA be used by an employer to provide health benefits to employees? [4]

12. Bleem Products has 27 employees, including 5 to 7 who could be considered management employees. Bleem is solely owned by Harold Bleem, an effective but frugal businessman. Bleem Products currently has no employer-provided health insurance. His seven management employees are demanding a health program for calendar year 2011 because they are not eligible for Medicaid and personal health insurance is prohibitively expensive. Suggest an economical approach by which Bleem can provide health insurance coverage for them. [4]

13. What methods of advance financing of retiree health insurance coverage involve (a) nondiscrimination rules and (b) current tax deduction of costs? [5]

14. Describe several advantages of corporate-owned life insurance as a method of financing retiree health insurance. [5]

15. On December 1, 2010, Nugent Corporation, a publicly traded corporation, enters into a 2-year employment agreement with its senior vice president, Elijah Eagle, providing for an annual salary of $600,000. In the event of a change of control Eagle will be entitled to a termination payment equal to 2.5 times the new annual salary rate and a retention bonus of $250,000, payable in $50,000 installments on the first day of each of the first 5 months following the closing of the transaction. Cosmos Development, Inc., a publicly traded corporation, makes a successful tender offer to Nugent's shareholders on January 10, 2011. Eagle's employment is terminated 6 months after the successful tender offer. Prior to entering into his new employment agreement, Eagle had received total compensation of $2,235,692 for the previous 5 years. [6]

    a. What is Eagle's base amount?

    b. What are Eagle's total parachute payments?

    c. What is Eagle's excess parachute payment?

16. Jim Washington is a U.S. citizen who is employed as a petroleum engineer by Diamond Drilling Resources, Inc., a U.S. corporation that provides oil drilling services in many countries throughout the world. In November, 2010, Jim is assigned to work in Amsterdam in the Netherlands for a period of 3 years. Jim's salary for 2011 is $85,000. In addition, his employer provides Jim with an annual housing allowance of $19,000. At various times during his foreign assignment, Jim is required to work at remote oil drilling sites in the North Sea. Nevertheless, Jim, his wife, Judy, and their two children rent an apartment in Amsterdam for $1,500 per month (including utilities). Jim and Judy expect to reside in this apartment during the period of Jim's foreign assignment. In 2011 Jim and Judy had taxable U.S. interest of $7,500 and taxable U.S. dividend income of $6,000. The Washingtons had no other income for the year and do not itemize deductions. [8]

a. Does Jim qualify for the foreign earned income and foreign housing expense exclusions for 2011?

b. How are the foreign earned income and foreign housing expense exclusions to which Jim may be entitled for 2011 calculated?

c. Assuming that the Netherlands imposes an income tax that is higher than that imposed by the U.S., is Jim better advised in 2011 to elect the foreign tax credit?

Answers to Review Questions

1. After 2010, if the plan is insured or self-insured, there are nondiscrimination rules for coverage and benefits. The plan must benefit 70 percent or more of all employees; 80 percent or more of all employees who are eligible to participate in the plan; or a nondiscriminatory classification of employees, as approved by the IRS. Under the plan, all benefits provided for highly compensated individuals (as defined in Sec. 105(h)), including dependent coverage, must be provided for all plan participants. Certain employees can be excluded in applying the coverage tests. [1]

2. For group term life insurance, the plan must benefit at least 70 percent of all employees; benefit a group of which at least 85 percent are not key employees; benefit a nondiscriminatory classification of employees, as determined by the IRS; or, in a cafeteria (Sec. 125) plan, meet the Sec. 125 nondiscrimination rules. In the group term plan, benefits must not discriminate in favor of key employees (as defined in the top-heavy rules, Code Sec. 416(i)), and all benefits available to key employees must be available to other plan participants. Life insurance coverage can be

equal to the same percentage of compensation for all participants. As with health and accident plans, certain employees can be excluded in applying the coverage tests. [1]

3. Other employee benefit plans that include rules against discriminating in favor of highly compensated or key employees include cafeteria (Sec. 125) plans and dependent care assistance programs. There have never been any nondiscrimination requirements for employer-paid disability plans. [1]

4. There are two benefits from group term life insurance plans: (a) the first $50,000 of insurance under the plan is tax free to covered employees and (b) amounts in excess of $50,000 are taxable under the Table I schedule. A group term plan is of no particular benefit to a highly compensated executive except for the exclusion of the first $50,000 of coverage. The Table I rates are not particularly favorable for large amounts of insurance or for insurance provided after age 65. Therefore, large amounts of insurance provided to executives probably should be provided outside the Sec. 79 plan. [2]

5. Postretirement insurance under a group term plan would be very costly to Arnold because of the dramatic increase in the cost of excess (over $50,000) coverage above age 64. The plan would actually be a tax burden to the retiree rather than a benefit. In this situation, it would probably be best to use an executive bonus type of additional insurance that is outside (carved out of) the company's group term plan. Additional insurance could also be provided under a split-dollar arrangement, but the bonus arrangement is simple and generally favorable. [2]

6. A carve-out life insurance plan can involve almost any kind of arrangement in which life insurance for highly compensated executives is provided outside the group insurance plan. Generally, the group insurance plan is restructured to provide relatively little coverage over $50,000. The $50,000 level, of course, remains favorable because of the tax exclusion. The group term plan remains nondiscriminatory since it in no way favors the highly compensated—in fact it discriminates against them. The insurance for executives is then provided through a bonus arrangement, a split-dollar arrangement, or other approaches, such as including life insurance in the company's qualified pension plan or a welfare benefit trust or VEBA. [2]

7. The carve-out concept relates to removing coverages over $50,000 from the group term Sec. 79 plan. No particular structure for the carved-out coverage is dictated, and any compensation-oriented form of life insurance planning can be used. [2]

8.

    a. A separate direct reimbursement arrangement will not provide tax-free health benefits to the covered executives in this example. The executives will pay taxes on their excess benefits under the plan—that is, any benefits that are provided to them that exceed the benefits provided to regular employees under the existing health insurance plan. A separate insured plan will provide tax-free health benefits to the covered executives, but the employer will be subject to substantial penalties as a consequence of maintaining a discriminatory insured health plan.

    b. Adopting either a separate insured plan or a discriminatory medical reimbursement plan for executives does not affect the tax-free status of the plan for noncovered employees. That is, the plan is not "disqualified"; instead, the key employees or the employer are penalized. [3]

9. Uninsured medical reimbursement plans are useful for employers that have relatively few lower paid employees. For example, a professional corporation with a doctor or dentist and no regular employees (or perhaps only one regular employee) might be able to use a direct medical reimbursement plan on a favorable basis, because costs for the regular employee would not be substantial. In these situations, the effect of the reimbursement plan is to make otherwise nondeductible medical expenses deductible. [3]

10. Prior to 2011 there was a significant tax difference between insured and uninsured plans. Thus, an important planning question was: "What is an insured plan?" The regulations under Code Sec. 105(h) indicate that for a plan to be insured, risk must be shifted from the employer to a third-party insurer. In this example, the IRS would probably argue that no risk has been shifted from the Gamma Company to the insurance company and, consequently, the nondiscrimination rules for medical reimbursement plans would apply. [3]

11. An HSA is an arrangement that provides high-deductible health insurance or HDHP (as defined in Code Sec. 223) together with a tax-free contribution to a tax-favored savings account for the covered individual. Employers can use the HSA concept to provide health benefits to employees by covering the group with a qualifying HDHP and making contributions to each covered employee's HSA account. The employer contributions can be made directly or

through employee salary reductions. Contributions are not taxable to employees (no income tax, FICA, or FUTA). [4]

12. Bleem Products could adopt an HSA-based health plan for a selected group of executives. If all the executives in the group have the same HDHP, then Bleem must make the same contribution for all executives in the group in order to meet the "comparability" requirement of the Regulations. This type of plan might be cheaper for Bleem than conventional health insurance coverage for the executives, taking into account all the benefits involved including the retirement savings element of the HSA to the executives. [4]

13. Funding retiree health insurance by increasing pension benefits, providing an incidental benefit in a qualified plan, or using a VEBA or other trust fund involves nondiscrimination rules. This approach cannot be used if the plan covers selected executives only. However, these approaches allow a current tax deduction for employer contributions. Therefore, there is a trade-off between obtaining a current tax deduction and employer discretion in designing the plan primarily for selected executives. [5]

14. The use of corporate-owned life insurance does not provide an initial tax deduction, but the overall financial result may be favorable. The investment accumulation on the policy is tax deferred to the employer, and death benefits payable to the employer are tax free. The employer's deduction is deferred until health insurance premiums are actually paid for retired employees, but the employer is substantially reimbursed for its costs under the plan. In addition, the insurance provides an asset to help cover the liability required under the FAS 106 requirements for postretirement benefits. This asset would be equal to the cash value of the life insurance policies at least, and some authorities would argue that the present value of the expected death benefits under the plan should also be counted as an asset. There are no nondiscrimination requirements for this method of financing. The plan can be restricted to the selected executives, with differing levels of benefits from one participant to another if the employer wishes. [5]

15. Code Sec. 280G restricts the deductibility of certain parachute payments received by disqualified individuals. A parachute payment is any payment in the nature of compensation to a disqualified individual which is contingent on a change in the ownership of a corporation or on a change in the ownership of a substantial portion of the assets of a corporation, to the extant that the aggregate present value of all such payments made or to be made to the disqualified individual equals or exceeds three

times the individual's base amount. The disqualified individual's base amount is the average annual compensation payable by the acquired corporation and includible in the individual's gross income over the five taxable years of such individual preceding the individual's taxable year in which the change of control occurs. In general, excess parachute payments are any parachute payments in excess of the base amount. On January 10, 2011, Nugent Corporation had a change of control and Eagle, a senior vice president, is a disqualified individual. [6]

a. Eagle's base amount is $447,138 ($2,235,692 ÷ 5)

b. Eagle's total parachute payments are $408,585 ($1,500,000 + $250,000) − (3 x $447,138).

c. Eagle's excess parachute payment is $1,302,862 ($1,750,000 − $447,138).

16. [8]

a. Jim and Judy are U.S. citizens and beginning in November, 2010 they will be residing in Amsterdam for a period of 3 years. In 2011 they will have lived abroad for a full taxable year. Given this fact, their tax home will be in the Netherlands. Finally, Jim received foreign source earned income in 2011. Consequently, Jim and Judy qualify to claim the foreign earned income and foreign housing expense exclusions on their 2011 federal income tax return.

b. Jim's gross income totals $117,500, including the $19,000 housing allowance. Jim's housing expenses are $18,000 ($1,500 x 12). The excess above the base amount (assuming it is $15,000) is $3,000. This is Jim's foreign housing expense exclusion for 2011.

Because Jim's foreign earned income of $104,000 ($85,000 salary plus $19,000 housing allowance) is more than the maximum exclusion of $92,900, Jim must reduce the maximum exclusion by the housing exclusion of $3,000. Thus, Jim's foreign earned income exclusion is $89,900. His total exclusion is thus the maximum of $92,900.

c. Since Jim is working in a high income tax country, it is probably advisable to forego the exclusion and take the foreign tax credit. The foreign tax credit should offset the U.S. tax liability and any excess foreign tax credit can be carried forward to future years. Clearly, Jim's taxes should be calculated under both scenarios to confirm this analysis.

Learning Objectives

An understanding of the material in this chapter should enable the student to

1. Distinguish between an *employee pension benefit plan* and an *employee welfare benefit plan* under ERISA and give some specific examples.

2. List some types of fringe benefit plans that are not considered employee welfare benefit plans under ERISA.

3. Describe the reporting and disclosure and fiduciary requirements imposed by ERISA and DOL regulations upon employee welfare benefit plans.

4. Describe the reporting and disclosure requirements for an employee welfare benefit plan that covers (a) 100 or more participants or (b) fewer than 100 participants.

5. Define a *party in interest*; and, given a particular set of facts, determine if a *prohibited transaction* has occurred.

6. Describe the fiduciary and reporting and disclosure requirements under ERISA applicable to nonqualified deferred-compensation plans.

7. Describe the reporting and disclosure, fiduciary, and other ERISA requirements for a nonqualified unfunded pension plan that provides benefits only for a select group of management or highly compensated employees (the *top-hat group*).

8. Describe the reporting and disclosure and fiduciary requirements under ERISA for a split-dollar plan or other life insurance plan that provides benefits only for the top-hat group.

9. Describe how federal age and sex discrimination rules apply to executive pension and welfare benefit plans.

10. Describe the accounting treatment of certain executive compensation plans.

This chapter discusses the Employee Retirement Income Security Act of 1974 (ERISA) that provides detailed reporting and disclosure requirements for most employee welfare benefit and pension benefit plans. These requirements are in addition to the administration and enforcement provisions and the fiduciary requirements of ERISA. These ERISA requirements are covered as they may apply to various employee welfare benefit and pension benefit plans.

This chapter also includes federal age and sex discrimination laws as they affect benefit plans. Finally, accounting standards for benefit plans are briefly discussed. These standards are not law as such, but they have much the same effect as law.

ERISA COVERAGE AND REPORTING AND DISCLOSURE REQUIREMENTS

ERISA—Scope of Coverage

The Employee Retirement Income Security Act of 1974 (ERISA) imposed extensive federal regulation on a broad range of employee benefit plans.

It will be helpful initially to discuss the scope of ERISA as it applies to employee welfare benefit and pension benefit plans. ERISA is set up as follows:

> Title I—Protection of Employee Benefit Rights
>> Part 1—Reporting and Disclosure
>>
>> Part 2—Participation and Vesting
>>
>> Part 3—Funding
>>
>> Part 4—Fiduciary Responsibility
>>
>> Part 5—Administration and Enforcement
>
> Title II—Amendments to the Internal Revenue Code Relating to Qualified Retirement Plans
>
> Title III—Jurisdiction, Administration, Enforcement, etc.
>
> Title IV—Plan Termination Insurance (Pension Benefit Guaranty Corporation)

For the most part, we will be concerned only with Title I, as it may apply to employee welfare benefit and pension benefit plans.

ERISA Covers Pension Plans and Welfare Plans

Under ERISA, employee benefit plans are divided into two types—pension plans and welfare plans. These definitions are broad, and most common employee benefits can be classified as either pension or welfare benefit plans. However, some plans do not appear to fit within either definition—for example, a plan providing reimbursement for employee moving expenses—and accordingly are not covered at all by any ERISA provision.

Statutory Exemptions from ERISA Coverage

ERISA Sec. 4 contains an exception from most or all of its provisions, including the reporting and disclosure requirements, for certain types of employer plans (both pension and welfare plans). These ERISA-exempt employer plans are

- plans of state, federal, local governments, or governmental organizations
- plans of churches, synagogues, or related organizations (These organizations, however, can elect to have their plans covered under ERISA.)
- plans maintained outside the United States for nonresident aliens
- unfunded excess-benefit plans (which are one type of nonqualified deferred-compensation plan)
- plans maintained solely to comply with workers' compensation, unemployment compensation, or disability insurance laws

Pension Plans—Coverage under ERISA

ERISA Sec. 3(2) defines an "employee pension benefit plan" and "pension plan" as

> any plan, fund, or program which is established or maintained by an employer or by an employee organization (such as a labor union), or by both, to the extent that by its express terms or as a result of surrounding circumstances such plan, fund, or program (1) provides retirement income to employees, or (2) results in a deferral of income by employees for periods extending to the termination of covered employment or beyond, regardless of the method of calculating the contributions made to the plan, the method of calculating the benefits under the plan, or the method of distributing benefits from the plan.

This definition includes all qualified pension, profit-sharing, stock bonus, and similar qualified plans; it does not include IRAs or Roth IRAs that are not employer sponsored. It also includes some nonqualified deferred-compensation plans. (These may, however, be eligible for exemption from funding requirements and reporting and disclosure requirements. See below.) In general, an ERISA pension plan is any employee benefit plan that involves deferral of an employee's compensation to his or her retirement date or later.

In addition to the statutory exemptions in ERISA itself (for government plans, church plans and so on), Sec. 2510.3-2 of the Labor Regulations gives partial exemption or special treatment to a number of other types of pension benefit plans for purposes of Title I of ERISA. These special regulatory exemptions are as follows:

- A severance-pay plan is not treated as a pension plan if

    1. Payments do not depend directly on the employee's retiring.
    2. Total payments under the plan are less than twice the employee's annual compensation during the year immediately preceding the separation from service.
    3. All payments to any employee are completed within 24 months of separation from service.

    A severance-pay plan that meets these criteria does not need to comply with the reporting and disclosure requirements for pension plans but must meet the more limited reporting and disclosure requirements for welfare plans, as discussed below. For example, welfare plans with fewer than 100 participants need not file an annual report (Form 5500 series) if benefits are fully insured or are paid by the employer out of its general assets.

- Supplemental payment plans that provide extra benefits to retirees to counteract inflation are exempt from numerous ERISA requirements under Department of Labor Regulations.

- Employer-provided IRAs and Sec. 403(b) TDA plans are subject to reduced ERISA reporting and disclosure requirements where there are no employer contributions; the employer is merely a conduit for paying employee contributions; and the employer has only incidental involvement in the administration and operation of the plans.

Welfare Plans—Coverage under ERISA

A welfare plan (also called a welfare benefit plan) is defined in Sec. 3(1) of ERISA as

> any plan, fund, or program . . . established or maintained by an employer or by an employee organization, or by both, . . . for the purpose of providing for its participants or their beneficiaries, through the purchase of insurance or otherwise, . . . medical, surgical, or hospital care or benefits, or benefits in the event of sickness, accident, disability, death or unemployment, or vacation benefits, apprenticeship or other training programs, or day care centers, scholarship funds, or prepaid legal services. Certain other plans described in federal labor law are also included.

The same list of ERISA-exempt plans (government plans, church plans, and so on) described above applies to welfare plans as well as to pension plans. Thus such plans are exempt from virtually all ERISA requirements whether they are pension or welfare plans.

For welfare plans, Sec. 2510.3-1 of the Labor Regulations provides exemptions and limitations from the applicability of Title I of ERISA. The following employment practices and benefits have been declared by regulation to be exempt from Title I of ERISA:

- overtime pay, shift pay, holiday premiums, and similar compensation paid for work done under other-than-normal circumstances
- compensation for absence from work due to sickness, vacation, holidays, military duty, jury duty, or sabbatical leave or training programs, if paid out of the general assets of the employer (that is, not funded in advance)
- recreational or dining facilities or first aid centers on the employer's premises
- holiday gifts
- group insurance programs offered to employees by an insurer under which no contribution is made by the employer, participation is voluntary, and the program is not actively sponsored by the employer
- unfunded tuition reimbursement or scholarship programs (other than Sec. 127 educational assistance plans) that are paid out of the employer's general assets

ERISA Provisions Applicable to Welfare Benefit Plans

Most of the plans discussed in this course, to the extent they are subject to the provisions of ERISA, are welfare benefit plans, so only the provisions of ERISA applicable to welfare benefit plans will be discussed here in detail. Nonqualified deferred-compensation plans (which are included within the definition of pension benefit plans under ERISA) will be discussed separately below.

In general, the provisions of ERISA applicable to welfare plans are Part 1, Reporting and Disclosure, Part 4, Fiduciary Responsibility, and Part 5, Administration and Enforcement. Part 2, Participation and Vesting, and Part 3, Funding, are not applicable to welfare benefit plans (ERISA Secs. 210(1) and 301(1)).

Reporting and Disclosure

There are two major reporting and disclosure requirements: a requirement to file an annual report with the Department of Labor and the IRS, generally on Form 5500 and a requirement to provide participants with a summary plan description (SPD). There are also a variety of recordkeeping and disclosure-upon-request provisions.

The reporting and disclosure requirements under ERISA and related Department of Labor regulations vary depending on the type of welfare benefit plan involved. For example, a plan that covers fewer than 100 participants is exempt from all reporting and disclosure provisions if benefits are paid solely from the general assets of the employer or provided exclusively through insurance contracts, the premiums of which are paid by the employer or partly with participant contributions.

Under the Department of Labor (DOL) ERISA regulations, there is an exemption from the annual report (Form 5500) filing for small insured welfare plans. A "small" plan for this purpose is one that has fewer than 100 participants at the beginning of the plan year and under which, if the employees contribute, the employer forwards employee contributions within 3 months of their receipt. However, the administrator of the otherwise exempted small plan must keep for the specified 6-year period the records that would be necessary to provide the data for a return/report if the Secretary of Labor requests one. A group insurance plan that covers fewer than 100 participants and that is part of an association group plan or multiemployer trust is also exempt from the reporting and disclosure provisions. An employee welfare benefit plan maintained primarily for the purpose of providing benefits for a select group of management or highly compensated employees, where benefits are paid solely from the general assets of the employer or through insurance contracts, the premiums for which are paid directly by the employer, is exempt from all reporting and disclosure requirements. Finally, a welfare benefit plan that covers 100 or more participants, except one providing benefits for a select group of management or highly compensated employees, is subject to all reporting and disclosure requirements.

Fiduciary Requirements

If one person is granted discretionary authority to hold and to administer assets belonging to another, the holder of such funds is legally described as a *fiduciary*. A funded employee-benefit plan, therefore, involves fiduciary relationships. In addition, ERISA imposes fiduciary requirements on a broad range of individuals and entities related to employee benefit plans. The fiduciary rules were intended to provide broad protection to employees, as well as to spell out the specific responsibilities of each person involved in designing and maintaining an employee benefit plan. Individuals and businesses involved with employee benefit plans have the responsibility of becoming aware of their fiduciary responsibilities and must do their best to comply with them or to structure their relationships so as to avoid them.

The definition of fiduciary is broad; it includes any person who (ERISA Sec. 3(21)):

- exercises any discretionary authority or discretionary control with respect to the management of the plan or exercises any authority or control with respect to the management or disposition of plan assets;
- renders investment advice for a fee or other compensation, direct or indirect, with respect to any plan asset, or has any authority or responsibility to do so; or
- has discretionary authority or discretionary responsibility in the administration of the plan.

This definition of fiduciary in ERISA generally includes the employer, the plan administrator, and the trustee. It also includes a wide variety of other people having relationships with an employee benefit plan. However, the Department of Labor has stated that an attorney, accountant, actuary, or consultant who renders legal, accounting, actuarial, or consulting services to the plan will not be considered a fiduciary solely as a result of performing their professional services.[108] These rules exclude broker/dealers, banks, and reporting dealers from being treated as fiduciaries simply as a result of receiving and executing buy-sell instructions from the plan. Furthermore, a person giving investment advice will be considered a fiduciary only with respect to the assets covered by that investment advice. The provision for fiduciary status where there is "discretionary authority" in the administration of a plan was probably not intended to target professional advisors; but such advisors must be careful to avoid expanding their activities to the fiduciary level in this regard. The issue is most acute when the client is also a friend or business associate, as is often the case with small business clients.

Every plan must specify a "named fiduciary" in the plan document. The purpose of this requirement is not to limit liability to named persons; rather it is to provide participants and the government with an easy target in case they decide to take legal action against the plan. Other unnamed fiduciaries can also be included in the legal action, of course.

The *duties of* fiduciaries are clearly specified in ERISA Sec. 404. These duties consist of the following:

- discharge duties with respect to a plan solely in the interest of the participants and the beneficiaries;
- act for the exclusive purpose of providing benefits to participants and their beneficiaries, and defraying the reasonable expenses of administering the plan;
- act with the care, skill, prudence, and diligence under the circumstances that prevail that a prudent man acting in a like capacity and familiar with such matters would use in the conduct of an enterprise of a like character and with like aims;
- diversify the investments of the plan to minimize the risk of large losses, unless under the circumstances it is clearly prudent not to do so;
- follow the provisions of the documents and instruments governing the plan, unless inconsistent with ER1SA provisions.

In interpreting the "prudent man" requirement, labor regulations indicate that the fiduciary, in making an investment, must determine that the particular investment is reasonably designed as part of the plan's portfolio to further the purposes of the plan, and must consider: (1) the composition of the portfolio with regard to diversification, (2) the liquidity and current return of the portfolio

---

108. DOL Reg. Sec. 2550.408b-2.

relative to the anticipated cash-flow requirements of the plan, and (3) the projected return of the portfolio relative to the funding objectives of the plan.[109]

> A fiduciary who fails to meet these requirements will be held personally liable for any plan losses that result from a breach in fiduciary duty. To protect plan beneficiaries, individual fiduciaries who handle plan assets must be bonded. Corporate fiduciaries—banks or trust companies—are not required to be bonded. If the employer handles only the funds that will be contributed to the trustee or insurer in payment of premiums, bonding is not required for the employer.

If the plan so provides, fiduciaries can delegate fiduciary responsibilities to other fiduciaries and, thereby avoid direct responsibility for performing the duty so delegated. For example, the employer can delegate the duties relating to the handling and investment of plan assets to a trustee, and the investment management duties can be delegated to an appointed investment manager. The plan must provide a definite procedure for delegating these duties. The delegation of a fiduciary duty does not remove all fiduciary responsibility; a fiduciary will be liable for a breach of fiduciary responsibility by any other fiduciary under the following circumstances (ERISA Sec. 405):

- If he participates knowingly in, or knowingly undertakes to conceal, an act or omission of another fiduciary knowing such act or omission is a breach;
- if he fails to comply with fiduciary duties in the administration of his specific responsibilities that give rise to his status as a fiduciary and, therefore, enables another fiduciary to commit a breach; or
- if he has knowledge of a breach by another fiduciary, unless he makes reasonable efforts under the circumstances to remedy the breach.

The broad scope of the fiduciary liabilities indicates that, in addition to careful delegation of fiduciary duties to well-chosen trustees and advisors, the employer should take care that its liability insurance coverage adequately covers any liabilities that might arise out of the fiduciary responsibility provisions. ERISA specifically prohibits a plan from excusing or exculpating any person from fiduciary liability, but individuals and employers are permitted to have appropriate insurance, and employers can indemnify (agree to

---

109. DOL Reg. Sec. 2550.404a-1.

reimburse) plan fiduciaries for losses they might incur as a result of fiduciary duties.

The following requirements must be met by every employee welfare benefit plan subject to the ERISA fiduciary requirements (Part 4 of Title I):

1. The plan must be established and maintained pursuant to a written instrument.
2. The written instrument is to provide for one or more named fiduciaries who are to have the authority to control and manage the operation and administration of the plan.
3. The plan must describe a procedure for the allocation of responsibilities for the operation and administration of the plan.
4. The plan must provide a procedure for amending the plan and for identifying those persons who have authority to amend the plan.
5. The plan must specify the basis on which payments are made to and from the plan, for example, who is to contribute to the plan and in what amounts. This requirement also involves establishment of a written claims procedure.

As a general rule, all assets of an employee welfare benefit plan are required to be held under a written trust by one or more trustees. However, the requirement of a trust does *not* apply to any plan assets that consist of *insurance contracts*, or where benefits are paid directly to plan participants *solely* from the *general assets* of the employer. Thus split-dollar and group permanent plans do not require the use of a written trust.

Prohibited Transactions

The ERISA fiduciary rules include provisions that impose civil liability upon fiduciaries who allow "prohibited transactions" to take place, that is, fiduciaries may be liable for plan losses. The fiduciary is also required to undo each prohibited transaction. In addition, the Department of Labor *may* impose discretionary 15 percent and 100 percent penalties on a party in interest, for each year that the prohibited transaction has not been corrected, which penalties are applied to the amount involved in the prohibited transaction. A plan fiduciary shall not cause a plan to engage in a transaction if he or she knows or should know that such transaction would be prohibited and would take place directly or indirectly between a plan and a "party in interest."

A "party in interest" is defined in ERISA Sec. 3(14) as

1. any fiduciary (including, but not limited to, any administrator, officer, trustee, or custodian), counsel, or employee of such employee benefit plan
2. a person providing services to such plan
3. an employer any of whose employees are covered by such plan
4. an employee organization any of whose members are covered by such plan
5. an owner, direct or indirect, of 50 percent or more of

    a. the combined voting power of all classes of stock entitled to vote or the total value of shares of all classes of stock of a corporation,
    b. the capital interest or the profits interest of a partnership, or
    c. the beneficial interest of a trust or unincorporated enterprise, which is an employer or an employee organization described in subparagraphs 3 or 4

6. a relative of any individual described in subparagraphs 1, 2, 3, or 5
7. a corporation, partnership, or trust or estate of which (or in which) 50 percent or more of

    a. the combined voting power of all classes of stock entitled to vote or the total value of shares of all classes of stock of such corporation,
    b. the capital interest or profits interest of such partnership, or
    c. the beneficial interest of such trust or estate is owned directly or indirectly or held by persons described in subparagraphs 1, 2, 3, 4, or 5

8. an employee, officer, director (or an individual having powers or responsibilities similar to those of officers or directors), or a 10 percent or more shareholder directly or indirectly of a person described in subparagraphs 2, 3, 4, 5, or 7, or of the employee benefit plan
9. a 10 percent or more (directly or indirectly in capital or profits) partner or joint venturer of a person described in subparagraphs 2, 3, 4, 5, or 7

A "prohibited transaction" under ERISA Sec. 406 is defined as any direct or indirect

1. sale or exchange, or leasing of any property between the plan and a party in interest
2. lending of money or other extension of credit between the plan and a party in interest
3. furnishing of goods, services, or facilities between the plan and a party in interest
4. transfer to, or use by or for the benefit of, a party in interest of any assets of the plan
5. acquisition, on behalf of the plan, of any employer security or employer real property in violation of Sec. 407(a)

A transfer of real or personal property by a party in interest to a plan shall be treated as a sale or exchange if the property is subject to a mortgage or similar lien that the plan assumes or if it is subject to a mortgage or similar lien that a party in interest placed on the property within the 10-year period ending on the date of the transfer.

If an insurance company issues policies to a plan and premiums are placed in the insurer's general asset account, the assets in the account will not be considered plan assets. Thus a subsequent transaction involving the general asset account and a party in interest, for example, the employer, will not be regarded per se as a prohibited transaction (ERISA IB 72-2). This exception, however, may not permit the employer to effect policy loans from the insurer since a pledging of plan assets would be involved. However, under a split-dollar plan where the cash values represent an interest of the employer, policy loans by the employer should be permitted since the cash values are not normally part of the benefits to be provided to the employee or his or her beneficiaries. Because of this uncertainty, an exemption may be sought from the Department of Labor.

Prohibited Transaction Exemptions (PTEs) Significant for Life Insurance

Because of the broad definitions in the prohibited transaction rules, a financial planning practice often engages in actions that could be considered prohibited transactions. In order to avoid burdening normal advisory practices with uncertainties about prohibited transactions, PTEs have been issued by the Department of Labor under ERISA Sec. 408(a) in a number of areas related to financial planning. There are several PTEs related to life insurance in particular.

Purchase of Life Insurance from an Employee Benefit Plan. On the face of it, many purchases of life insurance contracts from an employee benefit plan that a planner might like to recommend could be considered prohibited transactions. This is because the definition of party in interest is broad; for example, parties in interest include an owner of 50 percent or more of the business or a member of the family of such an owner. However, some transactions of this type are exempted if they meet the requirements of PTE 92-6.

PTE 92-6 exempts sales of life insurance or annuity contracts by an employee benefit plan to a participant or "relative" of the participant. The participant must be the insured under the contract. For purposes of PTE 92-6, a relative (1) is a relative as defined in Sec. 3(15) of ERISA (spouse, ancestor, lineal descendant, or spouse of a lineal descendent); or (2) is a member of the family as defined in Sec. 4975(e)(6) of the Internal Revenue Code (currently the same list as ERISA Sec. 3(15)); or (3) is a brother or sister of the insured (or a spouse of such brother or sister), and is the beneficiary under the contract.

Other requirements under PTE 92-6 include:

- The plan, but for the sale, would surrender the contract. (This requirement indicates the need for appropriate language in the plan requiring the plan to surrender the contract upon the termination of employment of one of the insureds.)
- If the purchaser is not the insured-participant, the insured-participant must be given an opportunity to purchase the contract first; PTE 92-6 dictates an administrative procedure that must be followed.
- The purchase price must put the plan in the same cash position as if it had retained the contract, surrendered it, and distributed any vested interest in the plan owed to the participant.

The Department of Labor confirmed in ERISA Opinion Letter 98-07A, 9/24/1998, that a second-to-die policy insuring the participant and his spouse is considered an "individual life insurance contract" that is governed by PTE 92-6.

Sale of Life Insurance to Employee Benefit Plan. There is a corresponding exemption for sales of life insurance contracts to an employee benefit plan, PTE 92-5. Such a sale, for example, could facilitate the use of life insurance in an employer-sponsored plan for an employee who has a personally-owned policy but has become uninsurable. The exemption applies to a sale, transfer, or exchange of an individual life insurance or annuity contract to an employee benefit plan from (1) a plan participant on whose life the contract was issued, or (2) from an employer any of whose employees are covered by the plan. The exemption is conditioned on the following:

- payment of a consideration based on policy valuation criteria described in PTE 92-5;
- no assumption of mortgage or lien;
- transaction that must be permitted by the plan; and
- a welfare benefit plan with no discrimination in favor of officers, shareholders, or highly compensated employees.

Receipt of Commissions from Employee Benefit Plan by Life Insurance Agents. A third exemption, PTE 84-24, addresses a number of situations involving the sale of life insurance and other investment products by a broker, agent, investment company or insurance company to an employer plan. PTE 84-24 sets out the conditions under which such sales are exempt from being treated as prohibited transactions. In particular, there is an exemption for the receipt by an insurance agent, broker, or pension consultant of a sales commission from an insurance company in connection with the purchase (using plan assets) of an insurance or annuity contract, under certain conditions:

- The transaction is carried out in the ordinary course of the agent's business.
- The transaction must be at least as favorable as an arm's-length transaction with an unrelated party.
- Total fees or commissions must not exceed reasonable compensation within the provisions of ERISA (Secs. 408(b)(2), 408(c)(2), and related IRC provisions).
- The agent must not be a plan trustee, plan administrator, fiduciary (with discretionary authority over plan assets), or employer with employees covered under the plan.
- The agent must file certain information with an independent fiduciary of the plan, including a disclosure of the agent's relationship to the insurance company and the *amount of any sales commissions*.

These PTEs have in general provided satisfactory working rules for pension consultants, insurance agents, and brokers in their normal course of business. However, those working in this area must recognize the importance of complying with the detailed requirements of these PTEs in every transaction that could be affected by them, in order to avoid prohibited transaction penalties.

In addition, if an agent or consultant has or acquires the status of a *fiduciary* under the plan, the general fiduciary requirements discussed earlier will apply to the agent or consultant. Under ERISA, the status of fiduciary is separate and apart from that of party in interest. The requirements for fiduciaries are broader and more stringent than the prohibited transaction rules alone. Compliance with the PTEs will avoid prohibited transaction penalties, but not the broader fiduciary requirements such as being liable for plan losses due to a breach of fiduciary responsibility. In general, consulting, insurance, and brokerage businesses try to avoid fiduciary status unless they wish to become so actively involved in plan design, investment, or administration that fiduciary status cannot be avoided.

Claims Procedure

All plans that are not totally excluded from ERISA must provide for a claims procedure. A claims procedure entails a written notice of claim denial including specific reasons as to why the plan is denying a claim, the terms of the plan on which the denial is based, and any additional information that, if submitted, will cause the claim to be allowed. Written notice must also inform a claimant as to the complete procedure for claim review.

A claim review procedure must be built into the plan and provide review by a named fiduciary upon written request, a review by the claimant of plan documents, and a provision allowing this claimant to submit written comments.

Administration and Enforcement (ERISA Secs. 501–514)

Any person who willfully violates a provision of Part I of Title I of ERISA may be subject to a fine, upon conviction, of not more than $5,000 or imprisonment for not more than one year, or both (corporations may be fined up to $100,000). A civil action may also be brought by a participant or beneficiary who is refused plan information by a plan administrator, as may be required by law, to recover plan benefits; to enforce or clarify his or her rights under the plan; to enjoin any act in violation of law or the terms of the plan; or to obtain other appropriate equitable relief.

ERISA Requirements Affecting Nonqualified Deferred-Compensation Plans

A nonqualified deferred-compensation plan is a pension plan for ERISA purposes that, therefore, is potentially exposed to the full ERISA regime applicable to qualified pension plans. However, there are significant special exemptions, and in practice, most nonqualified plans will be designed to rely on these ERISA exemptions. There are two significant exemptions discussed here: (a) unfunded excess-benefit plans, and (b) unfunded nonqualified deferred compensation for a "select group of management and highly compensated employees" (referred to as the "top-hat" group). This latter exemption is, in practice, the more significant in designing nonqualified deferred-compensation plans.

Unfunded Excess-Benefit Plans

An excess-benefit plan is a "plan maintained solely to provide benefits for certain employees in excess of limitations on contributions and benefits imposed on qualified plans by Sec. 415" (ERISA Sec. 3 (36)).

An unfunded excess-benefit plan, one where the employee must look to the employer's unsecured promise to pay for his or her benefits and where no assets have been set aside for the employee beyond the reach of the employer and its creditors, is totally exempt from the coverage of Title I of ERISA (ERISA Sec. 4(b)(5)).

The excess-benefit plan may appear attractive as a method of designing nonqualified plans. However, recent law reducing the compensation base for qualified plans to $245,000 (2011) (as indexed in Code Sec. 401(a)(17)) is generally more significant than the Sec. 415 limit in reducing benefits for highly compensated participants; a nonqualified plan that compensates for reduced benefits as a consequence of the $245,000 limit is not considered an excess-benefit plan. Therefore the current usefulness of excess-benefit plans is very limited.

Unfunded Nonqualified Deferred-Compensation Plans for the Top-Hat Group

If a plan is unfunded and maintained primarily for the purpose of providing deferred compensation for a select group of management or highly compensated employees, it is then subject to ERISA reporting and disclosure provisions. However, it is not subject to participation, vesting, funding, and fiduciary provisions (ERISA Secs. 201(2), 301(a)(3), 401(a)(1)).

DOL regulations also provide an exemption from the Form 5500 filing requirement, but in order to obtain the exemption from reporting and disclosure, an employer adopting a top-hat plan must file a letter with the DOL promptly after the plan is adopted containing (a) the name and address of the employer, (b) the employer's identification number, (c) the number of plans and number of participants, and (d) a declaration that the plan is maintained primarily to provide deferred compensation for a select group of management or highly compensated employees only and that the employer will furnish a copy of the plan document to the Department of Labor upon request.

ERISA has been amended to eliminate the requirement that summary plan descriptions must be filed with the DOL. However, employees covered by top-hat plans should be furnished with summary plan descriptions. Generally, the employees' written employment agreement containing the terms of the NQDC plan should meet this requirement.

Moreover, one of the critical elements of a top-hat plan is to make sure that all of the covered employees are part of a top-hat group. In light of this ERISA restriction, a top-hat plan should never be considered as a means of providing benefits to a large group of the employer's workforce, particularly if the group includes employees who are not true management or highly compensated employees.

Nonqualified Deferred Compensation Not Subject to the Top-Hat Exemption

Unfunded nonqualified deferred compensation that is not limited to the top-hat group is subject to very different rules. It is subject to a number of provisions of Title I; it must follow reporting and disclosure provisions, administration and enforcement procedures, participation (service and age), vesting, funding (unless it is a profit sharing plan or an allocated insurance contract plan), fiduciary responsibility provisions, and the written trust requirement. Furthermore, if the plan is funded, regardless of who participates in the plan, all the above provisions of Title I are similarly applicable. This includes reporting and disclosure, administration and enforcement, fiduciary responsibility, participation (must meet service and age requirements but can discriminate in favor of highly paid employees), funding (unless the plan is a profit sharing plan or uses allocated insurance contracts), vesting provisions, and the written trust requirement. Because of Code Sec. 83, the employee will be taxed on benefits in the year of vesting, even if benefits are not payable until many years in the future.

Because of the effect of ERISA, it is generally not practical to make use of funded NQDC plans or plans with coverage beyond the top-hat group, because such plans would be overly complicated to administer and could not meet the tax-deferral objectives that are generally sought in such plans.

ERISA Requirements Affecting Split-Dollar and Other Life Insurance Plans

Reporting and Disclosure

An endorsement-type split-dollar life insurance plan falls within the definition of an employee welfare benefit plan under ERISA. Thus, it would ordinarily be subject to all of the reporting and disclosure requirements unless a specific exemption applies. By regulation, however, where an endorsement-type split-dollar plan is primarily for the purpose of providing benefits for a select group of management or highly compensated employees, and the benefits are paid solely through insurance contracts, the premiums for which are paid directly by the employer, it is exempt from all reporting and disclosure requirements, including the Form 5500 and SPD requirements. The DOL may request copies of the split-dollar documents (DOL Reg. Sec. 2520.104-24).

A *contributory* endorsement-type split-dollar life insurance plan does not fall within the above exemption. The reason is that the exemption applies only where the premiums are paid directly by the employer from its general assets. Any time employee contributions are required or made, ERISA reporting and disclosure rules apply. Thus, a contributory endorsement-type split-dollar plan would be subject to reporting and disclosure requirements, but in most cases only those requirements applicable to employee welfare benefit plans covering fewer than 100 participants must be satisfied. Each participant and beneficiary eligible to receive benefits must receive a summary plan description, but this does not have to be filed with the Department of Labor.

Fiduciary Requirements

Since an endorsement-type split-dollar life insurance plan is an employee welfare benefit plan, it must meet the fiduciary requirements of ERISA unless it is exempt because it covers a top-hat group and is noncontributory. In those cases where a split-dollar life insurance plan is not exempt, the fiduciary requirements include a written instrument that provides for one or more named fiduciaries who are to have the authority to control and manage the operation and administration of the plan. The plan must also specify the nature of the benefits, the persons who are eligible to receive benefits, the basis for contributions to the plan, and a written claims procedure. However, a nonexempt split-dollar plan, while required to be in writing, does not require a written trust since the plan assets consist entirely of life insurance contracts.

Another important question is whether a life insurance agent who is involved in the sale of life insurance under a split-dollar plan will be required to execute commission disclosures based on the requirements of Prohibited Transaction Exemption 77-9. The agent's involvement in the sale of investment products would seem to result in his or her becoming a party in interest for prohibited transaction purposes, and it would be prudent to comply with the provisions of PTE 77-9. In addition, the rendering of investment advice could result in fiduciary status under ERISA or Code Sec. 4975(e)(3).

AGE AND SEX DISCRIMINATION RULES

Age Discrimination

The federal Age Discrimination in Employment Act (ADEA) provides that it is unlawful for an employer

1. to fail or refuse to hire or to discharge any individual or otherwise discriminate against any individual with respect to his compensation, terms, conditions, or privileges of employment, because of such individual's age;
2. to limit, segregate, or classify his employees in any way which would deprive or tend to deprive any individual of employment opportunities or otherwise adversely affect his or her status as an employee, because of such individual's age; or
3. to reduce the wage rate of any employee in order to comply with (ADEA).[110]

ADEA applies to workers and managers of any business that engages in interstate commerce (which the courts have defined very broadly) and employs at least 20 persons during the year.[111]

State laws are not preempted by ADEA. Therefore it is possible that benefit discrimination allowed under ADEA might be prohibited under applicable state law.

---

110. ADEA, §4(a); 29 USC §623(a).
111. 29 USC §630(b).

Pension Plans

Mandatory retirement at any age is prohibited by ADEA. However, mandatory retirement at age 65 is specifically permitted for an individual who has been in a "bona fide executive or high policy-making position" for at least 2 years before retirement and who is entitled to a minimum fully vested pension of at least $44,000 annually calculated as a straight life annuity.[112]

There are specific age-discrimination provisions in the Internal Revenue Code that are applicable to qualified plans.

Under Code Sec. 411(b)(2), a *defined-contribution* plan cannot reduce allocations (or the rate of allocations) of employer contributions, forfeitures, income, gains, or losses in a participant's account because of the participant's age. However, the plan can have a "cap" on the number of years during which employer contributions and forfeitures will be allocated, or the total amount of contributions and forfeitures, provided that it is not based on age as such. For example, a plan can provide that employer contributions and forfeitures will be allocated only over the participant's first 25 years of service. Few plans use this approach.

Correspondingly, under Code Sec. 411(b)(1)(H), in a *defined-benefit* plan, the benefit formula cannot cut off accruals at a specified age, but it can provide that benefits are accrued fully after a specified number of years of service, such as 25. Plans can continue to use age 65 as the "normal retirement age" for funding and benefit accrual purposes. If employees work past age 65, the Regulations provide alternative methods for benefit payment and/or accrual.[113]

Welfare Benefit Plans

ADEA also applies to welfare benefit plans.

ADEA contains a provision allowing an employer to "observe the terms of a bona fide . . . employee benefit plan . . . which is not a subterfuge to evade the purposes of [ADEA]."[114] For many years the courts and the regulatory agencies have interpreted this as an authorization for adopting rules allowing

---

112. ADEA, §12(c)(1), 29 USC §631(a)(1); 29 CRF (EEOC Reg.) §1627.17.

113. Treas. Reg. §1.411(b)-2(b)(4).

114. ADEA, §4(f)(2), 29 USC §623(f)(2). This exception does not permit involuntary retirement because of age or failure to hire because of age.

employers to use an "equal cost" approach. This approach was validated in the 1990 amendments to ADEA.

Sex Discrimination

Sex discrimination in employee benefit plans is governed primarily by the Civil Rights Act of 1964, which provides as follows:

1. It shall be an unlawful employment practice for an employer

    a. to fail or refuse to hire or to discharge any individual, or otherwise to discriminate against any individual with respect to his compensation, terms, conditions, or privileges of employment, because of such individual's race, color, religion, sex, or national origin; or

    b. to limit, segregate, or classify his employees or applicants for employment in any way which would deprive or tend to deprive any individual of employment opportunities or otherwise adversely affect his status as an employee, because of such individual's race, color, religion, sex, or national origin.[115]

The Civil Rights Act covers all employers in interstate commerce who have at least 15 employees for each working day in at least 20 calendar weeks in the current or preceding calendar year.[116]

There are no provisions in the Internal Revenue Code or ERISA directly dealing with sex discrimination, so court decisions and regulations under the Civil Rights Act are the primary source of authority in the benefits area.[117]

In the area of wage and benefit discrimination, the Civil Rights Act provisions overlap with another federal statute, the Equal Pay Act of 1963.[118] For most benefit purposes, it is adequate to discuss only the Civil Rights Act, since there are few, if any, benefit practices permitted by the Civil Rights Act that are prohibited by the Equal Pay Act. However, there is an important

---

115. Civil Rights Act of 1964, §703(a), 42 USC §2000e-2(a).

116. 42 USC §2000e(b).

117. Some commentators have theorized that the fiduciary provisions of ERISA require impartial dealing with plan participants, thus prohibiting discrimination because of sex.

118. 29 USC §206.

difference that affects smaller employers: the Equal Pay Act has *no small employer exception.*[119]

Pension Plans

Pension plans raise the issue of whether the law requires employers to make equal *contributions* or provide equal *benefits*. The court cases on this issue are not entirely clear, but the weight of Supreme Court decisions has convinced most commentators that an equal-benefit approach is required.[120] The equal-benefit approach would indicate the following guidelines:

- A defined-benefit plan should offer the same benefit for men and women retirees similarly situated (most have always done so).
- Employers with defined-benefit plans can use sex-based actuarial assumptions for funding purposes, since this does not affect employees' benefits.
- If a retirement plan includes an incidental life insurance benefit, the same amount of life insurance must be provided to men and women employees with the same retirement benefits. If the plan is contributory, contributions must be based on unisex tables.
- If a defined-contribution plan offers an annuity form of payout, either exclusively or as an option, unisex annuity rates must be used within the plan itself. (This will not prevent male retirees from taking a lump-sum distribution and using the money to purchase a sex-based annuity providing higher monthly payments from an insurance company.)

Life Insurance

The same Supreme Court cases cited for pension plans have convinced most commentators that the courts will uphold prohibitions against sex-based

---

119. Certain types of business are excepted, however, such as retail sales, fishing, agriculture, and newspaper publishing. 29 USC §§203(s), 213(a).

120. *Los Angeles Department of Water and Power v. Manhart*, 435 U.S. 702 (1978) involved a contributory pension plan of a municipality. The Court held that the plan could not require women to pay higher contributions than men to receive equal periodic benefits upon retirement. *Arizona Governing Committee v. Norris*, 103 S. Ct. 3492 (1983) involved a Sec. 457 deferred-compensation plan of a municipality. The plan provided a sex-based annuity table for retirees, so that for a given account balance, a female participant received a smaller monthly retirement payment. In both cases the Supreme Court found a violation of the Civil Rights Act.

life insurance benefits.[121] Therefore, any life insurance plan should provide the same amount of insurance to any participant, male or female, who is otherwise similarly situated (same compensation, same job classification, etc.). If plan participants must contribute to the plan (as in supplemental group coverage, for example), unisex premium rates must be used.

Health Insurance

In the area of health insurance, certain controversies have been settled only by federal legislation. Congress in 1978 added Sec. 701(k) to the Civil Rights Act to indicate that distinctions among employee benefits based on pregnancy or childbirth are considered sex related. EEOC interpretive guidelines based on this act[122] require pregnancy and childbirth-related medical expenses of employees to be treated the same as other medical expenses. Also, the EEOC guidelines require pregnancy benefits to be provided to spouses of male employees if spouses of female employees also receive health benefits.

Other EEOC regulations prohibit restricting spousal and family benefits to employees who are deemed "head of household" and also prohibit plans that provide benefits to spouses of male employees that are not available to female employees.[123]

ACCOUNTING FOR BENEFIT PLANS

Accounting rules, including those affecting employee benefit plans, are promulgated by the Financial Accounting Standards Board (FASB). The FASB is a private organization designated by the accounting profession to promulgate general principles, practices, and standards for accounting and financial disclosure. These FASB rules do not have the force of law as such, but they represent, de facto, the standards expected by shareholders, investors, and the government in financial reports of businesses; and they are generally followed by independent accountants for purposes of certifying financial statements. They are, therefore, quasi regulatory in effect and

---

121. Existing EEOC regulations prohibit sex discrimination in all fringe benefits, 29 CFR §§1604.9(b), 1620.4, 1604.9(e), 1620.5(e).

122. 44 Federal Register 23804 (April 20, 1979). The provision of these guidelines requiring pregnancy benefits to spouses of male employees was upheld by the Supreme Court in *Newport News Shipbuilding and Dry Dock Co. v. EEOC*, 103 S. Ct. 2622 (1983).

123. 29 CFR §§1604.9(c), 1604.9(d), 1620.5(c), 1620.5(d) (prop.).

should be considered along with state and federal government regulations in the design of executive benefit plans.

Pension Plans

The accounting rules for deferred compensation make no distinction between qualified and nonqualified plans as such. Instead, the applicable accounting rule depends on whether the plan constitutes one or more "individual deferred-compensation contracts" on the one hand, or a "pension plan" on the other. While the balance-sheet result is about the same either way, individual deferred-compensation contracts are governed by the older Accounting Principles Board (APB) Opinion No. 12, as amended by FAS 106. Pension plans, however, are governed by FAS 87.

Whether a plan is one or the other is to some extent a matter of the accountant's discretion. In general, if one or only a few executives are covered, APB No. 12 will be applied, while if the plan is a defined-benefit plan or a pension plan as defined in ERISA, FAS 87 will apply.[124]

Under APB No. 12, the benefits accrued under a deferred-compensation contract are charged to expense and spread ratably over the period of the executive's service. As amended by FAS 106, the period of service to be used is the period between the time the contract is entered into and the first year in which the executive is eligible for benefit payments (even if the executive might choose to further defer actual payment). Accrued benefits are charged to expense at their present value; the discount rate is not specified in APB No. 12, but accountants are likely to use current rates of return on high-quality fixed-income investments. No funding method is specified in APB No. 12, but apparently either a level-funding or accrued benefit approach can be used.

FASB Statement No. 87, "Employers' Accounting for Pensions," was put in final form in 1985. Highlights of FAS 87 are listed below:

---

124. See Tax Management Portfolio 393-2nd, "Accounting for Pensions and Deferred Compensation," Bureau of National Affairs, Inc., Washington, D.C., page A-6 for the authors' views of how this distinction is made. According to their rationale, it would appear that most accountants would not apply FAS 87 to an unfunded plan, but this is not clear from FAS 87 itself. Note: In 2007 Tax Management Portfolio 393-2nd was withdrawn permanently from the BNA Tax Management U.S. Income Portfolio Service. A discussion of accounting for pension plans and other postretirement benefits appears in BNA Tax and Accounting Portfolio 5108, "Pension Accounting."

1. Annual pension cost—the periodic cost charged against earnings, referred to as the "net periodic pension cost"—is determined under a uniform method prescribed by FAS 87. The employer may not simply charge the amount actually contributed to the plan to expense for the accounting year.

2. Generally the unit credit (accrued benefit) method is used in determining the net periodic pension cost, regardless of the actuarial method used by the plan.

3. If the net periodic pension cost differs from the employer's actual plan contribution for the year, the difference will be shown as an asset or liability on the balance sheet.

4. If the plan's past-service costs (accumulated benefit obligation) exceed the fair market value of plan assets, a liability referred to as the unfunded accumulated-benefit obligation must be reflected on the balance sheet. This liability is balanced by an intangible asset on the balance sheet.

5. A specific format is prescribed for various financial statement footnotes relating to the pension plan, such as the fair market value of plan assets and any unamortized prior service costs.

For a plan that is terminating during the year, FAS 88, "Employers' Accounting for Settlements and Curtailments of Defined-Benefit Pension Plans and Termination Benefits," provides rules for dealing with special accounting problems in plan termination.

Nonqualified and qualified plans must be reported separately by employers, since assets of qualified and nonqualified plans cannot be mingled. If a nonqualified plan is informally funded or financed—as such plans usually are—the plan is considered to have no assets for accounting purposes. This fact increases the magnitude of the reported liabilities. The assets used for informal financing are corporate assets, not plan assets.

These accounting rules increase the balance-sheet "visibility" of nonqualified plans, as compared with qualified plans, because the liability will generally rise steadily in a plan that is not formally funded. Planners can generally mitigate this disadvantage by using an informal-funding mechanism that produces a steadily increasing corporate asset, such as the cash value of an insurance policy; this asset can be pointed to as evidence of the company's financial responsibility with regard to the nonqualified plan liability.

Corporate-Owned Life Insurance

Corporate-owned life insurance, whether held as an informal-financing asset for a nonqualified pension plan (see above) or for other corporate or employee benefit purposes, is accounted for in accordance with FASB Technical Bulletin 85-4. The charge to corporate earnings is the premium less the cash value increase. Generally this produces a charge to earnings only in the first few years of the policy, after which there is a profit. The policy's cash value appears as an asset on the balance sheet.

FASB Statement No. 109 (1992; supersedes FAS 96, 1987) requires corporations to create a balance-sheet liability to reflect taxes anticipated to be payable in the future (deferred taxes). If the corporation holds property with unrealized gain, it must generally show a liability for taxes on that gain, even if the gain is not realized during the accounting year. This rule potentially has an impact on corporate-owned life insurance, such as that held in a split-dollar plan, informally funded deferred-compensation plan, or other plan. If the corporation's share of the policy's cash value exceeds the corporation's basis, there is a potentially taxable gain. However, in the great majority of plans using corporate-owned life insurance, the corporation intends to hold the policy until the insured dies, at which point the corporation's realized gain will be nontaxable, except for possible alternative minimum tax (AMT) liability.

FASB's previous statement on accounting for income taxes, FAS 96, stated the requirement of creating a tax liability in an inflexible way that appeared to apply to all insurance policies, regardless of whether the policy was likely to actually generate taxable income. However, FAS 109, which supersedes FAS 96, states that the difference between basis and cash value of a corporate-owned policy does not create a reportable liability if "the asset is expected to be recovered without tax consequence upon the death of the insured (there will be no taxable amount if the insurance policy is held until the death of the insured)."

FAS 109 does not directly discuss whether possible AMT on the death proceeds must be reflected as a balance-sheet liability. However, it can be argued that the principles of the FAS would require the potential AMT to be so reported.

Health and Other Welfare Benefit Plans

Health and life insurance benefit plans generally involve no significant accounting issues as long as the plans provide simply the usual year-to-year benefit and premium payment obligations. However, where employers provide benefits after employees retire, the FASB has recognized that there is a question as to how this obligation should be recognized for accounting purposes. The issue has become more important in light of recent court cases that restrict an employer's right to unilaterally modify or rescind benefits provided to retirees.

The FASB in 1989 issued an "exposure draft" of rules in this area, which was formalized as FAS 106, effective generally for fiscal years beginning after December 15, 1992, with a later date for certain small (under 500) nonpublic plans.

FAS 106 is based on the premise that postretirement benefits of all types are, like pension benefits, a form of deferred compensation that is earned year by year by employees while they are actively working for the employer. Accordingly FAS 106 requires an accrual of such benefits as they are earned, rather than as they are paid. This accrual will create a charge to earnings, and unfunded accrued benefits will create a growing balance-sheet liability.

FAS 106 covers medical and life insurance, tuition assistance, day care, legal services, and housing subsidies, as well as other benefits provided during retirement in return for prior employment services. Retiree medical benefits have by far the greatest potential financial impact. FAS 106 includes specific guidelines for valuing postretirement medical benefits.

This potential balance-sheet liability will cause employers to seek to provide either funded plans or asset reserves or other financing assets, such as life insurance contracts, to cover the liabilities created by postretirement benefits.

Under FAS 106, if assets are not segregated into a trust specifically for the purpose of funding the postretirement benefits, they are not "plan assets" that directly reduce the balance-sheet liability for postretirement benefits. Thus typical corporate-owned life insurance policies or asset reserves would not qualify as plan assets, nor would a Sec. 501(c)(9) trust (VEBA) if the VEBA included assets to fund benefits for active employees. However, Sec. 401(h) medical accounts probably would qualify.

Although informal financing of retiree benefits will not reduce the balance-sheet liability, the existence of assets can help to demonstrate the corporation's financial responsibility in planning to meet the projected liability. Corporate-owned life insurance can be used favorably for this purpose.

Equity-Based Plans (Employer Stock and Option Plans)

The issue of how to reflect stock options (offers to sell stock to a grantee at a specific price over a specified time period) granted to executives on the financial statements of the employer company has been controversial. Traditionally, options were not reflected on company financial statements unless they had an established value, such as options that are traded publicly on an established securities market. Most options are not so traded.

After a long controversy, in 2004 the FASB issued FAS 123 (revised) (FAS 123(R)), which establishes accounting standards for "share-based" compensation; that is, compensation based on the value of the employer's stock. This includes stock options, a very common form of executive compensation.

Under FAS statement 123(R), a company must recognize the cost of options or other share-based awards of compensation to an employee, at the "grant-date fair value of the award." This cost is recognized over the period during which the employee is required to provide services in exchange for the award of compensation.

Under prior guidance (Opinion 25), the grant of an option generally resulted in recognition of no compensation cost because of the difficulty of pricing options other than those traded on an established market. The new statement requires the company to value the options, whether they are traded or not.

Options are valued based on the observable market price of a similar option, or using a valuation technique such as an option pricing model.

CASE PROBLEMS

Case Problem 1

Hi-Fli Corporation has a qualified retirement plan that covers all full-time employees. The plan provides a retirement benefit at age 65 of 40 percent of final 5-years' average base pay. At a recent meeting of the company's board of directors, it was agreed that additional retirement and death benefits should be provided to certain key executives. It was also decided not to liberalize the provisions of the qualified plan since this would require increased benefits for rank-and-file employees in addition to the executive group.

The board of directors established a nonqualified deferred-compensation plan for key executives that would provide the following benefits:

1. Retirement benefits at age 65 equal to the amount accumulated for each participant based on an annual corporate contribution of 10 percent of base salary. Benefits would be payable for life with a 20-year period-certain feature.

2. If an executive dies prior to age 65 while in the employ of Hi-Fli, a death benefit will be paid to his beneficiary equal to three times his annual base compensation payable during the year of his death.

3. Payment of the benefits in (a) and (b) above are contingent upon the executive remaining in the employ of Hi-Fli Corporation until retirement or death.

4. In order to fund its obligation, Hi-Fli Corporation is considering the purchase of a paid-up-at-age-65 life insurance policy and a variable annuity on the life of each executive participant. The policies would be owned by Hi-Fli Corporation as unrestricted corporate assets. Premiums will be paid by Hi-Fli, and any policy benefits will be paid only to Hi-Fli.

Based on the above facts, describe the applicability, if any, of the reporting and disclosure requirements *and* the fiduciary requirements under ERISA for the nonqualified deferred-compensation plan.

Case Problem 2

Whizz Electronics Corporation is a publicly owned company with approximately 500 employees located in two branch offices in Pennsylvania and Delaware. It is engaged in the manufacture of electronic components for color television sets. Whizz Electronics provides its employees with a wide array of fringe benefits plans, including

1. a contributory basic hospitalization and medical insurance plan for all employees

2. noncontributory group term insurance of twice each employee's basic compensation

3. company dining room facilities for all executive employees (no cost to executives)

4. company cars for executives

5. moving cost reimbursements for new and transferred employees

6. noncontributory split-dollar life insurance for each of the 50 employees earning over $50,000 per year

7. insured contributory major medical and disability income plans for the 50 executives earning over $50,000 per year

The controller of Whizz Electronics wants to be informed by you, their benefits consultant, as to the general reporting and disclosure and any other requirements under ERISA, which must be met for each of the above plans.

CHAPTER REVIEW

Review Questions

1. What is the general definition of an employee pension benefit plan under ERISA? [1]

2. Name several types of employee pension benefit plans. [1]

3. What is the general definition of an employee welfare benefit plan under ERISA? [1]

4. List several specific examples of welfare benefit plans. [1]

5. List some examples of the types of fringe benefit plans that are not considered employee welfare benefit plans. [2]

6. Assuming that a corporation establishes an employee welfare benefit plan, in general what are ERISA reporting, disclosure, and fiduciary requirements? [3]

7. Jones Company has decided to establish a noncontributory group term life insurance plan covering all 150 full-time employees. What are the reporting and disclosure requirements for this plan? [4]

8. Would your answer to question 7 be different if the group term insurance plan was contributory? Explain. [4]

9. Suppose the plans in questions 7 and 8 covered less than 100 employees at all times. What would be the plan's reporting and disclosure requirements? [4]

10. Define a party in interest. [5]

11. Explain whether the following transactions are prohibited by ERISA: [5]

     a. the purchase of real estate by a funded nonqualified pension plan from the employer sponsoring the plan

     b. a policy loan by an endorsement method split-dollar life insurance plan to the employer sponsoring the plan

     c. sale of life insurance to an employee benefit plan by an insurance agent who has provided plan design advice and services to the plan

12. An employer would like to establish an employee pension benefit plan that will not be subject to the full reporting and disclosure requirements of ERISA. Advise the employer of two types of pension plans that might be used and the nature of each. [6]

13. Smith, Inc., would like to set up a nonqualified unfunded deferred-compensation plan for certain rank-and-file employees and executives. Explain the effect of the reporting and disclosure, fiduciary, and any other ERISA requirements on such a plan. [7]

14. Acme Corporation has established a noncontributory endorsement type split-dollar life insurance plan for 10 senior executives whose earned income is in excess of $250,000. To what extent, if any, will this plan be subject to reporting and disclosure requirements? [8]

15. Would your answer to question 14 above be different if the endorsement type split-dollar plan was contributory, in other words, if each employee paid a portion of the premium due? Explain. [8]

16. What are the fiduciary requirements for the endorsement type split-dollar plans described in questions 14 and 15, if any? [8]

17. Cholesterol King, Inc., a large corporate restaurant chain, adopts a disability program for its 25 executives who rank as vice presidents or higher, excluding executives over 60. [9]

     a. Chuck Tanner, a vice president aged 62, objects that the plan violates federal law. Is he right? If so, how could Cholesterol King bring the plan into compliance at minimum cost?

     b. Harley Flipper, aged 62, a kitchen worker at a Cholesterol King restaurant, makes the same objection. Is he right?

18. Compare the financial statement and balance-sheet treatment of a funded nonqualified deferred-compensation plan with those for a plan that is unfunded but informally financed using a life insurance contract. [10]

19. What is the balance-sheet impact of adopting a plan that promises to provide health insurance to certain currently active employees after these employees retire? [10]

Answers to Review Questions

1. ERISA defines an employee pension benefit plan to mean any plan, fund, or program that is established or maintained by an employer, an employee organization, or both. The plan, fund, or program either by its express terms or as a result of surrounding circumstances, provides retirement income to employees, or results in a deferral of income by employees for periods that extend to the termination of covered employment or beyond. You will note that this definition includes both qualified and nonqualified pension plans. It might also be noted that the word pension includes profit-sharing, stock bonus, defined-bonus, and other types of deferred-benefit and defined-contribution plans. [1]

2. The definition of an employee pension benefit plan under ERISA clearly includes any type of qualified retirement plan such as a defined-benefit or money-purchase pension plan, profit-sharing plan, stock bonus plan, and target benefit plan. Furthermore, any type of nonqualified deferred-compensation plan, whether funded or unfunded, would also be included if it provides for retirement income or the deferral of income for periods extending to the termination of covered employment or beyond.

    Other types of plans can create problems as to whether they fall within the definition. For example, a restricted property plan may or may not fall under this definition. It would be necessary to carefully examine the provisions of the restricted property plan as to when the property will be free of restrictions so that it will be subject to full enjoyment by the employee. Until clarification is received from the Department of Labor, it will not be possible to give a definite answer in cases of this type. However, a private Department of Labor ruling holds that restricted stock plans are exempt from ERISA. [1]

3. Under ERISA, an employee welfare benefit plan is defined as any plan, fund, or program established or maintained by an employer, an employee organization, or both, for the purpose of providing for its participants or their beneficiaries, through the purchase of insurance or otherwise, medical, surgical, or hospital care or benefits, or benefits in the event of sickness, accident, disability, death, or unemployment. This definition also includes vacation

benefits, apprenticeship or other training programs, day care centers, scholarship funds, and prepaid legal services. [1]

4. Some examples of employee welfare benefit plans include split-dollar life insurance plans, basic and major hospitalization and surgical plans, salary continuation or death benefit plans, and group insurance arrangements. [1]

5. Certain types of fringe benefit plans are not classified as employee welfare benefit plans for reporting and disclosure purposes. Executive dining rooms and supper costs, employee gifts and discount purchases, vacation pay, financial counseling for executives, tax preparation for executives, interest-free and low-interest loans to employees, and moving cost reimbursements are some of the employee fringe benefits that are not regarded as employee welfare benefit plans. [2]

6. The fiduciary requirements generally require the existence of a written plan setting forth the benefits to be provided and a procedure for the administration and amendment and payment of benefits under the plan. Thus, a written instrument must provide for one or more named fiduciaries who are to have authority to control and manage the operation and administration of the plan. A specific procedure for amending the plan must be stated, and the basis on which payments are made to and from the plan must be specifically indicated. Each named fiduciary must discharge his duties solely in the interest of plan participants with the care, skill, prudence, and diligence under the circumstances then prevailing that a prudent man acting in a like capacity and familiar with such matters would use in the conduct of such a plan. A fiduciary who fails to meet these requirements will be held personally liable. Fiduciary liability insurance is recommended to cover errors and omissions in this area.

    Although, as a general rule, all assets of an employee welfare benefit plan are required to be held under a written trust, this requirement does not apply to any plan assets that consist of insurance contracts or where benefits are paid directly to plan participants solely from the general assets of the employer. Thus, split-dollar, group permanent and group term insurance plans, long-term disability, and insured hospitalization coverage plans do not require the use of a written trust.

    If the plan covers fewer than 100 participants and benefits are paid solely from the general assets of the employer or provided exclusively through insurance contracts, the premiums of which are paid by the employer or partly with participant contributions, it is exempt from all reporting and disclosure requirements. Also, a group insurance plan that covers fewer than 100 participants and that is part of an association group plan or multiemployer trust is also exempt from reporting and disclosure provisions. An employee welfare benefit plan that is maintained primarily for the purpose of providing benefits for a select group of management or highly compensated employees, where benefits are paid solely from the general assets of the employer or through insurance contracts, the premiums for which are paid directly by the employer, is exempt from all reporting and disclosure requirements. Finally, a welfare benefit plan that covers 100 or more participants is subject to all reporting and disclosure requirements.

Also, welfare plans must generally furnish a summary plan description (SPD) to participants. Unfunded and fully insured welfare plans need not complete certain items of Form 5500.

By comparison, note that for employee pension benefit plans, if the plan is qualified, then it is subject to all of the reporting and disclosure requirements, with certain exceptions for fully insured plans. Nonqualified deferred-compensation plans, however, are treated somewhat differently (see below). [3]

7. A noncontributory group term life insurance plan covering 100 or more participants where coverage is not restricted to a select group of management or highly compensated employees is a type of employee welfare benefit plan that is subject to full reporting and disclosure requirements. A summary plan description must be furnished to each participant. Various other reports and information, under the Form 5500 series, must be filed and furnished to plan participants as outlined in this chapter. [4]

8. The reporting and disclosure requirements are the same for a contributory group term life insurance plan for 100 or more participants as they would be if the plan was noncontributory. [4]

9. An employee welfare benefit plan, such as a group term insurance program, which covers fewer than 100 participants at all times during a plan year, is exempt from certain reporting and disclosure requirements. Even if the plan is contributory, this partial exemption rule applies as long as participant contributions are forwarded to the insurance company within 3 months of receipt. This exemption from

certain reporting and disclosure requirements applies only where benefits are paid solely from the general assets of the employer or provided exclusively through insurance contracts or where benefits are paid partly from the employer's general assets and partly through insurance contracts. Where an employee welfare benefit plan covers fewer than 100 participants, there are no reports that the employer has to file with the Department of Labor. However, such plans must still furnish participants with a Summary Plan Description (or "ERISA Notice") that outlines the basic provisions of the plan and various other information, such as a claim denial procedure and information concerning plan changes. [4]

10. ERISA sets forth various provisions concerning prohibited transactions and the penalties that may be assessed for violations thereof. Under ERISA Sec. 408, a fiduciary who allows a prohibited transaction to take place must undo the transaction and may be liable for any losses that result. Under Code Sec. 4975 the government can impose 15 percent and 100 percent penalties on a party in interest, for each year that the prohibited transaction has not been corrected, with the penalties applied to the "amount involved" in the prohibited transaction. Generally, a prohibited transaction is a typical business transaction that takes place directly or indirectly between a plan and a party in interest. A party in interest is defined by ERISA as including a fiduciary; a person who provides services to the plan; an employer, any of whose employees are covered by such plans; and certain other parties, particularly those who own stock in the corporation, their relatives, and certain employees, officers, or directors. [5]

11.

    a. yes

    b. If the split dollar plan covers a top hat group, the plan is exempt from ERISA's fiduciary responsibility requirements. Consequently, the prohibited transaction rules do not apply. If the split dollar plan does not cover a top hat group, it is subject to the prohibited transaction rules, but the question becomes whether the policy loan is a transaction involving plan assets. If it is, then the loan would be a prohibited transaction. However, under a split dollar plan where the cash values represent an interest of the employer, policy loans by the employer should be permitted since the cash values are owned by the employer and are not part of the benefits to be provided by the plan.

c. yes, but a PTE is available (PTE 77-9).

A prohibited transaction is defined as any direct or indirect sale, exchange, or leasing of any property between a plan and a party in interest; the lending of money or other extension of credit between the plan and a party in interest; the furnishing of goods, services, or facilities between a plan and a party in interest; the transfer to, or use by or for the benefit of a party in interest, of any assets of the plan; or the acquisition, on behalf of the plan, of any employer security or employer real property in violation of ERISA. As a result, plans are prohibited from engaging in the preceding transactions, and those that do so can give rise to penalties to the plan fiduciary and party in interest involved.

A life insurance agent who provides plan-design services or who exercises persuasive control over plan investment decisions could be regarded under ERISA as a party in interest or a fiduciary because of the broad definitions of those terms. Thus, the agent's sale of life insurance to the plan would be a prohibited transaction.

However, Class Exemption 77-9, promulgated by the Labor Department under ERISA, would allow the agent to avoid this result if, prior to the sale, the agent discloses to the plan's independent fiduciary (1) a statement of his relationship to the insurance company and (2) a statement of commissions for the first and future years. The exemption would not apply unless the agent's compensation so disclosed was "reasonable." The government can inquire into this on a case-by-case basis.

Note that all plans are covered including fully insured plans that provide benefits for a select group of management or highly compensated employees. The above exemption does not apply where the agent serves as plan administrator, trustee, or as a fiduciary authorized in writing to deal with plan assets on a discretionary basis. [5]

12. Under ERISA, an unfunded nonqualified deferred-compensation plan for a select group of management or highly compensated employees (the "top-hat" group) is free of periodic reporting and disclosure and fiduciary requirements. The only exceptions are that the employer must file a written statement with the Department of Labor that includes basic information concerning the plan and must be willing to furnish the plan documents should the Department of

Labor so request. The plan must also establish a written claims procedure.

An unfunded plan presumably means one that is unfunded from a tax standpoint. This refers to a situation where the employee must rely only upon the unsecured promise of the employer to make retirement or death benefit payments. The employer should be able to finance its obligations internally through the purchase of life insurance, annuities, or any other investment media without such purchase being regarded as funding from a tax standpoint. The key point is that the asset purchased by the employer must remain an asset available to the employer's creditors.

An unfunded excess-benefit plan is exempt from all requirements of ERISA. This type of plan is defined by ERISA as a plan maintained by an employer solely for the purpose of providing benefits for certain employees in excess of the limitations on contributions and benefits imposed by Code Sec. 415 of ERISA. If the plan provides benefits to replace qualified plan benefits restricted by Sec. 401(a)(17) ($245,000 indexed compensation limit), it is not an ERISA excess-benefit plan. [6]

13. A nonqualified and unfunded deferred-compensation plan is regarded as an employee pension benefit plan under ERISA. Such plans are generally subject to the reporting and disclosure requirements, as well as participation and vesting requirements. However, an unfunded plan, which is designed primarily for the purpose of providing deferred compensation for a select group of management or highly compensated employees, is not subject to any reporting and disclosure or fiduciary responsibility requirements. Such plans do not have to meet the participation and vesting rules. The only requirement would be that the employer or plan administrator furnish a statement to the Department of Labor announcing the existence of the plan and certain other data, and that copies of the plan document be made available upon request. A written claims procedure is required.

Where an unfunded nonqualified plan is to cover rank-and-file employees as well as executives, the question arises as to whether the exemption from reporting and disclosure and other ERISA requirements will continue to apply. It is not completely clear whether a deferred-compensation plan for select management or highly compensated employees must confine participation exclusively to that group. Regardless of the final disposition of this question, it would appear that where several rank-and-file employees are included, all the reporting and disclosure requirements, participation, coverage, vesting, fiduciary responsibilities, and funding requirements of ERISA would have to be met. Thus, the use of a nonqualified unfunded deferred-compensation plan for rank-and-file employees is not a feasible arrangement under ERISA because of these requirements. Of primary concern would be the requirement of a funding policy that contradicts the very nature of an unfunded plan. [7]

14. An endorsement type split-dollar life insurance plan falls within the definition of an employee welfare benefit plan under ERISA. Thus, it would ordinarily be subject to all of the reporting and disclosure requirements unless a specific exemption applies. Where the endorsement type split-dollar plan is primarily for the purpose of providing benefits for a select group of management or highly compensated employees, and the benefits are paid solely through insurance contracts, the premiums for which are paid directly by the employer, it is exempt from all reporting and disclosure requirements. However, the Secretary of Labor can request copies of the split-dollar documents. [8]

15. A contributory endorsement type split-dollar life insurance plan would not fall within the exemption mentioned in answer 14 above. The reason is that the exemption applies only where the premiums are paid directly by the employer from its general assets. Any time employee contributions are required or made, ERISA reporting and disclosure rules apply. Thus, a contributory endorsement type split-dollar plan would be subject to the reporting and disclosure requirements, but in most cases only to those requirements applicable to employee welfare benefit plans that cover fewer than 100 participants. It appears that nothing will have to be reported to the Department of Labor, but each participant and beneficiary who receives benefits would have to receive a Summary Plan Description. [8]

16. Because an endorsement type split-dollar life insurance plan, whether contributory or not, is an employee welfare benefit plan, it must meet the fiduciary requirements of ERISA. These requirements include a written instrument that provides for one or more named fiduciaries who are to have authority to control and manage the operation and administration of the plan. The plan must also specify the nature of the benefits, the persons who are

eligible to receive benefits, the basis for contributions to the plan, and a written claims procedure.

However, the endorsement type split-dollar plan, while required to be in writing, does not require a written trust since the plan assets consist entirely of life insurance contracts. [8]

17. Cholesterol King is a large enough employer (20 or more employees) to be subject to federal age discrimination law. [9]

   a. Chuck Tanner's claim that the executive disability program violates age discrimination is valid—the program has discriminatory eligibility provisions. The program could be made lawful at minimum cost by covering all vice presidents and above, regardless of age, but scaling benefits back for older participants on an equal cost basis. If benefits are based on compensation, presumably the program would comply if costs for each participant represented the same percentage of each participant's compensation. This would result in different percentage-of-compensation benefits, with lesser percentages for older employees.

   b. Flipper's claim is not valid. The fact that a disability program exists does not mean that it must cover all older employees. The employer is free to cover any group of employees it wishes to cover—such as executives ranking as vice president or above—as long as the criteria for coverage do not exclude older employees.

18. On the balance sheet, there will be a liability that represents present value of the total accrued benefits to date of employees covered under the plan, less the value of plan assets. By definition an unfunded plan has no plan assets. But, with a funded plan, the full liability will be reduced by the value of assets used to fund the plan.

   With an unfunded plan, the full present value of the accrued benefits will be shown as a liability, even if the employer maintains an informal financing arrangement, such as corporate-owned life insurance. With informal financing, however, the value of the assets used to finance the plan will be shown on the balance sheet as an asset and can be identified as assets set aside to finance the plan, thus showing the employer's financial responsibility. [10]

19. Under FAS 106 the present value of the accrued postretirement health insurance benefits for currently active employees must be shown as a balance-sheet liability. [10]

Test your mastery of the material in GS 842 by reviewing this case study and preparing a recommendation for Frank Folio. Compare your recommendation with the Analysis on the next page. This analysis is not intended as a definitive answer, but just a guide to the issues. This case study is particularly helpful if it can be analyzed by a group of students, or several groups, with the results compared.

Frank Folio, aged 54, is president and CEO of Folio Title and Mortgage Services, Inc. The company provides mortgage, title insurance, and real estate management services. Frank, his mother Selma, and his wife Alice, aged 48, are the shareholders of the company. Frank is an entrepreneur who has parlayed an inheritance into a portfolio of good investments, including a number of small businesses in the building industry and related businesses. Alice also has a good deal of family money, much of which is invested in Frank's businesses. Frank and Alice have three children in college.

Folio Title was established by Frank about 10 years ago, partly to help finance his business ventures, but it now has many clients, mostly real estate investors in the area. It is profitable and has shown steady growth. His current business continuation and estate plans assume that Folio will continue to operate after Frank's retirement and death to continue to provide services to the family businesses.

Besides Frank, there are five employees who Frank considers to be key employees of the company. The two most important are the two vice presidents, Bill Brown, aged 38 and earning $150,000, and Eddie Walton, 47, vice-president for operations, earning $180,000. There are three other managers who have been with Frank from the beginning:

Employee	Age	Compensation
Mollie Stern	42	$100,000
Velma Marlow	44	$ 80,000
Nick Dilullo	35	$ 78,000

There are 20 other employees, who are mostly clerical. The company has a 401(k) plan with a safe-harbor mandatory contribution provision such that all employees currently have 401(k) accounts.

Bill and Eddie have relatively small 401(k) accounts and rollover IRAs from former jobs. (Bill—total about $200,000; Eddie—total about $350,000). Their only other major assets are homes worth about $400,000 each, with Bill's equity being about $100,000 and Eddie's about $250,000. Both have families with two children in school or college. Mollie and Velma have no significant assets except the equity in their homes, which is approximately $100,000 in both cases. Nick rents his home and as a result of a recent divorce has almost no significant assets.

The company has a Sec. 79 group term life insurance plan providing each employee a death benefit of twice their salary. Eddie has a personally-owned term policy for $100,000, and Bill and the other three managers have no personally-owned insurance. Bill has Type 1 diabetes, which is well-controlled and he has no active health problems.

Bill and Eddie have each asked Frank to look into enhancing their compensation by improving their retirement and other benefits. Frank has asked you as a financial planner to identify issues and recommend solutions. From his business experience and personality, Frank tends to be generous with his employees and wants to keep them for the long haul. Frank has decided that it would be a good idea to look also at the benefits picture for the three other key employees in addition to Bill and Eddie, since it is obvious that they also need some help with retirement savings issues. Frank isn't particularly interested in compensation plans for himself with the company, because he has substantial assets and from his standpoint he'd just as soon put those corporate dollars into the business, but he is willing to listen to ideas.

CASE STUDY ANALYSIS

1. Identify needs

    a. Current compensation needs for Bill and Eddie (children's education)
    b. Better life insurance protection, particularly Bill
    c. Improved retirement savings for Bill and Eddie
    d. Probably no current significant federal estate tax exposure for Bill and Eddie

e. Frank's financial planning needs go beyond what can be done with Folio Company alone

2. Current compensation

   a. Main issue here is, would just increasing salary or bonus be better than any other use of Company money? Probably not—the life insurance and retirement savings needs are real. But company could consider a small bonus program aimed at easing college costs for Bill and Eddie.

   b. Given reduction in capital-gain and dividend tax rates, does it still make sense to provide a tax-deferred benefit to an executive rather than a current taxable bonus that is invested?

      (1) Still marginally better to defer, depending on assumptions.

      (2) "Spendthrift" benefit of NQDC is still valuable.

3. Life insurance protection

   a. How much does each employee need?

   b. Carving Bill and Eddie (also Frank?) from the Sec. 79 plan could increase funds available for life insurance. Structure as

      (1) Simple bonus plan (bonus out premium amount) or

      (2) Endorsement-type nonequity split dollar.

         (a) Absent estate planning issues, is collateral assignment beneficial?

         (b) State-law loan restrictions relevant?

   c. Must cost out the alternatives

   d. One issue in particular—Bill's insurability. Would it be better to leave Bill in the Sec. 79 group?

      (1) Does Company have the flexibility to define groups however it wants? (Generally, yes under Sec. 79).

      (2) Compare premium costs.

   e. Frank seems ready to provide increase in insurance benefits, so company money is also available for premium dollars, not just the amounts freed from carveout.

4. Improved retirement savings

    a. Bill and Eddie face probably retirement income deficiencies.

        (1) Their 401(k) accounts could grow to the existing amount plus $1,500,000 or so (depending on assumptions including changes in 401(k) rules). (Assume that salaries and 401(k) contributions subject to same rate of inflation, so use current numbers). For Bill and Eddie, this is not enough to replace their current salaries in retirement. Gap is about $50,000 – $100,000 per year (current dollars). (Figures can be refined with some number-crunching)

    b. Look at qualified plan alternatives

        (1) Only a defined benefit plan would materially increase benefits for Frank and key employees

            (a) Cash-balance DC plan could be more cost effective if other employees are young, but cost-effectiveness is not one of Frank's stated objectives here; issue here is increasing benefits

        (2) Depending on employee census, DB plan could greatly increase costs for rank-and-file employees

        (3) Other employees probably satisfied with "rich" safe-harbor 401(k)

        (4) Since Frank would be the real beneficiary of a change to DB, this discussion should wait until Frank is ready to look at his own financial planning picture, if he hasn't done so already

        (5) May have to look at all of Frank's enterprises to determine required qualified plan coverage

    c. Nonqualified plan

        (1) Plan covering Bill and Eddie, or separate agreements for Bill and Eddie? Separate agreements probably better.

            (a) Does coverage of deferred compensation plan jeopardize "top-hat" plan status? No clear authority on this; most favorable case says coverage of up to 15 percent of employees does not jeopardize top-hat status under ERISA. Thus, there is a risk in extending the NQDC plan to the three other employees. It is important to retain the ERISA exemption from vesting and funding requirements.

(b) NQDC plan requires that the Company exist and be solvent at retirement of covered employees. Is this criterion met here?

(2) Benefit formula

(a) Salary continuation (fixed dollar amount or formula based on compensation) probably meets needs best but consider other formulas

(b) Salary reduction—probably neither Bill nor Eddie would want to reduce their current take-home, so salaries would have to be increased accordingly

(c) Equity-based formula—based on increase in company stock value or profits.

(a) Value of closely held-stock difficult to ascertain. However, if same valuation formula is used for initial valuation and for valuation at termination, employees should be treated fairly.

(b) If profits are used, what are accounting rules? How good is this formula for meeting needs of Bill and Eddie? Will Frank agree (or insist?)?

           (c) Formula based on "excess" value of underlying asset, such as insurance policy

                (a) Company is entitled to cash value increases up to fixed percentage, say 5 percent (reimburses company for use of money.)

                (b) Executive gets base amount plus increases above 5 percent.

           (c) Formula based on 401(k) plan to bring contribution up to 25 percent (or other percentage) of compensation—probably not appropriate here since 401(k) is already generous and is safe-harbor so no ADP reductions for highly compensated

(3) Death benefit

           (a) Total benefit should be coordinated with other insurance coverage (company-paid.)

           (b) Death benefit in NQDC is taxable to beneficiary, deductible to company, so this may not be the most tax-effective way to provide death benefit

(4) Disability benefit

           (a) Should benefit differ to reflect Bill's health situation?

(5) In-service withdrawals

           (a) Sec. 409A restricts to disability, unforeseeable emergency, etc.

(6) Informal financing asset

           (a) Life insurance—few competitors assuming assets are actually set aside

       (a) Provision of death benefit
           for early death

       (b) Tax-free buildup (company
           is tax owner)

       (c) Assets must be available to corporate
           creditors to avoid taxation under
           economic benefit theory

(7) Rabbi trust

    (a) Reasons for rabbi trust

       (a) Possible change in
           management

          (a) Can provide for
              payout on change
              in management

       (b) Future financial status of
           company

          (a) Trust can be
              irrevocable
              but still must
              be available
              to company
              creditors.
              "Trigger"
              provision or
              offshore trust not
              permitted under
              current law

       (b) Conclusion—rabbi trust
           would be a good protection
           for Bill and Eddie and
           other managers due to
           possibility of change in
           management before their
           possible retirement

          (a) Rabbi trust
              instrument should
              be designed so
              owners can't

defeat—for
example, by
adding additional
employees.

d. Equity-type benefits

- Depends on Folio family's concerns regarding dilution.
- Also possible to add a second class of nonvoting stock for employees; can initially be issued as restricted stock.